BEING LIBERAL IN AN ILLIBERAL AGE

BEING LIBERAL IN AN ILLIBERAL AGE

WHY I AM A UNITARIAN UNIVERSALIST

Jack Mendelsohn

Skinner House Books
Boston

Published by Skinner House Books, an imprint of the Unitarian Universalist Association, 25 Beacon Street, Boston, MA 02108-2800. First paperback printing by Beacon Press, 1984.

Printed in Canada.

ISBN 1-55896-332-4

99 98 97 96
10 9 8 7 6 5 4 3 2

Mendelsohn, Jack, 1918-
     Being liberal in an illiberal age : why I am a Unitarian
Universalist / Jack Mendelsohn.
         p. cm.
     Includes index.
     ISBN 1-55896-332-4
     1. Unitarian Universalist Association—Apologetic works.
2. Liberalism (Religion)—Unitarian Universalist churches.
3. Mendelsohn, Jack, 1918-   . I. Title.
BX9841.2.M46 1995
289.1'32—dc20   95-624
                             CIP

To All Those, Living and Dead, Who Are My Beloved Liberal Companions. Like the Wild Asses in the 39th Chapter of Job, We Roam the Barren Wilderness Searching After Every Green Thing.

Contents

Preface

You count your blessings, and you carry on. If I were to propose a creed for liberals, which I am not about to do, this would be it. The most powerful liberal instinct is a grating hunger for more freedom, more justice, more fairness, more inclusion, more fulfillment for more of earth's creatures. It is a hunger requiring a goatlike digestive system that can thrive on brush and weeds in the absence of rye grass and clover. Staying liberal means savoring small successes and digesting constant frustrations.

To a liberal, every age is illiberal. Forget perfection; that's not the issue. Remember instead the failings, the shortcomings, the repression, the egocentricities, the hypocrisies. In the human condition, they are unfailingly present. But so, too, is the struggle against them and the small successes, the blessings. Remember them as well!

I begin with the question, How shall we live while we live? What uses shall we make of our free will? These are the bedrock questions. In answering them it matters profoundly what our faith is, what we believe, and what choices we make about our loyalties and loves.

I made my fundamental choice long ago. I wanted freedom. Freedom to think, express, question, examine, grow, and change. Freedom to be myself. Freedom to prove, nurture, and develop myself. But freedom without a firm foundation of faith and a sense of history is perilous and fragile. Life's tragedies ride roughshod over a freedom without faith. I anchored my faith in the great legacy of the liberal spirit. I belong to that legacy and it belongs to me.

I wanted my life to count for something. I wanted my freedom and my faith to be embodied in works of love and justice. So I set myself the lifelong task of intimacy with ethical responsibilities and moral meanings. That task is as fresh to me today as it was when I entered the Harvard Divinity School in 1942. My failings have been, and are, depressingly frequent. I have needed much forgiveness from others and myself. But my sense of the holy in our relations with one another and my compassion have never ceased to grow.

I knew from the start that I did not want to go it alone, that I wanted to be rooted in religious community, to be part of a spiritual circle of approving and encouraging eyes, to savor the world and to save it, in the company of like-minded others—in worship, celebration, fellowship, study, service, spiritual discipline, and social action. Exercising my free will, I found this in the Unitarian Universalist movement and in each of the congregations it has been my privilege to serve.

If I had been looking for perfection, I would long since have excommunicated myself. Fortunately, being intimately acquainted with my own imperfections, I was not. We are not perfect. We are as subject as any to the ravages of the repressed unconscious and egocentrism. What saves us is that great old legacy of the liberal spirit. We will not stop examining. We will not stop questioning. We will test the validity of our concepts, our character, our reasoning, and our behavior. Our imperfections appear and reappear. But they do not get sanctified.

At our present point in civilization, many forces militate against a realization of depth religion. Organized religious bodies are frequently the worst offenders, treating communicants not as spiritually creative beings, but as objects to be "saved." To use Martin Buber's phraseology, the individual is dealt with not as a *Thou* (a person), but as an *It* (a thing). The natural tendency of most people is to behave as they are treated and to treat others in a similar fashion. Thus people come to think of themselves as functioning according to the same mechanical laws as their material possessions. If something goes wrong with your computer, you go to a service center to have it set right by experts. But persons are not computers. They become like computers when they lose faith in their own unique inner capacities. Then they click and buzz and whirr along, machines in a world of machines. Religion is external to them. It "fixes them up."

Essentially the same effect is felt from the crosscurrents of society. They disrupt us, alienate us from a sense of intimacy with our world, and eventually they alienate us from ourselves. The result is that we no longer live our lives from the inside out, but in terms of the various stereotypes imposed on us. We make machines that act more and more like persons, while persons act more and more like machines.

Simplify, simplify! said Thoreau, who could put down twenty-eight dollars for a refuge on Walden Pond and regain his soul by turning his back on the world. Thoreau, let us remember, had no family to support. Anyway, twenty-eight dollars would not buy much of a retreat these days.

Our predicament has burgeoned since Thoreau's time, and it has little to do with the pocketbook or the price structure. It involves the depth areas of human selves: feelings, emotions, values, conscience, reason, belonging. These are being crowded out by the ersatz products of the media, politics, marketing, and evangelism.

The function of depth religion in all of this is to take a stand, in community, for the inner person, to rescue the *Thou* from its *It* status, and to guide the *Thou* to the riches of untapped treasure within the depths and heights of persons.

As a Unitarian Universalist, I dedicate my life to the creative religious behavior of seeking persons, who learn to live in close touch with their times, who refuse to be psychically numbed to its problems, and who undertake to resolve them both within themselves and in their activities in the world. I can best summarize what I believe our liberal religious enterprise is up to with this paraphrase of John Winthrop's sermon to the Puritans approaching Massachusetts Bay in 1630 aboard the ship *Arabella*: We must love one another. We must bear one another's burdens. We must not look only on our own things, but also on the things of our sisters and brothers. We must rejoice together, mourn together, labor, suffer, and overcome together.

One truth is clear enough. We're all in it together. As Lewis Thomas wrote: "We have all the habits of a social species, more compulsively social than any other, even bees and ants. Our nest, or hive, is language; we are held together by speech. . . . Our great advantage over all other social animals is that we possess the kind of brain that permits us to change our minds. We are not obliged, as the ants are, to follow genetic blueprints for every last detail of our behavior. Our genes are more cryptic and ambiguous in their instructions: get along, says our DNA, talk to each other, figure out the world, be useful, and above all keep an eye out for affection." If ever there was an exhilarating description of liberalism, this is it.

The essential meaning of our lives, even in the midst of all that is so calamitous, is not in becoming part of a mechanical interplay of mechanical forces, but to seek more enthusiastically than ever in our shared thoughts and activities the evolving goals of our emerging spiritual selves.

Our present state is certainly oppressive, but it need not be the end of the road. Our capacity for folly is unmatched by any other species, but, as Thomas said, so too is our capacity to "talk to each other, figure out the world, be useful, and above all keep an eye out for affection." I am a liberal because I want to take my stand with a legacy, a spirit, that pulls for the positive possibilities in the human endowment. I am a Unitarian Universalist because I want to ally myself with others who are consciously striving, in a covenanted religious community, to explore and reveal the creative heights and depths within the human frame, one that fosters thinking, loving, and developing whole human beings.

The mysterious life force, of which we are remarkable manifestations, possesses a buoyant power, which in human terms can be fulfilled only as we better know and transcend ourselves. I am a Unitarian Universalist because our religion zestfully celebrates human reason, that unique gift for better knowing and transcending ourselves. I warmly applaud English psychologist Margaret Bowden when she says of reason, "We're not just talking about . . . logical-mathematical-scientific problem solving, we're talking about human life, human beings, human worth and human values, and if we're not, we jolly well should be."

It is the task of reason in this wider sense to point our way, to seek out the right direction for travel. It is by reason that we know what ought to be. It is by reason that we find meaning in moral decision. It is by reason that we grow responsible. It is by reason that we come to care for ideals, for standards, for criteria, for the arts of logical distinction and cultivated judgment. By reason we understand the meaning of self-giving and the importance of having a self to give. By reason we see that struggle for the life of others is as fundamental as struggle for the life of self; that interest in the life of others is deeply woven into the fabric of the life-process; that we are not born to be incarnate centers of selfishness. The self is private, personal, and precious, but it is not isolated from other selves. It is wholly unique, but it only shares not commands the universe.

All this we learn and know because the faculty of reason is our birthright. When loved and used, reason affirms that we are human because we are capable of being deepened and that until we are deepened we cannot know the fullness of joy.

I do not want to leave the impression that our garlanding of reason ignores faith. Far from it. Helped in recent years by the faith development thought of theologian James Fowler, we have begun to think of *faith* as a verb, not a noun; we faith together as a fundamental style of life, a way of relating to self, to others, to power(s), to boundaries such as death and finitude, and to sources of being, value, and meaning. We participate in a common faithing.

We faith to relate ourselves to creation not by having dominion, but as participants in a symbiotic arrangement, a wondrous, coherent body of connected life. We faith to relate to others in caring, not possessing, ways. We faith relationships as a source of common energy by which we find strength to live our lives with courage and compassion, to stand upon our own two feet, to seek our unique destinies, to make our special contributions, and to extend a helping hand. We faith a strong sense of religious community, not to shut ourselves in or others out, but to make us better people, to rekindle our joy and zest in living.

We faith a church that is not merely a structure, but a center of sanity and inspiration in a deranged world; that is not merely a place of private cultivation and retreat but a temple for renewing and revitalizing our beleaguered values; that stands as a symbol of humans aspiring together, tracking truth together, and demanding social justice together; that has within it the exuberance of play, the blessings of shared worship, a symmetry with life's rhythms; and that resonants with silence, song, critical inquiry, and social action.

We faith with and for our children and youth, that they will not be mirrors of ourselves, though they should fully know where we stand and may learn from us our best traits. But we faith their freedom to go forth to discover, multiply, and live their own values.

We faith to become more centered, more spontaneous, more genuine, more constant persons. But we faith also not to get so wrapped up in ourselves that we turn aside from the struggles against structures of injustice and oppression.

We faith not to love life but to hold it loosely, knowing that we must die, knowing that we must constantly strike a balance between what we desire and what we can do, that it is only in imaginary worlds that we can do whatever we wish or have whatever we want, that often we must choose and act amidst confounding paradoxes and ambiguities. We faith to know how important it is to be aware of small successes and happinesses, and that savoring them is itself an experience of liberation.

Human nature and its champion, liberalism, suffer these days from a wretched press. Those who would like nothing better than to take control of *our* lives are palpably encouraged that this is the best of all times for fastening on us their pet pieties, nostrums, orthodoxies, and chains. There will be fatal days for the liberal spirit, and for a human nature determined to take control of its own spiritual destiny and biological survival, if today's generation is without stalwarts who distill from the essence of the predicament the wonder of halting, imperfect, but coping solutions. Unitarian Universalism provides, not by any means an exclusive, but a special and inclusive place for such stalwarts. These many years of laboring in its vineyards have both chastened and deepened the pride I take in calling it the religion of my heart and mind.

My choice of Unitarian Universalist religion is a personal one, consciously made among possible alternatives, and does not in any way imply that we have a monopoly on the practice of the liberal spirit in religion. The very act of choosing, however, implies something that is dazzlingly unique about being human, something that is ultimately dependent on achieving relationships of functional congruence; that is, an experienced sense of belonging, of giving and receiving love and loyalty within a community of faith that was, is, and is to be.

The liberal spirit is today beleaguered and besieged, attacked from all sides, but particularly by a surging radical right in religion and politics. That this has always been so, in varying degrees, and is likely to go on being so is historically verifiable. But such verification comforts only in collaboration with the liberal will not to be morally confused within. Now is always the best time to redefine, revitalize, and reconnect the liberal spirit to the human future; and especially now, when we can starkly add, if there is to be a human future.

Jack Mendelsohn
Maynard, Massachusetts
January 1995

1

A Way of Walking and Acting in the World

Human life is a struggle — against frustration, ignorance, suffering, evil, the maddening inertia of things in general; but it is also a struggle for something which our experience tells us can be achieved in some measure.
Julian Huxley, *Evolution in Action*

The more we try to say precisely what is in our hearts, the more we find that we are speaking for multitudes of strangers the world over. The deeper we get down to our own fundamentals, the more deeply we represent those of other people. Like all human beings, I live on borrowed time. I never know when my time will run out, but I do know that it will run out. I have no way of knowing what tragedies will befall me at the next step, the next ring of the telephone, the next rising of the sun. My notion of spiritual fulfillment is learning how to accept this fate with a ringing affirmation of all that makes life worth living.

The liberal spirit is my inspiration to be a creative, cooperative human being, in spite of the fact that life may crush me at any moment and death may blot me out. As a skeptic about such matters, I cannot comfort myself with supernatural promises. I know that human existence contains irreducible elements of tragedy and incompleteness. I know that I can never really comprehend the totality of things. I am finite. For me the fundamental question of life is not why but how. How shall I live while I live? This is the bedrock question. In answering it, it matters very much what I believe. As we read in the Apocryphal book called *Ecclesiasticus*:

> Accept no person against thine own soul,
> And let no reverence for anyone cause thee to fall.
> But let the counsel of thine own heart stand:

1

For there is none more faithful unto thee than it.
For our minds are sometimes wont to bring us tidings,
More than seven watchmen, that sit above in a high tower.

It takes strong girders of conviction to keep the counsels of thine own liberal-spirited heart standing. Heinrich Heine, the German poet, was gazing with a friend at the cathedral in Amiens.

Asked the friend: "Tell me, Heinrich, why can't people build piles like this any more?"

Answered Heine: "My dear friend, in those days people had convictions. We moderns have opinions. And it takes more than opinions to build a Gothic cathedral."

I think of this exchange when I dwell on the massive attacks directed against the modern age, and its alleged inspiration, liberalism, usually uttered, in William F. Buckley, Jr., fashion, with a scornful curl of the lip.

Modernity's ambiguity, confusion, and sheer madness are enough to send the dazed rushing pell-mell toward certainty and direction. The limitless reaches of science and reason collapse into uncertainty and anxiety. "Where, oh where, is our center?" is a bleat of our times. The open mind? Why, it turns out to be nothing but a sieve. Even the most respected scientists say so. Take Niels Bohr's "Every sentence that I utter should be regarded by you not as an assertion but as a question." And Jacob Bronowski's "There is no absolute knowledge.... All information is imperfect." Modernity's only certainty is everlasting uncertainty. All that was thought to be solid dissolves in the air, adding to the pollution.

A generation hungering for certainties is like a vacuum. It sucks in evangelists of reactionary nostrums bearing conservative labels. Thus we are well launched into an era of regressive politics and regressive religion, in which the liberal spirit is at the head of a line of perceived evils, followed in no particular order by abortion, welfare, food stamps, affirmative action, sex education, the United Nations, aid to the Third World, disarmament, Soviet expansionism, and on and on.

What exactly is this satanic liberalism? To me, and by and large to history, it is a way of walking and acting in the world. It means celebrating and practicing the importance of persons: their inherent freedom to think, speak, associate, hear, read, see, and learn; not perfect freedom, but responsible freedom, become manifest in the particulars of our lives. It means warmly embracing political democracy and constitutional, compassionate government. Among its meanings are social justice, popular education, equal opportunity and access, peaceful resolution of conflict, broad tolerance of diversity, the scientific spirit of inquiry, a rational outlook, a relativistic philosophy and ethicosocial religion.

In my life, the liberal spirit is wholistic. It informs my being in all of its dimensions—spiritual, political, and social; private and public. I recognize, with appreciation and respect, that this is not a universal condition. There are numerous religious liberals who are conservative in their politics and religious conservatives who are liberal in their politics.

I claim no heavenly sanction for my all-embracing liberal way of walking in life's paths. Still, those who join me in trying to practice it are apt to be puzzled by the fervor with which it is smitten hip and thigh, not just by partisans of the right, but of the left as well.

Disparagement of liberalism from the right is normal and seemingly eternal. But today, the liberal spirit is exuberantly despised by many on the left. Black, feminist, and Third World liberationists, and many peace activists, often have that special Buckley-like curl to their lips when they pronounce the word *liberal*. Yet, as I shall point out, *liberation* and *liberal* come from the same Latin root. They are kin.

A solemn look back to Martin Luther King, Jr., may be instructive. Dr. King was steeped in liberalism. Liberals loved him when he spoke for nonviolence in Montgomery. Liberals loved him when he wrote his stirring letter from the Birmingham jail, where he was incarcerated for opposing Bull Connor's police dogs and fire hoses with freedom songs. Liberals loved him at the the Lincoln Memorial in 1963 when he linked his dream and the dream of black people with the liberal dream.

But how quickly frightened liberals deserted him when, at Riverside Church in 1963, he said that the struggle for justice at home and for an end to the war in Vietnam were one and the same. Liberal leaders raced to the television cameras and into print to accuse him of jeopardizing the civil rights movement by linking the two issues. We can only guess his thoughts when many of those same keepers of the liberal flame finally came around to saying what he had said three years earlier.

Liber, with whom both *liberal* and *liberation* are connected, was the Roman god of fertility and wine. It was natural, therefore, that *liberal* came to be applied to what was generous and open, to the unrestricted and unfettered, not bound by established mores to the orthodox and formal. Nor was it unnatural, in the eyes of certain respectables to whom the suggestion of a pregnant universe was distasteful if not downright threatening, that *liberal* evoked the licentious and chaotic. This we can understand. More difficult to understand are liberationists whose derision concentrates on liberalism rather than on reaction. Kinship struggles are often nasty.

To a certain extent, anti-liberal diatribes are a fashionable expression of human meanness and frustration. We all have a scurvy streak in us that we are bound to express. Now it is open season on liberals, who frequently respond by splenetically attacking one another.

Frustrations among liberationists are very real. They have to be vented somewhere. So why not on liberals, currently a pretty defenseless lot? In addition, the cyclicity of liberalism is an old story. Liberalism, religious and political, flowers, gets locked into transient programs, trends, parties, and tactics and withers, only to flower again. During its withering periods, reaction always takes heart, which is certainly true today, and liberals enter into a kind of choleric introspection. Nor is there anything historically original about those of more radical bent snapping at liberals for being mere reformers, when root-and-branch revolution is what is obviously needed. This too is an old story.

The trouble with too many liberals, according to radicalized blacks, women, youth, gays, and peace activists, is their complacent spirit. Yes, they have a decent concern for social change. But where is the passion? Where is the sense of their own oppression? Buried in middle-class standards. That's where it is. Tucked into the benefits that infuriatingly unjust social structures have bestowed upon them. Yes, they would like to share these benefits with the less fortunate, those who have been locked out and denied access, but at little or no cost to themselves and their children.

The evils of society burn a hole in the soul, say liberationists. We have a gut reaction, a kind of upset that can never be adequately expressed by the liberal's "decent concern."

How is this gulf to be bridged? I speak as a liberal in search of redemption and reconstruction — one whose soul is full of holes burned by the evils of society. If liberalism is to arise from whatever malaise withers it, if it is to reach out, it must be a humbled, radicalized, stretched, and shriven liberalism. It must be a liberalism with a monumental abhorrence of hypocrisy and cant. It must be a liberalism that knows, not just a decent concern for oppression, but a personal experience of it and a profound sense of agony and outrage. In brief, it must be a liberalism ecstatic enough and disciplined enough to celebrate, demand, organize, institutionalize, suffer for, and exult over profound social and individual change.

I speak then for a transformed liberalism. Scavenging for hope in this task does not mean donning "conservative" clothes and calling oneself a neoliberal. As for the self-styled conservatives of this age, typically they are nursers of their own resentments and defenders of their own interests. On the other hand, there is no genuinely effective radical movement. That leaves liberalism, however disarrayed and weary its troops, among whom there is a distressing loss of heart. But this is characteristic of liberalism, which is experiencing, as before, the agony of its success. Years ago, pioneers like Jane Addams and John Dewey helped launch a liberalism that was high on mental freedom and social compassion. They succeeded. Millions of people were introduced to new appreciations of economic equity and civic participation. The trouble with liberalism is that once it's successful as it has been in so many realms — from women's rights to minority rights, from universal public education to protection of the environment, from progressive taxation to Medicaid — liberals don't know what to do. All of this is accomplished, yet illiberalism flourishes. What should liberals do, not just to beat back reactionary assaults, but to gird for new positive thrusts?

Here are some possible revisions of the liberal idea, which once again might make it, in new shapes and forms, a powerful social force.

First there is the advocacy of a new theory of intellect, a new mode of perception, a new way of acting. Liberalism has always been right in its devotion to reason. But reason has been interpreted too narrowly for the present age. We assume that what we call reality exhausts reality, that what we call the human story is the real human story, and that our western symbols are universally binding to all humanity. Shall we try to persuade, or even force, all of earth's men and women to become like us? Do North American mind-sets and world views represent the best of what the world is capable? Will human value truly be advanced if North Americans make over the entire planet in their present image?

What liberals also need is an infusion of intelligent subjectivity, which is not a reaction against reason but an extension of reason, a way of looking at reality that snatches reason from the hands of textbook scientists, logicians, and technologists. What is needed is an expanded consciousness, capable of taking more seriously the data for reflection and reverence that come from feelings, instincts, insights—in short, from the whole realm of creative imagination. We keep trying to live like scientists, when in fact most of the important decisions we make—choosing a spouse, changing a job—are not scientific at all. And because we try to live like scientists, many in the world become convinced that we are spiritually underdeveloped and lacking in soul.

Liberals who permit new forms of consciousness to express themselves may get on the move again and be threatened by new successes. Wouldn't that be something?

A reminder is in order. Respecting ambiguity and distrusting absolutes is not bad. Questioning received opinion and the authority of doctrines that defy reason is a reassuring means of perceiving that irrationalism underlies many seductive "certainties" peddled by slick, thriving hucksters. The liberal spirit takes the questions of the age seriously and doesn't try to answer unasked or wasteful questions. It accepts our human finiteness and fallibility and rejects unrelenting certitude. This emphasis on openness (humility?), far from being like a sieve, can be a robust listening to other possibilities, as well as a shield against salvationist nostrums and premature closures.

Where, then, is the solid ground on which liberals plant their feet? How about a rich menu of values, goals, priorities, and agendas? There is a special kind of derision reserved for these "abstractions." But how impalpable are they really? Not at all, if you stop to think about how most of us try to live our lives. Values, goals, priorities, and agendas are the very stuff of the weal and woe of life. Bless the liberal spirit for beckoning us to treat the stuff with intense seriousness and saving humor.

The effectiveness is uneven, to be sure, but the liberal spirit helps its devotees to risk experiencing the tangles and riddles of modern life, free from blanched fevers where truth is never gray. The raw reality is that we live and die in the embrace of imperfection and relative judgments. Returning the embrace seems a reasonable faith by which to live.

Despite these earned hallelujas, liberalism faces the waning of the century with tired blood. It is so pummeled that many are diagnosing brain death. The heart still beats, diagnosticians say, and the outer extremities still respond in Pavlovian fashion to external stimuli. Some, whose wish is parent to the thought, claim that liberalism's death certificate and autopsy are at hand. They already know what the findings will be: death by hyper-confusion. Alas, a massive vascular accident induced by overextended uncertainty. Too much indulgence in paradoxes and ambiguities.

Others surmise that the overriding affliction of liberals is elitism: walling themselves into discrete, precious enclaves; each absorbed by some special cause, some unique set of ideas to play with. Requirements for admission can be seen as quite cliquish. Most people rebel against a steady diet of critical intellect. They hunger for transcendent nourishment and are frustrated by too much search and too little discovery. Frustration in turn will extend an uncritical welcome to almost any kind of metaphysical mooring, possibly something caring and sensitive, often commercial gimmickry, and in too many instances cruel claptrap. Yet, no amount of jeering and lecturing will discourage those who feel driven to take the gamble.

It is liberals who take a risk by denying the extreme spiritual discomfort of openness without commitment. Doubt is important in faith, but only if it is a means of keeping faith activated and enlivened. Doubt as an end in itself is deadly. There is nothing liberal about indifference to the human need for spiritual direction. To think so is to betray ignorance of the human condition.

We need to remind the world of the affirmations of liberalism if we expect it to listen to liberalism's complaints about quacks and rascals. The need for centering points in a careening world is real and rightful. Groundedness and rootedness are positives, not negatives. They are the crux of any transforming ministry to life. Liberals take notice. If we view liberalism as, in D. H. Lawrence's words, "an uprooted tree, with its roots in the air" (letter to the Reverend Robert Reid), nothing less than strenuous affirmation will supplant it. To say that we do not have the whole truth is not to say that we have no truth. Like Saint Paul, we see through a glass darkly, but we do see. Openness without wholeness and commitment is a clanging cymbal.

I was grateful when there came an invitation to share with a gathering of midwestern religious liberals the articles of liberal faith undergirding my social activism. It was an exciting task of self-examination and distillation — elementary and elemental. In the end I described four liberal/liberating convictions by which I live.

1. I am life that wills to live in the midst of life that wills to live.
2. Separating the essential from the nonessential is what I call being spiritual.

3. Power, ethically understood, is the ability to achieve moral purpose.
4. Nothing is settled; balance is blessedness.

Nietzsche wrote: "We are unknown, we knowers, to ourselves.... Of necessity we remain strangers to ourselves, we understand ourselves not, in our selves we are bound to be mistaken" (*Thus Spake Zarathustra*).

I respect the wisdom in this. But, as with so much of Nietzsche, it is overstated. I know myself imperfectly, but I am no complete stranger to myself and to what makes me tick. I am not "bound to be mistaken" in what I believe that I believe.

In addition to being a person, spouse, parent, and grandparent, I am a preacher, counselor, teacher, and would-be prophet. The sheer mess of human conditions that cry out for deliverance — from poverty, oppression, and bondage — appalls me. I experience human suffering and degradation as my own pain. I don't just read about them and think, Isn't that terrible? As a responsible advocate of human life and dignity, I hurt, and the hurt grips me at the roots of my being.

I also experience life as grace-filled wonder. Statistically, the possibility of any of us being here is so infinitesimal that the mere fact of our existence is confounding. As E. B. White put it in the *New Yorker*: "If the world were merely seductive, that would be easy. If it were merely challenging, that would be no problem. But I arise in the morning, torn between a desire to improve (or save) the world, and a desire to enjoy (or savor) the world. This makes it hard to plan the day."

As for the cosmic meanings of human life, I am content with a deep and abiding modesty. I simply do not know. But as for the finite meanings of human life, experienced in dazzlement and deliverance, in rights and repression, in surprise and struggle, in living and dying, I have no uncertainties. These meanings are real. They matter. I cannot and will not abdicate the quest for finite human fulfillment. If, cosmically speaking, human life is a trip to nowhere, so be it. I will not live my life, precious gift that it is, according to that rubric.

So, there is a special joy in sharing what sustains, directs, chastens, and validates my bittersweet journey along the boundaries of such a liberal faith.

Life as Gift

I am life that wills to live in the midst of life that wills to live. My life is a gift, a grace, if you wish. I had nothing to do with planning, creating, or initially shaping it. With my gift of life comes a unique endowment — human consciousness: a drive not only to be, but to be fulfilled. As I grew and developed, it was impressed upon me that my will to live and to be fulfilled existed in the midst of other wills to live and to be fulfilled. I learned that I could look out from within myself and see a life view, a world view. How then might I best express gratitude for my own gift of life? By reverencing not only my own will to live and to be fulfilled, but that of others. How could I do this? By sympathy, obviously. By self-development. By discipline. By encounter. By associated effort. We do not live alone. We live together. We depend on one another. To forget that is to become spiritually lost, like fiery particles flung off from the solar system and quenched meaninglessly in outer space.

For me, the great teacher of this spiritual and ethical affirmation of the gift of life is Albert Schweitzer, an exemplar of what I think is liberalism at its best, namely that progress does not come easily or automatically. Quite the contrary. His view of human beings (including himself, of course) was pessimistic. It was his willing, hoping, and acting that were optimistic. It is the same for me. I shut my eyes to none of human nature's aberrations. I do not believe that human reason is an all-sufficient force for good. My liberal faith is anchored in our membership in one another and in a consciously embraced ethical spirit generated by this truth.

Being Spiritual

Separating the essential from the nonessential is what I call being spiritual.

I found this phrase, years ago, floating in one of Corita Kent's gossamer paintings. It has since hung on my study wall, where I can contemplate it each morning.

There has never been, nor will there ever be, enough time or opportunity to learn everything, to do everything, or care evenhandedly about everything. We can never be completely satisfied or satisfiable, adjusted or adjustable. We continually run out of energy, ability, and courage. We are hurtable. The temptation is ever upon us to exercise influence we have not earned and do not possess.

To be spiritual, for me, means knowing all of this and still offering up thanks for the privilege of being what we are. There is in us the stuff out of which new, affirming experiences are fashioned. So build we up the human beings that we are.

"Love the moment," says Corita Kent, "and the energy...will spread beyond all boundaries.

"Flowers grow out of dark moments.

"Your each moment is vital because it affects the whole.

"Live in the dark moment.

"Life is a succession of moments; to live each one is to succeed."

So, it is not essential to me to set precise meanings to the word *God*. I know that only by living my limited moments will I grope toward truths about what God may be and what we are.

That's why I worry about dying, but not about death. Before I was born I knew nothing about life, and it certainly didn't worry me then. Death may be yet another state of being, or it may be a nonstate of nonbeing. I cannot know. Why should it worry me any more than life did before I was born?

But dying is an experience, an act in which I will be the central participant. It is essential to my spirituality to meditate upon that and to prepare for it as best I can, to think through the possible scenarios.

Like Henry David Thoreau, "I wish to learn what life has to teach, and not, when I come to die, discover that I have not lived." I want to immerse myself in the streams of intimacy and history. I want to live in this death-oriented world without letting death have power over me. I want to live in the fullest possible awareness of a true belonging, not just to those who are nearest and dearest to me, but to the times in which I live—the causes, emergencies, issues, desperations, and hopes.

Power and Moral Purpose

Power, ethically understood, is the ability to achieve moral purpose.

A crucial dimension of the gift of life and of its will to live in the midst of life that wills to live is the use of power. A liberal (and liberating) faith, in both its personal and communal forms, must come to terms with the realities of power. Social action is the exercise of power. Ethical social action is the exercise of power for implementing the demands of justice, equity, and love.

Power is two-dimensional. One dimension is an expression of ultimate reality, or, as many would say, of God's law and love. The other dimension is the exercise of human freedom. Understanding power as ultimate reality, or as God's law and love, means that in exercising it one is compelled by the ethical necessities of being fully human: to seek human community in the fulfillment of interdependent spiritual destinies, of life that wills to live in the midst of life that wills to live. Power understood as human freedom is our response to the possibilities in creation, which are both personal and institutional.

Power, ethically understood, is the ability to achieve moral purpose. It is the capacity, inherent in our being, "to bring good tidings to the afflicted; . . . to bind up the broken-hearted, to proclaim liberty to the captives, . . . to comfort all who mourn" (Isaiah 61:1-2).

The idea of power and the exercise of power must never be viewed as alien to the liberal spirit. Power is a basic dimension of being and a basic dimension of the personal and institutional liberal life. It is both desirable and necessary in implementing the demands of love and justice.

Martin Luther King, Jr., taught that "one of the greatest problems of history is that the concepts of love and power are usually contrasted as polar opposites. Love is identified with a resignation of power and power with a denial of love. . . . What is needed is a realization that power without love is reckless and abusive and that love without power is sentimental and anemic. Power at its best is love implementing the demands of justice. Justice at its best is love correcting everything that stands against love."*

These words, to me, are a veritable manifesto for an empowered liberalism. I say, Amen!

As a Team

Nothing is settled; balance is blessedness.

If I had to give a six-word definition of normative liberalism, this would be it. Take, for example, these two familiar areas of experience: innovation and tradition, and spiritual nurture and public action.

---

*Martin Luther King, Jr., *Where Do We Go From Here* (Boston: Beacon Press, 1968).

Innovation and Tradition.

In the Book of Acts (17:21) there is a description of those who hung around the Areopagus in Athens as "people who spent their time in nothing except telling and hearing something new." This is an impression we liberals frequently give. Trendy. Zealots of the latest. Innovators. Prizers of telling and hearing the new (as well we should be). But we also have a magnificent history, bequeathed to us by the labors and sufferings of forebears, known and unknown: thinkers, confessors, apostles, prophets, and martyrs. We are a rooted people, we liberals, who should be everlastingly respectful and proud of our tradition and inheritance.

Many of the problems of our common life in the liberal spirit rise from losing our sense of innovation or tradition. We get into trouble when we slip into an idolatry of only one. It is essential to our genius to love the making of new wine, but it is also essential to our genius to savor the mature, full-bodied wine of our heritage.

Nothing is settled; balance is blessedness.

Spiritual Nurture and Public Action.

Inward and outward; personal growth and social witness. Once again, nothing is settled; balance is blessedness. We have swung between these "birches" for as long as our history runneth.

Emerson put it this way: "These wonderful horses need to be driven by fine hands" (Society and Solitude). The liberal spirit is for healing our ever-battered souls: in solitude, in touching intimacies, in deep, searching disciplines. But we are in the world and must act in the world—as free individuals and as community persons. Nothing is finally settled by that either. We often act in hollowness. Spiritual preparation, private and communal, for acting in the world is crucial. Everything that has to do with our common humanity and how it is nourished is important. Everything that stretches from self to society and from society to self is important. These wonderful horses need to be driven, as a team, with fine hands. Balance is blessedness.

These days it is easy to despair of liberalism's weaknesses, so it is of consequence to be aware of our present and potential strengths. One of these is our enduring function of living on the boundaries—between mind and body, the internal and the external, freedom and necessity, individual and community.

We have never had a better opportunity to live not as one-side-or-the-other partisans of left brain–right brain, mysticism-empiricism, intuitive-rational, piety-society, nurture-nature, but as agile boundary-dwellers, at home on both sides of the borders: pilgrims of the reconciliations that must come if the human race is to survive.

As one familiar with significant voluntary associations of liberal bent, I know how rich the opportunities are for such valuing communities — as relatively stable, preventive arrangements against personal and social pathology and as centers for the generation of liberating change.

We liberals are members of a historic movement with accrued status and moral authority to stand as a counterpoint to the death of moral goodness. We who speak the language of the liberal spirit and live out of its bosom can be key figures in the struggle both to save and to savor the world. If this sounds inflated, remember that Daedalus's warning to his son Icarus was not just against flying too high. It was also against flying too low.

Security

I am not a liberal because it gives me security. No one should try the liberal spirit looking for that result. What liberalism appeals to in me is what Carl Sandburg, in "Man the Moon Shooter," described as the "moon shooter" part of our nature:

> The shapes of change
> ai ai they take their time
> asking what the dawn asks
> giving the answers evening gives
> till tomorrow moves in
> saying to...the moon shooter
> 'Now I am here — now read me —
> give me a name.'

We humans, in Sandburg's eyes, are moon shooters: restless, roving, inquisitive creatures, ever striving for unknown futures. There is no real stopping place, no status quo. There are always the next shapes of change to come.

It was Christmas Day, 1983, late afternoon. Our family, twelve in number, four generations, was in the midst of a high-decibel, high-calorie holiday dinner, when the phone rang. It was Jesse Jackson. "Jack," he said, "a Merry Christmas to you and Joan and the family."

"Same to you, Jesse, and to Jacqueline, and all your kids."

"Jack, I want you to go to Syria with me, to get Lieutenant Robert Goodman and bring him home."

"When do you plan to leave, Jesse?"

"Probably on Wednesday, three days from now. The Syrians say we can see Goodman and that Assad will talk with us. They say they aren't going to let him go, but I think we can get him. I want you with me."

"Jesse, let me talk it over with my family, and I'll get back to you."

The family talked. They were accustomed to the "moon shooter" nature of my relationship with Jesse Jackson. With their blessing, I flew off to Damascus on December 29, 1983, as a member of the Jackson mission. The rest is history. We brought Lieutenant Goodman home. Indeed, there are always the next shapes of change to come.

But what about rest for the weary soul? Moon shooting is exciting. But we are also creatures in need of tranquility. What place is there for inner quiet and peace? Not only do we need the thrill of change, of movement, but we also need dependable things, reliable things, steady things, things that stand fast while we think our way through the enigmas, puzzles, and horrors of a swiftly changing world.

Sandburg raises an ancient problem. We are indeed moon shooters, but we also long for solid ground beneath our feet. Where will we find that solid ground? In what thoughts, what beliefs, what faiths? In the midst of change, on what can we depend?

Robert Frost warmed to these questions in his narrative poem "The Star-Splitter," which tells the story of Brad McLaughlin, described by Frost as a "Hugger-mugger" New Hampshire farmer.

> He burned his house down for the fire insurance
> And spent the proceeds on a telescope
> To satisfy a life-long curiosity
> About our place among the infinities.

At first, Frost tells us, there was some mean laughter, but soon the townsfolk began to reflect:

If one by one we counted people out
For the least sin, it wouldn't take us long
To get so we had no one left to live with,
For to be social is to be forgiving.

So, Brad McLaughlin bought his telescope and took a job as ticket agent for the old Concord railroad, a job that gave him leisure for stargazing. He and his friend, the narrator, spent countless hours in the evening looking up "the brass barrel, velvet black inside, at a star quaking in the other end."

We've looked and looked, but after all where are we?
Do we know any better where we stand,
And how it stands between the night tonight
And (someone) with a smoky lantern chimney?
How different from the way it ever stood?

Frost has pondered the questions about security and raised some new ones about serenity. Is it abnormal to want serenity? Can we be moon shooters and still be serene? Can we find serenity in the stars or in anything outside our own being? If we cannot find serenity in the stars, can we find it in what the stars help us to learn about ourselves?

Let's go back again to that solid ground beneath our feet. In a spiritual sense, where are we likely to find it? By leaps of irrationality? In unquestioning obedience? Does this universe make life easier for us if we subscribe to the right creed, follow the right leader, or pledge the right allegiance? We must be morally myopic to think it is that kind of universe! Where then is security? Where is the solid ground? If we want an answer, a strong answer, one that does not try to blink the facts or sentimentalize the realities, we can hardly do better than the tough thoughts of the tender-spirited Emerson: "Nothing is secure but life, transition, the energizing spirit. No love can be bound by oath or covenant to secure it against a higher love. No truth so sublime but it may be trivial tomorrow in the light of new thoughts. People wish to be settled; only in so far as they are unsettled is there any hope." And then Emerson startles us with a conjecture that we never rise so high as when we know not whither we are going.

Obviously Emerson offers us little in the way of lulling assurance. If we never rise so high as when we know not whither we are going, most of us would have little trouble soaring free into the stratosphere. Perhaps there is more to this than first meets the eye. Possibly it is just such a time as ours, when it is impossible to know exactly where we are going, that we are literally forced by our problems and challenges to rise to new heights of coping and achieving. Is it, after all, so important to know precisely where we are going, as long as we know the general direction in which we want to travel and the stronger, warmer companions we will need for the journey? What more should we ask than the solid reliance on the faith that somehow, because of the nature of what is required of us, we will respond and rise higher than we dreamed possible? If only a wiser, nobler humanity is equal to our present problems, then a wiser, nobler humanity we will be.

By no stretch of the imagination can this be called security. At least it is not the kind of security that makes us feel smug and safe from the barbs of life. "Nothing is secure," says Emerson, "but life, transition, and the energizing spirit." With this perspective, we achieve a larger and revitalized conception of liberal faith. If we would find solid ground beneath our feet, we must have courage enough to give up illusions of a protected life and accept our role as servants of life, agents of transition, and incarnations of the energizing spirit, subject to all the stresses and shocks of life, but confident and buoyant through them all. This is the liberal spirit at its greatest, not a petty search for protection or a pinched hope of piecemeal benevolence, but the wonderful adventure of life itself, as solemn as a world that is dying and as supple as a world that is waiting to be born; as expectant as souls who see clearly what is required of them and rise empowered to make and meet a better future. This kind of liberal spirit *is* solid ground, and when we have discovered it and made it our own, nothing can take it away.

What of serenity? We will not find it in tranquilizing sermons that are on the self-help shelves of bookstores. Many of the pulpit recitals and cozy, expensive seminars devoted to serenity and success are geared to those who seek an easy way and can afford it. There is no easy way. The road to serenity is as rigorous as any we will ever travel. Serenity comes not from escaping the realities of life, but from being in the midst of them. The best human beings have always been those who achieved serenity by taking upon themselves the pain, fear, suffering, cruel passions, and murky guilts of human inhumanity toward other humans. Whether we speak of a Catholic Sister Teresa, a Jewish Martin Buber, or a Unitarian Joseph Tuckerman, we know that this is the truth of the matter. No one comes by serenity cheaply. To gain it, we have to meet its requirements; we have to do the deeds and make the choices that bring serenity in their wake. For each of us, it means making, not just alone, but in the disciplined company of others, the difficult choices, the demanding choices.

It means wading into the river of history and accepting one's place in it. It means breaking bread at a common table of memories and aspirations, rejoicing in identification with causes, emergencies, movements, parties. As William Ernest Hocking put it in *The Coming World Civilization:* "Failure to accept responsibility, refusal to take a stand on vital issues, timid rejection...of the ties of a true belonging, these are denials of life—in effect they are deeds of death."

The greatest and most emboldening of blessings is the will to care enough about the times in which we live to know where and to what moral ends we want to put our efforts on the line. This is, in Hocking's words, "life with shape and character." No one can consciously choose the lower against the higher and know inner peace. Serenity is involvement with the unserene.

We began with two poets: one who speaks of us as moon shooters, and another who spins a yarn about a farmer who sought solace in an ill-gotten telescope. We found them raising profound questions about security and serenity. In each case, the answer came back: Look within and look around you! The tasks of finding solid ground, of making peace with oneself and one's times, are tasks in the midst of change, challenge, and conflict. If we break under the weight of our burdens, we break, isolated, from within. If we master life, that mastery also comes from within, but is connected. All of life is change, and we cannot escape it. We look for strength and peace, and where do we find them but in being useful, being whole, being warm members of the human family, of adding our weight to what is called for by the deep nature of life.

That's what the liberal spirit is about, has always been about.

2

A Human Being, No More or Less

I came to see the damage that was done and the treasures that prevail.

Adrienne Rich, *Diving into the Wreck*

Humans are "glorious and happy," according to William Ellery Channing, not by what they have, but by what they are. They can receive nothing better or nobler than "the unfolding of their own spiritual nature." The liberal spirit's supreme gift to me was an introduction to the Unitarian Universalist religious community, where I found encouragement to unfold: the special joy of breaking out of the cocoon or of discovering a greater freedom in the exercise of my intelligence and in the growth of my experience of love, beauty, and justice.

Childhood is a quilt of many patches: sounds, smells, tears, playgrounds, back fences, anticipations. Mine was such a childhood, a compound of chance and purpose, marvel and misery. I remember with special warmth my maternal grandfather, Charles M. Torrey, of the Foxboro, Massachusetts, Torreys. He had been one of the early touring professional baseball players. It was he who guided my first nervous attempts at playing sandlot baseball. He gave me his very own cornet, battered and old, on which I learned the beginnings of the musical skills that eventually helped finance my college education.

I remember the summer, my twelfth, when I fastened a chinning bar on the back porch in the conviction that it would help to stretch my body to the more than six feet of height I so desperately desired. By the age of seventeen, the chinning bar long forgotten, I made it to six feet and three inches and stopped growing.

I remember the boyhood hours I spent poring over Uncle Lawrence Farwell's picture book of World War I. He had been an artilleryman in France, a feat I greatly admired. I nursed a morbid fear that there might never be another war in which I could perform valorous deeds. Such are the unpredictabilities of childhood! By the time we found ourselves in World War II, I was a confirmed pacifist, an ardent convert to nonviolence.

As I look back over the tender years, there is little that prophesied my eventual turn toward a Unitarian Universalist ministry, except that I was an avid reader. My room, to the dismay of my parents and, later, my grandparents, was forever strewn with books. At Christmas and birthdays there were only two kinds of gifts I really wanted: athletic equipment and books. As for religion, it was anything but a burden. None of my relatives pried into my religious thoughts, and I did very little prying of my own. My father, Jack Mendelsohn, Sr., born Jewish, was an uncomplicated person religiously and, like his father before him, nonobserving. Theology was about as pressing for him as witchcraft.

I worshipped my mother, Anna Melissa Torrey Mendelsohn, and was never given the opportunity to grow beyond a boy's craving for approval and affection. She was statuesque, red-headed, and very beautiful. Or so I remember. She was youthful. Even as a child, when anyone over twenty seemed ancient, I was deeply conscious of her youth. She played the piano professionally. That was how my father, then a music publisher, met her. She cooked wonderful soups and often held me in her lap. I needed her terribly and was painfully aware of it.

One day I ran home from school. I was six and a first grader in the old Morse School in Cambridge. The teacher left the room, and the children exploded into a chaos of screaming, jumping, and throwing erasers. Suddenly she was back, and I stood transfixed with eraser in hand. Enraged, she pulled me from the room and ordered me to stand alone in the hall until she was ready to deal with me. I was the only culprit she apprehended and humbled. Part of what I felt was fear, but a great part was outrage. In the face of massive injustice, I bolted from the corridor and ran home, where I knew there would be justice even though it would include punishment for my transgression. I was not disappointed. My mother deprived me of several privileges for a few days, but she also took me back to school, hand in hand, where she charmed and soothed the distraught teacher and returned me honorably to my peers.

This is the mother I remember. It was difficult for me to think of God as being other than a woman, like my mother.

Then life taught me something else.

I was eight and shared a room with my sister, Virginia, who was three years younger than I. One night I awoke in the darkness and peered into the hall where I caught a harrowing glimpse of my father helping my mother down the stairs. Her face was twisted with pain. It was the last time I saw her.

Years later I learned it was a miscarriage that took her to the hospital that night. My grandmother, Mary Spinney Torrey, came the next morning and an air of mystery hung on the house. The following night I awoke again and heard my grandmother and father whispering together. Soon they left, unaware that I was awake. But I knew what was happening. While my sister slept, I paced in the darkness of our parents' room, sobbing aloud, "She can't die. Oh, God, don't let her die!"

She did die, and at dawn my father and grandmother returned to tell us what I already knew. The cause of death, though it had no meaning for me at the time, was peritonitis, an abdominal inflammation. All that mattered to me was the loss of the most important person in the world. I was hurt and angry, desolate and resentful. For the first time in my life I had asked God for something. I had begged God for something! And God had turned and slapped me in the face, as I had seen some parents strike my playmates.

Since that moment religious questions have never been far from my thoughts. It may be a gift or a neurosis, but I am gripped with the habit of religious searching. It would be wrong, however, to give the impression of youthful zealotry or intense concentration.

Soon after my mother's death, my sister became a member of Aunt Mabel Farwell's household, and I went to live with my Torrey grandparents in Cambridge, Massachusetts. We were neighbors, just a few streets apart. My father, who had shifted from publishing music to selling furniture, took up residence in a New York City hotel. Though we saw him regularly, we were never again a united family.

My grandparents were quiet, steady, sober New Englanders. My grandfather had been a barnstorming baseball player in that pastime's pioneer years. Later, he had become a fireman and policeman in his native Foxboro, where my mother was laid to rest among her Torrey forebears. When I joined their household, my grandfather had long been a minor functionary with the Elliott Addressing Machine Company in Cambridge. My grandmother, who in her younger days was a solo whistler on the church and lodge circuit in Washington County, Maine, cooked, mended, busied herself about the house, and looked after me with untiring solicitude. The two of them played dominoes almost every night of the years I lived with them. They encouraged me to study, to play, and to bring my friends home. Athletic skills became a passion for me, equaled only by my determination to be a top student. I gravitated to friends who felt the same.

My grandparents and the Farwells were unenthusiastically associated with a neighborhood church, Pilgrim Congregational, a center of conservative, evangelical Christianity. Because God was a paradox to me, I became the most ardent and faithful churchgoer of the family. The minister, the Reverend Stanley Addison, kind and careworn, whose preaching voice always sounded tearful, had officiated at my mother's funeral and was keenly concerned about the welfare of my soul. The Sunday school superintendent, Dr. Arthur Miles, an austere, elderly dentist, believed in the fire of hell and was determined to guide me in another direction. From the beginning, I was both a protégé and a problem child. Our relationship developed steadily but never smoothly.

In the sense that I was determined to ask Why and How do you know, I suppose my religious future was set the night my mother died, but it would be years before I recognized it. If religion was to make sense to me, it had to provide room for my inquisitiveness and rebellion. Somehow it had to encompass the anguish and bewilderment I felt at God's failure to save my mother. It had to be wide enough to let me ask whether God was a demon, or whether God existed at all.

I expected to find answers in church, where the talk was interminably of God, Jesus, prayer, and salvation. I listened and grew confused and impudent. I tried to pray. I listened hard for God's voice. I wanted to feel Jesus's arms about me. I prayed and had the increasingly embarrassed feeling that no one was listening. If God possessed a voice, it was strangely silent in my presence. The more I thought about the Jesus who was being revealed to me in my religious education, the more unappealing and unreal he became.

What my religious tutors failed to realize was that a spell of dissent was upon me like a divine discontent. It was not about meek acceptance and a sense of sin that I wished to hear. I wanted to be challenged and shaken. I wanted my spirit to be given something to strive for. I wanted to know why the world could be at once wondrous and ugly. I wanted to know why I had both laughter and pain. If God had created me, I wanted to know who had created God. Instead, I was backed into a corner and was implored to surrender my soul to the Lord and Savior.

I stayed with the neighborhood church until I went to college and lived much of my social life under its care. I knew from the time I was twelve that I could never be a Christian as the word was interpreted there, but as a teen-ager I sang in the adult choir, as a high school senior I taught a Sunday school class of ten-year-old boys, and I rarely missed a Sunday evening Christian Endeavor meeting for youth. These Pilgrim Congregational people were my friends, my familiars, my community, and though they trembled for my soul on grounds I considered nonsensical, I respected their sincerity and was grateful for their affection.

Such religion as I possess was born of conflict and has been, in its development, a struggle *against* resentment of a wound inflicted upon me when I was unable to defend myself and *for* a positive, constructive, unfettered spiritual freedom. In college there were added dimensions of an awakened social conscience and a desire to commit my life to the service of others. The open-mindedness of classicism, the probing of philosophy, the measuring of science, and the eclecticism of anthropology impressed upon me the endless diversity of human spiritual searchings. A firm decision against religious sectarianism was inevitable. I have sought a spiritual life that offers not surrender and salvation but, in Albert Camus's words, "love of life in spite of life." I have striven to accept flaws and to find things to live for that transcend and conquer them.

Faith, Admiration, and Sympathy

For a time I was in a genuine dilemma about a career. After graduating from college, I spent three years testing the waters, first in the business world, then as a high school teacher and coach. I enjoyed both, gained confidence, and even accumulated savings. But all this time there was an underlying itch for the ministry. My philosophical views were radically at odds with traditional theology, yet I felt a deep affection for the *community* of the church, as I had experienced it. I kept thinking about what a profoundly useful vehicle it was, potentially, for moral improvement and social witness. The ministry, it seemed, offered one of the most rewarding and constructive careers to one whose mind responded enthusiastically to religious questions and who wanted, as I did, to cultivate skills in education, human relations, and the leadership of groups banded together to seek spiritual fortification, moral encouragement, and ethical effectiveness.

The passing years have only confirmed my early surmises about the ministry's possibilities. H. L. Mencken once described the clergy as ticket speculators outside the gates of heaven. It is not uncommon even now for skeptics and others to be anticlerical. There are always many justifying examples. In general, however, the modern, well-trained, and well-disciplined ministers, priests, or rabbis hold places of public respect equal ot those of scientists, educators, poets, and the like. They are regarded as makers and transmitters of culture, and as useful, responsible community figures who, more often than not, succeed in practicing what they preach.

Rather than being satirized, ministers often are objects of intense solicitude. There are frequent articles, reports, and studies about the plight of harassed, overworked, and underpaid clergy. Under headlines like "Why Ministers Are Breaking Down," they will list, anonymously, "brilliant" clerics who have been drained, exhausted, and washed up at what would otherwise be the height of their powers. Then follows an analysis of the minister's job — like an equestrian who is ordered to ride off in all directions at the same time. The blame often is placed squarely on congregations for failing to understand and appreciate the impossible demands made on their spiritual leaders.

My own feeling, developed over the years, is that the "driven" clergy are frequently the drivers. That is, they drive themselves for inner reasons they do not understand. The fact that many ministers do eventually end up in intensive therapy is not an offense attributable solely to voracious congregations. In fact, it is not an offense at all. Few congregations are exempt from the need for regular self-study and process review, preferably with skilled help. But in the selection and training of clergy early therapeutic "vaccination" and regular "booster shots" can fend off a lot of heartaches and breakdowns. We understand very easily the necessity of ministers' warmth toward others, but we are slower to realize the importance for clergy to like and respect themselves enough to cherish, conserve, and pace themselves.

Ministers can get themselves into all kinds of trouble. Few congregants really know how often ministers work thirteen or fourteen hours a day, seven days a week, months at a time, if that is what they choose to do. I say *choose* though the choice may not necessarily be conscious. But the fact remains that ministers may, if they know enough about themselves, choose to live relatively normal and balanced lives of work and play, study and recreation, activity and rest. In brief, ministers can learn to say no as well as yes. And I do not merely mean no to others. I mean no to themselves too.

One of the most important yeses ministers should learn to say to themselves is, Yes, I also am a person of flesh and not of stardust.

There are few professions in which there is not more work than a person can ever hope to get done. The ministry shares this plight, but the minister's task in coping with it is not essentially different from that in other responsible and burdened occupations.

Those who go into the ministry should expect to work hard and still live with the frustrations of never getting their work completed. The ability to pace themselves, conserve their energies, and diversify their interests and enjoyments is not something congregations can do for ministers. Congregations can do this with them, by making sensible and reasonable administrative arrangements and by fully assuming lay responsibilities, but first ministers must have the inner security to enable congregations to do that, and the will to get off their own backs. They must love and respect themselves and their congregants enough to want *all* in the community to be whole.

Mr. Justice Brennan of the United States Supreme Court received a letter that read in part: "Would you use your influence to help my boy to become a Judge. He don't like hard work and I figure that sitting on a bench would suit him just fine."

No man or woman who "don't like hard work" will find the ministry a congenial place. On the other hand, for those who are unable to learn to cherish themselves enough to live broadly and variously, with due respect for their own limitations and needs, the ministry is a poor place.

It is characteristic of congregations to want professional leaders to whom the religious life is an all-pervasive, full-time, and exacting calling that makes extraordinary claims on intelligence, sensitivity, and conscience. Ministers, in other words, are embodiments of spiritual specialization. This is not to say that laypersons desire ministers to be ethereal and otherworldly. The evidence from surveys done among Unitarian Universalist congregations indicates unmistakably that while preferred ministers are scholarly, idealistic, and responsive, they are also, by overwhelming choice, earthy and pragmatic.

The key attributes seem to be intensity and specialization. Laypersons sense that their religion is of necessity relatively cloistered. Preoccupations and distractions limit the scope of spiritual interest and cultivation. At first this sounds like a reversal of terms. After all, it is generally assumed that if anyone lives in a cloister, it is the clergy. But it depends on the kind of cloister we are talking about. If daily life, with its numerous demands and responses, is viewed as a cloister, then it is the layperson's life that is isolated from intimation and insights of spirit.

My years of association with laypersons, of enjoying the privilege of knowing them intimately, persuade me that this is a truth experienced deeply enough to be the basic motive of congregations in wanting ministers in their midst. Here are those whose only reason for being, as far as their professional lives are concerned, is to bring moral idealism to every realm of human experience. Here is a person who, by the deliberate deed of a congregation, is given the time, freedom, and sustenance to study, speak, and act on the ethical and spiritual issues of living and to help make more intelligible, to those who cannot claim such time and freedom, the religious resources available to them.

When congregations or parishioners experience disappointment, it is traceable mainly to a shattering of the image just described. If ministers fail, even unwittingly, to be the embodiments of the full-time religious life; if they fail, in some instance, to look at all aspects of life — personal, political, workaday, social — with religious insight and commitment, they are disappointments to those who accept their ministry.

I shudder as I write these words, because they mean that ministers are destined to fail in their chosen vocation. No matter how competent they become, they can never achieve enough. This makes of the ministry a very wide place and a very long road.

If the ministry is a call, it is a call not away from humanity but into it, deeply into it. It is not a summons to detachment, to become a Captain McWhirr, whom Joseph Conrad described in *Typhoon* as sailing "over the surface of the oceans as some . . . go skimming through years of existence to sink gently into a placid grave, ignorant of life to the last, without ever having been made to see all it may contain of perfidy, of violence and of error."

It is the most human thing in the world to flee from the slings and arrows of the mortal condition, and the ministry can be easily taken as a flight from being fully human — a kind of semidivine posture of being above the common embarrassment, doubt, and shame. But the only meaningful sense of the word *ministry* is one that speaks of a human fellowship of joy and pain and believes that persons do not come to themselves and to one another until they share the deepest levels of caring and compassion.

To minister — and here the word embraces laity and clergy alike — is to be called out of our pretensions, poses, and protective façades and into the great, open, windy world, where we are at least alive, even if tremblingly so, and where the chances of confirming the sanctities of our blundering hearts are endless.

To be a minister does not mean to be religious in a particular way, to cultivate certain techniques, which any bright woman or man can master, but to be a person. It is not some ecclesiastical act that makes a minister, but participation in the lives of humans, individual and associated, though it often brings one into painful relations.

The tremendous thing that is involved here is not a simple question of personal virtue or professional rectitude, but a genuine affirmation of the world: to love and live in the world for the world's own sake. And I am not talking about phony attempts to feint people into a position where the minister can get past their guard and whisper moral blandishments.

If we truly love the world, so that we can dare to defy it, we will have to get much closer to it than any phony worldliness permits. We will have to immerse ourselves in its sorrows, taste its bitter cups, and open our hearts to its most painful conflicts and tensions. Then and only then can our lives speak truth to the world in the spirit of love. In the more traditional religious ranks there is a caustic observation about clergy who stroke the cross but are very careful never to get crucified. Liberal ministers have their own unmoral equivalent in absent-minded wandering from room to room in humanity's tragic house, making gestures toward sisterhood and brotherhood, mumbling something about all-powerful reason, and contributing their own share of shallow faith with which religion so often pollutes the human atmosphere. In more ways than we like to contemplate, we disgrace with our actions the burning life-giving zeal we preach with our lips. Theodore Parker said: "I determined to preach nothing as religion which I had not experienced inwardly, and made my own, knowing it by heart."

What is it, then, that constitutes *ministry*? And I put it this way purposely to include the work of the laity as well as the clergy. Louis Lavelle describes it in his *Meaning of Holiness* when he speaks of those men and women who through their presence succeed in evoking in others an "interior quality."

The worst this world can visit on human spirit and flesh is the emptying of life, the sickening sense of nothingness. And in a world throbbing with technology and technique, with hard sell, hard play, and furious events, people spin until there is no inner life left in them. They become clothes without bodies and bodies without souls; they become not persons but masks, routines, objects, and roles: images without substance. Ministry is the restoration of an interior quality to life, a substance and a sustenance to the human interior. Ministry is the rehabilitation of people inwardly, an engagement in the kinds of relationships and advocacies that make persons of people, that imagine, anticipate, and empower the soul.

Wallace Stevens has a poem called "The Man with the Blue Guitar." It echoes Picasso's painting.

> The man bent over his guitar,
> A shearsman of sorts. The day was green
>
> They said, "You have a blue guitar,
> You do not play things as they are."
>
> The man replied, "Things as they are
> Are changed upon the blue guitar."
>
> And they said then, "But play you must,
> A tune beyond us, yet ourselves,
>
> A tune upon the blue guitar
> Of things exactly as they are."

A ministry is a blue guitar — something deeply embedded in the mystery of what we are as human beings. There can be no escape from doing something with things as they are, exactly as they are.

But one thing ministers cannot do. They cannot leave things as they are. They must play a tune beyond. Things must be changed on the blue guitar.

It is generally assumed that churches go looking for people. I went looking for a church — the right church for me. A consciousness of the possibilities in the Unitarian movement grew on me slowly. The merging of Unitarianism and Universalism was then only a dream. My Quaker acquaintances, who were aware of my unresolved dilemma, made gentle suggestions. As with so many I have met since, the unique qualities of Unitarian and Universalist churches were unknown to me. My first tentative visits were interesting but uninspiring. The intellectual caliber of the preaching was cuts above what I had known, but I happened to go to where the congregations were sparse, the ambience somewhat stiff, and the forms of worship too traditionally Protestant for my taste. But I took to reading whatever I could lay my hands on about the legacy of the liberal spirit in religion, which kept my curiosity alive. Then one Sunday in 1941 I found myself listening to John Haynes Holmes at New York's Community Church, an institution with a long Unitarian heritage. The congregation was then meeting in Town Hall, hardly an exalted setting; but Holmes created a temple of the human spirit just with his presence and preaching. The congregation was vibrant and an eloquent symbol of human diversity. The service was religious, deeply religious; yet there were no divisive, mind-splitting doctrinal elements.

During that hour I knew that if the Unitarian ministry was exciting enough to produce the fervent witness of a John Haynes Holmes, it might just possibly do the same for me. A door was open, and I wasted no time going through it. By the following summer I was enrolled in the Harvard Divinity School, with the warm encouragement and backing of the American Unitarian Association and its then-president Frederick May Eliot.

I had reservations then, just as I have now. I don't think that a religious liberal should ever be without them. As my first year of theological education began, I was asked by Stephen Fritchman, editor of the *Christian Register*, the official Unitarian magazine, to write an article on why I was entering the Unitarian ministry. In it I expressed my resentment at the bias that so obviously discouraged women from joining our ministry. My hope that this would end has, in recent years, been exultantly realized. Also, then, as now, I was distressed by the overwhelming number of white and middle-class people in our movement. Our denominational record of the number of blacks in the pulpit or the pew continues to be a sorry one indeed. My commitment to changing that record is strong, in faithfulness to the opportunities to unfold, which the Unitarian Universalist ministry has brought me. I am continually amazed and inspired by the growth of what Emerson called "faith, admiration and sympathy," which I find afforded by my calling, and especially by the congregations it has been my privilege to serve. Each has given memorable lessons of freedom in community.

3

Getting from Sunday to Monday

A person has no religion who has not slowly and painfully gathered one together, adding to it, shaping it; and one's religion is never complete and final, it seems, but must always be undergoing modification.
D.H. Lawrence, *letter to the Reverend Robert Reid*

There are very different notions of what precisely a religion is. Consider, for example, the covenant of All Souls Unitarian Universalist Church in Indianapolis. I served as minister there from 1954 to 1959, and during those years we planned, financed, and built an entirely new church plant. I remember having long conversations with the architects, expecially about how to express spatially the congregation's covenant: "Love is the spirit of this church and service is its law; to dwell together in peace, to seek the truth in love, and to help one another: This is our covenant." The architects sensitively probed with us why there were no theological doctrines set forth in this statement. It simply formulates a human purpose on which we are all united, we explained, and allows the widest possible latitude of individual theological belief. One of the architects asked whether a Baptist, Presbyterian, or Catholic could join our church. Of course, we answered, though practically speaking they might not want to because our statement leaves out matters that they might strongly want to include. But there are no barriers as far as we are concerned to anyone who wants to join us in furthering the purposes set forth in our covenant. This applies to Jews, Buddhists, Muslims, atheists, and agnostics, as well as to Christians.

Many years ago William Channing Gannett formulated the basic operational principles of our liberal religious movement in a brief statement that is as fresh as if it had just been written. He said: "*Freedom* is our method in religion; *reason* is our guide in religion; *fellowship* is our spirit in religion; *character* is our test in religion; *service* is our aim in religion." Once again, there is nothing about theological doctrine here; the concern is with a spirit, a method, a purpose.

We are forever being asked: But what, then, makes you a *church?* To those who ask, *church* obviously means required assent to certain concrete doctrinal beliefs. Not so among Unitarian Universalists. Whether the subject is God, Jesus, or immortality, there are widely varying convictions and questions among us, beneath which there is a unifying affirmation: the right of persons to make their own theological decisions. The prevailing notion of a church is that it conforms to a conventional pattern, which includes a creed, submission to authority (of holy writ, institution, hierarchy, and so on), and participation in prescribed rites and sacraments. To the uninitiated, the most puzzling feature of the Unitarian Universalist religion is its disregard of these ecclesiastical conventions. When they hear of this open process for the first time, some are confused. Others, coming suddenly upon it, fairly glow. "I've been a Unitarian Universalist for years without knowing it" is a familiar refrain. Many do not really know what to do with religiousness when it expresses itself outside the enclosures that convention has carefully labeled religion. For those not so inhibited in their spiritual pilgrimage, here, as a beginning, are some questions to try, to see if they have an intimate ring:

I simply cannot accept religious beliefs on trust alone. Is there a church for me?

I believe in many things: a deep religious chord within my being, essential human dignity, the efficacy of human effort, the search for larger truths, hunger for a caring community, the compelling need for ethical disciplines, the necessities of practiced human sisterhood and brotherhood; but I cannot bind my beliefs to a creedal test, nor place them beyond rational criticism. What church would welcome me?

In the end churches always seem to insist that the essence of their truth is revealed and complete. Does any church embrace the idea that even the essence of truth is an emerging, not a finished, thing?

Why shouldn't children be encouraged to discover religion in their own unfolding lives rather than have it drilled into them by indoctrination, no matter how well meaning? What church practices this?

Can any church be effective as a cohesive community and still urge its members to be their free, responsible, individual selves?

There is self-evident beauty and inspiration in all of the world's religious faiths. Is there a church that welcomes and reverences the insights of all significant spiritual systems?

Can persons from many religious backgrounds — Christian, Jewish, Buddhist, Muslim — find a church where all are welcome without conversion or renunciation?

I want to be free to wonder about — even doubt — the existence of God, the nature of God, the effectiveness of prayer, the value of the Bible, the possibility of immortality, and still be religious. Where is the church that does not label honest doubt "heresy" and where "heretics" are welcome?

If you find a gleam of recognition in these questions, if they reflect some of your own thoughts, experiences, and searching, there is probably an exciting place for you in the Unitarian Universalist fold.

For us, the vital task in religion is to get from Sunday to Monday: to carry our serious concern with spirituality and religious living from the protected atmosphere of a worship service into the flesh and blood realities of daily living. Religions generally emphasize salvation, and most religions speak of salvation in terms of creeds, ceremonies, sacraments, and cate-chisms. We speak warmly of salvation also, but in terms of character. We choose to think of it as dependent on deeds, not creeds. We also think of it as pertaining to the herein, not just the hereafter.

"What must I do to be saved?" That was the question the jailer asked the apostle Paul. His answer, as recorded in the Book of Acts, was crucial. One might say it marked a point of no return for orthodox Christianity. Recall this biblical incident: In the city of Philippi, in the Roman colony of Mace-donia, Paul and his associate, Silas, were brought before the local magis-trate for preaching religious doctrines frowned upon by the empire. After some manhandling by a mob, they were unceremoniously thrown into a prison cell where they immediately began praying and singing hymns. In the midst of this informal service, a violent earthquake shook the cell door open and split the prisoners' chains. The jailer, a sound sleeper who had evidently dozed through both the singing and the earthquake, thus proving himself to be a person of tolerably quiet conscience, awoke to find the prison doors open. Panic-stricken that he had permitted his prisoners to escape, he drew his sword to commit suicide. In the nick of time, Paul cried out: "Do not harm yourself. We are here." Overcome with gratitude, the jailer rushed toward Paul and Silas, pleading: "What must I do to be saved?" And Paul replied: "Believe in the Lord Jesus, and you will be saved, you and your household."

I want to be fair to Paul, whose hymn to love and "When I was a child...," both in I Corinthians, are among the most sublime of religious writings. What we have is a story *about* Paul, not *by* Paul. But be that as it may, whenever I read this story I think of all the answers Paul might have given. He might even have asked some questions of his own: "What do you mean *saved*? Do you mean how can you live a juster, kinder, more faithful life, or do you mean how can you get to heaven?"

Paul simply assumed, according to the story, as so many clergy have gone assuming ever since, that the jailer was only interested in getting his endangered soul into celestial safekeeping. He further assumed that no desire could be dearer to the jailer's heart than to escape this wicked world. No consideration was apparently given to the possibility that life is an exceedingly precious gift, that it is a great privilege to be alive and to have opportunities to do better with a life than one has done. Nothing of that. Paul, we are told, simply blurted out a formula. And not merely a formula, but, from his point of view, *the* formula: "Believe in the Lord Jesus, and you will be saved, you and your household."

Here was the track of authoritarianism on which orthodox Christianity would run from the days of the the Book of Acts to our own. Did it occur to Paul that the jailer might have some thoughts and insights of his own worth probing and nurturing? There is nothing of this in the story. Paul, it would seem, saw no reason to encourage the jailer to reflect on his traumatic experience, to ponder in his heart and conscience what might be found there. No words are attributed to Paul that might have moved Christianity in the direction of freedom and deepened accountability. Instead, a dogma is uttered, saying, in effect, this is not something to examine, to weigh, to test by experience. No, this is something you simply accept.

Unitarian Universalists don't buy it. The kind of religion that commands our allegiance is the kind that respects our ability to make considered religious decisions. In this sense, we feel much more at home with certain biblical portrayals of Jesus than with this depiction of Paul. The jailer asked a heartfelt question. He had been through a shattering experience. It made him think of ultimate things: "What must I do to be saved?" What a glorious opportunity for Paul to tell of Jesus's approach to the art of living. But there is not one word of the teachings of Jesus. All that is offered is a theological doctrine; nothing about love, nothing about an aspiring morality, nothing about bold goodwill.

Compare this with a similar recorded experience in the life of Jesus. A wealthy and deeply troubled young man came to Jesus with a question. "Rabbi," he asked, in more cultivated tones than the jailer's, "what must I do to inherit eternal life?" Jesus did not answer, "Believe in me and you will walk heaven's golden streets." Instead, we are told, Jesus encouraged the young man to guide his life by the great ethical teachings of the prophets. Forget about your wealth and bring riches to the lives of others!

The young man went away crestfallen, for he had great possessions. He wanted a formula. He would have liked talking with Paul much better. Perhaps this is why traditional Christianity became a religion *about* Jesus rather than a religion *of* Jesus. Yet, who knows what transformation might have occurred in the young man when, in the privacy of his thoughts, he began to reflect on the moral challenge the strange rabbi had given him.

For us, salvation is not an otherworldly journey, flown on wings of dogma. It is ethical striving and moral growth: respect for the personalities and experiences of others; faith in human dignity and potentiality; aversion to sanctimony and bigotry; reverence for the gift of life; confidence in a true harmony of mind and spirit, of nature and human nature; faith in the ability to give and receive love; and a quest for broad, encompassing religious expression—spiritual yet practical, personal and communal.

This is what we mean when we say we believe in salvation by character. Perhaps it would be more accurate to say that we believe salvation *is* character, for we do not mean that character saves us from the flames of hell or takes us to the bliss of heaven. We do not profess to know, as a community of faith, the precise dimensions of immortality. But we are sure of this: The inner life, shaped by the power of high and sane ideals, brings to human souls the finest, most enduring satisfactions and makes of our humanity a source of strength, even in utmost tribulation. This is what we mean by salvation, and what serves so well in life could not possibly serve less well in afterlife.

We believe that our humanness is punished *by* our sins, not *for* them, and that the evil we do lives with us. By the same token, we believe that we are enriched by our virtues, and that the good we do lives with us and beyond us as a benediction of peace in our own lives and in the life of humanity.

We believe that corporate religion—the church—has no higher object than helping us to get from Sunday to Monday, taking our Sunday professions into our Monday behavior; in short, when we talk of salvation, we talk of making religion a sustained and sustaining force in our daily lives. We do not say that religion has nothing to do with the afterlife, but we do say that it has everything to do with this life.

4

What Do You Say After You Say "I'm a Unitarian Universalist"?

Actually, we have to make the best judgments we can about what is right, and then we have to bet on it by trying to make ourselves act on it, without being sure about it.

Arnold Toynbee

In his delightful volume, *Born Again Unitarian Universalism*, F. Forrester Church, minister of All Souls Unitarian Church in New York City, recounts a conversation at a stiff dinner party. Seated between strangers and caught off guard, he let the cat slip out.

"You are a what?"

"A Unitarian Universalist."

"Oh, I see," he says, but obviously he doesn't. He is rescued by the woman to our right.

"I've never really understood just what it is you Unitarians believe. You *are* Christians, aren't you?"

"Not exactly. I mean, we were and some of us still are but most of us are not."

"You don't believe in Jesus?"

"Not in an orthodox way, certainly. Many of us value his teachings but few, if any of us, believe that he was resurrected on the third day or that he was God."

"What about immortality?"

"Well, I guess you'd have to say that we're pretty much divided on that one."

"But at least you all believe in God?" interrupts the man across the table. . . .

"Not exactly. Many of us do, if each in his or her own way. Others of us do not find the concept of God a useful one."

"What then *do* you believe?" our bewildered hostess politely asks.

A conversation of this kind is instantly recognized and appreciated by most Unitarian Universalists, with an "Ay, there's the rub." There is an initial difficulty that confronts us when we are asked point blank what we believe. Those who ask usually expect a creedal answer: "I (we) believe in God, the Father Almighty, etc." But we cannot give that kind of answer because we are a creedless church. There are two very compelling (to us) reasons for this. First, we are persuaded that it is spiritually depriving to state the intellectual content of religious belief in fixed and final form; we are convinced that humans are created to be capable of growth in their understandings of truth. So we have decided that a formal creed is a hindrance rather than a help in religion, and we have eliminated it from our church, choosing instead to set forth statements of purpose and principle, which by a democratic process of study and discussion we can refine as we see fit. Second, we are bound together by ties that we find deeper and more satisfying than those of creedal affirmation; we are bound together by a spirit of enriching our individual lives within a framework of caring community and of improving the social order. Within this unity of spirit we discover that it is invigorating to hold a wide variety of theological beliefs; we have no need of uniformity of belief among our members.

By its very nature, a creed is final and binding upon all who profess it. It is held to be outside the reach of questioning examination. Its origin in divine inspiration is assumed. Actually, if the historic church creeds were divinely revealed, they came into being in a strikingly human manner. There were more than two centuries of speculation, debate, and bitter strife before the first "final" Christian creed, the Nicene, became compulsory, on pain of excommunication, even death. It and its companion piece, the Apostles' Creed, cannot be viewed historically as anything but a string of compromises, based on an accommodation of contending views.

The traditional creeds are human creations, and they were probably the best attainable expressions of Christian belief in the third and fourth centuries. What we cannot accept is that these creeds should be binding on this and future generations. To us, the creation of a religious way of life is far too important to be left to the distant past's propounders of doctrine. We are Unitarian Universalists, not by substituting one confession of faith for another, but by opening our minds to receive truth and inspiration from every possible source — even from the ancient creeds, if by critical examination they throw genuine light on current concerns.

The most fundamental of all Unitarian Universalist principles, then, is personal freedom of religious belief — the principle of the free mind. But freedom, as Henry Whitney Bellows taught his congregation more than a century ago, "has no power to produce anything. It merely leaves the faculties free to act." Freedom is not aimless wandering with no duties attached. The freedom we hold so dear is the freedom of our faculties to act in behalf of what challenges and transforms our lives, our passage from birth to death. For us, this freedom to grow, to act, and to redeem is not based on external authority. It is established in our inward parts. No priest or pastor dictates. No Holy Writ dictates. No creed dictates what must be believed.

For those who are frankly appalled at the "burden" of such liberal spiritual freedom, the attractions of external authority are understandably great. I was once reproached by an acquaintance of impressive intellectual gifts and scientific achievements for doing a profound disservice by exhorting people to try to work out their own religious answers. "Religion," he said, "is a specialty that should be left to experts."

Unitarian Universalists are people who cannot leave their religious beliefs in the care of "experts." For us, the most vital faith about the human possibility is this: We must be free to grow in spirit. There is no area of life in which it is more important for us to be free than in the realm of spirit.

Those who honestly differ with us (and we respect them for it) argue that human nature requires authoritative religious guidance, or our inherent proneness to sin will corrupt and destroy. Yet when we begin to examine closely the "authoritative" religious guidance, what do we discover? The church that boasts authority to dictate beliefs is, whatever its claims, a human institution, and its "final truths" are only conclusions of previous leaders. The same is true of the Bible. It was written by mortals. No creed exists that was not originally hammered out, under pressure, by human beings like ourselves.

Churches, Bibles, and creeds are the creations of humans who once exercised their freedom to create. Is there any reason we should expect to do less? We accept the birth of a new age in all kinds of human undertakings; why not in religion as well? Human beings are still in the learning stage about everything from evolution to communication. All over the lot, concepts of truth and reality are in flux. The traditions and habits on which the religions of past millennia were founded have elements that are enduring and elements that are not. Either we go forward with religious sentiments and formulations appropriate for our time, or time will leave some radioactive remnant of us cringing in ancient spiritual caves.

The distinctive characteristic of religious liberals is their insistence that they will not lock their present and future in religion into the tutelage of the past. They will attempt to learn all that the past can teach, but they will do their own thinking about current matters of faith and belief.

Believing that spirituality is the power of understanding life, we Unitarian Universalists affirm within the community of the church our dependence on our thinking to generate significance and vitality. In Forrester Church's words (in *Born Again Unitarian Universalism*): "We value one another's thinking. We respect one another's search. We honor it even when it differs from our own. We resist imposing our perception of truth upon one another. Embracing a kind of theological pluralism, we affirm the human importance of our joint quest for meaning in life without insisting upon the ultimacy of any single set of theological criteria. . . . At our best, we move. . . to a fundamental trust in our own and one another's inherent ability to make life meaningful."

In a Unitarian Universalist congregation, an agnostic may sit beside one who believes in a personal God; at the after-service coffee hour a believer in reincarnation may stand chatting with one who affirms "utter extinction." Such are our diversities in theological belief.

We are together in our devotion to spiritual freedom; each challenged to live by a considered, examined, experienced covenant with self, others, and life as a whole; each understanding, even hoping, that beliefs may change as insights deepen and life teaches.

Earthy and Practical Reason

Since ours is such a free and creedless church, are we, as some claim, nothing but "a haven for people who can't quite make up their minds"? In *The Unitarian Universalist Pocket Guide,* David Rankin illustrates this charge: "One wit has written that a Unitarian Universalist is a person who walks a thin line between confusion and indecision.

"Another wit has written that if you are a Unitarian Universalist, bigots burn a question mark on your lawn."

"So much for wits!"

Yes, we have our anxious moments about the freedom we cherish. But second only to the free mind is our belief in reason and responsibility. Freedom requires responsibility, and responsibility requires reason. Humans must accept responsibility for their choices and for their acts. We believe that this sense of responsibility reflects the teachings of the great biblical prophets, from Amos to Jesus. We believe that our religious concept of moral and ethical responsibility is much more in tune with reality, and much more productive than the traditional doctrine of human nature's inherent depravity through "original sin."

"Why am I such a failure?" said the woman sitting in my study. She looked like anything but a failure. She and her husband and children were my good friends. I had been in their home many times and was impressed with the apparent affection and openness of family ties. Both parents worked. There were no unusual financial problems. Yet this woman was struggling with an insidious sense of guilt and inadequacy. A "tradition of inferiority" was poisoning her life.

Where does this tradition come from? For women, the punishing effects of this tradition are amplified by the deep strains of sexism embedded in our culture. But why are men, as well as women, so conscious of their failings and limitations that they are unable to think of good things as flowing from their lives? One of the most widespread causes, in my opinion, is the doctrine of original sin, stressed in early religious training and magnified until it comes to be regarded, deep in the recesses of personality, as an innate evil from which there is no real escape.

Please don't misunderstand me. I believe in sin. Looking within me and around me, how could I, or anyone, believe otherwise? But nothing is more appalling to me than the crippling effects of religions that fill persons with a sense of their hopeless condition, their wicked and disgraceful alienation from goodness and virtue. Each person experiences enough emotional conflict, enough harm done others, enough regret, enough self-reproach to give force to the doctrines of original sin and total depravity. The eloquent, remorseful outcry of the apostle Paul vividly expresses the traumatic clash between aspiration and action: "For the good that I would, I do not: but the evil which I would not, that I do. O wretched man that I am! Who shall deliver me from the body of this death?" (Romans 1).

With such a ghastly assessment of human nature, sharply contrasted with the perfection and beauty of God, how could one avoid the conclusion that the sources of the good life are nowhere to be found within the human frame? But a realistic study of human nature reveals a plethora of impulses and a rich diversity of motives within which the process of moral selection proceeds. We find some things are better and others worse, by trial and error, by measurements of happiness and welfare, by comparison and reflection. This is how we humans cultivate responsible behavior. For Unitarian Universalists, a chief resource is reason. With us reason holds a place ordinarily accorded to revelation in other religions. Those who are likely to behave best exercise their reason most.

Thus I, for one, remain hopeful about the human estate. I find a basic capacity for goodness in the human animal — a goodness that is not meaningfully negated by the "fall."

This does not mean that I am unmindful of the limitations of human reason, nor that I look upon it as an infallible guide. In the Unitarian Universalist way of life there are no infallible guides. But central to my faith and that of my liberal religious forebears, is the notion that reason is crucial to our functioning. How else shall we discuss our feelings of truth, beauty, and goodness? These matters do not, as some would say, defy discussion. Our religious community, our church, is grounded in just such communication. E. Burdette Backus, one of my early mentors in the ministry, used to describe our reasoning ability as an instrument that developed in the process of evolution, enabling us to satisfy our needs more adequately.

It had originally a very earthy and practical purpose, namely that of solving the problems that press in upon. . . daily life. Although it continues this immediately pressing function, it has far outsoared it and seeks to penetrate beyond the stars to find an answer to the riddle of the universe. Our reason makes many mistakes; it is frequently taken captive by our desires, so that we believe things not because they are true but because we want to believe them. It cannot give us absolute and final certainty, but it has established a substantial body of verified truth; it is steadily increasing the amount of that truth. For all its limitations it serves us very well, and those who advocate its abandonment are simply telling us as we grope our way through the dark by the light of a candle to blow out the light. (A Sermon)

Of course there are irrational elements in our experience of ourselves and, seemingly, of our cosmos. But to comprehend them, to understand them, perhaps even to transcend them — how else but by reason?

Unitarian Universalism, then, is a community of faith, with individual freedom as its method and with reason as its guide. It should not be assumed, however, that we practice reason in an austere and overly solemn manner. When we succeed in seizing upon the finer and more elevating aspects of experience, projecting them enlarged and colorfully enhanced upon the canvases of life, they become the source of the warmest joy and blessedness. Our purpose is to enable heart and mind to capture realizations of what life can be when humans live up to their best. Through expanded imagination, awakened conscience, and enriched beauty there springs into being a spiritual fellowship whose inspiration to deepen satisfaction and more ample living has magnificent force.

Susan B. Anthony, the famous champion of woman suffrage in the early days of that movement, and a Unitarian, celebrated our position on reason with a telling phrase: "Truth for authority, not authority for truth." That's it! Discover what commends itself to your reason as truth and then accept that as your authority. And by working at it faithfully, with one another's help, we can become better, wiser, and more loving human beings. We might even help this to become a better, wiser, and more loving world.

The path of the liberal religious journey leads from freedom, through reason, to a third fundamental principle: a generous, appreciative acceptance of differing views and practices.

Unity with Diversity

Churches are voluntary social institutions, sometimes warmly sociable, sometimes less so. Voluntary social institutions have an intriguing double function. They are at once the cause and the effect of the interests they represent. Nurturant families are the outgrowth of mutual love, and they are the producers of nurturing personalities. Admirable schools are products of concern for the learning process, and they inspire love of learning in those who participate in them. Churches are created by religious interest and enthusiasm, and participation in the activities of church life awaken and deepen spiritual aspirations.

If only the first part of this equation is emphasized, it encourages some to proclaim that churches are not necessary to the religious life ("I can get all the religion I need working in my garden"). When only the second part is stressed, it tempts some to conclude that churches are the sole source of spirituality. Each view is fragmentary and one-sided. All voluntary institutions are at once the yield and source of the convictions, carings, and concerns they embody. Concern for the environment draws people together into environmental and conservation associations, and these associations in turn stimulate higher levels of social policy and personal consciousness. Love of the spiritual life draws religionists together; organized religion encourages the further quest for spiritual affections and understandings.

Most churches find their bond in scriptural or creedal affirmations. Membership is based on a more or less uniform profession of theological belief, usually accompanied by a rite or rites.

We Unitarian Universalists fashion our bond differently. It is our faith and practice that people can covenant to work together for the deepening of spiritual life, the strengthening of moral character, and the improvement of society without conforming to a set pattern of theological doctrines. In fact, we go well beyond this to declare our conviction that differing theological views are natural and healthy and that attempts to enforce conformity are deadening and potentially destructive. History is witness to the horrors of religious intolerance.

We hold that churches are voluntary communities striving for togetherness in difference, for fellowship combined with individual freedom, for the right to be oneself joined with vital participation in society. The goal of organized Unitarian Universalism is to provide maximum freedom combined with full fellowship for each individual. Truth, we recognize, is vast and many-sided. Why should we all have the same theology? It is a basic part of our faith that people of widely differing religious backgrounds and meaningful symbol systems can work cheerfully and productively together under the same denominational roof, strengthening and challenging one another, for the great common tasks of making human life more splendid, more precious, and more secure. This stance is an eminently practical one of measuring religion by the fruit it bears rather than the bark it wears. By making this concept explicit in the organized life of the church, we unfurl standards of value found within experience itself and make them subject to the judgment and conscience of the people who actually constitute the community of the institution.

Serious seekers of what Unitarian Universalists *really* believe must first be encouraged to set aside their predilection for the theological definitions that describe most churches. They must also be urged to suspend the notion that there are only two alternatives: accepting a creedal religion or rejecting church life altogether. Ours is very definitely a different kind of church, which requires a different kind of definition. Yet, let there be no mistake about the fact that the Unitarian Universalist fellowship is a purposeful, positive, organized religious movement, dedicated to the spiritual, moral, and social fulfillment of the gift of life. Let those who believe that they must surrender their intellectual freedom in order to enter a community of faith take notice.

Our churches reach out to all who catch a vision of filling the empty places in their lives by placing principles of freedom, responsibility, reason, and tolerance above uniform theological doctrines. Our churches are free associations of those who fashion their own personal theologies, unconstrained by institutional dogmas or ecclesiastical authorities. Our covenant is to strive together by every honest means to discover and nurture the highest forms of life that creative experience can devise. Religion for us is no insulated segment of life. It is our entire being in search of meaning.

We are respectful of the history out of which we have come and through which we have endured for more than four hundred years. But we are bound by no historic model. We continue to evolve by the light of our growing understanding of ourselves and our world. We feel obliged by the very urgency of religion to seek and experiment with more effective forms of teaching our members, young and old, with more compelling and inspiring arts of worship, with more energetic and adequate methods of public witness, and with more moving and sustaining sources of comfort and courage in the high adventure of living our lives in examined, loving, and transforming ways.

5

How Did We Get This Way?

Heir of all the ages, I,
Heir of all that they have wrought,
Struggle stern, adventure high,
All their wealth of precious thought.

Julia Caroline Ripley Doar, *a hymn*

The plane on which I traveled landed at the Athens airport in the eerie half-light of dawn. By the time customs formalities were over, the rising sun had placed a halo on the nearby hills. A taxi sped me along the Pireus and headed up a broad avenue toward the city's heart. Suddenly, there it was. The Acropolis, silhouetted against a brilliant morning sky! Transported through time as well as space, I had arrived at one of the cradles of my liberal faith. It wasn't Unitarian Universalism Socrates had in mind, but he was seeding the soil when he said to Crito: "Do not mind whether the teachers of philosophy are good or bad, but think only of Philosophy herself. Try to examine her well and truly; and if she be evil, seek to turn all away from her; but if she be what I believe she is, then follow her and serve her, and be of good cheer."

With such words were laid the foundations of the free human spirit, the examined life, and the endless quest for elusive, redemptive truth. Ancient Athens was one of the planting places of liberal religion. Take the word *heretic* and forget for the moment how it has been loaded with negative baggage. *Heretic* is a Greek word that means "able to choose." Think of that. Heretics are persons of independent mind who, as Socrates taught, do not simply accept beliefs because they happen to be dominant in the society or because they are taught by their churches, but they accept them on the basis of their own testing, their own independent thought. They consider different possibilities and are able to choose.

47

On another journey, it was my good fortune to spend an hour in Israel with the great Jewish philosopher and theologian, Martin Buber. He was a gnome-like man, barely five feet tall, with a huge head and a magnificent, flowing white beard. His eyes were large, brown, and compassionate. His study, in a shaded, one-story, stuccoed house in Jerusalem, deserved a Dickens to describe: Victorian desk and divan, a lamp that must have been designed soon after the invention of the electric light bulb, random heaps of books, brochures, pamphlets, periodicals, and manuscripts.

As he began to talk, I scribbled furiously. Suddenly there was silence, and when I looked up, Buber was smiling. "Mr. Mendelsohn," he said, "either you can take notes without really listening, or you can really listen without taking notes." It was said with no trace of harshness. Firmly, I closed my notebook and "really listened." He said: "Throughout the world, there is a spiritual front on which a secret, silent struggle is being waged between the desire to be on life's side and the desire to destroy. This is the most important front of all — more important than any military, political, or economic front. It is the front on which *souls are moulded.*"

My question was the obvious one: "What can individuals do to tip the balance?"

Buber gazed out the window for a moment; then he turned to me and said: "No one can chart a day-to-day course for anyone else. Life can only be determined by each situation as it arises. We all have our chances. From the time we rise in the morning until the time we retire at night we have meetings with others. Sometimes we even meet ourselves! We see our families at breakfast. We go to work with others. We meet people in the streets. We attend gatherings with others. Always there are others. What we do with each of these meetings is what counts. The future is more determined by this than by ideologies and proclamations."

In sitting with Buber I felt that I was in the presence of another remarkable Hebrew prophet — one whose lineage extended directly to Amos, Hosea, Isaiah, Jeremiah, and Jesus. I was moved, as in Athens, by a sense of discovery of the roots of my Unitarian Universalist religion.

Modern liberal religion gratefully acknowledges its debt to these two founts of reverence for human dignity and ethical imperatives: ancient Athens and ancient Israel. And I, for one, acknowledge also that just as Socrates was not much heeded in ancient Athens, neither was Buber, an advocate of Jewish-Arab reconciliation, much heeded in modern Israel.

The Christian origins of our movement are anchored in a long, shared history of reverence for the moral example and teachings of Jesus, as exemplified in the Beatitudes and the Sermon on the Mount. We realize that there are many complications in making a historical assessment of Jesus. Most of us hold that, on the basis of the evidence available to us, Jesus was faithful even unto death to the messianic Judaism into which he was born and did not intend to found a new religion. It was followers and interpreters like Paul who transformed Jesus into a Savior Christ — God's chosen atoner for the sins of humankind.

In a technical sense, early Christianity was neither Trinitarian nor Unitarian. For nearly three centuries after Jesus's death, no specific doctrine of this type was enforced as part of an official Christian creed. When doctrinal controversies became too heated to contain, the Roman emperor Constantine summoned church leaders to a council at Nicaea where, in 325 — almost three hundred years after the death of Jesus — the Nicene Creed was voted into existence. The godhood of Jesus thus became the official orthodoxy of the Christian religion. The Nicene formula declared, by a divided vote, that Jesus was of the same essential substance as God. It is characteristic of Unitarian Universalists, including those who retain and cherish a Christian identity, to reject the validity of the Nicene decision and to emphasize instead the symbolic and human meanings of Jesus.

A half-century later, at another gathering of church leaders, the General Council of Constantinople, the assembled dignitaries added the Holy Spirit to their formula, thus completing the Trinity. I have simplified the history, but essentially this was the very human manner in which the Trinitarian dogma of Father, Son, and Holy Spirit came into being. From the beginning, there were dedicated Christians who felt that the spiritual message and moral leadership of Jesus were being swamped in a sea of metaphysics, but it quickly became apparent that those who would not bow before the Trinitarian formula were to be expelled, condemned, and even executed for their heresy, their insistence on being able to choose.

It is worth noting that the only sources we have of the actual teachings of Jesus are the first three Gospels — Matthew, Mark, and Luke. The Gospel of John was not written to emphasize Jesus's teachings. More recent discoveries — the Gospel of Thomas, for example — add little. In their present form, Matthew, Mark, and Luke (though they contain earlier materials) were written one to two generations after Jesus's death. There is not the remotest suggestion in them of a Trinitarian formula. Indeed, Jesus—or any other Jew of his age—would have been shocked by the "blasphemy" of such a concept.

Earl Morse Wilbur, in *Our Unitarian Heritage*, writes:

"During long centuries of their national humiliation no other conviction had been so deeply burned into the consciousness of the Jewish people as their belief in the absolute and unqualified oneness of God. In fact, down to this very day, nothing else has proved such an impassable barrier to the reception of Christianity by the Jews, as has the doctrine of the Trinity, which has seemed to them to undermine the very cornerstone of their religion."*

It is a minor but interesting fact of Christian history that, as late as the fifth century, in an enclave east of the Jordan, a lonely handful of Jewish Christians, known as Ebionites, clung to their original beliefs in the unity of God and the pure humanity and natural birth of Jesus.

From the time of Jesus to the Council of Chalcedon, roughly 450 years, orthodox Christian doctrine, against which European Unitarianism and Universalism were eventually to protest, emerged with the belief that God, while one, exists in three persons, and that one of these persons (Jesus) has two natures (divine and human).

It is all too easy for contemporary religious freethinkers to look back on the controversies that shook the early Christian Church and conclude that centuries were spent in absurd strife over the forms rather than the substance of spiritual life. From Nicaea to Chalcedon, the councils seem to have labored mightily to bring forth vaporous verbal formulas. It must not be overlooked, however, that to Christian believers of the third and fourth centuries the very essence, and perhaps even the existence, of their faith hung on the resolutions of deep conflicts. In fairness, it must be granted that the struggles represented the emotional religious perplexities of the time.

Wilbur wrote:

The character and methods of the Councils that established these doctrines are not, it is true, calculated to give us great reverence for their Christian character, nor much respect for their opinions; while the

---

*Earl Morse Wilbur, *Our Unitarian Heritage* (Boston: Beacon Press, 1929, 1935), p. 9.

repeated interference of the civil power to enforce decisions of doctrine in its own interest was as vicious as it well could be. Yet the changes of thought. . . do not quite deserve to be called, as they often have been, "corruptions of Christianity." No one tried, or wished to "corrupt" the Christian faith. It was, indeed, a vast change from the simple religion of the sermon on the mount and the parables of Jesus to the theology of the Nicene and Athanasian Creeds; and the whole emphasis shifted from a religion of the heart and life to abstract speculations of the head. Yet when we have made all deductions for the political intrigues and the mean jealousies and the unscrupulous ambitions that so often accompanied them, we find at the bottom of these controversies an earnest and honest desire in the best minds to state the theory of the new Christian religion in terms which the cultured old world of Greek thought could accept. *

Anyone who has ever struggled for a cause can appreciate the fervor attached to the doctrines of the Trinity and the deity of Jesus. For early Christians their emergence was experienced as a life-and-death exertion. Once achieved, they must be defended as the essence of the Christian faith. Whoever questioned or disavowed them seemed to endanger the very soul of Christianity. It is always a temptation to identify orthodoxy with religion itself. Christians fell victim to the temptation. They came to look upon dissent as the most heinous and contemptible of crimes. Centuries later, when a few brave and enterprising spirits began to compare the creeds with the Gospels and concluded that they preferred a belief in God's unity and Jesus's humanity to the enigmas of the Trinity and the God-Man, they were fanatically attacked. The most extreme punishments — torture and burning — were considered to be no more than what these "enemies" of religion justly deserved.

Thus, through all the early history of liberal religious impulses within the Christian fold, there is a strain of violent persecution. Tragedy and death stalked those who first laid the foundations in Europe of the movement that was to bear the Unitarian and Universalist names. And it was not only the Trinity and the God-Man that were to come under critical scrutiny; other zealously guarded doctrines were also questioned. First to be challenged was Augustine's doctrine, later elaborated by Luther and Calvin, that

---

*Our Unitarian Heritage, pp. 32-33.

human nature, even in infancy, is totally corrupted by original sin. Next, another of Augustine's dogmas — a great favorite of Calvin — that Almighty God had decided at creation time which human souls to save and which to confine to eternal damnation — was denied. Finally, the notion of vicarious atonement — that Jesus provided salvation by paying for the sins of human-kind — was questioned and discarded.

Thus the forerunners of Unitarianism and Universalism struck not only at the two central doctrines of orthodox Christianity, but at three derivative ones as well. From the beginning they staked the merit of their argument on a plea that the five dogmas were not only inconsistent with Scripture, but offensive to reason and the moral sense.

Nothing that could properly be called a Unitarian or Universalist move-ment came into existence until the Reformation was in full flow; but this does not mean that there were no pioneers of liberal religious thought prior to the sixteenth century. Such a one, for example, was Origen, born in Alexandria in C.E. 185, who was the most productive and liberal of early Christian writers and thinkers. His was a remarkably open-minded and open-ended presentation of Christianity, worthy of Erasmus, who arrived on the scene nearly 1300 years later. Origen, as a pioneer of the liberal reli-gious tradition, richly deserves recognition not normally given to him. Soundly schooled in the science, philosophy, and theology of his time, he insisted that faith and knowledge were complementary, not antagonistic, and that religion was enriched not endangered by a rational search for truth. Absent from his makeup was the bigotry of so many of his Christian peers who were then bent on erasing the rich spiritual heritage of Greek and Stoic philosophy. He believed that the Bible was to be studied reverently but critically, and he denied that it was necessary to accept the Bible literally in all instances.

A biographer, Fred G. Bratton, writes: "From the standpoint of charm and versatility, Origen is one of the most appealing characters in history. His independence of mind prejudiced orthodoxy against him so that he was never beatified, but not all saints are canonized. Owing to his compara-tively liberal views, the historic Christian Church has never given him his rightful place either as a thinker or as a Christian character."*

---

*Fred G. Bratton, *The Legacy of the Liberal Spirit* (Magnolia, Mass.: Peter Smith, n.d.), pp. 8, 9.

What were some of his "comparatively liberal views"? He was the first analytical theologian. What mattered to Origen was not the confirmation of orthodox doctrines, but the fullest possible application of reasoned thought to the issues of the religious life. He was inclined to reject anything that was unreconcilable with reason. Where Tertullian would later exclaim of his Christian orthodoxy: "I believe it because it is absurd," and Augustine insisted: "I would not believe. . . if the authority of the. . . Church did not compel me," Origen consistently promoted rationality as the basis of belief.

He was a forerunner of Luther in upholding faith as the soul of the religious life, but he would have been appalled at Luther's vituperative rejection of good works. Origen saw a symbiotic relationship between faith and works, with faith rendered worthless unless expressed in ethical conduct. Throughout his writings it is the moral emphasis, as well as the celebration of reason, that stamp him as a fountainhead of the liberal tradition. By renouncing dogma, by disclaiming prejudice and ignorance, by respecting the insights of the Classical as well as the Christian world, by honoring reason, and by upholding the ethical imperatives of faith, Origen richly earned a primary place in our affection.

Another memorable but neglected figure was the English monk, Pelagius, whose lifetime extended roughly from C.E. 360 to 420. His major contribution was a courageously creative advocacy of moral free will and spiritual liberty at a time when Augustine, with his insistence on the total depravity of human nature, stood astride the Christian scene like an unchallengeable colossus. Pelagius, like Origen, preached a Christian faith blessed by God with freedom of moral choice. Because Pelagius was a scholar of impressive learning and a person of undeniably honorable character, Augustine saw him as a threat to orthodoxy.

The two engaged in intense formal debates. "If I ought, I can," proclaimed Pelagius. Augustine argued back that human nature, though created upright by God, had, of its own free will, become depraved and was justly condemned to beget "a posterity in the same state of depravity and condemnation."

Dean Inge once said: "A religion succeeds, not because it is true, but because it suits its worshipers." There seems little doubt that a majority of Christians of the fifth century resonated with Augustine's enthusiasm for human depravity and condemnation. The faithful repudiated Pelagius, along with his confidence in their moral competence. One consequence was the adoption of Cyprian's doctrine which said that in view of human depravity there could be no salvation outside the Church. Christians would wait a long time for a reassertion of the universalistic, encouraging faith of Pelagius that sin is, as he put it, "a thing of will and not of nature."

I like to think of Origen and Pelagius as bridges over which Hebrew ethical religion and Classical philosophy made their way across the stream of Christian orthodoxy into the developing liberal religion of the contemporary world. Perhaps there would have been others to do their pioneering work if they had never lived, and, in fact, there were others who would nurture the seeds of reason and moral freedom in religion, keeping them alive for the day when the climate would change and they could burst forth to challenge orthodoxy. I like to think of Origen and Pelagius as having won great, though suppressed, victories for the free human spirit. I fear that most Unitarian Universalists remain unaware of the outstanding debt owed by all liberal religionists to these two uncanonized saints of the Catholic Church.

With the ferment of the Protestant Reformation, many adventurous opportunities were opened for a more liberal spirit in religion, despite fierce opposition from such major Reformers as Luther and Calvin. Sibling to the Reformation was the Renaissance, preparer of medievalism's ultimate downfall. Revolutionary theories of the universe shattered biblical cosmology, questioned Aristotelian logic, and undermined medieval supernaturalism. The tiny sailing ships of Columbus, Magellan, and Vasco da Gama proved the earth's roundness by refusing to drop off the edge of the ocean. World trade shifted from the Adriatic to the Atlantic to the Pacific. Minds stretched to embrace new global frontiers.

Great centers of art and scholarship were created in Florence, Rome, Augsburg. Creativity was encouraged and subsidized. Genius was celebrated, individualism honored, freedom praised. A new trust in human nature arose. Scientific exploration and the use of reason grew in luxuriant revolt against absolutism and finality.

Too little is made by biographers of Leonardo da Vinci's prophetic religious spirit. His genius as artist and scientist is warmly recognized, but he was equally impressive as an advanced and independent thinker in religion. Deeply committed to religion as a moral rather than a creedal imperative, Leonardo was an eloquent critic of clericalism, fanaticism, superstition, and dogma. He spoke with frank disapproval, before either

Erasmus or Luther, of the worship of Mary and the saints, the sale of indulgences, and the exploitation of the sacrament of confession.

He recognized the implications of the philosophical conflict between mental freedom and authoritarianism and was a solid partisan of freedom. He wrote: "When beseiged by ambitious tyrants, I find the means of defense in order to preserve the chief gift of nature which is liberty." Impatient with the church-controlled science of his time and smarting under the ban imposed on his anatomical studies, Leonardo wrote: "Those sciences are vain and full of errors which are not born of experience, mother of all certitude, and which do not terminate in observation. . . I will make experiment before I proceed because my intention is first to set forth the facts and then to demonstrate the reason why such experience is constrained to work in such fashion. And this is the rule to be followed by the investigators of natural phenomena: while nature begins from causes and ends with experience, we must follow a contrary procedure, that is, begin from experience and with that discover the causes."

Leonardo was the best of the Renaissance spirit incarnate, a liberal mind come into being. It was the Renaissance as well as the Reformation that pointed ahead to what we Unitarian Universalists became.

The Reformation was a herald with a mixed message. Luther and Calvin replaced the authority of the Pope with that of Scripture, but left essentially unchallenged the Latin theological orthodoxy of the Church. They altered the techniques for attaining salvation, and by making Scripture rather than the Holy See the ultimate source of spiritual authority, they guaranteed a multiplicity of competing sects within the Christian world. They did not, except indirectly, encourage the life of reason in religion or cultivate a greater trust in the possibilities of human nature. They did, however, assert a priesthood of *all* believers, and by so doing opened the gates to those who would be architects of freer communions of faith.

Fourteen years after Martin Luther nailed his ninety-five theses to the Wittenberg Castle Church door, Michael Servetus startled Christendom with a furiously written book entitled *On the Errors of the Trinity.* It was an angry, strident denunciation of the dogma of the Trinity as upheld by Reformation and Catholic authorities alike. The most widely quoted of Servetus's phrases is: "Your Trinity is a product of subtlety and madness. The Gospel knows nothing of it."

The author of these no-nonsense blasphemies was nineteen years of age.

His style was chaotic and intemperate, but demonstrated a remarkable range of reading and learning. The book was placed on sale in the Rhine cities and spread swiftly through Switzerland, Germany, and northern Italy. It appears that Servetus, in his youthful zeal, actually believed for a time that the major Reformers would see the light and embrace his arguments as soon as they could carefully consider them. Luther quickly quashed that hope when he labeled the book "abominably wicked." Other condemnations rose in a fierce storm.

A shaken Servetus asked to be allowed to write a second book in which he would attempt to correct the mistakes of the first. At Basel he was given indulgence to do so. The result was a slimmer volume with the more conciliatory title *Dialogues on the Trinity.* He excised some of the objectionable passages of his earlier effort and tried to express himself in language more nearly like that of recognized Church teachers. In substance, however, he restated the vigorous dissents. Rather than pacifying his critics, he inflamed them. Lacking both friends and money, he took up medicine and disappeared from public view for more than twenty years.

A quarter of a century later, when he was on trial for his life for surfacing and reasserting his old cause, his books on the Trinity had been so successfully suppressed that not a single copy could be found for use in Calvin's court.

Martyrdom was Michael Servetus's grisly reward. Calvin had him burned at a Geneva stake after Servetus insisted, despite dire warnings, on expanding his earlier books into a new polemical work.

What alarming teachings did these volumes contain? Servetus claimed straight out that God is indivisible and that there is no Trinity taught in the Bible. Creedalisms such as Trinity, essence, and substance, he said, are inventions, foreign to Scripture. The Trinity and the doctrine of two natures in Christ actually discourage the devout from being wholehearted Christians because they are illogical, unreasonable, and contradictory. They raise unanswerable questions, lead to crises of conscience, and leave people, in effect, with no God at all. Moreover, said Servetus with missionary zeal, they are a stumbling block to the conversion of Jews and Moslems. The mission of Christianity, to spread across the face of the earth, he concluded, requires the uprooting of these doctrines.

Unitarian Origins

It is inappropriate to claim Servetus as a Unitarian. He was an anti-Trinitarian. His approach to theology was very much his own, and we honor him for that and for his courage. But he sought out no religious community of freer faith, nor did he attract one. His contribution was to give dramatic impact to the issue of dissent in Christian thought and practice. The burning of Servetus, not by the Pope of Rome but by the great reformer of Geneva, raised searching questions about the cruelty of religious intolerance. Castellio's memorable rebuke spoke for growing numbers: "To burn a man alive does not defend a doctrine. It slays a person."

Movements sprang up in Poland and Transylvania, which were the cradles of European Unitarianism. They were non-Trinitarian, but of greater consequence was their devotion in Christian practice to principles of spiritual liberty, reason, and tolerance. The movement in Poland was headed by the saintly, scholarly reformer Faustus Socinus. He organized liberal congregations, persuaded them to give up extreme positions, and defended them in their controversies with both Catholic and Protestant opponents. The movement spread rapidly, attracting many of the most enlightened and gifted of Poles. In spite of harsh persecution, a lasting imprint was left on Polish culture. Church records were eventually put to the torch, but it is generally believed that by 1618 there were more than three hundred Socinian congregations.

Persecution mounted under Jesuit leadership, until it became an all-out war of extermination. To the very end of their existence, the Socinians carried on an active program of education and advocacy in and beyond Poland. They were bold and enterprising in spreading their liberalized Christianity, but depended on reasoned discussion rather than impassioned crusades. They quite deliberately tried to set an example of good temper and mild speech in religious disputation and won many to their cause. In the end they went under before onslaughts of persecution. Their self-imposed moral standards were no match for the Counter-Reformation's decision to root out of Poland every vestige of the Socinian "heresy." Socinus himself was attacked in the streets of Krakow. His face was smeared and his mouth filled with mud. This was the first of a series of assaults that left him first broken, then dead.

A systematic extermination policy completely destroyed the Socinian movement in Poland. Exiles scattered over the face of Europe: a tragic and plaintive chapter in the history of religious persecution. A few found their way to a haven in Transylvania where, for some time, there had been well-organized churches of their own type and outlook. Under the leadership of the charismatic Francis David, Transylvania had become the scene of a vital liberal Christian movement actually bearing the name *Unitarian*. It is worth noting that the label was not self-chosen. It was bestowed on Francis David's followers, as a term of vituperation, by Trinitarian critics. It stuck and assumed a life of its own. These Transylvanian liberal Christians stressed the human qualities of Jesus, the moral and spiritual teachings of Jesus, the right of congregations to choose the kind of preaching they wanted, the virtues of religious freedom and toleration. By the late sixteenth century, there were more than four hundred Unitarian congregations in the area, and they are there still. I write with special feeling about this because my wife, Joan, and I have enjoyed their warm hospitality and shared their joys and sorrows. I have preached in their churches and met with their leaders, their children, and their theological students. Four hundred years of history have bestowed on their liberal faith a remarkable maturity and steadfastness.

At the peak of his career, Francis David was Transylvania's outstanding religious figure and one of Europe's ablest preachers and theologians. Under his guidance, the only Unitarian king in history, John Sigismund of Transylvania, issued the western world's first edict of religious freedom and toleration. It read in part: "Preachers shall be allowed to preach the Gospel everywhere, each according to his own understanding of it. If the community wish to accept such preaching, well and good; if not, they shall not be compelled, but shall be allowed to keep the preachers they prefer. No one shall be made to suffer on account of religion, since faith is the gift of God."

This bill of rights in religion marks a precious moment in Unitarian Universalist history, for it kept liberal religious faith and practice from being destroyed as it was in Poland and elsewhere. This is not to say that Transylvanian Unitarians escaped persecution. Sigismund's successors were persuaded to adopt anti-Unitarian policies. By 1574 David's preaching and teaching were under hostile scrutiny, and within a year many of his noted followers were deprived of their rights and property. Some were tortured and mutilated; others were executed. By 1579, David was thrown into prison, where he died of exposure, hunger, and disease. Nevertheless, the spirit of religious liberty, preached by David and promulgated by Sigismund, was never completely crushed. The Unitarian congregations persisted and survived. Now part of Romania, they are tolerated but closely regulated. Once again, they need the full force of David's humane, inspiring example of unswerving loyalty to his free faith.

The saga of Unitarian pioneering in England is more merciful than on the Continent. While it is true that the first stages of the English Reformation were marked by occasional executions and frequent imprisonments, there was a gradual, if grudging, official toleration of dissent. Long before Unitarians attempted to organize themselves, capital punishment and imprisonment for religious dissidents were banished from the English scene. Civil persecutions endured, but the stake, gallows, and dungeon disappeared as deterrents to religious nonconformity.

Socinianism influenced progressive religious thinkers well into the eighteenth century. Early English Unitarians acknowledged their debt to the Polish movement by applying three principles: they advocated Socinian tolerance of differences in belief, applied the Socinian test of reason to religious doctrines, and preached the Socinian concepts of God, Jesus, and atonement.

England's developing Unitarian movement was star-studded with such notables as Isaac Newton, John Locke, Margaret Fell, John Biddle, and, for a time, William Penn. The person who most deserves credit as the actual founder of the Unitarian Church in England was Theophilus Lindsay, a Church of England cleric turned liberal. Laying aside the traditional, white surplice of his office, Lindsay conducted the first official Unitarian service in a London auction room. A large congregation, which included Benjamin Franklin and Joseph Priestley, participated. The date was April 17, 1774.

Lindsay's motivations are best understood by reviewing the affirmations that he described as the unifying bonds of the new Unitarian Church in England:

"That there is One God, one single person, who is God, the sole creator and sovereign lord of all things;

"That the holy Jesus was a man of the jewish nation, the servant of this God, highly honored and distinguished by him; and,

"That the Spirit, or Holy Spirit, was not a person, or intelligent being; but only the extraordinary power or gift of God, imparted, first (Acts 1, 2) to our Lord Jesus Christ himself, in his life-time; and

afterwards, to the apostles, and many of the first christians, to
impower them to preach and propagate the gospel with success: and

"That this was the doctrine concerning God, and Christ, and the
holy Spirit, which was taught by the apostles, and preached to jews
and heathens."*

This statement would strike most of us as quaint and tangential. It is to
be appreciated for the startling departure it represented in its own age.

Coupled with Lindsay, was the scientist, author, and minister Joseph
Priestley. Celebrated as the discoverer of oxygen, Priestley was also the best
known and most influential of early English Unitarians. He gave intellectual brilliance and prodigious scholarship to the development of Unitarian
religion and, together with Lindsay, stimulated a mushrooming of
Unitarian institutions. With incredible energy, he lavished his quick mind
and warm spirit on preaching, pamphleteering, scientific research, and the
espousal of many liberal and unpopular social and political causes, including the French Revolution. Inflamed by exasperated leaders of the Established Church, a Birmingham mob chose Bastille Day, July 14, 1791, to
attack and burn down Priestley's home, laboratory, library, and Unitarian
chapel. Priestley made a hairbreadth escape, fleeing to London, where he
immediately wrote and dispatched a sermon to be read to his congregation
on the following Sunday, using as his text: "Father, forgive them; for they
know not what they do."

Discouraged by the prevailing political and ecclesiastical climate, and
beckoned by an invitation from his friend Thomas Jefferson, he sailed, in
1794, to the United States. In Northumberland, Pennsylvania, he gathered
around him the first congregation in the new nation to call itself Unitarian.

The roots of American Unitarianism were already deep by the time
Priestley arrived. Liberal breezes had long been blowing through the dour
Calvinism of the pre-Revolutionary colonies. Increasing numbers of ministers and laity were calling for a greater use of reason in the interpretation
of Scripture, for a questioning of the doctrines of depravity and predestina-
tion, for a consideration of potential human goodness and the exercise of
free moral will, and for a belief in the unity of God. Priestley's powerful

---

*Quoted by David B. Parke in *Epic of Unitarianism* (Boston: Beacon Press,
1957), p. 47.

presence encouraged the progress of such liberalism, but it is in figures such as Charles Chauncy, Jonathan Mayhew, and the pioneer Universalist John Murray that we should look for our Unitarian origins in America. These combined a bold humanist spirit with their Christian piety and a dauntless rationalism with their godliness. Determined at first to challenge only the dogmatism of the dominant religious institutions, the liberal leaders found themselves pressed inexorably toward a genuine break. The bonds were finally severed in the first quarter of the nineteenth century, when Unitarianism emerged as a self-consciously distinct form of organized religious life. As described by David Parke: "Freed from the shackles of tradition and circumstance, Unitarianism embraced Unitarian Christianity, Transcendentalism, and Naturalism in such rapid succession that the radicalism of Boston in 1819 was the conservatism of Cambridge in 1838 and anachronism of Chicago in 1880. Unitarianism also became the mind and pen of America as the Nation sought to discover where she was, where she had been, and where she was going. It was a magnificent century, one, like those of Jesus and Luther, to be re-lived and ploughed back into the future."*

Two colossi of the "magnificent century" were William Ellery Channing and Theodore Parker. Each could boast of sturdy Yankee and Revolutionary lineage. The first Channing came to the colonies from Dorsetshire, England, in 1711, and the Parkers were residents of Lexington, Massachusetts, for nearly two centuries before Theodore was born. Each had one foot firmly planted in New England morality and the other foot in the Enlightenment's rationalism. Both were prodigious readers and scholars. Both were forceful preachers.

Channing achieved his religious liberalism through an evolution from Calvinist training and belief. In his youth he believed that God had elected from the beginning those who would be saved and those who would be damned, and that human nature (including his own) was sunk in hopeless depravity. In maturity he believed that God bestows love upon all. His espousal of Unitarianism was determined by a growing conviction that human nature is endowed with an intrinsic moral sense that gives the power to perceive and choose good. Short, slight, supremely self-disciplined, Channing projected an image of humility, intellectuality, com-

---

*Parke, *Epic of Unitarianism,* p. 68.

passion, moral strength, social vision, and natural leadership. His only ministry, from 1803 to 1842, was in Boston's Federal Street Church (later relocated and renamed Arlington Street Church). It proved to be a succession of great events. In his book-lined study were organized not only the American Unitarian Association, but new societies for the promotion of world peace, early childhood and adult education, social work and ministries to the poor, prison reform, care for the mentally ill, and temperance. He became one of the most prestigious voices raised against slavery and for abolition. Nothing was more compelling to Channing than the defense and enhancement of human dignity. He worked to rouse New England and the nation from the comas of Calvinism and materialism. He felt that religious leaders had become priestly rather than prophetic, while for many of the laity the real god was commerce. He was determined to stir the spiritual imagination, light a fire of moral responsibility, and make the living of a life greater than the making of a living.

Using writing desk, pulpit, and lecture platform as tools, he had an astonishing influence in three major areas: the liberalization of theology, the implementation of social reform, and the stimulation of a literary and cultural renaissance. Not the least of his accomplishments was to give emotional support and practical encouragement to a vanguard of empowerment-bent women, including Dorothea Dix, Elizabeth Peabody, Lydia Maria Child, and Margaret Fuller.

It is now hard to believe that *any* sermon could create the stir that Channing's Baltimore address did at the ordination of Jared Sparks in 1819. Yet, nearly every leading Unitarian minister made the exhausting horse-drawn journey to be present. Thousands of copies of the sermon were prepared in advance for immediate circulation. Like Luther's Wittenberg theses, Channing's statements at Baltimore were destined to compel people to take a stand on fundamental religious issues.

Channing scored orthodox theology for according humans no freedom but that of being damned or saved by an arbitrary God. In a Baltimore address he called this an insult both to God and to humans. He went on to object strongly "to the contemptuous manner in which human reason is often spoke of by our adversaries. . . . We indeed grant, that the use of reason in religion is accompanied with danger. But we ask any honest person to look upon the history of the Church, and say, whether the renunciation of it is not still more dangerous."

Turning to his belief in the unity and benevolence of God, Channing said: "We cannot bow before a being, however great and powerful, who governs tyrannically. We respect nothing but excellence, whether on earth or in heaven. We venerate, not the loftiness of God's throne, but the equity and goodness in which it is established. We believe that God is infinitely good, kind, benevolent, in the proper sense of these words; good in disposition, as well as in act; good not to a few, but to all; good to every individual, as well as to the general system."

Trying to summarize Channing's influence is like trying to summarize an epoch. Perhaps he did it best himself when he wrote: "I have lost no occasion for expressing my deep attachment to liberty in all its forms, civil, political, religious; to liberty of thought, speech and the press, and of giving utterance to my abhorrence of all forms of oppression."

If Channing was the most influential figure yet produced by American Unitarianism, Theodore Parker was the most remarkable. At the height of his preaching career in Boston's Music Hall, he spoke Sunday after Sunday to congregations of three thousand or more. His grandfather, Lexington's Captain John Parker, had delivered himself of one of the Revolution's immortal phrases, when in 1775 he said of the advancing British: "If they mean to have a war, let it begin here." Years later, when Parker made up his mind to defy the Fugitive Slave Law, he recalled his grandfather's famous words and wrote:

I have had to arm myself. I have written my sermons with a pistol in my desk—loaded, a cap on the nipple, and ready for action. This I have done in Boston, in the midst of the 19th century; been obliged to do it to defend the innocent members of my church, women as well as men. You know I do not like fighting. . . but what could I do? I was born in the little town where the first bloodshed of the Revolution began. My grandfather drew the first sword in the Revolution. With these memories in me, when a parishioner, a fugitive from slavery, a woman, pursued by kidnappers, came to my house, what could I do less than take her in and defend her to the last?"*

Parker made religion more than an ecclesiastical exercise. He took it from the pulpit onto the highways and into the cities and towns of expand-

---

*Parke, *Epic of Unitarianism,* p. 117.

ing America. This is literally true in terms of his Herculean lecture tours, and figuratively true by reason of the subjects over which his mind and pen ranged. He was a pathfinder in the practical applications of religion and a trailblazer in confronting secular issues with spiritual standards. He was, in Henry Steele Commager's words, "the conscience of the North—of such men as Charles Sumner and John Hale and Abraham Lincoln, and of countless thousands of ordinary men and women who were troubled by the contrast between the faith they professed and the practices they tolerated."*

To Parker, there were no exemptions from the imperatives of moral law; getting from Sunday to Monday, from the observances of religion to the practice of religion in every kind of human relationship, was the real business of the church. He recognized no compartmentalizing of the spiritual from the secular. To him they were one, and human beings were bound, if their faith be true, to be deeply involved in correcting the injustices of the political, commercial, and social order.

His ministry began in West Roxbury, Massachusetts, where he promised his congregation "to preach nothing as religion that I have not experienced inwardly and made my own." Many hours were spent in the well-stocked libraries for which Boston was noted. He nurtured his mind, ministered devotedly to the seventy families of his congregation, wrote essays and articles for transcendentalist publications, and took an active interest in the affairs of the nearby utopian Brook Farm community.

Then came Emerson's Harvard Divinity School Address: "Historic Christianity has fallen into the error that corrupts all attempts to communicate religion. As it appears to us, and as it has appeared for ages, it is not the doctrine of the soul, but an exaggeration of the personal, the positive, the ritual. It has dwelt, it dwells, with noxious exaggeration about the *person* of Jesus. The soul knows no persons. It invites (all) to expand to the full circle of the universe, and will have no preferences but those of spontaneous love."

Parker was stirred and depressed. Emerson's repudiation of miracles, his human-centered sovereignty of spirit, his celebration of "moral science" thrilled Parker. But Emerson had turned his back on the Unitarian parish

---

*Theodore Parker, *Yankee Crusader* (Boston: Little, Brown, 1936), preface.

ministry and sought other channels for his talents and energies. Parker brooded over whether the ministry was a wide enough place for him and decided that it was. He would remain in the pulpit and do everything in his power to make the church an instrument for the very things he and Emerson wanted.

By moving into downtown Boston, Parker gained a national platform at the Twenty Eighth Congregational Society. His sermons recognized the profound revelations taking place in science and philosophy. They were circulated, read, and discussed from one end of the country to the other, and in Europe as well. Like Emerson, he insisted that miracles proved nothing about religion. The permanent truths of the spiritual life are confirmed by experience and practice. The forms of Christianity change, the substance of religion remains. "If it could be proved," he said in a sermon entitled "Permanent and Transient Christianity," "that the gospels were a fabrication and that Jesus of Nazareth never lived, Christianity would still stand firm and fear no evil." Scientific truths do not rest on the word of their discoverer. Gravity does not operate because Newton said so. The same is true of the truths of religion. Confirm them by experience, and not by whether Jesus spoke them, or the Bible records them, or doctrine upholds them!

No part of my legacy as a Unitarian Universalist minister is more precious to me than the portion created by Theodore Parker. He was a prophet of righteousness, justice, and mercy who believed, as I do, in the progressive development of the church. "The church," he wrote, "should be the means of reforming the world. . . . It should therefore bring up the ideas of the times, the sentiments of the times and the actions of the times, and judge them by the universal standard."

Parker scandalized many of his Unitarian colleagues, just as Emerson did, and strenuous efforts were made to expel him from the Unitarian ministry. It was a time for many of the more cautious Unitarians to attempt appeasement of the orthodox. Parker's outspokenness was an embarrassment. It was, for me, a godsend to succeeding generations. Parker was the wave of the future for the kind of Unitarianism that could attract and hold the likes of me. It is his spirit that has prevailed sufficiently to preserve a genius for which liberal religion is especially suited — a genius that he himself described: "Progressive development does not end with us; we have seen only the beginnings; the future triumphs must be vastly greater than all accomplished yet."

The Universalists

There is one terror I would banish from every heart in the world if I could: the fear of hell. In the early years of my ministry, I was asked by a couple who were strangers to me if I would conduct a funeral service for a family member. I listened, shaken, as they described their last experience with death, the death of a baby born to close relatives. The officiating minister felt compelled by his doctrinal belief to announce that the infant was burning in hell because she had died unbaptized. With all due respect for the sincerity of that minister's belief in infant damnation, I felt then, as I feel now, that for anyone to make a statement like that to grief-stricken parents is not only incredibly cruel but also the opposite of all that I hold to be religious.

Were this an isolated case we might sadly let it pass; but with the passing years I have been approached over and over again in similar circumstances because it was known that I did not believe in hell and would not use a funeral as an occasion to harrow grief.

To their everlasting credit, our Universalist forebears were lifting their voices aginst the cruel myth of hell as early as the last half of the eighteenth century. In England and in the American colonies, brave spirits began to preach that it was unthinkable for God, as a loving creator-parent, to damn any of God's children everlastingly to hell. How could the offspring of a good God be willfully consigned to damnation by that same God? The creedal assumptions formulated at Nicaea must be in error. Even though the Nicaean Council had pointed out that God's justice *required* the punishment of sin, it was self-evident that a good and perfect God created humans to grow eternally in the goodness of their creator.

In the 1740s these "heretical" notions were preached in Pennsylvania by George de Benneville, a scholar and physician, born in England of Protestant French parents, members of the nobility. After his parents' death, he was taken under the wing of his godmother, Queen Anne of England. She appointed him midshipman in the Royal Navy when he was twelve. He later was educated at the University of Padua and at seventeen, in France, was converted to Universalism. For preaching unconventional religious views, he was imprisoned and tried for treason. Sentenced to death, he was, at the last moment, reprieved. In 1741, at the age of thirty-eight, and by invitation of Christopher Sower, a Universalist Quaker, he arrived in Philadelphia, where booksellers were already displaying Universalist writings. He established his home near Reading, Pennsylvania, and used one room as a chapel and a day school for a newly gathered Universalist congregation of fifty.

In the 1760s, in England, the espousal of Universalist ideas brought about the excommunication of John Murray, a zealous lay teacher and preacher of Methodism and a familiar of John Wesley, George Whitefield, and other pioneers of that movement. Murray was successful in business, married, and the father of an infant. Through the influence of James Relly of London, Murray became a convinced Universalist. He must have wondered about the wisdom of his conversion. His seemingly solid life fell apart. Death took his wife and child; his business failed; he was imprisoned for debt. By the time he won his release, he was in a deep depression. He resolved to bury himself in what he thought of as the wilderness of America and never to preach again.

Through a series of circumstances, which he ever after believed to be providential, he found himself strolling in 1770 along the New Jersey shore near Barnegat Bay, where he had arrived as the captain of a small vessel that he had promised to sail to New York as soon as the wind permitted. A stranger named Thomas Potter approached Murray and said: "The wind will never change, sir, until you have delivered to us, in that meeting house, a message from God." Potter, a local settler with strong, unconventional religious views, had constructed a meetinghouse but had been unable to find a minister to his taste. There was no change in the wind. Murray yielded to Potter's persuasion. He preached. Still gun-shy from his earlier experience, he preached what he thought of as a crypto-Universalist sermon. No matter. The wind changed in more ways than one, and Murray became something of an instant celebrity. Soon there were invitations from up and down the East Coast, including Gloucester, Massachusetts, where Murray settled as a minister of a small Universalist group and met Judith Sargent, a young widow, who became his second wife.

Judith Sargent Murray, member of a prominent Massachusetts family, was both a Universalist who proclaimed the final harmony of all human souls with God and a vivid, vital early feminist. Her essay, *On the Equality of the Sexes,* published in 1790 in *The Massachusetts Magazine,* is an extraordinary manifesto, in which she declares: "Yes, ye lordly, ye haughty sex, our souls are by nature *equal* to yours; the same breath of God animates, enlivens, and invigorates us; and that we are not fallen lower than yourselves, let those witness who have greatly towered above the various discouragements by which they have been so heavily oppressed."

George de Benneville and the Murrays are among the most deservedly revered of those who established the Universalist movement on this continent; but their coworkers, often very ordinary and unassuming folks, made of early Universalism a genuine enterprise of common people, buoyed by the faith that the love of God will ultimately prevail over human sinfulness. They were certain of this because they believed the love of God to be the most powerful force in the universe.

The Calvinist majority was understandably disturbed by such perilous wandering from sound doctrine. It was expected from arrogant Unitarians, but this was a threat from a new quarter. There was immediate denunciation of the Universalists as an errant and irresponsible lot bent on encouraging loose lives of wickedness, in the deluded belief that no matter what they did, they could count on escaping the torments of hell. They are free thinkers and godless misinterpreters of a just God, said the Calvinist accusers, no better than Unitarians! In many towns and villages, children were sternly instructed by their pastors and parents not to look a known Universalist in the eye lest Satan lay a curse upon them.

Bracing themselves against the storm of abuse, Universalists steadfastly defended the moral character of God, insisting that God is by nature loving, rational, and redemptive. Sin, they said, is finite (reminiscent of Pelagius). Punishment is remedial, not vindictive. A future of social humanism and humanitarianism in Universalist development was forecast by this early emphasis on the ethical and redemptive aspects of God's nature, and therefore of religious living.

The movement grew slowly, for the tempest of vilification was so strong that as late as 1800 only a handful of churches had been formed. Then there appeared on the New England scene a rebel preacher and self-taught theologian of outstanding ability. His name was Hosea Ballou, and he was a courageous, scholarly, and eloquently persuasive Universalist leader. He was born and reared a Calvinistic Baptist on a small Richmond, New Hampshire, farm. Somewhere along the line he was impressed with the "awful doctrine," as Universalism was called, and began to ride the circuit, preaching the universal salvation of all of God's children. Dressed in homespun, the tall, athletic Ballou made a strong impression on admirers and critics alike. His sermons were peppered with wit and earthy stories of the land and its people. The like-minded loved his humor. Those offended by his theology thought he was bitter and sarcastic. A well-remembered anec-dote illustrates why. In a discussion period following one of his sermons, he was angrily challenged: "What would you do with a man who died reeking in sin and crime?" "I think it would be a good plan to bury him," he answered.

The year 1803 was a lively one for Ballou and the struggling Universalist movement. At the Universalist General Convention of 1802, a committee including Ballou had been appointed to draw up a plan of faith and fellow-ship for Universalists. The move was controversial because of prevalent opposition among Universalists to "human creeds," though Articles of Faith had been adopted by a Universalist convention in Philadelphia in 1790. Strong feelings about creeds were running when the 1803 convention met in Winchester, New Hampshire.

The Winchester Profession, as it came to be known, was adopted, but only after vigorous debate and adoption of an amendment allaying fears that the profession might one day be used as an instrument of oppression or exclusion. The document emphasized standard Universalist views of God's universal love and the example and leadership of Jesus. It represented not only a further rupture with orthodoxy, but a departure from some of John Murray's tenets. Murray held orthodox beliefs about atonement and Christ's role as divine atoner.

For Ballou, the Winchester Profession served as a starting point for views that he progressively expanded. In 1805, he published his celebrated *Treatise on the Atonement,* in which he effectively demolished atonement as a Universalist concept. He greatly expanded the idea of a loving God. Christ is not God, he said, but God's messenger of love and reconciliation. He added the phrase "salvation by character." As for the punishment of sin, he stated that it was instantaneous, constant, and inevitable; but it was not everlasting, for the self-evident reason that everlasting punishment makes no sense. Unless punishment has character for its purpose, it is vicious and cruel. The only defensible reason for punishment is growth in righteous-ness. He asked: "Is God any less intelligent than any parent? Would a par-ent see any point in punishing a child forever? Would that improve the child?"

Ballou made a statement that was as Unitarian as any of his time. His thought resembled Channing's to a remarkable degree, with the added luster that it anticipated many of the things Channing would say only in subsequent years. Most of the Universalist congregations and ministers followed Ballou's lead, making their movement an organized Unitarian Universalist movement fifteen to twenty years before Unitarians, as such, gave themselves official form.

Sadly, there was never any enthusiasm among emerging Unitarian leaders for close ties with embattled Universalists. One might assume that when Ballou, clearly a leading light of Universalism, came to Boston in 1817 to minister to a major Universalist congregation on School Street, he might have been embraced by the Unitarians as an ally. Instead, he was coldly ignored. Unitarians were afraid of being bracketed with Universalists by the orthodox. Their heretical views of Christ's nature were radical enough; God forbid that they be labeled universal salvationists as well. From 1815 to 1840, as Unitarians were seceding from Calvinists and Calvinists were repudiating Unitarians, the Universalists, whose cause was virtually identical on the issues involved, looked longingly for encouragement, cooperation, understanding, and fellowship from Unitarians. Universalism did not possess the social and cultural status of Unitarianism, and reinforcement was desperately needed. It was not forthcoming.

The situation pained Hosea Ballou, who wrote a poignant sermon addressed to Unitarians. He selected the pertinent text "Nevertheless, I have somewhat against thee." He wrote eloquently of the affinity of the two groups. He rehearsed their common aspirations and frustrations and called for an intellectual and spiritual unity. He chided Unitarians for currying favor with groups much less friendly to Unitarian ideas, while snubbing Universalism. Many of us who patiently pressed for the merger of the two bodies, which at long last took place, felt that Hosea Ballou's spirit smiled upon our efforts. One of my favorite anecdotes about him is the following.

On a preaching engagement, he arrived at the home where he was to be put up and was greeted by his hostess, who had mop in hand.

"This is Mr. Ballou, I suppose?"

"Yes, madam. My name is Ballou."

"Well, Mr. Ballou, they say you hold that all will be saved. Do you really believe that doctrine?"

"Yes, madam. I really believe it."

"Why sir! Do you really believe that all are going to be saved just such creatures as they are?"

Seeing that she did not understand the nature of salvation as he understood it, Ballou asked: "What is that you have in your hand, dear woman?"

"Why it is my mop."

"Your mop? Well, what are you going to do with it?"

"I am going to mop up my floor. I always do it on Saturday afternoon."

"Well, sister, I understand you. Are you going to mop it up just as it is?"

"Mop it up just as it is?"

"Yes, you wished to know if I hold that all will be saved just as they are. Do you intend to mop up the floor just as it is?"

"Why, I mop it up to clean it."

"True. You do not require it to be made clean before you will consent to mop it up. God saves us to purify us; that's what salvation is designed for. God does not require us to be pure in order to save us."

During the latter part of the nineteenth century, Universalism, like Unitarianism, was deeply stirred by the rise of critical biblical scholarship and studies in evolution. As Max A. Kapp described, "Darwinianism (from 1859 on) posed a challenge to all Bible-centered faith: Universalism... not without pangs, accepted the implications of the theory of evolution and other scientific findings. . . . A marked shift of emphasis has gradually taken place so that 'salvation' no longer suggests to most Universalists an event in the after-life, but a process of self-fulfillment and social transformation."

As late as 1899 a Universalist statement of faith adopted in Boston read: "We believe in the Bible as containing a revelation from God." But by 1955 a profession approved in Washington stated: "We avow our faith in the authority of truth, known or to be known." It is impossible to miss the broadening of view inherent in these statements.

In this century the same degree of theological diversity developed among Universalists as among Unitarians. There were theists, humanists, naturalists, and mystics. There were Universalists who retained a loyal, albeit liberal, identification with Christianity, and Universalists who chose not to be known as Christians. All Universalists came to accept what they called the liberty clause, which meant simply that no creedal test might be used for determining who should or should not be a Universalist.

I am deeply fond of the Universalist name. The Unitarian name is precious to me both personally and historically. But simply as a word, laying aside for a moment the aura of history, it does not possess the magnificent, contemporary fitness of Universalism. It was a bit awesome, as we moved toward the merger of our faiths to contemplate calling ourselves Unitarian Universalists or Universalist Unitarians, but I warmly favored retaining both names and am content with the designation that was adopted — the Unitarian Universalist Association.

When the historic merger of 1961 finally took place, it united more than six hundred Unitarian congregations with nearly four hundred Universalist congregations. Since both bodies had what is called congregational polity, there was no change of governance at the local level. *Congregational polity* simply means that the seat of authority is in the local church or fellowship, rather than in a synod, presbytery, or bishopric. It is the democratic town-meeting principle in action in religion.

I look back with satisfaction on my warm support of the merger. Its overall result has been to strengthen the free church in its fundamental tasks. The liberal church should be one of the most contemporary and realistic of institutions. It should seek every legitimate means to rationalize and invigorate its internal administration. Combining the supplementary and complementary energies of Unitarians and Universalists was a logical move in this direction. The broader our base of human resources, the more likely it is that we will do an effective job of imparting creative moral inspiration to people's lives. The greater the invasions of freedom and civil liberty in the larger society, the more urgent it is to cherish and enlarge the practice of freedom in smaller religious communities. Obviously, this cannot happen by accident. Intelligent planning and wise organization are required. In today's world, freedom is threatened by assault and adulteration, but it is also weakened by prosaic institutional arrangements. The merger of Universalists and Unitarians was an imaginative venture, in keeping with progressive approaches to institutional life. It enlarges our horizons and invigorates the general climate of liberal religion.

The vital role of the liberal church is one of leavening. We must be the yeast of spiritual liberty that is forever working and increasing. We must be bearers and breeders of freedom. For us, denominational arrangments are not matters of authority but effective implementations of the services we require and the causes we espouse. Authority does not inhere in structures themselves, but only in the consistency and adequacy of evidence in any proposal or proposition and in demonstrations of character and competence on the part of persons charged with leadership responsibilities. Thus titles and positions bestow no automatic power. Free men and women do not bow before offices. Respect is not accorded to positions as such. For the sake of the creative uses of freedom, we devise bylaws, boards, committees, offices, and positions. These are established, not to restrict, limit, or circumscribe freedom, but to enable us to reach out beyond present customs and boundaries into unexplored realms, and to do so with maximum effectiveness. This requires maturity, not only in individuals, but in the techniques of planning and implementing. The democratic process is of great importance to us. The institution must grow in depth and breadth, along with the people who comprise it.

The history of the merger is an engaging tale of triumph over many tribulations. For more than a century the two groups grew increasingly, albeit warily, conscious of one another. Their separate histories are notched with efforts to effect a closer relationship. There are also long-standing grievances. Tufts College, for example, owes its beginnings to Universalists who were devoted to providing higher education free of creedal tests. But these founders made no secret of their wish to establish a first-rank college as an alternative to Unitarian-dominated Harvard. They did not want their Universalist youth subjected to the snobbishness and elitism of Harvard's Unitarians.

On more than a dozen occasions resolutions were introduced calling for some kind of union of the two movements. Somehow, the practicalities of getting together dampened whatever ardor there was. In 1899 a motion adopted by both bodies established a joint committee to "seek coordination — not consolidation; unity, not union." There were no notable results. In 1908 a National Federation of Religious Liberals was established. It was, on paper, a considerable coup, for the membership was to include not only Unitarians and Universalists, but Quakers and the Central Conference of American Rabbis. Alas, little came of the effort. In 1923 Universalists were courted by the National Convention of Congregational Churches, and each group appointed a Committee on Comity and Unity. Four foot-dragging years later, the Universalist Committee met with an interested group of Unitarians to discuss setting up a Congregational-Universalist-Unitarian organization; but the whole movement fell through. By 1933 still another council was incorporated in Massachusetts, known as the Free Church of America. Nearly one hundred Universalist and Unitarian congregations affiliated, along with one Methodist church, one independent church, and three Community churches. It was never possible to raise enough money for either a staff or a program (the word *free* was apparently interpreted in a financial as well as a spiritual sense), so the movement withered.

In 1947 a joint Universalist-Unitarian commission was established to lay the groundwork for federal union, and after an overwhelmingly favorable plebiscite among all member congregations of both bodies, the commission was instructed to draw up and present a practical plan. By 1951 the commission was ready to recommend an immediate union in religious education, publications, and public relations, with a gradual trend toward a complete merger. The report was ratified by both bodies, and the Council of Liberal Churches (Universalist-Unitarian) was organized in 1953. Meanwhile, the youth groups of the two bodies voted to dissolve their separate structures and merge. The result was Liberal Religous Youth, since reorganized and renamed Young Religious Unitarian Universalists. Just as the merger seemed to be an untroubling enterprise for youth, so it was for religious educators, who, from the first days of the Council of Liberal Churches, proceeded to work smoothly together across all previous denominational lines. The recommendation was then made and accepted that a commission be set up to bring the question of a complete merger to a head.

In May 1960, in Boston, by overwhelming vote, the two denominational structures became one.

6

Christian or More Than Christian?

All creatures weak or strong,
Great or small
Seen or unseen,
Near or far, —
May all be blessed with peace.
Let all-embracing thoughts
For all that lives be thine.

Sutta-Nipata, *Hindu Scripture*

I have blocked out where I was when in 1982 I first heard the news that the Israeli army, navy, and air force were attacking Lebanon with the suddenness and violence of a tornado. I remember the chills that ran up my spine. To me, this was personal. Over the years, I had spent many days and nights becoming acquainted with the men, women, and children — Israeli, Lebanese, Palestinian; Jewish, Christian, Moslem — who were once again caught in a terrible web of slaughter and destruction. I had recently, in the company of Jesse Jackson, sat down with political and religious leaders of Israel, with Lebanon's major factions, and with the Palestine Liberation Organization. We had listened to their grievances, rages, and fears and pleaded with them to find a different way, to break out of their desperate cycle of pain, to give up military "solutions," armed struggle, terrorism, to sit down, in mutual recognition, at the bargaining table.

My life has been rich with opportunities to make junkets of this kind, to meet with, mingle with, and write about the peoples of the world in all of their luxuriant diversity. My respect for this diversity has grown deep, along with my horror at the brutalizing intolerance one faith seems to breed against another faith. All over the globe, the religious beliefs and aspirations of people empower their determination to achieve a better life. All over that same globe, these same religious beliefs and aspirations breed violence and vengeance.

What is a Unitarian Universalist's approach to the world's vast pattern of religions? Has liberal religion grown beyond its Judeo-Christian cradle and become something more universal? Or is it a unique expression of a Christianity that views without prejudice or missionary yearnings the spiritual traditions of others?

When the Unitarian Universalist Association was formed in 1961, the principles to which it was dedicated were these:

> Support the free and disciplined search for truth as the foundation of religious fellowship;
> Cherish and spread the universal truths taught by the great prophets and teachers of humanity in every age and tradition, immemorially summarized in the Judeo-Christian heritage as love to God and love to humankind;
> Affirm, defend, and promote the supreme worth and dignity of every human personality, and the use of the democratic method in human relationships;
> Implement the vision of one world by striving for a world community founded on ideals of brotherhood [sic], justice, and peace. (UUA bylaws)

True to our penchant for self-examination, we have spent recent years in a denominationwide exploration of fresh ways to state our principles, taking special note of the concerns of the UUA Women and Religion Committee and the UU Women's Federation. A new statement of principles, now before us for final adoption at the 1985 General Assembly, reads as follows:

> We, the member congregations of the Unitarian Universalist Association, covenant to affirm and promote:
>
> - The inherent worth and dignity of every person;
> - Justice, equity and compassion in human relations;
> - Acceptance of one another and encouragement to spiritual growth in our congregations;
> - A free and responsible search for truth and meaning;
> - The rights of conscience and the use of democratic process within our congregations and in society at large;

- The goal of world community with peace, liberty and justice for all;
- Respect for the interdependent web of all existence of which we are a part.

The living tradition we share draws from many sources:
- Direct experience of that transcending mystery and wonder, affirmed in all cultures, which moves us to a renewal of the spirit and an openness to the forces which create and uphold life;
- Words and deeds of prophetic women and men which challenge us to confront powers and structures of evil with justice, compassion, and the transforming power of love;
- Wisdom from the world's religions which inspires us in our ethical and spiritual life;
- Jewish and Christian teachings which call us to respond to God's love by loving our neighbors as ourselves;
- Humanistic teachings which counsel us to heed the guidance of reason and the results of science, and warn us against idolatries of the mind and spirit.

Grateful for the religious pluralism which enriches and ennobles our faith, we are inspired to deepen our understanding and expand our vision. As free congregations we enter into this covenant, promising to one another our mutual trust and support.

This new statement is certainly wordier, but it is also remarkably inclusive. It could not be otherwise, considering the many currents that run strong in our movement. It is an urgent reminder to ourselves of our world's need for new approaches to faith, one that feeds the hungers of the human spirit without asking us to divide into hostile sects or split our minds into segments. The absence of such a faith—a faith expressed in the idiom of our age, at peace with its scientific method, awakening a real and deep interest in the soul, appealing to the highest and profoundest sentiments of our nature, permeating every facet of our being, and directing its enormous powers into channels that are creative and uniting—is a great spiritual tragedy in our troubled world. I could not remain within the Unitarian Universalist fold unless I felt that we were genuinely striving to build and exemplify such a faith.

A significant minority within our ranks deeply cherish their Christian identity. Organized in the Unitarian Universalist Christian Fellowship, they keep warmly alive in our midst an appreciation of our Christian roots and a reverence for the life and teachings of Jesus. I rejoice in this, just as I do in the lively identity maintenance cultivated by Unitarian-Universalists for Jewish Awareness. I am willing to call myself a Christian and a Jew, but only if in the next breath I am permitted to say that in varying degrees I am also a Hindu, a Moslem, a Buddhist, a Humanist, a Stoic, and an admirer of Akhenaton, Zoroaster, Confucius, Lao-tze, Simone de Beauvoir, and Black Elk.

Channing was thinking only of Christianity when he said: "We must shun the spirit of sectarianism as from hell. We must shudder at the thought of shutting up God in any denomination." I, as a present-day Unitarian Universalist, would extend the sentiment to include all the world's religions. Overwhelmingly, the organized faiths, from Christianity to communism, still remain bastions of the tense, closed, heresy-hunting mind. I cannot choose for others, but I can choose for myself. I can give my loyalty to a religious community whose aim is to unite the universal sources of divine-human inspiration. For me such a community must shun the spirit of sectarianism and shudder at the thought of shutting up God.

There are dangers in this appraoch, and not those imagined by the many determined souls, usually anonymous, who have tried over the years, by postal service and telephone, to save my soul because I do not accept the exclusive saviorship of Christ. The dangers I have in mind inhere in any reach that may exceed our grasp. What I and most of my coreligionists are striving to achieve can easily become a leaky bucket for sloppy thinking. It can be a way of avoiding genuine issues in aimless and untested benevolence. It is easy, at a distance, to build illusions about the other great religions. We are close enough to Christianity and Judaism to be realistic about their excesses, egotisms, and dogmatisms, but when we speak of the far-away faiths, particularly Eastern ones, our voices tend to take on hushed tones; our eyes acquire a starry glow; our worship services dwell sentimentally on Zen, Krishna, and Taoist poetry. Somehow we are not impressed that exotic faiths also have their excesses, egotisms, and dogmatisms. We are understandably upset about Christian encroachments on public schools, legislatures, courts, and abortion rights, or Jewish encroachments on the rights of Palestinians; but we are somehow much less alert to invasions, often violent, into the lives of peoples in Moslem, Buddhist, or Hindu lands.

It is very attractive for us to think of ourselves as a bridge for the world's religions. After all, we have no exclusionary myths to defend, no creeds to enforce. We are open to all that is ethically best in the world's religions, and through freedom, reason, and tolerance, we feel prepared to touch each of the great faiths sympathetically and draw together their moral teachings. It is a grave mistake, however, to view this as a superficial task. Most of the hungry, diseased, and superstition-ridden folk — and they are the vast majority of the world's peoples — haven't the vaguest idea what we are talking about. I am only saying that it is extremely important for *us* to know what we are talking about.

We speak over and over again of our acceptance of change, and we are properly critical of those who resist change. Yet the kind of change we know and understand is comparatively mild and orderly. There are vast areas of the world where change, when it comes, is like a volcano. It erupts with formidable fury. Most of us have known very little of that kind of change.

When the General Assembly of the Unitarian Universalist Association met in Boston in June 1969, it found itself faced with a nerve-shattering schism over black empowerment, from which we are still trying to recover. In the middle 1960s, there was broad support in our ranks for the civil rights movement led by Martin Luther King. In keeping with a growing militancy among black civil rights activists, Unitarian Universalist blacks formed a Black Unitarian Universalist Caucus, recruited a cadre of white supporters, of whom I was one, and confronted our movement with a series of racial justice demands, including special funding and black leadership for an aggressive denominational assault on racism, our own, as well as that of the larger society. At the General Assembly in Cleveland in June 1968, the demands of the caucus were approved by a two-thirds majority vote, but there were deep lacerations.

As the Commission on Appraisal (1984) described in a report: "The black empowerment issue hit the Unitarian Universalists particularly hard. . . . The issue was especially painful. . . because, as primarily middle-class whites who make democratic practice an exercise in religion and who are proud of their traditions of social progress, hearing that they are a racist church compounded a guilt they already felt for not having more members of color."

By 1969, in Boston, the guilt, for many, had turned into resentment. Continued funding for the Black Affairs Council barely survived. In 1970, it ended amid waves of stress, anger, disillusionment, and the dwindling of blacks from denominational involvement.

Perceptions of why we botched the test of black empowerment will probably always vary widely. The confrontational tactics of the Black Caucus made sense to those who used them because, out of their experience, they truly believed it was the only way their needs would be understood and addressed. While some of us whites could identify with that, many could not. The abrasive strategy of "demands," even though for a genuine transfer of power to black leadership, was traumatically offensive to the way we normally did business. As the Commission on Appraisal report put it: "Those who are not oppressed must overcome their own preconceptions in order truly to side with the oppressed." This did not happen. To me a great opportunity was lost. We were confronted with a demand for change that came upon us with a fierce, unfamiliar passion. Since there is enough fault to spread around liberally, finger pointing is absurd. It is my sense, not without foundation, that we are experiencing the rise of fresh corporate responses to the issue of racism as a compelling priority.

But to return to our desire to play a universalizing role in the world community of faiths, I again emphasize the pitfalls of romanticizing the task. We must be careful how we tread in areas that are not very real to our experience, like the late 1960s' thrust for black empowerment. It would be a sobering error to assume that we of the western Unitarian Universalist movement are now prepared to live in the world community. We are not. At the most rudimentary level, the unvarnished sights, sounds, smells, passions, and credulities of the vast bulk of the world's peoples would certainly frighten and perhaps sicken us if we were thrown suddenly into their midst.

What we do have to our credit is an honest desire to play a useful, constructive, and uniting role. We will learn soon enough that some of our notions about spiritual unity and global religious fellowship are realizable only in part, over long periods of time, and as a result of infinite patience. Basically, ours is a nature that seeks peace and pursues it. We will develop a more agonized appreciation of how unreal peace can seem to the emaciated parents of starving children who have been exploited. We will increasingly discover that world community is not an abstraction about which we can make inspiring poems, but a fearsome concreteness of honesty and corruption, cleanliness and filth, kindness and barbarism, hope and hunger, ballots and bullets. This consciousness is growing in us, and we are right to cultivate it, because the world community *is* a reality and we must begin to treat it as such. We will become better, stronger people than we are — sadder and wiser. We will make more room in our hearts and minds for tragedy, because widespread tragedy is one of the hallmarks of the present world community, and total tragedy could become its end result.

We will not desert our humanism. Instead, it will become sturdier and more reliable because it learns to accept the very real presence of despair in people's lives. We will not forsake our optimism, but it will become a chastened optimism based more on our human ability to transcend error and cruelty than on the possibility of completely abolishing them.

Like all others on the North American continent, we religious liberals live in the shadow of colossal United States military and economic power which, much of the time, seems incredibly deficient in ideas of how to nourish the human spirit. Successive government administrations continue to assume that there must be a moral flaw in those who do not instantly recognize the rightness and piety of our intentions. To our credit, Unitarian Universalists have been sufficiently sensitive to identify this tendency as religious idolatry. We are not alone in this; but we, along with others, do speak out candidly against the shameful practice of conscripting God as a tribal deity who smiles upon whatever any particular president decides is in "our national security interest"; a God who is "on our side," a God itching to discomfit "godless communism." We are keen enough to sense that a religiosity that is merely an accessory of national purpose is a religiosity the Soviet leadership could tolerate as well.

There is little mystery about the spiritual need of an emerging world community. Albert Einstein once said that nuclear weapons had changed everything except the way humans think. Our profoundest spiritual need is for a new understanding of what it means to be human in a world that the human mind has succeeded in placing at ultimate risk. It must be an understanding illusionless enough to respect our limitations within a universe incomparably greater than ourselves and to reevaluate our potential for fashioning a sane, compassionate, and productive life within that frame. It must also be an understanding frank enough to accept ourselves as part of a naturalistic order, creatures who emerged from primordial earth, subject to destructive impulses that can be elaborated by the intricate cunning of a remarkable brain; but also creatures with transforming capabilities of thought, imagination, self-awareness, and caring cooperation. Further, it must be an understanding courageous enough to assert that humans are part of a moral order that knows no boundaries of sect or creed, outside of which we lose our meaning, but within which true redemption and transformation may be found.

Arnold Toynbee was Christian to the core, in belief and in practice. But his was also one of the new minds the world needs, and he spoke for Unitarian Universalists when he wrote:

> In the world in which we now find ourselves, the adherents of the different living religions ought to be readier to tolerate, respect, and revere one another's religious heritages because, in our generation, there is not anyone alive who is effectively in a position to judge between his own religion and his neighbors's. . . . If we do not feel that. . . we are confessing to a lack of faith in the truth and value of the religion that happens to be ours. On the other hand, if we do have faith in it, we shall have no fear that it will fail to play its full part in helping human souls to enter into communion with the presence behind the phenomena and to bring themselves into harmony with this Absolute Reality. The missions of the higher religions are not competitive; they are complementary. We can believe in our own religion without having to feel that it is the sole means of salvation.*

Those of us who dream of an onrushing day when all will become even as we are, need to take Toynbee to heart. He is talking to us as well as to others. For ourselves, we must have a view of life that sustains us and prepares us for living in the thorny world community of which we are a part. But we must not assume that we can immediately communicate our religious viewpoint to our world neighbors in convincing particulars. After all, we are not notably successful in communicating it to neighbors here at home. We must, in fact, strip ourselves of the irrelevant belief that for their own good all should accept our definition of what is rational. We must divest ourselves of the basically smug assumption that human progress and felicity are possible only in terms of our realities.

Liberal religion is something that can and does contribute to our becoming more serviceable participants in an emerging world community, as David Rankin enumerates in his eloquent essay "Defining Our Faith" on Unitarian Universalist beliefs:

---

*Arnold Toynbee, *An Historian's Approach to Religion* (New York: Oxford University Press, 1979), pp. 297-98.

Like the Roman Catholics, we have a long tradition — extending back to the sun-baked desert of ancient Israel, the small rural villages of Transylvania, and the rocky shores of early New England.

Like the Jews, we have our heroes and heroines — Servetus, David, and Fuller; Murray, Channing, and Emerson; Barton, Anthony, and Steinmetz — to name only a few.

Like the Baptists, we have a system of democratic polity — with the congregation as the ultimate authority, an elected Board of Trustees, and a pulpit characterized by freedom of expression.

Like the Confucianists, we have emphasized the capacity for reason — possessing a thirst for the fruits of wisdom and knowledge, and a reverent feeling toward the achievements of the mind.

Like the Hindus, we have an eclectic system of theology — encouraging each individual to develop a personal faith which is not dependent on external demand.

Like the Humanists, we have our roots in the experience of the world — as it is known through the medium of touch, and sight, and sound, and taste, and smell.

Like the Buddhists, we have an accent on the individual — on the beauty, the mystery, and the holiness of each man, woman and child — as each is a sacred vessel.

The liberal spirit in religion, as we Unitarian Universalists know it, grew out of the Judeo-Christian tradition and is part of that tradition. But for most of us, it has grown to be more. Looking about us, we see that the liberal spirit has appeared in greater or lesser degree in all of the great faiths. It emerged in Hinduism in Buddha's teachings, then later as the Brahma-Samaj. It appeared in cultic Judaism as the ethical thundering of the early prophets, then again in the efforts of Jesus to purify the moral imperatives of his ancestral faith. It sprang to life among the great philosophers of ancient Greece. Its story is that of the bursting of the cocoons religions spin around themselves. All the world faiths, as we see them today, are mixtures of contradictory impulses; the thrust to the closed, the particular, the chosen, and the thrust to the open, the universal, the all-embracing.

Invariably, the narrowing instinct of each religion is deeply rooted in its past, beneath a hard crust of "exclusive" revelation. The devotees of God's incarnation in Christ must contend with the devotees of Allah's whisperings directly into the ear of Mohammed. But every faith also has its universalizing proclivity; one that is basically spiritual rather than mythical, ethical rather than doctrinal, social rather than sectarian. It is in this realm that the great faiths are in harmony:

In Hinduism: Systems of faith differ, but God is one.

In Buddhism: The good person's purpose is to increase the mercy, charity, kindness, and piety of all humankind.

In Judaism: Who gains wisdom: Those who are willing to receive instruction from all sources.

In Zoroastrianism: Diversity of worship has divided the human race into many creeds. From among all their dogmas I have selected one — divine love.

In Shintoism: Regard heaven as your father, earth as your mother, and all things as your brothers and sisters.

In Confucianism: Love cannot be outnumbered.

In Christianity: Let us therefore follow after the things that make for peace and the things wherewith we may edify one another.

There is a distinctive note in each of the great religions. They cannot be better described than as the many strings of the harp. Their harmony flows from dealing with the same materials: human nature, human dependence on the transcendent, and human interdependence. Their highest aspirations are universal.

The religious liberalism of the western world arose as the universalizing impulse within Judeo-Christianity and has grown gradually in its awareness of kinship with the same impulse in other great faiths. This is what led Emerson to study Asian religions and to their lasting imprint on his life and thought. This is what drew from his lips the passage in his Harvard Divinity School Address of July 15, 1838, that scandalized so many of his Unitarian peers: "Attach thyself not to the Christian symbol, but to the moral sentiment which carries innumerable Christianities, humanities and divinities in its bosom."

Channing, despite his staunch attachment to the Christian symbol, was moved to write: "Virtue is no local thing. It is not honorable because born in this community or that, but for its own, independent, lasting beauty." And he defined the bond of "the universal church" as one from which none could be "excommunicated" except by themselves, by "the death of goodness" in their own hearts.

In 1936, a newly established Commission on Appraisal of the American Unitarian Association issued a landmark report:

> What is needed is an association of free churches that will stand and fight for the central philosophy and values of liberal religion. . . . These churches. . . will be thoroughly emancipated from the sectarian spirit, from the tendency to set themselves up as small, select, superior groups of men and women to whom by some mysterious dispensation an exclusive gift of truth has been granted. They will cultivate an intensive sense of fellowship within their own ranks, but they will be keenly aware of the world-wide aspects of their liberal faith, recognizing the kinship of liberals across all barriers of race, nationality or traditional religious background.

No document has ever been more prophetic. It recognized and gave impetus to an unmistakable trend. It reads today like a spiritual blueprint for a Unitarianism Universalism of the 1980s, witnessing the oneness of the universe, the oneness of the human family, the oneness of discovered and discoverable truth, the universal validity of free inquiry, and the dawn of universal humanity. We are not anti-Christian any more than we are anti-Moslem or anti-Buddhist. In fact, we are not anti anything except ignorance, dogmatism, bigotry, poverty, injustice, war, tyranny, and hypocrisy.

Our liberal faith is far from fully stretched to meet the spiritual needs of a new age. But we are beckoned to transform our faith into an adequate working force whose energies will not rest nor cease to mature as long as brotherhood/sisterhood, justice and peace are the poorly realized dreams rather than the realities of our common life. In a time as dangerous to the human future as ours, the character of our liberal religious movement dare not stop short of the universal claims upon it.

7

The Who, What, and Where of God

Go not, my soul, in search of him; thou wilt not find him there —
Or in the depths of shadow dim, or heights of upper air.
For not in far-off realms of space the Spirit hath its throne;
In ev'ry heart it findeth place and waiteth to be known.

Frederick Lucian Hosmer, "Hymns for the Celebration of Life"

All mother goddesses spin and weave....Everything that is
comes out of them: They weave the world tapestry out of genesis
and demise, "threads appearing and disappearing rhythmically."
Helen Diner, *Mothers and Amazons*

Rich indeed have been our discoveries "in far-off realms of space." Our
spaceships and satellites, marvels of human technology, have girdled the
earth, landed on the moon, and orbited planets. Yet none aboard them, or
guiding them, would take issue with Hosmer. There are no sightings out
there of heaven's location or God's throne. What is out there, our com-
puter-directed invasions confirm, is perhaps the most significant scientific
discovery of our age — infinite geometric space, within which, for practical
human purposes, God is silent.

God does not speak in rational science's space. And it was Pascal, prescient and deeply Christian, who foresaw it when he wrote: "The eternal
silences of the infinite frighten me."

From Pascal to the latest mind-boggling refinement in computer circui-
try miniaturization, the impact on liberal religion is profound. The
achievements of the scientific method inspire reverence in the minds of religious liberals. But there is confusion and sadness in their hearts. Science as
science renounces all moral norms save the search for what is truly true and

really real. Where, then, do we anchor all of the other moral issues and meanings of life? In a well-known anecdote, Napoleon asked a scientist where God figured in his model of the heavens. "Sir," the scientist answered, "I have no need of that hypothesis in my work." No need of that hypothesis in our scientific work perhaps. But what of the rest of life? Is there no need in that for all that is meant by "God's love of us" and "our love of God"? As Hosmer put it, "not in far-off realms of space. . . ."; but what of "In ev'ry heart it findeth place and waiteth to be known"?

On yet another "God" front — feminist theology — religious liberals have responded, not with confusion and sadness, but with passionate enthusiasm. If in infinite geometric space there is no heavenly throne from which God roars "I am the Lord, thy God," isn't it equally bizarre to picture God as of one — or of any — gender? In part, God's maleness results from simple anthropomorphism, but it is also a product of the specifically Judeo-Christian conception of God, which was, and is, patriarchal. As feminist theologians like Rosemary Radford Ruether and Mary Daly have abundantly demonstrated, there was another early vision of deity within Judeo-Christianity, widespread until fiercely suppressed, which worshipped either a female goddess or a female aspect of divinity. Feminist theology's use of women's experience has been a critical force in liberal religion, along with science, in compelling a searching reexamination of the who, what, and where of God.

God as Problem

Male terminology has so permeated discussions of God as problem, that it is practically impossible to write much of what follows without using masculine characterizations.

Even to suggest that God might be a problem remains for many, despite science and feminist theology, a scandal and a blasphemy. Not so among Unitarian Universalists. God is a problem for several reasons; first because *God* is a word used to cover a multiplicity of meanings. Popularly, the word is used as if everyone understood the same things by it; but how can anyone, with reasonable consideration, claim that Albert Einstein's *God* is the same as Jerry Falwell's, or Rosemary Ruether's the same as Phyllis Schlafly's? This is one of the problems of God: a problem of language, of semantics, of perceptions. As my colleague Wallace Robbins once said: "Don't slap God on the back; you'll miss."

Another reason God is a problem grows out of what people sometimes know, but mostly do not know, about the historical evolution of God concepts. The God of a Hindu priest is a quite different product of spiritual development from the God of a Roman Catholic priest. Through the ages, the various divinities experienced and imagined by the human race have been of infinite and splendid variety. It is a great pity that they are not better known. A deeper appreciation of their richly diverse functions and natures might temper many of the hostilities among peoples of differing beliefs. Humanity's gods can only be known by those who take the trouble to investigate origins and comparative histories, and since so few bother, God *is* a problem of divisive misunderstandings and bitterness.

Still another problem is the symbolism of God. Religion deals with great, sweeping issues of destiny. When you ask someone how to get to the nearest post office, you anticipate a simple, direct answer. But when you ask someone sitting next to you on a plane, Where are we all going? you do not expect to be told Peoria. Religion strives for an overall account of the sum of things. It has an interest in totality, and God is the symbol most commonly used to express this cosmic perspective. But it is a tremendously large and encompassing symbol. Within its misty infinities, it is easy to become confused. Confused people lose their patience with one another. They find themselves contending for concrete definitions, and in the name of such definitions, massive slaughters have taken place.

Reasonable, temperate people come along who say that such strife is senseless. There is no way to prove *anything* about God, so why squander precious energies trying? Isn't it better simply to put the problem aside until we have more to go on? Meanwhile we can turn our attention to matters that yield to our current skills and knowledge. For the present, at least, the proper study for humans is humans. Let religion throw its entire and undistracted force into the struggle to extricate the human enterprise from its present dire failings and dilemmas. Someday we may know enough to make responsible statements about God. At present this is not possible.

I have described here the view of a significant company of sincerely religious persons both within and outside the Unitarian Universalist body. Yet many are not so willing to suspend their quest for God. Asking ultimate questions may be impractical, but one of reason's compulsions is asking.

We recognize from the start that it is undesirable to press for conformity of profession about the nature of God. As I have suggested, for some it seems better to leave the symbol *God* in abeyance until there is more to go on. For others, it is a symbol representing, however intangibly, the precious quest for deeper and deeper meanings. None of us tries to compel others to believe one thing or another about God, but every Unitarian Universalist assumes an obligation to know as fully as possible the facets of human experience out of which theologies arise.

The human race has told itself many stories about human origins, destinies, and relationships with forces called gods and God. These stories have two common elements: they reflect the ordinary anxieties and strivings of daily life, and they recognize the existence of forces humans may never actually see or touch, but which must be taken into account in describing the realities of birth-to-death human living. Inevitably these stories raise puzzling questions. Are humans but meaningless specks in infinite wastes of space and time, helpless victims of random forces, careless products of invisible energies, creatures like the fisherman in Hemingway's *The Old Man and the Sea* who catches the largest fish of his scrabbly career only to have it devoured by sharks before he can bring it to shore? Are good and evil as casual, as coincidental, as impersonal as the catch and the shark? Are humans, as Lewis Mumford posed it, "a smoking candle with a charred wick . . . a poor flame flickering in a wind that will speedily extinguish it"?

Or are humans the epicenter of divine attention, the wayward children of a majestic deity, creatures who have flaunted their rebellious will in the face of a Father-God and placed their souls in eternal jeopardy? Have they, by their disobedience, thrust themselves out of a Garden of Eden where they were at one with all creation? Is their nature both earthly and divine, but so steeped in the sins of assertiveness and pride that it cannot overcome damnation except through the gift of divine grace? Is it true that humans can find the answers they seek only if they prepare themselves, by the right beliefs, for another world and turn all their hopes and energies toward it?

This is the story orthodox Christianity tells to the world, and with certain variations (some of them important), it is a story told by many religions. Actually, the notion that earthly life is a vale of human sin from which there is rescue only by divine fiat is far older than Christianity.

How do people think their way through such dilemmas as the traditional myths pose? They do so, quite naturally, within their own limits. Since their own earthly lives have a beginning and an end, they think of the universe in the same way. It, too, must begin and end. Humans understand best the things they themselves have a hand in creating. In an effort to understand the universe, they assume that there must be a creator who stands outside creation and controls it. Early metaphysical thinking was done at a time when kings or their equivalent ruled with despotic authority over property, behavior, ideas, and even life. Representative democracy and the consent of the governed were far in the future. Consequently, people thought about the most powerful gods, or God, as both male and almighty.

It is difficult for most Unitarian Universalists to understand why people have continued through the ages to fashion God in this image. Even more to the point, since Pascal anyway, is the question of God as creator. If God is creator, was he himself uncreated? John Stuart Mill, in his autobiography, wrote: "My father taught me that the question 'Who made me?' cannot be answered, since it immediately suggests the further question 'Who made God?' Here in this very simple sentence is the enormous fallacy in all the so-called proofs of God's existence as a First Cause. If everything must have a cause, then God too must be caused. If there is anything without a cause, it might just as well be you as God."

Bertrand Russell ran one of his celebrated numbers on the Mill conundrum, pointing out that it is like the ancient Hindu view that the world is resting upon an elephant and the elephant upon a tortoise. When someone asks, "What about the tortoise?" the Hindu says, "Let's change the subject."

The argument for God as creator, as Kant and many others have pointed out, is unconvincing. Logic throws no obstacle to the notion that the universe has *always* existed. But the human imagination shrinks from this. The need to think in terms of beginnings and ends is strong; so humans speculate about God as creator and first cause, and lead themselves to the conviction that God, though in the midst of his creation, is separated from it by incalculable distance. God is in the midst of the human scene (immanent), indeed is within each one of us, yet dwarfs the whole of creation by his awesome power and perfection. Is it not fair to say that such a God, in terms of reason, is actually more of a problem than the problems his existence is presumed to solve?

Baffled by the very mysteries they create for themselves, humans, the ineffable theologians, plunge into further contradictions. On the one hand, God is pictured as pure spirit: nameless, fathomless, infinite; on the other hand, he incarnates himself as Krishna in Hinduism, as Buddha in (some forms of) Buddhism, as Christ in Christianity. The intention is admirable enough: it is to account in some way for the existence of a divine element in human life and to give to it an intimate reality. But for our lives to have the meaning and purpose we require of them, is it necessary for us to confound ourselves by setting forth these competing incarnations as material facts? Is it necessary to try to make an uncreated creator out of God—a cosmic, male satrap? Will we slide into moral nihilism unless we think of the cosmic process as a predetermined plan existing first in the mind of God and then unfolding itself like a giant edict before our eyes?

The persistent habit of traditional religions is to shape their demands upon communicants around a God who is responsible for everything that is and is to be. God, in the classic phraseology, is all-powerful, all-knowing, and omnipresent. In the Ninetieth Psalm's flowing description:

> Lord, thou hast been our dwelling place in all generations.
> Before the mountains were brought forth,
> Or ever thou hadst formed the earth and the world,
> Even from everlasting to everlasting, thou art God.

God, in other words, is at the beginning of all things and in a position of active, conscious responsibility for everything.

A Unitarian Universalist does not shrink from recognizing that such a God is a staggering dilemma. If God is put at the beginning, as the creator of all things, the power responsible for all things, he becomes a monstrous being. This, in truth, is what many sensitive spiritual souls, down through the centuries, have intuited. Any God who is responsible for everything is, at least in part, a god of violence, pain, misery, injustice, and cruelty. As a piece of folk wisdom has it: "If God is God, then God is not good; if God is good, then God is not God. Take the even; take the odd."

If you try to apologize for this God, who has presumably produced a creation at least half lost to the powers of evil, by saying that he promises redemption for the elect, you merely turn a brutal deity into a demented one. What would we think, for example, of a human father who deliberately torments his children with debasement and terror, then turns around and lavishes favors on one of them while leaving the others to tremble and whimper? As shocking as such an act would be, it is less so than the behavior of an Almighty who is capable of condemning human beings to an eternity of awful suffering for sins committed in the briefest of lifetimes in a world for which this King of the Universe is avowedly responsible.

Here is a savagely disproportionate system of punishment that is an insult not only to reason but to justice as well.

Yet, children are being indoctrinated every day with such teachings. The daughter of one of my colleagues came home on the verge of hysteria because a playmate told her that if she was bad God would send her to burn forever in hell. She was reminded of the mild disciplines she experienced at home, when they were absolutely necessary, and was told that if Mommy and Daddy could be that gentle when provoked, how much more gentle God must be.

It is a reasonably good answer to a child, yet it begs the question. If God is really at the beginning of things, if God truly controls, then it is small wonder that he could shock Voltaire with the slaughter of innocents. We can imagine what Voltaire would say about a God who permits his creatures to build crematories in Buchenwald, to atom-bomb Hiroshima, to exterminate Afghan villages, and to practice apartheid in South Africa.

Neither faith nor reason can refuse to face such questions. If divine planning actually presides over all the occasions of human life, then God, from a human point of view, is part demon. If God is all-powerful, responsible for all that happens, capable of heeding even the sparrow's fall, then he can hardly be a loving God. By the same token, if God, from a human point of view, is truly a loving God, he cannot by any means be all-powerful. Indeed, it is precisely this that led in ancient times to divine dualisms, a God of good locked in combat with a God of evil, and both contending for the control of human affairs. Zoroastrianism and early Manichean Christianity are examples. In our day, there is renewed interest in what used to be called a limited God: a God who is loving but not all-powerful; a God who struggles against primordial, untamed chaos and evil. Attesting to a widespread sympathetic response is the popularity of books, sermons, and church school curriculum units around the general theme of why bad things happen to good people. The difficulties of dealing with two supreme deities, or one limited God, are no less vexing to faith and reason than those associated with one God, omnipotent, omniscient, and omnipresent.

It is questions such as these that form some of our strongest bonds of liberal religious fellowship. We know that the issues are real, pertinent, and searching. We know that they cannot be dismissed with pulpit platitudes. We draw together in common revulsion before those who speak of God as some kind of cosmic Big Brother who will set everything right if we just put his name on enough coins, stamps, public buildings, and schoolroom walls.

Unitarian Universalists share a realization that if the traditional Almighty is real, he is beyond human comprehension and unworthy of human worship. We are inclined, in this instance, to agree with Julius Penrose in James Cozzen's novel *By Love Possessed* that theology is "the homage. . . nonsense pays to sense."

In what ways, then, do we characteristically look for solutions to the problem of God? There are three main lines of direction: God and the human search for self; God and idealized reality; God and the search for meaning and purpose.

May the Inner and the Outer Person Be One

What motivates people in their religious beliefs? The picture that emerges from research is hardly cause for unalloyed rejoicing. A project done for the American Anthropological Association reports the sad finding that intense religiousness springs more often from fear and anger than from love and peace. This would seem to confirm what psychotherapists have long noted when treating persons whose emotional distresses include a pronounced religious element. Mary McCarthy underscores this in a paragraph in *Memories of a Catholic Girlhood:* "From what I have seen, I am driven to the conclusion that religion is only good for good people, and I do not mean this as a paradox, but simply as an observable fact. Only good people can afford to be religious. For others, it is too great a temptation—a temptation to the deadly sins of pride and anger, chiefly, but one might also add sloth. My Grandmother McCarthy, I am sure, would have been a better woman if she had been an atheist or an agnostic."

Religious belief may all too easily become a weapon in the hands of infantile adults, justifying and sanctifying hostile and fear-ridden behavior. For many of us the search for God is a search for self. So far so good. But if we find God too easily and in too stereotyped a form, we are likely to end with a none-too-admirable self. God can be a vehicle for immaturity.

Until the beginning of our century, nearly all matters concerning the human psyche were referred to theologians and philosophers. In the late eighteenth century, for example, psychology was taught in the same departments at Harvard and Yale as angelology. Ancient Athens, with its deeper respect for psychological insights, turned to philosophers for guidance. Thus Socrates, in one of his infrequent prayers, gave this memorable prescription for spiritual health: "Beloved Pan, and all ye other gods that haunt this place, give me beauty in the inward soul, and may the inner and the outer. . . be at one."

Centuries later, Augustine, a person of many facets, developed a keen eye for psychological truths. He taught that persons find themselves only when they are able to penetrate deeply enough into their experience to unite the subjective and objective aspects of their lives. It is also at this point, Augustine said, that a person finds God.

If we continue up the slopes of history to the nineteenth century, before the advent of Sigmund Freud, we find the most penetrating psychological insights being offered by Kierkegaard and Nietzsche, both philosophers and both intensely interested in religion. Contrary to a widespread impression of his work, it was Nietzsche who sensed more clearly than most that without corresponding advances in human moral character, technical progress could lead to ethical nihilism. In reaction to this grave danger, he wrote his familiar dramatic parable of the madman who comes into a village asking, "Where is God?" The people laugh and answer that God has emigrated, gone on a trip. The madman then cries: "I will tell you where God has gone. We have killed him, you and I. We have unchained this earth from its sun. God remains dead, and we have killed him." At this point, the madman lapses into silence, gazing at the people. They, too, become silent, looking at him. Then he speaks his final words: "I come too early. This tremendous event is still on its way."

Nietzsche was issuing an indictment against a mechanization of life that crushes the self and the ethical sense. The "tremendous event. . . still on its way" was, as he accurately predicted, the onrushing fury of twentieth-century collectivism (George Orwell's *1984*), with its transformation of persons into automatons without heart or soul.

The developing science of psychology became itself a portion of the mechanistic tendency. Pavlov's conditioned-response experiments in the Soviet Union and B.F. Skinner's behaviorism in the United States cannot be called premeditated attempts to dehumanize humans. Far from it. Both had the underlying humanistic purpose of discovering better ways to release persons from the tyranny of fear and hostility. But from these and similar efforts an attempt continues to construct a total psychological view of human behavior based on mechanistic principles, disregarding such

unquantifiable abstractions as mind and consciousness. This flaw is
alarming to most religious liberals. Humans ought never to be just conditioned creatures, the complete captives of a chain of stimulus and response.
Humans transcend conditioning. They exercise choice by virtue of their
capacity for self-awareness. Their margins of choice are narrow — to this
extent behavioral psychology is correct — but within such margins they find
the meaning of freedom and responsibility. Here, also, is the dwelling place
of their higher religious yearnings and their quest to understand the purposes of their being.

Most psychologists today are unwilling to be classified among the mechanistic thinkers. The tide in psychology, as among practitioners of the
harder sciences, is toward a more open view. This is not to say that the
wider scientific horizons offer proof, however fuzzy, of particular concep-
tions of God. But it is now scientifically respectable to examine what, for
many, had been a closed area and to seek ideas of a ground of being that
sustain and magnify the human sense of freedom and ethical responsibility.

The coming of Sigmund Freud, interestingly enough, helped to turn the
search for God inward. Freud's work had a shattering effect on traditional
understandings of faith and morals. He demonstrated that many of the real
reasons for our behavior have little to do with conscious theological beliefs,
but stem instead from wishes, fears, and experiences of which we have no
conscious awareness. With Freud's findings as guides, it was possible to
demonstrate that pious behavior is often motivated by repressed hate of self
rather than by love of God. Freud hovers behind Mary McCarthy's pained
observation that only people who are good to begin with should risk the
temptation of becoming ardent religious believers.

The popularization of Freud's theories sent waves of alarm through the
minds of many sincere ethical and religious thinkers. It seemed that a new
type of determinism was being forced on the human species, this time in
the guise of unconscious drives and instincts. Freud himself argued that the
Judeo-Christian concept of God was an extension of infantile dependency.

Once again, however, the meanings suggested by Freud's pioneering
work have been broadened by the trend away from a mechanistic interpretation of science. Psycholanalytic thinkers such as Jung, Adler, Horney,
Fromm, and Kohut have built on Freud's discoveries and have used the
fruits of his genius to encourage a deepened and more positive interest in
the role of ethics and religion. It became possible to assert that ethics cannot
be attained by being dishonest with oneself, and that the idea of God as a

cosmic father who will always take care of his right-believing children is inadequate. Freud's historic accomplishment, broadened by those who came after him, puts a fresh gloss on Socrates's prayer. The oneness of the inner and the outer person, a unity of the self, is the basis for sound ethics and creative religious beliefs.

Liberal religion is not driven by a conflict between psychology and religion. To us, psychoanalysis and psychotherapy are not substitutes for religion, but are exciting, useful tools for helping to clear away some of the debris of anxiety, guilt, and hostility that keeps us from enlarging our precious margins of freedom. Our purpose is to arrive at ethical and religious beliefs that will be most expressive of the self and of the real situation in which we live. Augustine said that persons find God when they find self. There is nothing in modern psychology that should persuade anyone, in the name of science, to dispute Augustine's contention. A concept of God emerging from a unified, unblocked, fully functioning self bears its own spiritual warrant. To plumb the levels of the unconscious is to tap springs of insight, creativity, and energy beyond anything most people are conscious of possessing. For many of us, the discovery of self is indeed, as Augustine suggested, the beginning of a discovery of an experience of God.

If self-discovery results in greater self-affirmation, what happens to the traditional idea of dependence on God? This is a serious issue, if for no other reason than that it divides people into conflicting camps. From the evangelical side come the common, comforting affirmations: "What a friend we have in Jesus" and "God will take care of you." From the brasher advocates of psychological scientism we hear warnings to depend on no one or nothing but one's self or suffer the consequences of immaturity and crippled self-regard.

It is wise to rephrase the problem. How can we, on one hand, resolve to be accountable to ourselves and to others for our own actions, develop and use our own powers, and mind that each person take responsibility in the long run for the development of her or his own life and, on the other hand, acknowledge that we exist in a world of "givens" that are much weightier than we are no matter how faithfully we apply ourselves to high moral tasks?

When the question is asked in this manner, we can reasonably hope to demonstrate that truly creative people are those who affirm themselves and their talents to the fullest extent but at the same time acknowledge their dependence both on life's unmerited favors, forces, and circumstances and on their need for others. We might call this a Unitarian Universalist's tri-partite principle of self-assertion, grace, and community. We all have resources of creativity for which we are starkly and relentlessly responsible. At the same time, we live in circumstances over which we exercise little or no control. And we are in this condition together. How we are to adjust ourselves to this reality is each person's basic religious challenge. Ours is not the effrontery of rejecting the solution of those who *do* accept the "revealed" answers of traditional theology and find by doing so that they are able to keep growing, make fuller use of their powers, and deepen their humility and capacity for awe, wonder, and service. But for us, Freud was right in saying that the idea of God can be used for anything but con-structive ethical and religious purposes. By the same token, we also disci-pline ourselves to remember that a superficial skepticism, untempered by an abiding sense of the mysteries of which we are a part, *can* be an unwhole-some spiritual arrogance.

Fortunately, there is a healthy kind of pride in one's own powers that goes hand in hand with humility, and it delineates liberal religion at its best. For lack of a better term, we call it self-esteem: a willingness to assert, with-out guilt, our capacities for freedom, responsibility, creativity, and com-munity, while affirming, without anxiety, our constant dependence on forces beyond ourselves. Never need we fear to assert ourselves as long as we are able to feel a proportionate awe in realizing that truth is always greater than our grasp of it. Indeed, the truth we do *not* know grows larger precisely as we discover more truth. We are free to rejoice in the use of our talents, to exult in our abilities to feel, create, and grow, in proportion to our wonder at the vast mystery of grace that surrounds us. To esteem our-selves properly means that we esteem also the people about us and the indescribable, immeasurable reality of which we are all part. For many of us, God is this reality. Self-assertion and dependence are reconciled. The religious person and the spiritually healthy person become one.

To Find the Province of the Divine

Let me return for a moment to James Cozzen's novel *By Love Possessed.* Arthur Winner, Jr., the central figure, is musing about the religious views of his father:

In short, did the Man of Reason ever accept the story of the incar-nate godhead, or the story of the risen Christ. . . ? The Man of Reason had done the reading of his day and what was he being told (by his friend, the rector) but the very stuff of myth—the woman got with child by the deity in time to bear the infant savior at the winter solstice; the grievous formal murder of the theanthropos whose earth-breaking return from the dead must occur near the vernal equinox. Could the Man of Reason credit the dreadful drama's orthodox accounting-for? Could ethical assent ever be given by him to all the shocking, the really monstrous, dogma of the atonement implied? What was here but allegorical fantasy, a laborious attempt in symbols to relate the finite known to the infinite unknown? You received such stories, not as shedding light on, but as admitting, the mystery awesome and permanent of life.

Those who have borne with my self-revelations in this book so far will instantly recognize why these lines touch and delight me. I arrived long ago where Arthur Winner, Sr., arrived, with a sureness of feeling that the God whose substance can be verified only by such tortuous dogmas as the atonement is a God who sheds no light on the awesome and permanent mysteries of life. Then what does a person do? If that person is Arthur Winner, Sr., he remains in the Episcopal Church, telling himself that the stuff of myth has long been the sacred fiction of his family and of his class, a fable so honored that it has a vested right.

Another option is one claimed by me and my chosen coreligionists, who seek the province of the divine in precincts other than those established for the veneration of ancient myths and creeds. We look for sustaining and satisfying intimations of God within the vested right of the free mind.

Such a coreligionist, for example, was Baruch Spinoza, master mathematician and philosopher of the seventeenth century's liberal Dutch Republic. In 1656, Spinoza was excommunicated from the Jewish community of Amsterdam for "abominable heresies." His crime was seeking an experience of God acceptable to people of reason, independent thought, and ethical sensitivity—not a God of revelation, but a God of nature.

Spinoza began with nature and divided it into two parts. One part is the active, invisible, vital process of nature: its creative force; the other is the massive product of creative force: the tangible, individual items, modes, or forms such as trees, winds, waters, hills, fields, stones, flowers, mountains, animals, and human beings. For Spinoza, God *as substance* is the first part of nature, and God *as extension* is the second. God is the vital, creative process and force beneath and within all things. God is the universe and all that is in it.

Spinoza then asked what we mean when we speak of the help of God. He answered that the help of God means the fixed and unchangeable order of nature, or the chain of natural events. The universal laws of nature and the decrees of God are one and the same. To use Spinoza's words: "From the infinite nature of God, all things follow by the same necessity, and in the same way, as it follows from the nature of a triangle, from eternity to eternity, that its three angles are equal to two right angles" (*Treatise on God and Man*).

What the laws of the triangle are to all triangles, God is to the world. Therefore, since the will of God and the laws of nature are one and the same, it follows that all events in human life, and outside it, are governed by dependable, invariable laws, and not by the whim of an autocrat seated in the heavens. Spinoza concluded that our gravest human error is to try to make God a conscious creature like ourselves, with changeable desires and purposes. Our problem of evil, in which we attempt to reconcile the ills of life with the presumed goodness of God, is a purely human problem having nothing to do with God. Spinoza chided those who forgot the lesson of Job that God is beyond our human problems of good and evil. Good and evil are relative to human tastes and experiences. They have no meaning in the universe as a whole.

As to the question of whether God is in any sense a person, Spinoza answers no. If triangles could speak, they would describe God as triangular. If circles could speak, they would describe God as circular. If horses could speak, they would describe God as horselike. It is natural but incorrect for humans to ascribe their own attributes to God.

The will of God, Spinoza continues, is the sum of all causes and all laws. The intellect of God is the sum of all mind. The mental and molecular processes that constitute the double reality of the universe — their causes and their laws — *are* God. Because this is a lawful universe, we must apply a measured understanding to human actions. As reason provides us with the perception of God behind the flux of things in the universe, so reason enables us to discover law in the flux of human desires and purposes. The action of reason is human liberty, and it is the only real freedom available to us. We are free to the extent that we know and understand ourselves, our fellows, and the world in which we live. Thus do we fortify ourselves to bear both faces of fortune. God is not a capricious personality, absorbed in the private affairs of worshippers, but the invariable, sustaining order of the universe. Moral persons, perceiving things through this eye of eternity, rise above fitful yearnings to identify their personal pleasures and desires with God and achieve a high serenity of contemplation and ethical wisdom.

Little wonder that Spinoza is the prototype of many present-day Unitarian Universalists. His was a lasting, impressive monument of brave faith in a magnificently credible and impersonal God. The province of the divine discovered by this inspired grinder of lenses plays a vital role still in the making of liberal religious minds.

James Luther Adams, the foremost theologian and ethicist of contemporary Unitarian Universalism, grapples directly with what is meant by "the love of God." He describes it as "the giving of oneself to the power that holds the world together and that, when we are tearing it apart, persuades us to come to ourselves and start on new beginnings" (*The Love of God*). Why is this kind of love reliable? Because it alone "has within it the seeds of becoming, even in the face of tragedy and death—when it keeps confidence, saying, 'Into thy hands I commend my spirit.'" What is also reliable about this kind of love is the special respect it engenders for the necessary diversity of human beings. Because this love is a giving over of self to a process of transformation, all persons who experience it in their relations to each other and in their diversity "become mutually supporting and enhancing rather than mutually impoverishing."

The seemingly intractable antagonism between egoism and altruism is "transcended in the devotion to the good of others, which is at the same time the fulfillment of the good of the self." As Adams expresses it: "In the fellowship of the love of God one loses life to find it. And yet the loss and the finding are more than the process of self-realization. We become new creatures. This is the work of God that brings the self to something more than and beyond the self, beyond even the 'highest self.'" Adams warns that no rosy path is promised by this kind of love. "It may lead to what Thomas à Kempis calls 'the royal way of the cross,' a way which God as well as man traverses, not for the sake of suffering in itself to be sure, but for the sake of suffering, separated humankind. A comprehending mutuality rooted in immemorial being stirs. . .itself anew to heal and unite what has been wounded and separated."

Adams reasons that the love of God is a love we can give only because it was first given to us. "Ultimately, it is not even ours to give, for it is not in our keeping. It is in the keeping of a power that we can never fully know, of a power that we must in faith trust. Humanity's expression of it is a response to an antecedent glory and promise, the ground of meaning and the ever new resource for its fulfillment."

Is there a test we can apply? Indeed there is, says Adams. "By their fruits shall ye know them." To learn what is meant by professed love of God, watch "what sort of behavior issues from it." The best way to demonstrate the power of a religious-ethical profession is "to show what difference it makes in action." In fact, we commonly apply this test in personal behavior terms, noting that love of God that is deficient in "individual integrity, in humility, and in affectionate concern for others, is counterfeit."

But Adams is not content to let the matter rest in personal attitudes and behavior alone. He insists that love of God is clearly and relevantly manifest only "when we know what it means for institutional behavior, when we know what kind of family, or economic system, or political order it demands." As an example of decisive difference, he compares and contrasts the family patterns of "the old Lutherans and the Quakers." Their words about the love of God are, on the surface, much the same. "The one group," however, "sanctioned a sort of patriarchal family in which the authoritarian father was the vicar of God in the home, and love of God among the children was supposed to produce instant, unquestioning obedience; the other group preferred a family in which a more permissive, persuasive atmosphere prevailed. Yet both groups avowed the love of God as proclaimed in the Gospels." Adams concludes that the true meanings of professed religious imperatives become concrete only when seen in a social context: "Often the meaning of an ethical generality can be determined by observing what its proponents wish to change in society or to preserve unchanged."

The profound impact that James Luther Adams had on the theological quest of Unitarian Universalists is perhaps best summarized in his words: "Those who interpret the love of God as movement toward a community of freedom and mutuality will be able to vindicate the claim that they serve a power that is reliable, only by yielding to that power in the midst of a world that is suffering, divided by cleavages of race, class, and nation. What is at stake is the creation of a world in which this kind of love of God becomes incarnate in a more just and free society."

Rosemary Radford Ruether, a feminist Christian theologian, has no organic bond with Unitarian Universalism, but her nonsexist understandings of God are a bracing tonic for many within our ranks. With bold strokes, she challenges ages-old interpretations of religious experience that are rooted in a male elitist perspective. Women, she writes, have been systematically subordinated and negated in a system of language about God, "man," nature, sin, and redemption that is male-centered. With unassailable scholarly credentials, she mines the teachings of the Bible and the writings of ancient Goddess-oriented cultures, concluding that the patriarchal bias in religion was not always so nor need it be today. Widening her embrace to include the liberation theologies of all oppressed peoples, she points the way to a fuller vision of God/ess, one that undergirds a positive, egalitarian faith.

To fill in the picture, I will let Ruether speak for herself in an imaginary interview, with all of her answers drawn from her book *Sexism and God-Talk*.

JM: How would you describe the critical principle of feminist theology?

RRR: "[It] is the promotion of the full humanity of women. Whatever denies, diminishes, or distorts the full humanity of women is, therefore, appraised as not redemptive, [and] must be presumed not to reflect the divine or an authentic relation to the divine, ... or a community of redemption."

JM: Can you phrase this in more positive terms?

RRR: "[Gladly.] What does promote the full humanity of women is the Holy, it does reflect true relation to the divine, it is the true nature of things, the authentic message of redemption and the mission of redemptive community. But the meaning of this positive principle—namely, the full humanity of women—is not fully known. What we have known is ... the denigration and marginalization of women's humanity. Still, the humanity of women ... has not been destroyed. It has constantly affirmed itself, often in only limited and subversive ways, and it has been touchstone against which we test and criticize all that diminishes us. In the process we experience our larger potential that allows us to begin to imagine a world without sexism. ... The uniqueness of feminist theology is not the critical principle, full humanity, but the fact that women claim this principle for themselves. Women name themselves [as *imago dei*, in the image of God] as subjects of authentic and full humanity."

JM: Would you explain again how you think sexism has corrupted this principle?

RRR: "[By] the naming of males as norms of authentic humanity. . . .

This distorts and contradicts the theological paradigm of *imago dei*/Christ. Defined as male humanity against or above women, as ruling-class humanity above servant classes, the *imago dei*/Christ paradigm becomes an instrument of sin rather than a disclosure of the divine and an instrument of grace."

JM: Doesn't this imply that "women cannot simply reverse the sin of sexism[;] cannot simply scapegoat males for historical evil in a way that makes themselves only innocent victims"?

RRR: "Women cannot [and must not] affirm themselves as *imago dei* and subjects of full human potential in a way that diminishes male humanity. Women, as the denigrated half of the human species, must reach for a continually expanding definition of inclusive humanity — inclusive of both genders, inclusive of all social groups and races. Any principle of religion or society that marginalizes one group of persons as less than fully human diminishes us all. In rejecting androcentrism (males as norms of humanity), women must also criticize all other forms of chauvinism: making white Westerners the norm of humanity, making Christians the norm of humanity, making privileged classes the norm of humanity. Women must also criticize humanocentrism, that is, making humans the norm and crown of creation in a way that diminishes the other beings in the community of creation."

JM: But isn't there a danger here of leveling everything into a deadening kind of sameness?

RRR: "This is not a question of sameness but of recognition of value, which at the same time affirms genuine variety and particularity. It reaches for a new mode of relationship, neither a hierarchical model that diminishes the potential of the 'other' nor an 'equality' defined by a ruling norm drawn from the dominant group; rather a mutuality that allows us to affirm different ways of being."

JM: One last question. It is about your use of the term God/ess. What do you mean by it?

RRR: "If all human language for God/ess is analogy, if taking a particular human image literally is idolatry, then male language for the divine must lose its privileged place.... Images of God/ess must include female roles and experiences. Images of God/ess must be drawn from the activities of peasants and working people, people at the bottom of society. Most of all, images of God/ess must be transformative, pointing us back to our authentic potential and forward to new redeemed possibilities.... Feminist theology needs to affirm the God of Exodus, of liberation and new being, but as rooted in ... God/ess as Matrix, as source and ground of our being [and] ... of our being-new [who] does not lead us back to a stifled, dependent self or uproot us in a spirit-trip outside the earth.... The liberating encounter with God/ess is always an encounter with our authentic selves resurrected from underneath the alienated self. It is not experienced against, but in and through relationships, healing our broken relations with our bodies, with other people, with nature. We have no adequate name for the true God/ess, the 'I am who I shall become.' Intimations of Her/His name will appear as we emerge from false naming of God/ess modeled on patriarchal alienation."

Through the use of unique, individual expressions such as we find in Spinoza, Adams, and Ruether, I have attempted to sketch some of the God and God/ess concepts available to and influencing the theologies of various Unitarian Universalists. Once again it is important to stress the range of diversity not only permitted but encouraged in our free fellowship of religious seekers and affirmers. For us, faith is forever struggling to come into existence. It is a design still fully to emerge, a rationality still to be achieved, a justice still to be established, a love still to be fulfilled.

Whatever Yields to Human Guidance

Finally, we turn our attention to still another faith stance, one that exercises great influence not only among us, but also among concerned and thoughtful people the world around. It is religious Humanism, an ethically based spiritual position that abjures theological supernaturalism and metaphysical dualism even as it resists and rejects all-out secularism.

According to Francis Bacon, we humans are empowered not only to live more creatively within the natural world but also to shape more creatively a moral world. We can accept responsibility for bettering the ethical environment, taking firmer command of our lives, finding new ways of seeing old facts and patterns, going beneath appearances to deeper levels of meaning and purpose. Bacon believed, far ahead of his time, that there is no better way to become fully human than to give birth to a conscious faith that is one's own. He was a post-Reformation herald of what we now know as religious Humanism, which may or may not be, as an English bishop has said, the religion of "fifty percent of the intelligent people of the modern world," but is, by all recent surveys, the religion of a plurality of contemporary Unitarian Universalists.

Religious Humanism has ancient foundations. A millennium before the birth of Jesus, the Aeolians, Dorians, and Ionians swept into Greece from the north, bringing their gods with them. For centuries, the wisest among them wrestled with the task of accommodating these gods to a new land and a new way of life. Their speculations became steadily more obscure. Finally, some 450 years before the Christian era, a voice spoke out in ringing protest against the unintelligible popular theology. It was Protagoras's voice: "As for the Gods, I do not know whether they exist or not. Life is too short for such difficult enquiries. . . . Humans are the measure of all things."

For his outburst of frustration, Protagoras was exiled. Seeking haven in Sicily, he was lost at sea. Inquisitors poked into the corners and closets of his homeland, ferreting every copy of his books they could find and burning it in the public square. Nevertheless, Protagoras is justly remembered as the pioneer humanist. His is still the classical definition of Humanism — an approach to faith, thought, and action that assigns an overriding interest to the human rather than to the supernatural.

In current terms, people look at the enormous religious energies expended on scanning, worshipping, supplicating, and propitiating a God who may or may not exist, and, like Protagoras, they say: "Wait a minute! I don't want any part of this. Life is too short and too endangered. Let's change the focus to what we know exists — human beings and their demonstrated capabilities for good and evil. Let's concentrate our moral passions on what we can do about that!"

Bertrand Russell said his humanist faith sprung ultimately from an admiration of two human qualities: kindly feeling and veracity. Speaking of kindly feeling, he wrote that "most of the social and political evils of the world arise through absence of sympathy and presence of hatred, envy, or fear. . . . Every kind of hostile action or feeling provokes a reaction by which it is increased and so generates a progeny of violence and injustice which has a terrible vitality. This can only be met by cultivating in ourselves and attempting to generate in the young feelings of friendliness rather than hostility, of well-wishing rather than malevolence, and of cooperation rather than competition" (*Lecture on Humanism*).

Russell said that when he is asked why he believes this, he does not appeal to any supernatural authority, but only to the common human wish for happiness: "A world full of hate is a world full of sorrow. . . . From the point of view of worldly wisdom, hostile feeling and limitation of sympathy are folly. Their fruits are war, death, oppression, and torture, not only for their original victims but, in the long run, also for their perpetrators or their descendants."

The opposite is also true, Russell said. If we could all learn to love our neighbors, the world would very rapidly become a better place for us all. This is why he regards veracity as second only to kindly feeling. The key to veracity is believing according to evidence and not because a belief is comfortable or a source of power, pride, or pleasure. Self-deception—the absence of veracity—is the classic enemy of love of truth. In Russell's words: "It is very easy for those who have exceptional power to persuade themselves that the system by which they profit gives more happiness to underdogs than they would enjoy under a more just system. And, even where no obvious bias is involved, it is only by means of veracity that we can acquire the scientific knowledge required to bring about our common purposes."

Russell asks that we reflect on how many cherished prejudices had to be abandoned in the development of modern medicine and hygiene, and how many wars would have been prevented by a just estimate of the prospects rather than one based on conceit and wishful thinking. He proposes that we apply these considerations especially to religious beliefs. Unproven and unprovable "revelations" are not really needed to help us see that human welfare requires a less ferocious ethic. More and more people are unable to accept traditional beliefs anyway. To think that apart from these beliefs there is no foundation for kindly behavior is to invite disaster. That is why, Russell concludes, "it is important to show that no supernatural reasons are needed to make humans kind and to prove that only through kindness can the human race achieve happiness."

As we turn to a crisp summary of Humanism's major affirmations, let me first distinguish the movement in religious thought from the school in general culture that also calls itself humanism, and whose most celebrated advocates of the recent past include Irving Babbitt and Paul Elmer More. The link between the two is that both are fundamentally concerned with the human condition, and especially with the distinctive values that humans are capable of realizing. Beyond this link, however, there are marked differences, greatest perhaps in religious matters. Babbitt had little sympathy for religious interests. More, on the other hand, championed Anglo-Catholicism, a position far from religious Humanism.

The primary professions of religious Humanism are these:

Concerning the human moral situation. Any honest reading of history reveals that moral values are relative to changing human experience. The shareable social values, however, maintain and enhance their excellence in the face of all doubt and criticism.

Humans need not only the satisfaction of particular wants but also the attainment of integrated personalities. This result is best achieved by earnest devotion to the shareable social goods. Such devotion is the essence of religion.

Concerning metaphysics. Scientific method is the most dependable guide to truth about the world. The universe is an objective order, which takes no account of human good or evil except so far as humans control parts of it toward their own ends.

There are no guarantees of good's ultimate victory, nor of the eternal preservation of human values. Intelligent devotion to the highest values does not require such guarantees. The ultimate faith in religion is faith in the worthwhileness of human good.

Concerning social ethics. The most important values that maintain their excellence in the face of all doubt and criticism are scientific truth (veracity), moral and artistic creativity, and love (kindness and justice). The joy of comradeship (community) in the quest for these values is a more than adequate compensation for faith in a supernatural helper, savior, or judge.

All social institutions, including the church, must be progressively but determinedly transformed toward expressing and giving full scope to these values.

In 1945, at the time of my ordination, there was considerable fusillading within Unitarian and Universalist ranks between our liberal Christian theists and our humanists. In both groups there were firebrands who viewed one another as deadening or dangerous to the task of revitalizing liberal religion. In retrospect, the controversy, though awkward, cleared the air. One of those most helpful in a resynthesizing process was the late Dr. Charles E. Park, for many years the eloquent and scholarly minister of Boston's First Church. Park's credentials as a Christian Unitarian were impeccable, so he was listened to when in a sermon he described the prophetic role of Humanism as

a protest against unprofitable speculation concerning matters which, by their very nature, lie beyond the reach of human comprehension;

and an appeal to philosophy to give the first freshness of its vigor to problems that fall within its scope. It appears periodically in the history of thought, to keep philosophy within its proper bounds. When scribes, rabbis, and Pharisees in Palestine could find nothing better to do than to get themselves all snarled up in useless conjectures as to the meaning and scope of their precious Law, Jesus appeared teaching the importance of considering the dignity of human nature, the potential capabilities of the human spirit

Did Park mean that Jesus was a humanist? Certainly not in the word's strict sense. What Park meant is that Jesus fulfilled the *spirit* of Humanism. "We may call Jesus an unconscious Humanist," said Park, "for if you take away the humanistic element in his teachings there is little left." With equal fairness, we could say the same of Spinoza, Adams, and Ruether. Contrary to Alexander Pope's advice, they "presume to scan God" in depth. And they fulfill the spirit of Humanism. Humanity is the measure of their moral passion.

I make this point to dispel a confusion that arises from trying to build walls around Humanism or theism to separate them sharply and distinctly from one another, as if religious liberals can be faithful to the ideals of Humanism only by banishing God from their vocabulary and vice versa. This can happen only when we forget that we are supposed to be a community of open-minded seekers, all of us blessed with independence of mind and spirit, free to arrive at honest convictions without prejudice to our good standing, and deserving respect for the integrity of our motives. These are our distinguishing characteristics, and not whether we choose to call ourselves theists, humanists, or something else.

It may be that I cherish my Unitarian Universalist affiliation most of all because every congregation I have served harbors a mixture of theists and humanists, Christians and non-Christians. They are, in my opinion, exceedingly good for one another. The theist, whether of the Spinoza, Adams, or Ruether type, exemplifies a persistence in the search for God which is by no means lacking in fruitful results. As Park put it: "Gleams and flashes of insight do come from the surrounding darkness, and help to lighten our way through life's maze." The humanist, meanwhile, keeps reminding that the more insistently we turn toward whatever yields to human guidance, the sooner and better we shall know the immense capacities for good of the human spirit.

Here I Stand

It would be ungracious to conclude this chapter without giving my personal faith stance. I will do it briefly because there have been ample intimations of it in the preceding pages.

In 1947, prior to becoming minister of the Unitarian congregation of Rockford, Illinois, I met with their ministerial search committee. Seated beside me was Cousie Fox, a lifelong church member. Hers was the first question. "Are you a humanist or a theist?" My answer was immediate and honest. "Both!" So it was then, and so it remains.

I affirm heart and soul all of Humanism's major premises of faith, just as I listed them. In profoundly humanistic terms, I strive to practice and live my religion as the natural functioning of my personhood in pursuit of a full, free, and socially useful life. I believe that we humans are neither saints nor irredeemable sinners. I believe that we can get somewhere better than where we've gotten so far, that we can improve, that we have within ourselves all the capacities for solving the problems we can reasonably expect to solve. I believe that faith's most critical role is to inspire and strengthen attitudes that will bring humans to the fullest possible consciousness of their freedom, their reason, their aesthetic depths, and their moral capabilities. The joy of comradeship and community in this quest is more than adequate compensation for my nonexistent faith in a supernatural helper, savior, or judge.

I am not willing, however, to abandon imaginary interactions between myself and an ultimate something else in nature which is called God or, now, God/ess. I would not insist that the name *must* be given and indeed, I use it sparingly. There is in me a deep distaste for the slovenly, exploitative ways in which it is merchandised by pulpiteers and politicians. Also, I am concerned that associations of the term with the supernatural are so widespread that any use of it is certain to give rise to misconceptions and be taken as a concession to traditional ideas.

I am a devout believer in applying the experimental method to theology, as well as to physics, chemistry, and musical composition. Down the centuries, questions about the existence and nature of God have been answered with abstractions dictated by cramped theories of knowledge. Immobilized by a long-standing dualism of the mind and its object, thought could conceive of God only as an object separate from humans. Thus, God must be either a figment of the human mind or an Other beyond the reach of human understanding, except through revelation. If God is inaccessible to the human mind, the religiously inclined have only two logical paths open to them. They may become thoroughgoing humanists, content with a conclusion that God is, at present, unknown or unknowable. Or, confessing the inability of philosophy to verify God's existence, they may seek a direct experience of God in the self, in nature, or in a revelation that is of a different order than human reason and knowledge. This was Kant's response to philosophical frustration, and it has been the basis of many theologies since.

The experimental approach to the inquiry centers on actual, observable human experience and asks what this tells us about the nature of God. It is impossible to do this without exploring the history of religions. From such an exploration it becomes clear that the lesser and greater gods of all religions have been the life process itself, idealized and personified. All gods are clothed in the habits and moral codes of their worshippers and invariably reflect the changes that influence the customs, outlooks, and goals of their people. When the followers are warlike, the god is warlike; when the followers are peace loving, the god is peace loving; when the people live under a king, the god is a monarch; when the believers (as among the Enlightenment worthies) espouse and promote democratic ideals, their god underwrites freedom, reason, and justice. Thus God, at all times and in all places is the spirit of a people as they experience and interpret their existence. To the extent that the world of humanity is embraced, God is the spirit of humanity. Insofar as the universe is consciously conceived as a unity, God is the spirit of the universe.

The prophets of ancient Israel foretold that as humanity's splintered segments achieve a greater sense of commonality, God emerges as truly the Lord of all, with universal commandments of righteousness, justice, mercy, and love. Indeed, as commerce, art, science, and moral interchange level the barriers of human isolation, this is increasingly so. Even so, nationalism, sectarianism, racism, and ethnicity stubbornly and aggressively prevail. At root, God is still conceived of as the soul of particular communal values, particular social traditions, particular loves and hates.

The advantage of such an overview—to say nothing of its existential truth—is that philosophical frustrations about God's "existence" are no longer involved. If the world is a reality, then so is the God who is the living experience, in one form or another, of all people in the world. Whatever reality there is in the lives of individuals, clans, nations, or humanity is imparted in kind and degree to God, and with the flourishing of feminist theology, to God/ess. I readily grant that the total reality of God is greater than any individual's or group's experience of it to date, which is what is so challenging to me about the continuing quest.

Now positively: God, to me, is the Spirit of a spiritual universe in which I share with all life an interdependent destiny. God is that ultimate reality that interacts with all my doings and strivings, both instinctive and intelligent and, in the end, quite literally determines to what degree they are responsible for conserving, transmitting, rectifying, and expanding those values, which alone can redeem and preserve the human community. God enfolds and permeates the so-called material world in which the conditions and actions of living occur. Thus, God is both transcendent as creativity and immanent as the creative event. God, in brief, is the glorious sum of the living process, in which I, as a person, and we, as a human community, live, strive, and die. God is the existence I share with all that is or is to be. God is Being lifted to the utmost limits of my spiritual insight and exertion. God is as genuine as my own nature and as boundless as my most imaginative hopes for spiritual enlightenment. With every deepening of my insight, every strengthening of my moral will, every expansion of my understanding of truth, every experience of beloved community, God is better known to me, more reverently loved, more personally and profoundly experienced.

What the Unitarian Universalist fellowship offers me is the encouragement to be utterly my most responsible self in matters of theological belief. When I use the word *God* or *God/ess,* it is with the full understanding that I speak from personal conviction and experience, and not from any desire to impose my "revelation" on others. By the same token, I not only speak as conscience dictates, but I also listen to what others are saying with an eagerness that comes from wanting to catch the gleams and flashes of their intimations of spirit. Thus does my experience of God increase.

8

With Their Own Eyes

Some beliefs are like walled gardens. They encourage exclusiveness, and the feeling of being especially privileged. Other beliefs are expansive and lead the way into wider and deeper sympathies.
Sophia Lyon Fahs, *Today's Children and Yesterday's Heritage*

Of all the good reasons I can list for being a Unitarian Universalist, none is more personally exciting to me than our work with children and youth. Over the years, it has seemed to me that new and better ways of religious learning and growth are coming into being. The reason is plain: the individual child, rather than a Bible or catechism, is at the center of our concern, which means that we are forever challenged to examine and improve what we are doing. Are our efforts "expansive" enough? Do they "lead the way into wider and deeper sympathies?" The director for religious education of the Unitarian Universalist Association, citing the radical Catholic educator Thomas Groome as his inspiration, describes this as "a process of reflection upon action, a process which invites one to name one's own knowing, invites deep exploration of how one came to that knowing, provides challenge with visions and stories of one's own faith tradition, adds the best insights of one's own day, moves from that vision to the reality of one's own life, invites a dialectic among the ideas and a dialog within the church community, and leads one to answer the question, 'What will I do now?' It leads always to action and again to reflection (Berry Street lecture, by Eugene Navias, 1983)."

The Bible is a significant part of our curriculum, but only as it contributes to the broader goals of religious learning and growth for the children entrusted to our care, *and* for the adults to whom that care is entrusted. Let me explain.

Some time ago, a stranger telephoned me and, without preliminaries,

113

asked: "Is the Bible God's own word, or just a bunch of fairy tales?" Feeling that a minister's task is kindliness even toward the belligerent, I answered in my most considerate manner that I believed the Bible to be neither God's own word nor a bunch of fairy tales. I could not tell at that point whether my caller was a divine-inspiration or fairy-tale partisan. "It's got to be one or the other!" he said, providing the semanticist in me with another classic example of the excluded middle. "If it isn't God's word, then it's just a bunch of fairy tales." As it turned out, this particular examiner of my theology was a divine revelationist, bent on giving me yet another chance to mend my ways and save my soul. But he might well have been a zealot of the other school.

In working with the religious learning and growth of children, we recognize first of all that the Bible is no simple either/or matter. We live in a complicated climate of opinion about the Bible. At one extreme are those who despise the Bible for its violence, superstition, and chauvinism. For them, it is an emotionally loaded symbol, just as it is for "true Biblical believers." Only they would just like to get rid of it. To those who feel this way, I can only say that, like it or not, the Bible is a major source of our ideas, habits, and attitudes. From it have come many of our laws, social institutions, morals, and folkways—good and bad. It is a factor in our lives to be dealt with sensibly, feelingly, and intelligently. To reject it out of hand is to betray an emotional ignorance of the enormous spectrum of human experience the Bible contains.

At the opposite pole are those to whom the Bible is the Word, with a capital W, of God, with a capital G—verbally inspired by God the Father, dictated by God the Holy Ghost, and revealing through God the Son, without jot or tittle of error, the divine scheme of eternal salvation. This view is filled with arrogance. Those who refuse to accept it are immediately labeled as reeking with sin. Its purveyors speak to the needs of untold millions of biblical certainty seekers. A Moral Majority leader in the Midwest encourages his followers to conduct search-and-destroy missions for books in their local libraries that are anti-Bible. "If they . . . feel like burning them, fine," he says. A pastor in Michigan uses a home-made "electric stool" and a twelve-volt battery to shock his young Bible students into "hearing God's word."

From time to time I deliberately practice the hair shirt spiritual discipline of forcing myself to watch some of the celebrated television evangelists preach their biblical fundamentalism and right-wing politics. Via the electronic church, backed by state-of-the-art computerized mailings, they have made a quantum leap, both in reaching mass markets and raising funds. According to my own count, the total audience to which Jesus preached did not exceed twenty thousand persons. Today's electronic preachers speak regularly to millions. One of them, Dr. Oral Roberts, Bible in hand, recently reported to viewers that Jesus had appeared to him in a vision; the vision was "about nine hundred feet tall"; Jesus lifted the unfinished Tulsa hospital Roberts is building high in the air and simultaneously promised that funds would be forthcoming to complete the structure. After sharing his vision with his followers, by direct mail as well as by television, Roberts received almost $5 million in donations, which works out to approximately $5,555 per foot for a nine-hundred-foot Jesus.

Some of this money comes from corporate and individual angels, but more impressive are the amounts that come from tens of thousands of persons and families of modest means and with a deep need to have the supernatural qualities of Holy Writ affirmed. A Methodist minister I knew used to call this a "wooden-headed way of handling the Bible" that was "responsible for a bibically illiterate generation." So, this is a concern that many nonfundamentalist Christians and Jews share with Unitarian Universalists, yet how tardy and hesitant is the carrying over of this concern into the religious education of children. For the most part, churches and synagogues continue in the old way, identifying religious education with the teaching of the Scriptures just as though we still believed them to be an infallible revelation, continue to indoctrinate young minds with certain beliefs regarded as necessary to salvation and to surround those beliefs with an emotional pattern of fear and hope whose purpose is to keep children bound to those dogmas when they are grown. However well intentioned this may be, it remains, in my view, a tragic mistake. It serves neither the best interests of the children, nor the best interests of the adult community of which these children are destined to become members.

What has happened to bring about the changed attitude toward the Bible described by my Methodist minister friend? What has happened to deepen the concern of Unitarian Universalist families about *how* the Bible is used in the religious education of children? The basic answers, of course, are the fruits of biblical scholarship and a revolutionized view of what constitutes religious "learning" for a child. For a century and a half, scholars have devoted their lives to intensive critical studies of the Bible, steadily discovering more about its origins, texts, and contexts. How many laypersons know the meaning of the word *Bible*? It is an English rendering of a Greek word describing the inner bark of a reed which was once used as paper. The plural of this word, *ta biblia*, was used by early Greek-speaking Christians to characterize their most revered writings and simply meant "the books." Later, Latin translators mistakenly used the singular in place of the plural and thus launched the erroneous impression that the Bible is a single, unified book.

In medieval times, scribes attempted to correct the error by using another word, *bibliotheca*, which means "library." They were justified in this, because the Bible is a collection of books, a library, which does not express a single theme but encompasses a diversity of subject matters. For example, the gloomy, sophisticated, skeptical viewpoint of the author of Ecclesiastes clashes sharply with the cosmic optimism of Isaiah. They write of two different world views and two different sets of spiritual experiences. Existence is morally meaningless to one, full of moral meaning to the other. Yet, there they are in the same Bible, both canonized. The explanation is that the books of the Bible were written over a millennium by authors of widely divergent outlooks and purposes. It is not at all unnatural that the Book of Judges varies profoundly from the Book of James in moral stance and tone.

Another simple historical fact, known by surprisingly few, is that the earliest Christians had no scriptures of their own. There was, as yet, no "New" Testament; consequently there was no "Old" Testament either. The first Christian Bible was the Jewish Bible, the Torah, which was Jesus's Bible as well. First- and second- generation Christians lived in eager anticipation of the return of Jesus the Christ, the Anointed One, the Messiah. Since the Savior was soon to mount his throne as ruler of earth, there was little reason to add to the existing holy books of the Jews. It was enough to tell and retell the wonder stories of Jesus by word of mouth. When congregations gathered for religious services, there would be recitations from the Jewish Scriptures, with additional renderings of Paul's letters and those of other apostles.

A fair summary of what scholarship tells us about Jewish Scripture is that we are dealing with a wonderfully diversified product of nearly a thousand years of a people's religious and cultural development. What emerges from a painstaking sifting of Genesis, Exodus, Leviticus, Numbers, and Deuteronomy is a patchwork accomplished by editors who combined primitive folklore and myth with legendary accounts of how the Hebrew tribes came into existence and developed into a nation. There are ancient legal codes and manuals of hygiene, early battle songs and poems, of which the Song of Deborah may well be the oldest recorded material in the Bible. All of this is woven by succeeding generations of editors into an epic story.

The original authors of the myths, legends, traditions, and histories are unknown. The later editors are unknown. We do know, however, that the cutting and pasting process went on for several hundred years. We also know that during this period the Hebrews emerged from primitive forms of religion, such as magic arks and animal sacrifices, to much more elevated forms, and that this advancement can be plainly traced through the Jewish Scriptures. Some eight hundred years before Jesus, there arose among the Hebrews those remarkable reformers known as the prophets. In all, these Scriptures contain a dozen brief prophetic books, the long Isaiah (which is actually several books) and the two major works attributed to Jeremiah. By this time the Hebrew religion had evolved into monotheism and produced an inspired ethical universalism, of which the prophets were the formulators and articulators.

The collection of Hebrew holy books, this fantastic library of the Jewish experience, was translated into Greek for the use of dispersed Greek-speaking Jewish communities scattered over the Mediterranean region. It was taken up by the early Christian congregations and adopted as their own. In this manner it was subjected to the re-interpretations that made it over into a familiar segment of the Christian salvation story.

As the years rolled on and the certainty of Christ's imminent return faded, there arose, understandably, a need for Scriptures that were distinctly Christian. The churches were fractured by internal conflicts and disputes, even as they were oppressed by persecution. The authority and inspiration of Scriptures of "the new dispensation" were required. Appeals were made to the letters of Paul and others. Reverence for the remembered teachings and wonder works of Jesus was transformed into a demand for permanent, authoritative accounts. Unhappily for us, the earliest texts of these memoirs are lost. They did, however, form the basis of what we have: the Gospels of what Christians insisted was the *New* Testament, automatically relegating the Hebrew Scriptures to the status of Old.

Still, we remain much in the dark, for the original manuscripts of the Gospels have never been found. We possess only relatively late translations and copies of material that was first written down long after Jesus. There are formidable problems of textual and historical interpretation.

What we do know is that three of the Gospels (Matthew, Mark, and Luke) are based on two primary sources: a collection of the sayings of Jesus, which Matthew and Luke treat in different ways, and an earlier form of Mark's Gospel. The Gospel of John is regarded by most scholars as historically less accurate. It was composed much later than the other three and is less factual. It is impossible to reconcile the Gospel of John with its counterparts.

Reverence for the collection of works now known as the New Testament steadily increased. But there were also tensions. Some church leaders were suspicious of books that might outstrip their personal authority, but at the same time, the bishops, as they had come to be called, recognized the need for written works to consolidate their power, as well as to inform the faithful. The dilemma was solved by claiming that the added volumes were really a part of the Sacred Scriptures—a *New* Testament as distinguished from the Old—and that only the properly designated authorities of the Church could interpret it.

Even with so brief and sketchy an introduction as this, the question of whether the Bible is a book dictated by God becomes facetious. The Bible is replete with inaccuracies, inconsistencies, and errors, which should surprise no one in so great a compendium, compiled over a millennium from numberless sources, authors, editors, and copyists. The Bible is a saga not of one religion but of many, some of which exist side by side. I recently led a workshop called "The Nine Religions of the Bible" for my Bedford, Massachusetts, congregation. It turned out to be an exciting and informative way of starting with Genesis and ending with Revelation, and making some sense of an evolutionary whole.

Basically it is a bit unfair to attribute this aggregate to God. The Bible was inspired bit by bit and part by part by the experiences of people over centuries. An obvious extension of this is that scripture is still being written and will continue to be written as long as there are men and women who are spiritually sensitive to what is happening to them and their world. It is much better to accept the Judeo-Christian Bible for its uniqueness as a library of ancient human experience and to know and love it for this, than to surround it with a supernatural aura. The inspiration of the real Bible is wisdom distilled from struggle and insight gained from the hard evolution of human life. The Bible makes just claims upon us, not in terms of divine authorship, but on the basis of the everlasting quest for the redeemed life and the assurance that humans, in their search for deeper meanings and larger purposes, must progress from lesser to greater truths.

We Unitarian Universalists include the Bible in our learning and growth programs for children, youth, and adults; but we take special care with children. There are many good stories, words of wisdom, and inspiring thoughts in the Bible. Knowing more about them from a historical perspective helps our children to express and defend their own developing beliefs. Ours is a culture deeply, if often confusingly, permeated by the Judeo-Christian tradition. Anyone who does not know anything about David or Ruth or Jesus or Mary and Martha is culturally illiterate. That's not playing fair with our young. They deserve, at the very least, to have their curiosity stimulated about the legends, myths, stories, teachings, and symbols that pervade our culture.

The care we exercise is to encourage our children to approach the Bible with unawed candor, on the assumption that it was written by human beings like ourselves. The care we exercise with ourselves as parents and other adult mentors is twofold: first, we are genuine about overcoming our own biblical illiteracy; second, we respect the ability of children to grasp only what they have the capacity to understand and absorb, and this is limited by age level and development. We do not try to infiltrate the religious consciousness of a second-grader with all of the profound issues of the Book of Job, yet a second-grader can wrestle with the fundamental fact that bad things do happen to good people, and vice versa.

Unitarian Universalist parents sometimes look longingly at the supposed biblical literacy drilled into the heads of children in traditional Sunday schools. But the results can be startling. One study I am familiar with was of a group of fifty college sophomores, selected on the basis of demonstrated scholastic aptitude and achievement. The students had experienced Bible training as children in either orthodox Protestant or Catholic churches. They were then given a five-week refresher course followed by an examination, which demonstrated that only eight or nine had anything resembling a solid knowledge of the Bible. The rest were swamped in confusion. They had no real conception of the differences between the Hebrew and Christian Scriptures. Many thought that Jesus appears in both. Some thought Jesus gave the Ten Commandments to Moses. A few thought he was Job's companion. The prevailing sentiment was that everything in the Bible happened at about the same time and in the same place. Most thought of the Bible as teaching a single, clear ethical code throughout. The majority, in spite of massive confusion about its contents, insisted that the Bible was to be accepted as a whole. There were no marked differences between Protestant and Roman Catholic students.

The only possible conclusion from this particular study, and it is borne out by others, is that the undiscriminating goal of simply "teaching the Bible" can do more harm than good. Given the approach widely used, it cannot be otherwise. In Unitarian Universalist programs of religious learning and growth, biblical materials are delicately and discriminatingly used with children, not because we want to deprive them of biblical knowledge and inspiration, but because we want them to have a chance, gradually and developmentally, to know the Bible as it is. We believe this can happen only incrementally, with the best results emerging at the upper age levels, and only if parents and families join wholeheartedly in the process with ministers, directors of religious education, and church school teachers.

I have the benefit of a good deal of continuing education in the literature of the Bible. My own earlier jumble of misinformation has long since been unscrambled, so it is no longer easy for me to re-experience that jumble in the midst of my exposure to a conventional Sunday school. But by the gift of imagination, I can lay out a likely scenario. Once upon a time, a white-bearded giant named God, who lived in the sky but sometimes visited the earth, told a king to kill everybody except his own relatives (the story of Samuel, Saul and the Amalekites), and at about the same time God was telling a man named Noah to build a great ship in which to save his family and two of each kind of animal (because God was going to drown everyone else) and that there was a man named Jesus living in the same place who taught that God loved everybody but was still going to burn all the bad people. (It is worth noting that children are aware of the fact that they are often "bad.")

My heart goes out to youngsters who are "learning" that the good Jesus and the savage David were both faithful servants of God, and that tricky Jacob was a favorite of God and was rewarded, while the good Jesus was allowed to die on a cross; and that God slew all the first-born children of Egypt because the Egyptian ruler was quarreling with Moses.

Exaggerated as I make it sound, this is precisely the kind of problem we face when it comes to teaching the Bible indiscriminately to children. Think of all the little ones who have been taught this way and have never gotten over it.

We are not likely to repeat this error in Unitarian Universalist religious education, because we are concerned first with the child's spiritual development and not with a hasty administration of biblical salvation. We want our children to know and appreciate the Bible for what it is, and we are determined that, to the best of our ability, they will have access to the kind of knowing and understanding they can later trust and respect.

Here is how we might undertake this task in any one of our church schools, with the expectation, of course, of cooperation at home. To five- and six-year-olds we introduce for discussion some of the simplest Bible stories, such as the Passover and Christmas legends, and some of the most familiar teachings, such as the Golden Rule. With seven- and eight-year-olds we begin to make use of educationally sound Bible storybooks such as the story of Joseph with its dramatic human interest as a family-centered tale of jealousy, achievement, and forgiveness. We encourage the children to act out the religious legends and myths of many different peoples in addition to those of the Bible.

Nine- and ten-year-olds may become acquainted with the creation stories of Genesis (there are two, not, as popularly believed, one) and have an opportunity to compare them with other creation stories and with scientific theories of the universe.

At the age of eleven and twelve, youngsters are ready for their first serious probes of the life and teachings of Jesus. As teenagers, they can begin to fill in backgrounds for Jesus in the historical drama of ancient Israel and become familiar with the great prophets and their ethical concerns. High school students are encouraged to come of age with deeper first-hand explorations of their own Unitarian Universalist heritage and the roles in that of Judaism, Jesus, the beginnings of Christianity, and the practices of various Christian groups.

Throughout this process, our young participate in services of celebration and worship, often intergenerational. Particularly at high holiday times — Rosh Hashanah, Christmas, Easter — these services embrace biblical stories, rituals, symbols, and songs.

Please understand that I have been writing only of the dimension of our approach to children's religious learning and growth that deals specifically with the Bible. I have done so at some length to clarify, as well, prevalent adult Unitarian Universalist perceptions and understandings of the Bible. There is far, far more than the Bible in our religious education efforts as a whole. Our fundamental concern in religious learning and growth for children is that they have a foundation of understanding, awakened interest, and enriched experience to appreciate not only the Bible, as they become really capable of comprehending it, but also many other founts of spiritual inspiration as well.

The Great End in Religious Instruction

I honor the sincerity of those traditional Christian communions whose approach to religious education rests on human nature's alienation from God, with reunion possible only by learning and internalizing a doctrinal plan of salvation. Children, according to this view, must be taught the saving revelation, which alone can rescue them from inherited original sin.

Religious education in Unitarian Universalist circles is founded on the conviction that human nature, rather than alienating us from God, binds us to the universe and to all that sustains it. The human nature of children is neither inherently wicked nor inherently good. It is potentially both. Within the natural needs, urges, impulses, drives, and curiosity of children is the very stuff of which a religious education should be fashioned. We are respectful of the degree to which "genes are destiny." We are enthusiastic about the degree to which children, as a crucial portion of their genetic destiny, are natural and creative learners — unless and until their natural and creative bent is stifled and destroyed.

What we strive to offer children is loving, informed nurture for achieving a religion, a spirituality that is truly their own and is shareable. If our young are to have a religion of their own, we of the liberal religious community must do everything in our power to teach by example, as well as by precept. We must demonstrate that all of us are about the business of discovering religion for ourselves.

"Thou shalt love thy neighbor as thyself." This is the kind of injunction children have been memorizing in Sunday schools for generations. But if the premise is that the child is lost until saved by grace, conversion, and creedal belief, what possible meaning can the injunction have? It is a simple reality that you cannot love your neighbor effectively if you feel contempt for self, if you cannot, dare not, and have not the freedom to trust and respect yourself. Unless girls and boys are able to believe that they are worth loving, there is no logic in expecting them to love their neighbors. To help our children to build an awareness of their own worth, and thus to create a genuine foundation for respecting the worth of others, is one of our supreme aims in religious education—from the cradle on.

In Herb Gardner's play *A Thousand Clowns* the central character, Murray, tells what he wants for a young nephew who has been left in his care: "I want him to be sure he'll know when he's chickening out on himself. I want him to get to know exactly the special thing he is or else he won't notice when it starts to go. I want him to stay awake and know who the phonies are. I want him to know how to holler and put up an argument. I want a little guts to show before I can let him go. I want to be sure he sees all the wild possibilities. . . . And I want him to know the subtle, sneaky, important reason why he was born a human being and not a chair."

Murray's passionate words go to the heart of what religious education means to us, with this significant addition: one of the most important reasons for being born a human being and not a chair is to learn the wonders of community—of practicing mutuality, interdependence, and involvement. Otherwise Murray is right on target, expressing what I want for my children and yours, for my grandchildren and yours. It is what I want for every child in the congregation I serve, for every child in the world. It is what I want for myself, and for you.

A key clue to what Unitarian Universalist religious education is up to is that a child's religion grows out of natural, not supernatural, experience. Religion is not something "revealed" to a child, or thrust upon a child; it is something to be nurtured and encouraged in a child's unfolding life. We believe that spirituality will grow naturally out of a child's everyday living and maturing, which is why we emphasize the enrichment of experiences in the here and now rather than confining ourselves to rehearsals of the deeds of Jesus and other biblical worthies. We believe that young people are ready for direct, immediate experiences of birth, growth, death, nature, love, hate, joy, and suffering—the fierce yet wondrous ambiguities of life.

Out of such experiences come the beginnings of religion. We believe that a primary order of business of the teaching and learning congregation is to help children to articulate such experiences in their own words and ways, *before* their minds have been frozen by adult explanations. Instead of being taught to memorize traditional prayers and litanies for the sole reason of repeating them parrotlike, our children are encouraged to recognize and respect the Lord's Prayer, for example, and the Twenty-third Psalm. But more important, they are encouraged to speak of their awes, enthusiasms, fears, and questionings in their own unconstrained way. Heartening youngsters to search the mysteries of their here-and-now experiences is to us the soundest beginning of a religion that will deepen and mature. All along the way, as they become ready for it, their searchings can be profitably and excitingly compared to those of an Isaiah, a Jesus, a Sojourner Truth, or a Gandhi.

A century and a half ago, William Ellery Channing did a remarkable job of formulating the aims of methods of liberal religious education as it applies to the young at home and at church. His insight continues to serve as a reality check whenever we slip into purely secular means of achieving religious goals. Channing wrote:

> The great end in religious instruction, whether in the Sunday School or family, is, not to stamp our minds irresistibly on the young, but to stir up their own; not to make them see with our eyes, but to look inquiringly and steadily with their own; not to give them a definite amount of knowledge, but to inspire a fervent love of truth; not to form an outward regularity, but to quicken and strengthen the power of thought; not to bind them by ineradicable prejudices to our particular sect or peculiar notions, but to prepare them for impartial, conscientious judging of whatever subjects may, in the course of Providence, be offered to their decision; not to impose religion upon them in the form of arbitrary rules which rest on no foundation but our own word and will, but to awaken the consciousness, the moral discernment, so that they may discern and approve for themselves what is everlastingly right and good. (*The Sunday School Discourse*)

One can readily see why this statement still stands both as a reminder of our inevitable shortcomings and as the ideal for which we strive.

Our children are not, cannot, and should not be quarantined from traditional and orthodox religious beliefs. They are bound to bump into them head-on among their playmates, to say nothing of relatives, baby-sitters, and born-again Christian teachers. This is an inevitable complication in guiding a child's religious development along liberal lines, but it is also an opportunity.

My colleague, Tony Larsen, who left a Roman Catholic order to take up studies for the Unitarian Universalist ministry, has a unique perspective:

Believe me, most UU children I know would *not* have been a match for me when I was a kid. When I was young I went around the neighborhood spreading the fear of hell and the wrath of God; and was I good at it. Sometimes I'd walk around in my little priest outfit and sprinkle holy water here and there. And sometimes I'd invite the other kids to come to the church my dad built for me in the back-yard, and I'd tell them all about the Catholic religion. If the kids were Catholic but not going to church, I'd remind them of the hell-fire awaiting them if they should die. And if the kids were Protestant, I'd tell them that being Protestant didn't *automatically* keep them out of heaven, but it sure made it difficult to get there. I mean, I was the kind of kid that most Unitarian Universalist parents try to protect their children from.

The point Larsen makes is this: Yes, we want our children to make their own religious choices, to develop naturally a religious faith anchored in their own experience. No, we don't want to push beliefs on them, or shove our religion down their throats. Yes, we want our children to grow up spiritually free. "That's nice," he says, "and I agree. But that doesn't mean that you can't give a plug for your religion. . . you can at least *share* your beliefs with them." Larsen sadly concludes, with considerable intergenerational experience, that many Unitarian Universalist young people "do *not* know what their parents believe about God, and afterlife and Christianity. And most parents don't know what their *kids* believe. . . . Is it too much heresy to suggest that you sit down together and talk about your beliefs? That's not shoving your religion down their throats. Sharing is a little different from shoving."

Larsen's plea touches a sensitive nerve, and deserves to. Our philosophy of religious education represents a revolutionary departure from traditional Sunday school techniques.

We do not teach a finished gospel. But that doesn't mean we are bereft of convictions and devotions that give direction to our lives and are shareable with our young. I have filled these pages with convictions and devotions we have in common.

We do everything possible to avoid an atmosphere in which children might feel that their natural curiosity is being repressed. But isn't it a natural part of their curiosity to want to know why our church commitment is powerfully attractive to us, and why we might reasonably hope that they will choose to remain Unitarian Universalists when they grow up, though we'll go right on loving them whether they do or not?

We never suggest that truth, beauty, and goodness are to be cherished simply because they are honored in our church and our religion. But they *are* honored in our church, which is going to need people like them to keep up the honoring. There's no reason our young shouldn't be helped to know how to put up an argument when they are challenged on the street, or in the classroom, or at the beach, about being headed for hell because of their beliefs and their church affiliation. In Tony Larsen's words: "If *you* don't prepare your kids in religion, there may be a little Tony Larsen in your neighborhood who *will*."

We are enjoying a dynamic time of rebirth in Unitarian Universalist religious education: more children and youth, more families, more trained ministers and directors, new curriculum and teaching guides. And there is a new emphasis as well, one that says the entire program of a liberal church should be considered an adventure in religious learning and growth. Perhaps this is best described as a holistic approach. It gives equal emphasis to children and adults. It gives equal emphasis to worship, fellowship, social action, and education. The old model of religious education as a "school" for children, while the adults worship, is giving way to one in which religious learning and growth take place in the context of the religious community as a whole. We are increasingly convinced that our religious communities are strengthened by the creative interchange of people of all ages who share deeply with one another and, to the greatest extent possible, do their religious growing and learning in one another's presence. Eugene Navias, in his 1983 Berry Street lecture, expresses it this way: "I would hold that for each of us to be fully human is to be using our endowment for growth throughout our lifespan, that to be fully human is to be developing our complementary human capacities of the spirit, soul, reason, passion, imagination and intuition in ways which lead to our greatest liberation and most just action. To be fully human is to get our powers together to become most integrated, whole, and in that sense, 'religious.'"

Parents who think they can put their children in Sunday school for one or two hours a week to "get" religious education will not be comfortable in one of our churches. Our outreach is to those who wish to enter *with* their children (if they have them, if not, with the children of others) upon an adventure in lifelong religious learning and growth. Should this strike a responsive chord, make contact with your nearest Unitarian Universalist congregation. Or, if you're not yet ready for that, write to: Religious Education Section, Unitarian Universalist Association, 25 Beacon Street, Boston, MA 02108.

In all of this we have tried not to overlook individuals and families who live at too great a distance from a Unitarian Universalist church or who are homebound. For them there is our Church of the Larger Fellowship, with headquarters, a minister, and a religious education director at 25 Beacon Street, Boston MA 02108, which sends religious education materials, books, sermons, and a regular newsletter to all who affiliate with this imaginative outreach to the isolated.

If Channing set the course for Unitarian Universalist religious education with his memorable 1837 address to the Sunday School Society, Sophia Lyon Fahs did more than any other individual in this century to steer us toward the tangible fulfillment of his hopes. She died a few years ago after a long, productive life of bringing into being the resources, curricular and human, for contemporary liberal religious education. The enduring quality of her inspiration is best exemplified in her own words: "Some beliefs are like blinders, shutting off the power to choose one's own direction. Other beliefs are like gateways opening wide vistas for exploration. Some beliefs weaken a person's selfhood. They blight the growth of resourcefulness. Other beliefs nurture self-confidence and enrich the feeling of personal worth. Some beliefs are rigid, like the body of death, impotent in a changing world. Other beliefs are pliable, like the young sapling, ever growing with the upward thrust of life" (*Today's Children and Yesterday's Heritage*).

9

Taking the Time to Care

We are learning that a standard of social ethics is not attained by traveling a sequestered byway, but by mixing on the thronged and common road where all must turn out for one another, and at least see the size of one another's burdens.

Jane Addams, *Democracy and Social Ethics*

"Why are you doing this?" The year was 1947 and my questioner was dean of the faculty of the medical school in Vienna. World War II was over, but its gruesome reminders were everywhere. We were sitting in a three-hundred-year-old room of Vienna's bullet-riddled central hospital. The day's surgery and seminar sessions were ended. I was there as secretary to a team of prominent American and Swiss physicians sponsored by the Unitarian Service Committee (later merged with the Universalist Service Committee to become the Unitarian Universalist Service Committee). Our purpose was to do all we could to provide Austrian doctors with the latest skills and techniques in medicine and surgery. The once-proud center of the healing arts had suffered terribly from the ravages of Nazism and war. The Unitarian Service Committee, with the full cooperation of the newly established democratic government of Austria, the World Health Organization, and the four-power military occupation, had organized a mission of twelve specialists to act as midwives at the rebirth of Austrian medicine.

"Why are you doing this?" the dean asked. Earlier he had quizzed me about the religious interests of the twelve team-members. He raised his eyebrows when I told him that only two of the doctors were Unitarians, and that was quite by happenstance. "Do you expect to get Unitarian converts by this program?" he asked. I told him that we only wanted to do something useful for Austrians. "The work of the Service Committee is entirely non-sectarian," I explained. "Why are you doing this?" he inquired, shaking his head.

For most Unitarian Universalists, religion means little if it does not include enlightened conscience in action. We continually remind ourselves that the word *ethics* is shorthand for actions arising out of faith and from within community. Or, as Jane Addams put it: "To attain individual morality in an age demanding social morality. . . is utterly to fail to apprehend the situation." Yet, we are not missionary minded. We send no missionaries over the face of the earth to convert others to our way of believing. In fact, as I explained, we generally feel that people of other religions have as much to teach us as we have to teach them.

We have the moral equivalents of missionary activities, one of the most dramatic of which is the Unitarian Universalist Service Committee (UUSC). Independent of the Unitarian Universalist Association, the UUSC works in close harmony with it and shares the same basic, supportive constituency. Established in 1940 to rescue Jewish and other refugees from Nazi Europe, the UUSC has kept pace with the changing needs of our changing times. Kindled by compassionate imagination and fanned by a desire to share skills, resources, and goodwill with people the world around, it has carried out, over the years, a remarkable array of programs ranging from direct assistance for victims of war, repression, and hunger to community development and advocacy projects at home and abroad.

At present, typical UUSC efforts include:

A family-life education program in Senegal. This is a joint project with the Federation of Senegalese Women's Associations. It helps rural young women migrating to Dakar, the capital, and is partially funded by the Public Welfare Foundation.

Fact-finding missions, community development networking, human rights monitoring, and emergency relief in Central America. I write these words just as I have returned from Central America, where I found widespread respect for the Service Committee's work and for the UUSC's Human Rights Education director, under whose guidance there have been, since 1978, many congressional fact-finding missions. As a result of in-depth experience, the UUSC continues to raise with key decision makers in the United States the toughest questions about U.S. policy in the region. And, in order to provide new opportunities for Unitarian Universalists interested in direct involvement in Central American concerns, a staff person was appointed in the Boston office of the UUSC to produce an action organizer's handbook on Central American issues.

U.S. programs on aging, criminal justice, and native Americans. The Service Committee's Creative Living Environments in Old Age supports a pilot project in Naples, Florida, to build an interracial community center and housing complex. In addition, the board, staff, and volunteers help to create a criminal justice system that is fairer to all through the UUSC's National Moratorium on Prison Construction. Energetic support continues for various projects in cooperation with native Americans on nutrition; home gardening for self-sufficiency; land, water, and mineral rights; examination of imprisonment rates for native Americans; and an oral history project.

There are many other UUSC projects deserving mention. All characterize our conviction that dignity is best preserved by partnerships rather than handouts and by nonsectarian efforts rather than proselytizing.

I can only repeat what I said many years ago to that Austrian dean. We support the work of the Service Committee and participate as volunteers in it because it represents our profound spiritual need to mingle "on the thronged and common road where all must turn out for one another, and at least see the size of one another's burdens." We do not expect anyone to pat us on the head for being "good," and we do not expect anyone to become "converted" in return. We work *with* and not just *for* others. If it is possible for us to bring help, or know-how, or advocacy, or whatever where it is needed, we want to try to meet the need, but only in keeping with what others express to be their desires. We never try to impose a project on unwilling recipients.

We have consistently tried to adjust our programs to changing world patterns. We sincerely try not to succumb to the temptation to tell people what they ought to be doing. Our ability to work is stringently circumscribed by funds made available through voluntary contributions and grants, so it is of the utmost importance that we choose wisely among the overwhelming needs of an age of revolutionary change and disruption. We have learned the dangers of entering into a tug of war for the affections of people on the basis of who offers the better handouts. Our projects are never conceived of as competition or as bringing the "light" of salvation. We only wish to join hands with people struggling for their own lives and dignity. By so doing we feel that we are demonstrating to ourselves that religion is far more than a Sunday morning gesture to God. Behind the UUSC there is a powerful religious motivation, but it is not one of seeking converts. It is the motivation of demonstrating that mutuality is the way to One World, One Humanity.

Strength and Promise

As a nation, the United States views itself as the greatest example of power and plenty the world has ever known. Yet, in the midst of our vaunted technological millennium, we walk daily on the brink of a catastrophe so great that we can hardly grasp its possible consequences. Nor is the threat of nuclear holocaust the only symptom of distress in our otherwise upbeat and affluent way of life. The economic cornucopia we prize so highly is mocked by spreading slums, deepening poverty, stubborn racial injustice, a deteriorating environment, a bottomless pit of military expenditures, and a general retreat from compassion both in and out of government. In the world at large, U.S. policies contribute to a distribution of wealth so inequitable that thoughtful people are haunted by the fear of consequences.

The point I want to make about these evils is that, while we generally deplore them, we consistently refuse to recognize our responsibility for them, instead telling ourselves that it is the wicked who are to blame. In World War I it was Kaiser Wilhelm and the Huns. A generation later it was Hitler, Mussolini, Tojo, and Stalin (until he became our wartime ally, after which he reverted to devil status). Hitler, of course, blamed it all on the Jews, with one of history's most hideous results. Today it is blamed on communists (Chinese and Yugoslav varieties currently excepted), among whose secret minions, according to the new religious right, are feminists, liberals, and environmentalists. Some blame it all on the AFL-CIO, others on the military-industrial complex, others on sinful human nature, and still others on "deluded do-gooders." Most of us want desperately to believe in some sort of devil who is responsible for the evils that beset us. Religious fundamentalists have the advantage of being able to blame Satan, while political conservatives can blame the American Civil Liberties Union.

We Unitarian Universalists, if we are true to our conscience and reason, must be content with the uncomfortable truth that we, individually and collectively, create by our own actions and inactions the world in which we live and suffer or rejoice. We know that no class, race, religion, political party, economic system, dictator, rebel can be absolved from responsibility or singled out as the only villain. So, if we were to get down on our knees and pray "Oh God, bring peace to our world by helping us to realize that it is *we* who must wage peace, by our attitudes, thoughts, and acts," we could pray with a clear conscience.

Because humans are human and love to blame devils for their difficulties, religions often are sadly ineffective against the world's ills, though this is by no means a fatal flaw in religion. There is in religion a high tradition concerned with the *all* of life and dedicated to its enhancement. The great Hebrew prophets insisted that God is concerned with the well-being of *all* peoples. One of the finest sayings attributed to Jesus is "But whosoever would be great among you, shall be your helper; and whosoever would be first among you, shall be servant of all." This principle is applicable to every kind of human relations: of spouses, parents and children, teachers and pupils, employers and employees, privileged and underprivileged, and nations. Religion fails, not because of an internal defect, but because it is lived in fallible people. A confession of faith is never a substitute for responsible action.

Religion may be a matter of prayer, but prayer without responsible action is a mockery. Religious faith may at times be a necessary retreat from the world, but retreat without a vigorous return to responsible action is contempt for life.

In the heat of the civil rights struggles of the 1960s I wrote a book called *The Martyrs: Sixteen Who Gave Their Lives for Racial Justice.* Ten of the sixteen who died in the cause of civil rights were black, six were white — eleven men, one woman, four children. All were murdered in Alabama and Mississippi, by dynamite or by gun. In gathering the material, I spent many hours talking with white clergy in the towns and cities where the killings had occurred. Three of the dead, George Lee, James Reeb, and Jonathan Daniels, had been ministers. I divided the pastors I had interviewed into three groups. There were those who had risked their all by calling on their congregations to accept desegregation and to condemn violence. Some had already been fired, others expected the same, and a few thought they could make it through. A second group were pastors of prestigious parishes. Although most favored the civil rights cause and abhorred violence, they felt constrained to preserve the unity of their congregations by keeping silent in order "to be effective in the future." The third and largest group consisted of pastors who, again for the most part, favored the end of Jim Crow, but who were still dealing with the problem, as they essentially expressed it, "by praying for guidance," which seemed to mean praying for guidance on how to say something without being heard.

I do not stand in judgment of these pastors. I am reasonably certain that

I would not be found in the third group. But without actually being in that situation and having to make a decision about my personal course, I cannot say with assurance whether I would take my stand with the first group or the second. I can only say where I *hope* I would be found. Those of us who defend religion by relating it to the problems and conditions of life know that the ultimate test is responsible action from which there is no escape when greater and lesser values are in conflict. We know that in order to win a hearing for a worthy concept of religion there is no way of avoiding the pain of choice.

The dismal showing so often made by religious leaders and organized religious groups can be largely attributed to the narrow notion that religion is a system of props and supports for the individual. Actually, I do not contest that this is one of religion's significant and powerful functions. Few of us can do without spiritual support and solace, but a religious expression that turns only inward, that fails to help us face and carry through the moral responsibilities inherent in the economic, political, and social structures, is in decay. Religion's high tradition as a vehicle of deepening social conscience is brought to shame if a church focuses primarily on rituals and "feel good" fellowship. Not that there is anything innately wrong with rituals and "feel good" fellowship. Far from it. But history most honors religionists who, from the depths of their faith and fellowship, cry out against economic and social evils, paint a glowing picture of life as it should be when it is lived in mutual respect and service, and exalt the earth as a sacred trust for all.

Hearing this, one is bound to say: But wait. What can a mere handful do in a world like ours? On many issues we can't even agree among ourselves. How can we expect to do more than learn to live with all the grace and resignation we can muster?

Unitarian Universalists *are* a mere handful. Though our adult membership on the North American continent is increasing at an encouraging pace, we still number only about 140,000 in a huge sea of religious orthodoxy. Child and youth enrollments in our congregations, now gaining substantially, are about to pass the 40,000 mark, but they are only a tiny segment of the whole. With each passing month our membership is growing, but we are still talking of exceedingly modest totals in comparison with the statistics of other major religious bodies. Organized congregations are forming or are soon to be formed in dozens of new locations, adding to the more than 1,000 already dotting the continent's cities and towns. Still, this is nothing when compared with the number of Methodists, Baptists, or Roman Catholics.

In a mere handful, however, there is the power to move mountains, redress grievances, and change the climate of a community. Over the years I have preached scores of sermons at services in which my colleagues were being installed in new ministries. Invariably the participants include local priests, rabbis, and ministers of other denominations, who just as invariably express their gratitude for the tonic effect on the community and their own pastorates of the Unitarian Universalist presence. We are appreciated!

From so small an acorn has grown an amazing oak. Unitarian Universalists at the White House have included John Adams, Thomas Jefferson, John Quincy Adams, Millard Fillmore, and William Howard Taft. Adlai E. Stevenson didn't make it, but there are millions who still wish he had. Seventeen of the seventy-seven Olympians in the U.S. Hall of Fame came from our ranks. Equally impressive is the roll of literary figures: the Longfellows, Oliver Wendell Holmes, Louisa May Alcott, Ralph Cullen Bryan, Margaret Fuller, Edward Everett Hale, Ralph Waldo Emerson, James Russell Lowell, Nathaniel Hawthorne, Bret Harte, Catharine Sedgewick. Nor should we forget great historians such as George Bancroft, John Lothrop Morley, Francis Parkman, and William Prescott.

Because of our emphasis on service and social change, our movement has produced an amazing number of pioneers. Championing the anti-slavery cause were such figures as Maria Chapman, Lydia Maria Child, and Samuel J. May. Stalwarts for women's rights and human rights in general were Lucy Stone, Judith Sargent Murray, Julia Ward Howe, Elizabeth Cady Stanton, and Susan B. Anthony. In education some of the familiar names are Horace Mann, initiator of universal, nonsectarian, public education; Elizabeth Palmer Peabody, first to establish a kindergarten; Cyrus Pierce, pioneer crusader for teacher training programs; and Peter Cooper, founder of the famed Cooper Union in New York.

We can also include, among the most honored of humanitarians, Joseph Tuckerman, architect of the profession of social work; Dorothea Lynde Dix, whose boundless energies launched reform movements in prisons, charity institutions, and care for the mentally ill; Samuel G. Howe, who founded the first school for the blind; and Henry Bergh who helped establish the Society for the Prevention of Cruelty to Children and founded the American Society for the Prevention of Cruelty to Animals. Others who made memorable application of their religious ideals to public welfare include George William Curtis, pioneer advocate of civil service; Mary Livermore and Henry Bellows, early leaders of the United States Sanitary Commission, which later, under the inspired guidance of Clara Barton, became the Red Cross; and Whitney M. Young, Jr., who led the Urban League to unprecedented growth and effectiveness.

Similar lists could be enumerated of Unitarian Universalists who laid foundations for modern science, medicine, and the arts. These leaders are but a few of the many who justify the pride Unitarian Universalists feel about the influence of our religious movement. It has been all out of proportion to our numbers in moving public opinion forward, initiating social change, and making history. Fortunately we can turn to the present with comparable satisfaction to find a brilliant array of leaders acting as articulators and exemplars of our way of life. Indeed the list is so extensive I beg off from the risk, and the injustice, of singling out a few to the exclusion of the equally deserving many.

The strength of Unitarian Universalism is the strength of those who, though only a relative handful, are determined not to let the complexities of life deaden the imagination to care. The promise of our faith is crisply summarized in the aspiration: Give us the serenity to accept what cannot be changed, the courage to change what can be changed, and the wisdom to know one from the other. Or, as Jesse Jackson puts it: "If you try you *may* fail; if you don't try you're *sure* to fail."

Let me offer two practical examples of how it works when, out of aroused consciences, people say: "Our vision is always incomplete. No matter. We must move from questions we cannot answer to answers we cannot evade."

That's what happened when, on October 15, 1973, the congregation of the First Unitarian Church of Chicago and I, as senior minister, joined thirty other plaintiff organizations and individuals in a class action suit against the Chicago Police Red Squad. The purpose was to lay bare and, hopefully, to abolish the systematic spying done on us and many other lawful religious and secular groups whose "sin" was apparently that of sustained criticism of various aspects of the Richard Daley administration. A major vehicle for this criticism was the Alliance to End Repression, a broad coalition of Chicago-area civic, religious, and community groups that developed as a result of the police execution of Black Panther leaders in December 1969. I was one of the founders of the alliance and served as its first chairperson. My congregation belonged to it and made a significant financial contribution each year to the budget of the alliance, whose overall objective was strict observance of constitutional guarantees coupled with reform of all facets of the judicial system.

Our lawsuit required years of patient, unflappable effort, but had spectacular results. The Red Squad was abolished. We gained access to all of their files in undeleted form, an unprecedented accomplishment. We won a broad federal injunction, which for the first time outlawed political spying by a city's police department and set forth the toughest set of restrictions on intelligence agencies at all levels of government (including the FBI and CIA). A decade later, claims for civil damages resulting from the spying were still being litigated. In 1983, the alliance went back to court to block the implementation of new FBI rules, contending successfully that at least four provisions violate the injunction agreed to in the Red Squad suit. In matters like these, the beat goes on. The need for vigilance is eternal.

How does this costly involvement by congregation and minister reflect my understanding of Unitarian Universalist religious and social principles? For us there is an inescapable, commanding necessity to rebuke arrogant official power and defend freedom of voluntary association. This necessity arises out of our faith in human freedom, reason, and responsibility. It is rooted in our collective memory of the indivisible nature of lawful liberty and the awful consequences of lawless official power. We must assert and insist, by word and deed, that in a democratic society laws must be respected first and foremost by those who make and enforce them.

Is it more important to speak out as an institution, or as an individual? Conscience is individual, but it is also organic and social. Both aspects of conscience are precious in our heritage. But to insist on only going it alone is to fail to grasp the human situation. I believe that, until we roll up our sleeves and join hands as a community of faith, we cannot fully experience the redemptive power of our convictions or our witness. A community of faith that does not try to mold history is not only undependable but, in the end, impotent.

My second example evokes the oft-heard plaintive question, What can one or two of us possibly do for a better world? At our 1982 General Assembly, Unitarian Universalists saluted Jo and Nick Seidita, a middle-aged California couple, for their extraordinary efforts in the nuclear weapons freeze movement. In December 1980, Nick drafted the nuclear weapons freeze resolution, which was overwhelmingly adopted, along with a plan for implementation by our 1981 General Assembly. Not content to sit back and wait, Jo and Nick began in their own Pacific Southwest UU district to build support. Meanwhile, they inspired their own UU congregation in Sepulveda to contribute $3,000 toward the initiation of the California Freeze Campaign.

With this seed money, through home petition parties and the help of hundreds who volunteered, they sent packets to social studies teachers in every accredited high school in California. Meanwhile, for several months Jo worked full time as a volunteer organizer for the California Nuclear Weapons Freeze Referendum. Despite vigorous opposition by the Reagan administration, the freeze was approved by a substantial majority.

They were only two, but Nick and Jo Seidita, with the support of their congregation, reached out to the Unitarian Universalist Association, and to their entire state, to influence dramatically the growing awareness of and commitment to the need for freezing and reversing the nuclear arms' race. The citation given to them closed with these words: "With pride and pleasure we present the 1982 Holmes-Weatherly Award to Jo and Nick Seidita of Sepulveda, California: committed workers for peace, who have inspired and organized, and shown us the way. May their efforts and ours continue until the ground swell for nuclear control passes from a dream into reality."

Religion Must Be Acted Out

The two examples of acting out our religion, corporately and personally, were known to me intimately and firsthand. I might have chosen and examined scores of others with similar results. A few who think and act clearly and intelligently, and who feel deeply their spiritual responsibility, possess influence vastly out of proportion to their numbers. In whatever concrete ways they may decide to exercise their power, the vital matter to remember is the foundations on which that power rests:

1. Religion is concerned with the *all* of life. The world is not cut into two mutually exclusive segments—one containing secular affairs that religion must disregard, the other composed of religious beliefs and rituals.

2. Religion sees all humankind riding in the same boat, not bobbing about on a lot of separate life rafts bearing the labels "denominations," "nations," "cultures," or "races." We ride out the storms together, or we go down together.

3. It is not enough for us to profess oneness with others; we must act it out. More than wearing the garment of religious identification, we must welcome its ethical and moral responsibilities.

The substance of religion is in persons who deeply yearn to learn what is good and how it may be obtained; it is not merely the claim of personal sacredness, but the binding of oneself to others through respect and sensitivity toward the sacredness of all. It is not enough to boast of the gift of rational intelligence. The substance of religion is to nurture reason—to work it, to apply it, and to defend it.

My colleague and friend, William F. Schulz, wrote: "If the equation (Plato's) 'Being = Power' holds for individuals, then it is even more evident a characteristic of institutions. By its very being-in-the-world the church posesses power. By their property and their wealth; by their prestige and by their people; by their ministries, mailing lists and mimeos; by their visibility and by their vision, our local societies and our Association are *de facto* possessors of power. We cannot avoid it."

So, the issue is never whether or not we possess power, or whether or not we can use it. We do, and we can. What is impossible is avoiding its use. Not to decide in the face of injustice is to decide to let injustice stand. The issue, then, is always how best to decide on the side of our ideals, how best to incarnate in our actions what we stand for.

The Power of the Word

Unitarian Universalists are notably unenthusiastic about proselytizing, but there is a mounting zeal among us for telling our side of the story. Our use of radio and television is on the rise. My own interest in this dates to 1954, when in Indianapolis I began a subcareer of regular appearances on radio and television. I have kept at it ever since, impressed by the evidence that these powerful media are rich sources for new Unitarian Universalists. I am ever more convinced that there are hundreds of thousands of unchurched religious liberals out there who are still completely unaware of what Unitarian Universalism represents.

For this reason, I have paid special attention in recent years to "Cambridge Forum," a uniquely respected Unitarian Universalist voice in public affairs broadcasting. With headquarters at the First Parish in Cambridge, Massachusetts, "Cambridge Forum" regularly reaches an audience of millions through its weekly programs on public radio stations and its frequent use of the special series approach on public television stations. The role of "Cambridge Forum" is that of presenting nonsectarian, informed discussion on the great issues of our time and of nurturing a sense of hope that there *are* better choices and actions for us in this complex, troubled world, if only we take the trouble to care and to learn. It is the purpose of "Cambridge Forum" to provide guidance and inspiration for doing this, thus both strengthening the Unitarian Universalist movement and aiding in the personal and social development of those it can reach.

Another approach is that of Univision, an organization that produces twenty-three minutes of material aimed particularly at cable television audiences and that stresses Unitarian Universalist views on the Bible, the family, the church, and religious experience. Churches are encouraged to make arrangements to use the taped material with their cable or broadcast television operators and to provide five-to-seven minutes of their own local material.

In steadily growing numbers, our congregations and ministers, in addition to devising local tie-ins with "Cambridge Forum" and Univision, are creating their own ways of reaching radio and television audiences with Unitarian Universalist values. May their tribe grow! Culturally, we are conditioned to think of organized religion in terms of the conventional tri-umvirate — Protestant, Catholic, and Jewish. But in a very real sense, we are the largest and most significant segment of a *fourth* faith — religious liberalism.

Any form of personal arm twisting to join a church is repugnant to us, but the response to our outreach efforts indicates that it would be short-sighted and selfish to withhold information on something about which we are so enthusiastic and which strikes such a responsive chord in so many who were previously unaware of our existence. Ours is a live and thrilling option for the many who are dissatisfied with traditional religious institu-tions but who do not yet know that another and deeply appealing alterna-tive is available. Our new members repeatedly tell us of their intense regret at having gone so many years without discovering the Unitarian Univer-salist church. "We simply did not know that such a religious movement existed, and no one bothered to tell us," they say. We now sense, with fresh appreciation, our obligation to spread as widely as possible a knowledge of our history, aims, principles, values, and the basis of our church life. More than ever before the time is ripe to resist religious homogenization by bringing together as many as possible of those who desire to advance the cause of freedom and human fulfillment through liberal religion.

One of our most effective tools is the written word. Through the Uni-tarian Universalist Association, we support a broad publications program, which includes pamphlets, books, newsletters, and a newspaper. Elements of this program are:

Beacon Press. A major trade publishing house wholly owned by the Unitarian Universalist Association. Founded in 1854, Beacon Press produces books of a serious, general, and often controversial nature. Beacon Press hardcover and paperback editions are prominently displayed in bookstores throughout the continent and in many countries overseas. It is the purpose of Beacon Press to make a spirited contribution to the world's cultural, intellectual, and religious life through an energetic program of quality publishing that emphasizes the pre-eminence of the human spirit. Beacon Press is a religious publishing house in the sense that it promotes the Unitarian Universalist view that religious values must be lived out in the world. It has been a leader in publishing black writers such as James Baldwin, Sterling Brown, Martin Luther King, Jr., Paul Robeson, and June Jordan. In the field of women's studies, its record is outstanding, featuring celebrated theologian Rosemary Radford Ruether and radical feminist philosopher Mary Daly. In 1947 Beacon Press had a mere seventeen titles on its backlist. Today Beacon's robust backlist comprises nearly three hundred titles in sociology, philosophy, art, literature, communications, black studies, women's issues, political science, religion, and current affairs.

In the words of a Beacon Press director: "Though Unitarian Universalists do not necessarily agree on politics, life styles, or priorities, they do agree that it is important to carry forward a free and disciplined search for truth and justice against forces of conformism, ignorance, and fear. They believe they should do what they can to help people become informed of the critical issues of their times so that they can live more effective, caring, and responsible lives."

Pamphlet Commission. A rich array of attractively styled and crisply written pamphlets on virtually all aspects of the religious life is available for seekers, potential members, new members, and established members. These pamphlets are distributed by the hundreds of thousands in our churches and other gathering places and are used in a multitude of ways by organized groups throughout our denomination.

The UU World. A denominational newspaper, in tabloid format, is mailed to about 100,000 households twelve times a year. It carries religious news and inspirational material, programs of local congregations, ideas, views, plans, schedules, opinions, letters, book reviews, and information about Unitarian Universalist Association (UUA) services, materials, and programs.

Social Outreach

Our impact is also felt on the denominational level by the Section on Social Responsibility, a division of our headquarters staff. Each general assembly of the UUA passes resolutions on the prominent social issues of the day. It is the task of the UUA to implement these resolutions and to translate rhetoric into action. The Section of Social Responsibility is responsible for this task. In addition to a small headquarters staff, the Social Responsibility section includes the Office of Gay Concerns, the Committee on Aging, and the UUA Washington, D.C., Office of Social Concerns, which represents the UUA before Congress and the executive branch. Seeking to educate and stimulate our own constituency, the section also provides education and advocacy services to local congregations and helps mobilize a Unitarian Universalist presence at events of significance for social change.

By no means do we try to go it alone. Coalition building is essential in expressing social concern. To this end, the UUA plays an active role in the Interfaith Center for Corporate Responsibility, the National Coalition for Abortion Rights, the Religious Committee for the ERA, the Coalition to End the Death Penalty, and the Coalition for a New Foreign and Military Policy. Through liaison representatives, we are in regular contact with the National Farm Workers Ministry, the National Coalition Against Censorship, the National Organization of Women, the National Urban League, and other action groups.

Constrained only by a limited staff and budget, the Section on Social Responsibility channels our institutional energies and human resources to a wide variety of fronts, from women's rights to apartheid, from racism to corporate responsibility, from disarmament to civil liberties to economic justice. An appropriate humility marks what we can do, but an equally appropriate zeal marks our determination to do all we possibly can.

Founded in 1961 to provide Unitarian Universalists with a direct link to the United Nations, the Unitarian Universalist United Nations Office (UU-UN) is an affiliate of the UUA supported by direct contributions from individuals, churches, women's groups, and grant-making organizations in Canada and the United States. The UU-UN is an accredited nongovernmental organization in consultative status with the world body. From its New York office overlooking the UN, it serves as a rallying point for our churches and their members, encouraging direct participation through annual workshops and seminars, visits to UN sessions, a newsletter on developments in the world community, sponsorship of UN Sunday, program planning guidelines, and detailed special reports on current affairs.

One of our latest and most welcome creations is the Unitarian Universalist Peace Network established in 1984 to link the peace advocacy efforts of five international religious organizations representing ten million members, sixty nations, fifteen languages, and every continent. Based in Philadelphia, the UU Peace Network coalesces and coordinates the peace interests of the International Association for Religious Freedom (IARF), which includes Hindus, Buddhists, Shintoists, Moslems, and forty-three other groups; the Unitarian Universalist Association; the Unitarian Universalist Service Committee; the Unitarian Universalist Peace Fellowship; and the UU-UN. Announcing the network's establishment, the Reverend Eugene Pickett, president of the UUA and treasurer of the IARF, said: "What is significant about this effort is that it will focus our collective Unitarian Universalist influence in the interest of a world free from nuclear arms. It is also a truly cooperative undertaking which brings five denominationally related groups together in a concerted effort to deal with the most important issue before the world — its preservation."

Woven together with all of the above is an array of organizations affiliated with the Unitarian Universalist Association, but self-governing and autonomous. Each draws its support from within our total, varied constituency. Each expresses a concern for some aspect of the human condition, some ideal to be fostered, some need to be met, some interest to be pursued. These include the Unitarian Universalist Women's Federation, the Society for Alcohol Education, the Unitarian Universalist Urban Church Coalition, Unitarian Universalists for Justice in the Middle East, the PSI Symposium, the Benevolent Fraternity of Unitarian Churches, and the Lesbian-Gay Caucus.

On the Move

News from the Unitarian Universalist world has never been more exciting. Major adventures are under way or on the drafting board at every level of our movement. Our ministry is strong. We have received an $11 million fund for theological education. Two hundred and thirty-two students, the largest number in our history, more than half of whom are women, are preparing for our ministry.

We have inaugurated a new youth organization, Young Religious Unitarian Universalists, which is flourishing. Our congregations are doing more building, expanding, and renovating than ever before. Thanks to the Women's Federation, the Women and Religion Committee, and Beacon Press we are taking to heart new insights from feminist theology and thought. Our Extension Department is working overtime to keep up with the demand for new congregations. The energies generated by the Urban Church Coalition, the Committee on Urban Concerns and Ministry, and the Whitney M. Young, Jr., Fund are pushing us to strengthen our urban churches. We are girding ourselves to work aggressively once again to make our denomination racially and ethnically inclusive.

New ideas, fresh approaches, experimentation, and wise planning and action are combining to give the Unitarian Universalist tradition revived and revised relevance to the religious needs and shifting patterns of our time. This must not, and does not, mean that we will grow careless of the profound distinction between being an ecclesiastical and missionary assembly line and being a religious fellowship bent on uniting the efforts of the largest possible number of like-minded people. Our present strength and future promise promote confidence that our era of greatest usefulness and effectiveness is dawning. The sole stumbling block to moving vigorously ahead lies at the heart of our spiritual life. We must not stumble there. We must summon recurring infusions of spiritual sensitivity and insight. In doing so, we will only be replicating what has characterized our movement at its best from the beginning.

I cannot begin to describe adequately the gratitude I feel for the privilege of being a Unitarian Universalist minister at this particular juncture in history. We find ourselves exploring new horizons of witness, service, and growth. To be able to say that I am part of this unfolding destiny, that I am able to make some contribution to its fulfillment, is to express my utter joy at being a member of a unique ministry serving a unique movement. I am a free person living deeply in the community of a free religious faith, which is bent on making freedom prosper at a time when the "better angels" of the human spirit are everywhere under attack.

What I care about most on a day-by-day basis is that our faith appeals to, and gives inspiration to, persons — ordinary and extraordinary persons — with special sparks of courage, who say and do difficult and different things, who think new thoughts (at least to them), and who follow small insights in the absence of big ones.

I acknowledge with humility and gratitude that we have no exclusive claims to the liberal spirit, nor to social concern and service. Under many labels, people are committed to essentially the same goals and hopes that motivate us. The collaborative power of interfaith and ecumenical efforts is one of our most buoyant sources of hope. I agree with the Reverend Harry Nevels, an Episcopal priest in inner-city Cleveland, when he says: "We've taken a step when we work together without asking each other what church do you come from."

Let's face it. We are overwhelmingly white. We are overwhelmingly comfortable to affluent on the economic scale. We are mostly suburban. The happy truth is that we don't really want to stay this way. It violates something deep in our souls. So we are struggling, in a variety of ways, to reach out to those who are diverse in terms of race, ethnic background, location, and socioeconomic status. One of our visions is to help congregations to duplicate the full racial integration of such models as First Unitarian in Chicago, All Souls in Washington, D.C., and Community in New York City. But we are also beginning to look to different models. In Boston, the Unitarian Universalist Association is assisting the storefront Church of the United Community, where the congregation is composed of welfare mothers and children, union workers, Hispanics, blacks, and whites. On Chicago's changing North Side, Unitarian Universalists, along with the United Church of Christ, are revitalizing the Peoples Church as a center of community life and worship. Multiple congregations — interracial, Asian, and Hispanic — are planned as part of this renewal. A Korean Fellowship is an integral part of the First Unitarian Church of Los Angeles and is led by our first Korean minister, the Reverend Hyun Hwan Kim.

Still, the blunt truth is that while we have four black members on the UUA Board of Trustees, we have only three settled black ministers.

Will we have vision enough to accept the challenge, *really* change, and own the discomfort of such change? The gap between things as they are and things as they ought to be will remain an offense until it is bridged.

10

The Courage to Be

Keep your heart with all diligence, for out of it are the issues of life.
— *Proverbs*

There is no faith without separation.
— Paul Tillich, *The Dynamics of Faith*

Christmas is often a perverse reminder of the many reasons we have for feeling unjoyous. Our Unitarian Universalist forebear, Charles Dickens, captured the essence of this experience and of overcoming it in *A Christmas Carol*.

The central characters begin as cogs. Bob Cratchit is not really a person, but a tool, a thing, a machine, hired to turn out as much work as possible. Scrooge is a stick figure, fashioned of cupidity, alienation, and self-hate. Both live in a social situation of moral anarchy. Dickens's answer, appropriate to the crisis, is that love can overcome such radical alienation and weave bonds even between people who lack shared customs and beliefs.

We know that Dickens brought off the miracle of showing Scrooge the power of love, the courage to be new. We face a task more difficult than Scrooge's or Dickens's, not only because our task is real, but because the forces of estrangement and spiritual numbness are stronger now than in the London of Tiny Tim. In a way this can be turned to our advantage, for we have no choice but to recognize and accept the implications of our predicament.

The love that saved Scrooge is now a necessity, not just an option; and it must be love in the tough and universal sense of community and of daring, personal transformation. A fragmented, holocaust-prone world needs people capable of such love to put it together. This putting together is not an abstraction. It needs to be present and real, right now.

I am grateful to *Good News,* the publication of the Unitarian Universalist Christian Fellowship, for the story of a small boy, alone in his bed in the dark. He was afraid, so he called his Dad. Seizing the teachable moment, his Dad said: "My son, you need not fear. God is everywhere. God is with you." And with that he left. Soon the boy was crying again. And again Dad came, administered the same good advice: "Don't be afraid. God is near," and he left. But yet a third time the fear rose, and the boy cried out. This time, the Dad with ever so slight an edge in his voice, asked him: "Son, what did I tell you?" and was told, "Yes, Dad, I know God is everywhere, but sometimes I need someone with skin."

There is power to create in our life circles, intimate and remote, precious bonds of tough and universal love. But it isn't easy. We all know that. We have to incarnate love within our skins.

For many of us, the inexorable limits of life are never more apparent or gripping than in the midst of the Christmas season. We know, for example, that we will never be great as the world measures greatness. We know that we will never be truly saintly. We know that we will never be untainted by life's corrosions, compromises, and hypocrisies. We will never be immune to aging, illness, grievous losses, and bereavements, to crises large and small, to vanished hopes and broken dreams.

The one thing we do need to know, and to encourage one another to know, is what I find at the heart of Dickens's story. It is not God who drives us into anxiety and depression over what is lacking within our skins. We do that to ourselves and to one another. The only status, the only real possibility we need is the one we already have. And we have it as a gift. The gift of life. God is not up there, out there, or everywhere, demanding that we prove ourselves worthy of the gift, only that we express ourselves as conscious receivers of the gift. What a different world we would live in if all of us did that—proving less, expressing more of our simple appreciation, in courage and faithfulness, for that gift of life which is incarnated within our skins. Think how much less anxiety, depression, and weariness there would be! Until then, we are at war with ourselves, making casualties of others.

I have written with fervor in this volume about the blessings of community. I will write more before I finish. But for a few pages, I want to meditate as powerfully as I can upon the individuals who make up communities.

It is as persons, within our self-contained skins, that we experience the ultimate sense of uniqueness and the ultimate anguish of aloneness. The marks of our selfness are unequivocally stamped upon our behavior, whether we are assembled in community or off on a stroll alone. How we walk, sound, write letters, turn our heads is infallibly unique. No one is quite like any other. We are unduplicatable individuals. When we gather in communities, each of us asserts and speaks the lines of an identity that is unique. This takes a great deal of time and energy. To the extent that we permit ourselves to become caricatures of our uniqueness, it is difficult for communities to get much done. We need not become caricatures of ourselves. The best way to avoid it is to do some solid thinking about our uniqueness as aloneness.

Is it really true that each of us is alone? Is not our aloneness largely dissolved in the intimacies of love and fellowship? Do not an ideally married couple overcome separateness? "Love consists in this," wrote Rainer Maria Rilke in *Letters to a Young Poet,* "that two solitudes protect, and touch, and greet one another." Because we are human, we remain alone even in the most affectionate unions. We do not penetrate (indeed, we have no right to try to penetrate) into one another's innermost center of being, no matter how strong our love, because it is our human greatness to have an unassailable inner core which is ours alone.

I went through an uncomfortable period in our denomination when many became engulfed in the encounter movement and obsessed with a need to have everyone "let it all hang out." There is much good to be gained from the insights of this movement. But there is a danger in it, difficult to guard against. It is the danger of trashing something very precious to me in my religious affiliation: recognition and respect for the *impenetrable* center of every person's being. Like anyone else, I have inhibitions, which others can help me overcome. But an ultimate solitude of soul in which to find my deepest convictions is the reality of my being, not an inhibition. This is another way of my saying that creation may be a badly botched job, but I love it. I stand alone in creation, encased within my own mortal skin; and, wonder of wonders, I am conscious of this because I am a person. Knowing that I stand separate, I can look out upon the world and love it and cooperate with others who also stand separate, to savor and transform it. This, I say, as Paul Tillich did, is where faith enters and makes its presence profoundly felt. Only as I have the courage to accept my supreme aloneness and vulnerability can I turn to full participation. Only as I am brave enough to know that, even in my own warm home I am but on a visit, only as I can face the fact that everything I build will someday crumble am I free to give that which endures on this earth; the spirit in which I live my life and do my part. This I pass on to my wife, my children and grandchildren, my friends, my parishioners, my colleagues and associates. I live so that the human spirit may live in the only way it can live—within the human skin. Any faith smaller than this will not console me in my transitory defeats, nor comfort me in my times of despair, nor give me the courage to push through.

Shakespeare has Cassius say to Brutus in *Julius Caesar:*

> There is a tide in the affairs of men,
> Which, taken at the flood, leads on to fortune;
> Omitted, all the voyage of their life
> Is bound in shallows and in miseries.

I do not believe that there is any *one* moment that "taken at the flood," leads us to the fulfilling courage to stand and be ourselves. All we are and believe, all we do and work for and love, is constantly under the threat of "shallows" and "miseries." Yet the tides keep rising. We salvage. We compensate. We cultivate the strength that comes with sharing, with caring, with reaching out, with bestowing, where we can, the meanings we discover in the core of our aloneness. This is the truth of Whitehead's famous definition that religion is what we do with our "solitariness." There is reverence in my religion for my solitariness. There is no compulsion in liberal religion to intrude upon my aloneness with public revelations and salvation systems. My solitariness is honored. There is respect for my experience of the human condition and for the way in which I choose to enter into communion with others. There is recognition that the real religious decision for me is what I decide to do, together with others, and that the role of the church is not to bend my will but to give strength and flexibility to my willing. The will is in the self. Out of the self comes the character of the deeds that make for individuality.

In our intermediate fate, there is no substantial variety, because we are all subject to anxiety, accident, and disappointment. In our ultimate fate, there is no variety whatsoever, because we all must die. But it matters greatly how we deal with our anxieties, accidents, and disappointments. It matters greatly what we believe in while we are around. It matters to *us,* even if it may not matter to the universe, what purposes we set for the days of our years. I am a Unitarian Universalist because I do not require or want revelatory proof of purpose. I have faith in purpose in the midst of the unknown because I know that the purposes I choose in my aloneness are themselves sources of courage, balance, and compensation.

To live is to grow, and to grow means to change enough to be able to play a creative part in change itself. I am acquainted with a play-therapy clinic for children, where the first reaction of one child who was brought for treatment was to raise his arm in protection or attack whenever an adult approached. Flight or fight. One of the therapists worked and worked with this child until that exquisite moment when an accepting smile finally broke through on the boy's face, and he dropped his arm, his symbol of fear.

The history books will never celebrate this therapist as one of earth's great liberators. Her name will never be joined with Sojourner Truth, Emma Goldman, and Margaret Sanger, but in essence, she is a liberator of the most precious human qualities: courage and trust. In this, she deserves to rank with the greatest, because she shares the emancipating intentions of those who are greatest. And so may we all.

I cannot prove the purposes through which we find the courage to take our stand on the side of life. I do believe in these purposes, and not just naïvely. I believe in them because I am so sure of the liberating possibilities in men and women. The comfort of my religion rests not on any of the conventional but questionable "proofs" of God's personal concern and care, but on the encouragement I find in my aloneness, and in an appreciation of the aloneness of others, to accept and trust life without such proofs. If the world of nature is impersonal, so be it. If the universe plays no favorites — as Einstein put it, "God does not play dice" — isn't that after all a necessary condition of whatever dependability we can find? My liberal religion offers me the comfort of spiritual solitude in a world where I can rise in hope to meet, or compensate for, most of my problems; where, in fact, I can intelligently anticipate many of the stresses I must solve or bear. In brief, mine is a religion that cares more about me as a person — my potential resources and strengths — than it does about theological explanations or atonements of the dilemmas and failures that beset me. My courage to be is not mediated by priests or revelations. It is cultivated in the recesses of my essential aloneness and challenged by the opportunities of communion with others. I know that my ultimate fate is not in my hands; but my human version of fate is. The element of tragedy I cannot always control; but beyond tragedy I may choose the purposes by which my life will be guided. My human limitations I cannot abolish; but within the limitations are the meanings I am free to create.

I count it as one of the great and good fortunes of my generation that a superb poet, yearning for a metaphor of the twentieth century's spiritual dilemmas, turned to the Book of Job. In writing *J.B.,* Archibald MacLeish ran a literary gauntlet. The Book of Job is probably the most sublime piece of Hebrew literature that has come down to us. It is no small problem to do justice in a modern work to its insight, its imagery, its richness of symbolism, and its depth of feeling. MacLeish has given us a worthy Job of our time, and he tests his fidelity in terms of our calamities and explanations. In a highly imaginative setting, MacLeish successfully avoids sanctimoniousness and religious sentimentality without losing any of the intimacy of the grandeur of J.B.'s terrible trials. I love the way he has Zuss and Nickles play God and Satan by donning a pair of appropriate masks. It is wonderful to have them speaking through their masks with heavenly detachment and then removing their masks to make very human and salty comments about supernatural affairs. The masks produce what is for me one of the most moving perceptions of the entire drama. Nickles, after putting his mask on for the first time, tears it off in a kind of cold sweat. "Those eyes *see*," he says.

> They see the *world*. They see it.
> From going to and fro in the earth.
> From walking up and down, they see it.
> I know what Hell is now — to *see*.
> Consciousness of consciousness...

Has anyone ever experienced a moment of searing, conscious insight without knowing what Nickles meant when he ripped off his mask? To know life is to *see* — to be gripped by the terrible pain and wonder of it.

As a poet, MacLeish was very much of this world. His J.B. is also very much of this world. J.B. is a hearty, prosperous business executive, surrounded by a Hallmark-card family of bright, healthy children, and loved by an intelligent, attractive wife. He thinks well of his fellows and is sincerely grateful to God for his abundance and good fortune. Then God begins to enlighten him about the true nature of life. Afflictions stab with senseless abandon and brutality. One by one his children are destroyed. To cap all this, his business is wiped out, leaving him penniless and suffering from hideous radiation burns. In a final blow, his wife walks out on him for failing to defend himself.

At this point, MacLeish introduces the typical soothsayers of our generation — a Marxist, a psychoanalyst, and a conventional preacher — who

explain J.B.'s catastrophes and console him with their characteristic
panaceas. His first comforter, the Marxist, tells J.B. that he is being
punished by historical necessity:

> God is History. If you offend Him
> Will not History dispense with you?
> History has no time for innocence.

The second comforter, the psychoanalyst, informs J.B. that he is
punishing himself unnecessarily in depths of unconscious, mindless guilt.

The third, a ponderous, pastoral type, insists that J.B. is being punished
for the unpardonable sin of having been born:

> ... Guilt is reality!
> The one reality there is!
> All mankind are guilty always!

J.B., in his misery, rejects all three. "What is my fault?" he cries.
"What have I done?" The clergyman thunders back:

> What is your fault? Man's heart is evil!
> What have you done? Man's will is evil!
> Your fault, your sin, are heart and will:
> .... Your sin is
> Simple. You were born a man!

J.B. crouches lower in his rags and agony, and speaks very softly:

> Yours is the cruelest comfort of them all,
> Making the Creator of the Universe
> The miscreator of mankind —
> A party to the crimes He punishes...

At this point MacLeish makes the same abrupt switch we find in the
ancient Book of Job. God relents and rewards J.B. for his unwavering
loyalty. He restores to J.B. his wife, family, affluence, and health. To say
that this resolution cheats is to put it mildly.

What really matters in J.B., as it does in Job, is not that a happy ending is awkwardly patched on, but that there is an epilogue of interpretations and affirmations that go to the heart of the human dilemma. There are, first, the unforgettable words placed in God's mouth by the authors of Job and retained nearly intact by MacLeish:

> Where wast thou when I laid the foundations of earth...
> Hast thou commanded the morning
> Can'st thou bind the sweet influence of the Pleiades?

Who are humans to feel that they must have an explanation for everything? Who are humans to believe that their pain and pleasure can only be understood as reward and punishment, as the willful giving or withholding of their God? Is it humans who give the horse strength or make the eagle rise? Reward and punishment are not God's themes; they are human themes. The universe does not reward or punish; it simply is. God does not reward or punish. God is.

And to this J.B. and his wife respond, as we, if we have the wisdom, will also respond. Into any life may come events too terrible to understand, but not because they were willed by a malignant universe. The universe is neither just nor unjust; the universe does not bless or curse. The human answer is not to seek justice in the heavens, but to seek it in the human frame. "You wanted justice, and there was none," J.B.'s wife says. But she offers her love.

The universe gives life—the precious gift of life—and the human response is love: love of God, love of the universe, for making life possible, and love of all those who share the gift. This kind of love is the seat of justice. It is wholly that of humans to give or withhold.

In this violent century, J.B. and J.B.'s wife are abstracts of each and every one of us. As such they are written larger than life, so that their plight overwhelms us not only with pity and terror, but also with reverence for the human race. We are human and we are mortal. We did not create the universe, and we need not despair that we cannot explain all its mysteries and paradoxes. We know that human suffering is pervasive, that it can come to us, and that when it does we must bear it and cope with it. We know also that it comes to others, and that when it does, our task is not to justify or judge but to ease and comfort and uphold. We are born into a world of many evils for human beings. In some of them, we are directly implicated. In some of them, we are not. Our task is not so much to know from whence these evils come, as how they may be resisted, or borne, or overcome.

We speak of justice, but the lesson of Job and J.B. is that the only justice we will find is that which is fashioned by the human spirit. We speak of love, but the lesson of Job and J.B. is that the only love we will know is that which we exchange with one another. The Book of Job was written to challenge the monstrous doctrine that God willfully and personally rewards and punishes. J.B. was written to remind us that if we look to heaven for an explanation of our generation's travails and terrors we will find only emptiness and despair. The universe creates but does not legislate. Justice is a human genius, not a divine one. It may err and be corrected. Misfortune is a human experience, not a cosmic punishment. If all things are to come out right in the end, we do not know it. What we do know is that there is no substitute for blowing on the coals of the human heart.

The answer to what we call the injustices of life is love — our love of life in spite of life. The universe gives life, and humans give life soul, but only if they love in the midst of their thralldom, in spite of suffering, injustice, and death. From Job to J.B. the lesson is this: we are *not* called upon to justify the ways of God; we are always called upon to justify our own ways.

In Job and J.B. I find stirring parables of what my religion means to my courage to be. I do not love life because God will take care of me. My reason tells me that the universe is not organized to look after my personal welfare. The universe has given me life. By placing that life in a body separate from all other bodies, the universe has also granted me an unassailable core of inner being that is mine and mine alone to cultivate and deepen. No priest or revelation can mediate between my solitariness and life as a whole. I love life because, although it leaves me in an ultimate sense alone, it brings me into communion with everyone else's aloneness. In solitariness I sense how intimately I am linked to all those from whom I am separated. My religion is the finding of self and others. It is not only my courage to be myself, in all my stark individuality and aloneness, but also my basic source of the power to live serviceably with others.

Immortality for Skeptics

What happens to this life I prize so highly when, in me, it dies? What befalls this core of inner being that is mine and mine alone when death overtakes my body? Is death the end, or is it a beginning? One of our pamphlets, *Unitarian Universalist Views of Death and Immortality*, presents six personal testimonies, widely different in spirit, tone, and substance. I recommend this pamphlet. It dramatizes the range of beliefs around which we encourage discussion, open and frank, in our religious community. Such discussions, and my reflections on them, have brought me to the views I share with you here. They are mine. May they be of some help in sorting out your own.

Those who find sustaining hope in the Christian doctrine of personal immortality are struggling in their own way with a universal problem. I do not find this doctrine to be helpful, but I level no charge of self-delusion against those who do. We live in a universe of fantastic possibilities, and with each passing year developments in the physical sciences make the possibilities even more fantastic. I have dealt too long and too intimately with people facing death to feel anything but compassion and sympathy for the various means by which faith and fortitude are mobilized.

I summon to mind sitting at the bedside of a friend who knew that within days cancer would snuff out his life. I asked how he felt about what lay ahead. He told me that he was able to feel quite serene about death. He felt, with Socrates and Elisabeth Kübler-Ross, that death cannot be a harsh or evil thing. He went on: "I would be less than honest, however, if I did not tell you I have qualms about *dying.*" Again, the distinction between death and dying I wrote of in an earlier chapter. How valid a distinction it is. Death is unknown, but it is the destiny of all living creatures. Death is either nothingness or another realm of being, and surely neither merits terror. We remain alone in our anticipations of dying. No communication with others can remove this aloneness. Those who love us can touch and protect, but they cannot share or hide the fact that it is our dying and ours alone that awaits. Can we stand this? The world's many theologies of immortality and afterlife bear witness to our doubt that we can stand it without the comfort of a faith certain.

Yet, there are those of us who find small solace in promises of resurrection and eternal life. Most religious liberals are among this group. I myself am unimpressed by the traditional Easter message. It seems to me to be a quite inadequate way of celebrating spring's renewal and rebirth. My ministry is basically to those whose thoughts and experiences lead them to question the Christian faith in resurrection and a personal, eternal, heavenly afterlife, and to seek something more nearly suited to their emotional and rational needs. There is nothing strange or perverse in this point of view. It grows on a person with reflection. It may flicker first as a reaction against the Christian gospel. If Jesus was a divine being, his rising from the dead says nothing about a mere human's ability to conquer death. People are not deities; they are human beings. To celebrate the resurrection of a deity tells us nothing about the prospects for human beings. In good logic, only those who disbelieve in the deity of Jesus should be able to derive any real comfort from the story of his resurrection. It seems to have no proper place in a contemporary, rational view of reality. That early Christians believed in a resurrection is no sound reason, in itself, for believing it today. Everybody believed in supernatural happenings and wonders two thousand years ago. They believed, for example, that mental illness was caused by an invasion of tiny devils into a person's body. In spite of the tremendous amount we still don't understand about mental illness, we at least know that miniature devils are not the explanation. It can be said with much the same reassurance that we also know better about resurrections. Moreover, our study of history makes clear that Jesus did not bring the hope of personal afterlife into the world, because not only the hope but the belief in it was held by peoples long before his time.

Elisabeth Kübler-Ross now numbers herself among those who tell us that, quite aside from Jesus's role, there is a growing body of clinical evidence of personal immortality. There are reputable researchers who work full-time on the remembered experiences of patients who returned to life after being "medically" dead. These accounts have a ring of authenticity about them and reassuring descriptions of personally felt peace, serenity, and beauty. But after examining this literature, an honest mind can conclude that it is still speculation, not proof.

There have long been impressive forms of poetically expressed beliefs in personal survival after death. They come from persons, such as Evelyn Underhill and William Wordsworth, who base their faith on what they call intimations and intuitions of inner experience. Emerson had similar feelings and wrote:

> What is excellent,
> As God lives, is permanent;
> Hearts are dust, heart's loves remain;
> Heart's love will meet thee again.

Yet, even under the spell of beautiful thoughts so beautifully expressed, there are some of us who are not persuaded by our sense of human worth to require a personal continuance after death. In other words, traditional concepts of immortality do not become more valid simply because they are associated with a morally satisfying view of human life. Feeling, of itself, no matter how elevated, does not signify personal survival. Compassionate human behavior is not inspiring because it whispers to us of some concrete plan of immortality; it is inspiring in itself and on its own merits. The teachings of Jesus are not guides to ethical growth because they are linked to beliefs about his resurrection. They are guides because their worth is implicit in human conduct.

Why I exist, nobody on earth is capable of telling me; but since I do exist, let me strive to give my existence a brightness and glory by setting for myself the loftiest goals I can reasonably hope to achieve. This is my religious view. Is there a kind of immortality that fits and augments such a view? To me there is, and I am joined in it by many of my fellow Unitarian Universalists. Interestingly enough, there is nothing new about this view. Since long before the time of Jesus it has been cultivated by some of the Chinese religions. It has been known and cherished by Buddhists for nearly twenty-five hundred years. It is belief in the immortality of character, of conduct and thought, of influence. In no way does this take from me the loneliness of dying. I know that dying is something I must face alone and with honest apprehension. But I have something to live and die for: not a personal survival, which would (and may) greatly surprise me, but a present and lasting immortality of influence in which I can and do believe.

Whatever such an observation may be worth, this is truly a democratic idea of immortality. It is an affirmation that everyone is immortal since whatever we do lives on somehow, somewhere, somewhen. The evil we do is as immortal as the good. There is an immortality of the ignoble as well as the noble, of the brutish as well as the sublime, of selfishness as well as generosity, of stupidity as well as wisdom. Immortality is complete. It encompasses the whole of what one is.

When we reason together about the truths and mysteries of life, there is one all-powerful reality: the humanity of which we are individual expressions is a product of the sense and nonsense of our forebears. We are the living immortality of those who came before us. In like manner, those who come after us will be the harvest of the wisdom and folly we ourselves are sowing. To let this reality permeate and drench our consciousness is to introduce ourselves to a grand conception of immortality which makes yearnings for some form of personal afterlife seem less consequential. So long as there is an ongoing stream of humanity I have life. This is my certain immortality. I am a renewed and renewing link in the chain of humanity. My memory and particularity are personal, transitory, finite; my substance is boundless and infinite. The immortality in which I believe affirms first and foremost my unity with humankind. My unity with humankind gives meaning to my desire to practice reverence for life. It is pride in being and pride in belonging to all being. I do not welcome the fact that dying waits for me. Yet, I know that I must die, and I will attempt to do so with all the fortitude and dignity circumstances and forethought permit.

Death, on the other hand, presents me with no special problem. It cannot be an evil condition. Of immortality, my mind and heart cherish the kind I have described. My religious community affirms rather than denies the freedom with which I have discussed these matters. As a Unitarian Universalist I grant that there may be a personal existence after death. Many of my coreligionists believe there is. No one can really tell. But there is one assured immortality, the realism of which we can know in advance. It connects us with every human being who shares this earth with us. It joins us in unbroken line with all who have mortally passed from this earth before us. It unites us with all who are yet to be born. By the glow of this idea of immortality, I have long aided and abetted Helen Caldicott's crusade against the nuclear arms race, and I resonate with her words: "It is time for people to rise to their full moral and spiritual height, to take the world on their shoulders like Atlas ... and to say *I* will save the earth. . . . No other generation has inherited this enormous responsibility and the privilege of saving all past and all future generations. Think of the variety of delicate butterflies; of the gorgeous birds, of the fish in the sea; of the flowers; of the proud lions and tigers and of the wondrous prehistoric elephants and hippopotamuses; think of what we are about to destroy" (*Missile Envy*).

For those of us who can no longer live under the spell of traditional beliefs in resurrections and personal afterlives, the larger message of immortality need not be lost. Fundamentally, it is a message of renewed, redeemed, ongoing life and of the wonder that our thoughts and deeds are our real immortality.

If Jesus Is the Answer

They pop into view all over the continent — signboards, billboards, and bumper stickers bearing the message "Christ Is the Answer." If Christ is the answer, what are the questions? An answer, unless it is preceded by a meaningful question, is not much of an answer. One of Steve Allen's old routines, "The Question Man," satirized the vacuity of quiz programs and games. Appearing as a seedy, rumpled professorial type, Allen provided the questions for people's answers. Behind the satire is a basic truth. It is frequently easier to supply answers than it is to ask the right questions. Unitarian Universalism is an "asking" religion, and unashamedly so. There are no qualms about asking what should be a very obvious question: How do we know who Jesus is or was?

The answer must be discovered in the writings about him, and these are the Gospels. Nothing is known of Jesus except what is found in them. All other literature of his time and place is lacking in a single, meaningful reference. The letters of Paul have much to say *about* Jesus, but Paul acknowledges that he never knew Jesus in the flesh. What Paul wrote was interpretation. If this is true of Paul, it is even more true of at least one of the Gospels, John. If Paul was far removed from the personality of Jesus, then John, according to most scholars, was even farther removed. So, what we have left to answer our question must be found in Matthew, Mark, and Luke. We know nothing about these books from any independent source, and we know little if anything about their authors. Scholars generally agree that the names, Matthew, Mark, and Luke, have meager historical credibility. Whatever validity these Gospels possess must be confirmed within the text of the books themselves. When we turn to an examination of the Gospel material, we find that in large part the three are identical, so that the whole material about Jesus is about one-third of what it seems to be. Most scholars believe that Matthew and Luke copied extensively from Mark and that what is distinctive in their accounts came from written recollections that have never been recovered. This suggests that Matthew and Luke had no first-hand knowledge of Jesus. But what about Mark? Did he know Jesus in the flesh? If he did, the acquaintanceship must have been distant. There is not a single reference in Mark to the appearance or mannerisms of Jesus, something that seems unlikely if the author had had contact with such an apparently vivid personality. We are forced to conclude that the author of Mark's Gospel could have known people who *did* know Jesus, and he may even have been a younger contemporary. Matthew and Luke wrote a generation later, and John nearly a century later.

Having taken this quick tour through the scholarly realms of New Testament study, we find some questions to be inescapable. How can a person be the answer about whom there is no first-hand knowledge, and very sparse second- or third-hand information? Historical knowledge may not be the only means of judging, but what other justifications are there for the claim that Jesus is the answer?

Intelligent, sensitive, dedicated people, who are fully aware of the implications of biblical scholarship, still say that Jesus is the answer, as they did when the World Council of Churches met in Vancouver in the summer of 1983. We, who are puzzled by this, owe it to ourselves to try to understand their position. One fruitful approach is to acquaint ourselves with how heavily Christian theologians lean on a Danish genius of the nineteenth century, Søren Kierkegaard, who probed the mysteries of faith through the existentialist technique of looking deeply within himself. By doing this, Kierkegaard was convinced that his inner self was a chaos of untruth, sinfulness, and alienation from God. If humans are created in the image of God, how can this be? Kierkegaard insisted that God dwells not within the human frame. Saving grace must come from outside. The deeper we probe into ourselves, the further we are from ultimate truth.

By looking to our own resources, we have widened the gulf between ourselves and God. Sin has conquered our precious free will. The more we struggle to pull ourselves up by our bootstraps to touch the reality of God, the more we sink into a slough of despond. Even a knowledge of God's love overwhelms us and makes us more hopelessly conscious of sin. The only answer is for God to take the initiative. God can do this in two ways. One is to lift humans to the level of God; the other is for God to accept the debasement of becoming human. Kierkegaard argued that the first course is unthinkable. He did not adequately explain why it is unthinkable, but he dismissed the possibility. The second choice is the only defensible one. God, said Kierkegaard, came over to humans by becoming human in the form of Jesus Christ.

This startling act is not without its drawbacks, according to Kierkegaard. The human mind is affronted, and the affront cuts in two directions. Jesus's claim to be the Christ/God is odiously offensive to human reason. Any such claim is insulting. At the same time, it is an attack on human reason to expect that God would dream of becoming human. The mind rebels at the absurdity of God becoming a carpenter whose fate is to die on a cross as a common criminal in the insignificant land of Palestine.

With genuine savor, Kierkegaard shaped the paradox and declared that only the love of God makes it possible for the mind to accept such an irrational truth. But in order to be a Christian, Kierkegaard concluded, you must crush reason and take a leap of faith. Thus, becoming a Christian is an agonizing experience that bears no resemblance to what Kierkegaard called the "perpetual Sunday twaddle about Christianity's ... sweet consolation." Kierkegaard's Christianity consists of no reasonable summons to tread conventional paths of public piety. It is an uncompromising repudiation of reason in favor of a shattering, transporting faith. This is what makes Jesus the answer, not whether scholarly examination of the Bible delineates and confirms his mission. It is all right for a Christian to be intellectually interested in rational studies of religion, but salvation is another matter. Without the leap of faith, there is no salvation. Jesus is the answer not in reason but in faith.

Kierkegaard sharpens the issue magnificently and makes the next question inescapable. Am I prepared to leave reason behind to go soaring into what he calls faith? The answer, obviously, is a resounding no. I have no argument with the notion that Kierkegaard was an authentic font of Christian theology, but he has failed to persuade me to abandon my mind. I *do* have a mind. It may not be an overly impressive one, but such as it is, it is mine. However I may have come to possess it—whether from God, or from genes and chromosomes, or from culture and education, or from a combination of all these and more—I am determined to make the best of it in my religious life. If rational intelligence is part of my given endowment, it is logically given to be exercised rather than exorcised. If Jesus is the answer only if I cast out my reasoning abilities, he cannot be the answer for me.

Fair enough, my orthodox friends may say. You cannot accept by a leap of faith that Jesus is the answer. What about his unsurpassed moral teachings? Can't your reason accept these as an authentic revelation of God's saving power?

Historically, Unitarian Universalists have professed reverence for the teachings of Jesus. In fact, an idealized interpretation of Jesus as teacher and prophet has characterized our development and still does. Some among us consider themselves to be true Christians, not in a Kierkegaardian sense, but in terms of the reverence in which they hold and desire to emulate the teachings of Jesus. In the last decade and a half, our ranks, Christian and non-Christian alike, have been deeply challenged by Christian liberation theology. Arising first in Latin America, then in the larger Third World, then among blacks, women, youth, and gays, liberation theology has mightily empowered Christian commitment to the poor, the dispossessed, the scorned, and the abused. To liberation theology, Christianity in its most fundamental impulse is a religion of the underdog, and Jesus is the supreme symbol of that impulse. In Jesus is found the ultimate person "for others" — the saving exemplar of total commitment, in love and sacrifice, to the struggles of one's fellow beings. Jesus is "the place to be." And the place of this Christ is in the midst of the struggle for justice, political empowerment, and peace. It is in the world, in the midst of human sin, suffering, and degradation, with the needy and oppressed.

If our Unitarian Universalist religion means anything, it means the right to choose this kind of identification with Jesus. Many of us have been moved by it. Still there are difficulties; not with the prophetic commitments of Christian liberation theology, but with the role assigned to the teachings of Jesus. If the teachings of Jesus are the answer, which teachings and which Jesus is meant? "Render unto Caesar that which is Caesar's, and unto God that which is God's" (Matthew 22). According to the Gospels, Jesus taught it, but where in it is encouragement to stand against the Caesars of this world?

An attentive reading of the Gospels can be an unnerving experience. When Jesus called for turning the other cheek, he seemed not to allow for compelling exceptions. There are many situations in which turning the other cheek is not only moral but highly practical conduct. On other occasions it might be a way of risking not only one's own safety but that of others as well. If I spotted a man about to detonate an explosive in a crowded Boston subway station, I would be inclined to try to stop him forcibly. Turning the other cheek has something less than universal application in struggles to overturn painful injustices.

It can be argued that Jesus believed in the ultimate conquest of good over evil and based his teaching on such a belief. I happen to believe that there is nothing inevitable about this. In fact, most of the good that counts is doggedly and forcefully implemented. What I am saying is simply that I am against turning the other cheek when it is stupid and unreasonable to do so. On the other hand, I recognize how plausible and effective turning the other cheek can be in a large percentage of the stresses that afflict ordinary human relations. I attempt, therefore, to practice it, subject to the guidance of reason and situation, and I honor Jesus for the advocacy of it. Then I remember that in another portion of the Gospels Jesus used excessively violent language against the Pharisees and Sadducees. No cheek turning there. Which was the real Jesus? Was he both or neither? "Do not think that I have come to bring peace, but a sword. For I have come to set a man against his father, and a daughter against her mother, and a daughter-in-law against her mother-in-law; and a man's foes will be those of his own household" (Matthew 10:34–36). Can this be the same Jesus who in the same Gospel is reported to have said: "Love your enemies...."?

The logical inference is that the true followers of Jesus will stir up hostilities even within their own families but will proceed to love the enemies they have made. In truth, there is no logic in a juxtaposition of these two teachings except the logic of anyone's human inconsistencies. But if these are two sides of Jesus's personality, which am I to accept as the answer?

Actually, what religious liberals generally have in mind when they speak of their reverence for the moral leadership of Jesus are his most apt and penetrating parables, plus that remarkable collection of sayings in Chapters 5, 6, and 7 of the Gospel of Matthew, known misleadingly as the Sermon on the Mount. I can warmly endorse the notion that these are moving and inspiring ethical teachings. I cannot, however, close my mind to other teachings attributed to Jesus, which strike me as being anything but ennobling. Taking the Gospel narratives as they stand, Jesus believed in hell. As you know, I do not myself feel that anyone who is deeply humane can believe in everlasting punishment. But Jesus as depicted in the Gospels did believe in it, and one finds his fury vented on those who would not heed his preaching—a mode of expression, some would say, that is not uncommon among preachers, but that does raise questions. We find the Gospels placing on Jesus's lips: "You serpents, you generation of vipers, how can you escape the damnation of hell?" To my mind, this is not the most admirable tone he might have taken.

The point I am trying to make, and it seems to me to be a very important one, is that the Jesus portrayed in the Gospels is an elusive figure, as Albert Schweitzer so amply demonstrated. What we really seem to mean when we say that the "spirit of Jesus" is the answer to our problems is that we would like to try to the best of our ability to live by the moral precepts we choose to identify with Jesus. Christian liberation theologians do it their way, and they have my empathy. The Jerry Falwells of this world do it their way, and they do not have my empathy. Many of my coreligionists identify with the moral goals Jesus represents to them, namely compassion, unselfishness, self-sacrifice, love, faithfulness, and goodwill. No one should be upset if I suggest that the admirable goals represented by this chosen idealization of Jesus can be duplicated in all of the world's great religions.

Jesus is, and will remain, an enduring idealization of much that religious liberals hold dear in the religious life. By the same token, religious liberals should be as anxious to avoid fuzzy thinking about Jesus as about other religious symbols. The book is not closed on questions and answers about Jesus. The Dead Sea Scrolls brought fresh excitement to the subject. Other finds of similarly provocative material may well turn up.

To me, the important thing about Jesus is not that he was *just* human, but that the human race is capable of producing him. And not him alone, but others like him. And not only in ancient times, but now.

Let Us Pray

Prayer is both a problem and a challenge to religious liberals. It must have been a problem to my parents, but not much of a challenge. The only prayer they taught me as a small child was the familiar "Now I lay me down to sleep . . ." I am satisfied that it did me no harm, but it took me many years to conquer negative feelings toward prayer and to find a constructive place for it in my religious life. I still experience waves of revulsion at the content of certain types of public prayer, but I can hear Robert Louis Stevenson with joy and inspiration: "The day returns and brings us the petty round of irritating concerns and duties. Help us . . . to perform them with laughter and kind faces; let cheerfulness abound with industry. Give us to go blithely on our business all this day, bring us to our resting beds weary and content and undishonored, and grant us in the end the gift of sleep."

This, I would say, is an eminently worthy prayer that anyone could repeat without feeling craven. Like John Tyndall, I think "solemnly of the feeling which prompts prayer. It is a power which I should like to see guided, not extinguished—devoted to practicable objects instead of wasted upon air." Prayer should trouble the conscientious religious liberal. In many of its customary forms, it is primitive, naïve, and frequently selfish. Who can attribute nobility to attempts to cajole and wheedle God into giving us what we personally want, or into bending the order of nature or history for our personal benefit? Huckleberry Finn was a classic practitioner of the kind of prayer that backlashes. His Aunt Polly gave him a fishing pole. She also told him that if he prayed hard enough, God would hear and respond. Huck took this literally. Several nights in a row he closeted himself in his room and prayed for some fishhooks. He did not receive them. Obviously, there was something wrong with the whole idea of prayer, so Huck gave it up.

This is a familiar problem. It illustrates the importance of the assumptions we make about prayer. If prayer is viewed as a method of getting what we want, as a kind of cosmic lever for prying personally desired answers out of the Almighty, then, like Huck, we are doomed to futility and frustration. Like him, we will renounce prayer as a snare and a delusion, and we would be quite right about this particular kind of praying.

But suppose we start from an entirely different assumption. Suppose we think of prayer not as a means of commandeering God's attention for our personal wants, but as an approach to the deepest truths about ourselves. Suppose we think of it as a way of shedding new light on our relations with others or with God. Suppose we think of it as an essential religious striving to touch truth and tap resources within and beyond ourselves. What then? Do not great possibilities open before us? I talked recently with a parishioner who was suffering from a series of devastating blows. "The temptation is overwhelming," she told me, "to believe that God has simply abandoned me. Then I remind myself that God doesn't move in and out of our lives, and that the real challenge for me is not to abandon God." There is a heap of wisdom in her words. I will never forget them.

There are many means for getting what we think we want in this world. Money is one. Prestige, power, and privilege are others. There are various kinds of "pull" we can exert. For adults as well as for children, sometimes a tantrum will produce favorable results. Political leverage can often accomplish wonders. Prayer is not like these. Rather, it is an effort to reach deep and to reach out and to *become* what we would like to be, and need to be, and ought to be. Proper prayer is not a petition to escape realities. It is an effort to face up to realities, to understand them, to deal with them. It is an expression of the desire to grow in spiritual stature, in courage, in strength, and in faith. The purpose of prayer is to transform those doing the praying, to lift them out of fear and selfishness into serenity, patience, determination, belonging. If we begin to approach prayer in this manner, it assumes an entirely new significance.

There are many recognitions of this kind of prayer. In an ancient and beautiful book, the *Theologica Germanica,* we read that our purpose in prayer is to "be to the eternal goodness what our own hands are to us." Each person has hidden energies that deserve to be released. Within all of us dwell imprisoned splendors of hope, aspiration, and spiritual transformation. In fact, this particular path of prayer has been worn by the passage, through the ages, of all sorts of men and women who have sought and found an open way to sustain religious truth. Jesus traveled it, and so did Buddha, Lao-tze, Phillis Wheatley, and Gandhi. This is a journey that may be taken by any. Each of the world's religions and races has contributed to our knowledge of the terrain. This inward excursion to the growth and transformation of the human spirit is one of the truest marks of the universality of religion. In spite of all the external differences of the faiths by which humans live, the inward pilgrimage is everywhere much the same. Aldous Huxley called it the perennial philosophy. Buddha named it the noble eightfold path. Others have called it simply "the way." On this journey no one need be separated from others by differences of doctrine. All are friends and companions.

We are first made aware of our need for a deepening of the inward life in various ways. Awareness may arise from a haunting sense of dissatisfaction with ourselves as we are. Or, we may become bored and weary with too much surface activity, which leaves little or no time for thought, reflection, or meditation. We may feel that there must be more comprehensive meanings to life than those we have so far discovered. Our lives may receive a severe shock or a whole series of them, shaking us to the foundations; so we pause and take stock. We ask questions about what we are doing and why we are doing it. We make an effort to find out what our lives should mean, what they do mean, and what they could mean.

Here, in this process of self-examination, the sifting and judging of our desires go on. Here we can slowly learn what is one of the first and deepest lessons of religious growth: that the requirements of love, justice, peacemaking, and truth may well run contrary to some of our personal desires and inclinations. The profoundest fulfillment of our lives is *not* to be found in getting what we think we want, but in giving what is needed. Here we are made humble and eventually wiser. Until we have experienced this process, our religion has not really begun to ripen. It does not much matter how it comes about — in church or out, verbally or silently, invoking God by name or not. What matters is that it *does* happen, and that when it happens we know we are involved in the first, tentative steps of a genuine prayer experience.

Quite rightly, psychologists tell us that these initial, hesitant breakthroughs are fraught with dangers. Self-searching, without positive steps, can lead to self-abasement, discouragement, and despair. We must push beyond our all-too-evident weaknesses and failings. We must find and recognize the strengths we have, and our hopes. This is the seeking aspect of prayer, only it must be a seeking that is disciplined and cleansed of narcissism. As Phillips Brooks expressed it in a sermon: "Do not pray for easy lives. Pray to be stronger. . . . Do not pray for tasks equal to your powers. Pray for powers equal to your tasks." Once entered upon this inward journey, we have an obligation to seek the strength and courage equal to great tasks. This is the positive part of prayer, its outreach. Much honesty of soul is required. There is plenty of space for centering but none for sentimentality in this kind of praying.

Finally, there is the aspect of patience. Lives conditioned to constant activity and diversion do not readily appreciate the value and necessity of simply waiting in silence, in expectation, in appreciation of things to come. One of the most colorful and promising dimensions of the human spirit is its ability to experience sudden flashes of insight and clarity. All at once a sense of direction emerges out of chaos. Formidable obstacles melt away. A decision is suddenly plain. Norbert Wiener used to tell his students that solutions to seemingly insoluble mathematical problems frequently came to him in the dead of night when his mind was presumably at rest.

Sometimes we seem to have nothing to offer but our perplexity, our indecision, our confusion. Then out of the silence, the waiting, the expectation, and the appreciation of things to come, a light breaks through. Is a prayer answered? Yes, but not in a supernatural or miraculous sense. It is simply true that some of our most important moral decisions and spiritual discoveries come upon us with surprise and wonder when we are receptive and ready to use them.

These, then, are aspects of prayer that recommend themselves to a person like myself, who does not hesitate to register his distaste for prayers seeking a winning lottery ticket, victory, safety, fishhooks, or the discomfiting of enemies.

Prayer based on self-examination, on an honest ordering of our minds, and on the ability to wait in expectation and appreciation of untapped and unrevealed spiritual resources, is, to me, prayer at its best. In the words of Lon Ray Call: 'Prayer doesn't change things, but it changes people and people change things. Let us pray."

Index

Adams, James Luther, 101-102, 105, 109

Adams, John, 135

Adams, John Quincy, 135

Addams, Jane, 5, 130; *Democracy and Social Ethics*, 129

Addison, Reverend Stanley, 22

Adler, Alfred, 96

Agnostic, 40

Alcott, Louisa May, 135

Allen, Steve, 160

Alliance to End Repression, 136-137

All Souls Unitarian Church (New York City), 37

All Souls Unitarian Universalist Church (Indianapolis), 31

American Anthropological Association, 94

American Revolution, 63

American Society for the Prevention of Cruelty to Animals, 135

American Unitarian Association, 62, 85

Androcentrism, 104

Anne, Queen, of England, 66

Anthony, Susan B., 43, 83, 135

Apostles' Creed, 38

Arlington Street Church (Boston), 62

Athanasian Creed, 51

Athens, ancient, 47, 48, 94-95

Atonement: notion of vicarious, 52; treatise on, 69

Augustine, Saint, 51-52, 53, 95, 97

Babbitt, Irving, 107

Backus, E. Burdette, 42

Bacon, Francis, 105

Baldwin, James, 141

Ballou, Hosea, 68-71; *Treatise on Atonement*, 69

Bancroft, George, 135

Baptists, 83

Barton, Clara, 136

Beacon Press, 141, 144

Beatitudes, 49

Bellows, Henry Whitney, 39, 136

Benevolent Fraternity of Unitarian Churches, 143

Benneville, George de, 66-67, 68

Bergh, Henry, 135

Bible, 52; use of, in religious education of children, 113-122 *passim*

Biddle, John, 59

Black Affairs Council, 79

Black empowerment, 79-80

Black Panthers, 136

Black Unitarian Universalist Caucus, 79-80

Bohr, Niels, 2

Book of Acts, 12, 33, 34

Bowden, Margaret, 178

PRAISE FOR NATALIE MACLEAN'S

UNQUENCHABLE!

"A rollicking travelogue of her journeys around the world in search of the best vino that won't break the bank." —*The Washington Post*

"There are very few people in the wine world that I think 'get it,' and Natalie is one of those people that brings more fun to a buttoned-up and stodgy game." —**Gary Vaynerchuk, author of** *The Thank You Economy* and host of *Wine Library TV*

"Highly educational and witty. Neophytes and professionals will drink this up." —*Wine Enthusiast Magazine*

"I learned so much from Natalie MacLean's humorous, literate, lively adventures in search of great buys in wine. Fun to read, her book introduces you to many winemakers who could be in novels, to out-of-the-way places you want to add to your travel list, and, most of all, to an appreciation of vino as integral to the joy of living. I'm restocking my racks with her smart suggestions." —**Frances Mayes, author of** *Under the Tuscan Sun*

"One of the best wine books I've read recently. . . . I enjoyed it so much I read it in an afternoon—and then rushed right out and bought several of her suggested wines. It would make a terrific holiday gift for the wine lover in your life." —**Victoria von Biel, Forbes.com**

"If you're looking for unpretentious, forthright wine advice, look no farther. In *Unquenchable!*, Natalie MacLean travels the globe with a curious palate and a meager pocketbook to search for the world's best wine values. The result is a delightful adventure—part travel story, part wine journal—that will convince even the most cynical wine lover that there are still affordable treasures to be had." —**Dr. Deborah Harkness, author of** *A Discovery of Witches* **and** blog editor of *Good Wine Under $20*

continued . . .

"MacLean is a charming and disarming author, freely admitting to her love of a bargain (so long as it is delicious) and the intoxicating fun of having wine in her glass. Verdict: a light, informative adventure in wine appreciation that should have broad appeal. Highly recommended."   —*Library Journal*

"Our book of the year is Natalie MacLean's *Unquenchable!* . . . the writing is both entertaining and informative. Each chapter ends with suggested wines, food, and additional reading."

—**Tom Marquardt and Patrick Darr**, *The Annapolis Capital Gazette*

"Natalie MacLean has done it again! . . . A treasure trove of worldly wines that are kind to our pocketbook and keep your taste buds tantalized. All this wine is wrapped up into a book filled with adventures."

—*Eat Love Savor* **magazine**

"A must for those seeking to learn about affordable wine through the entertaining adventures of a vital, charismatic wine expert."

—**Mark Oldman**, *Drink Bravely*

"It's a breezy, fun exploration of wine-producing regions that price-conscious shoppers should get to know."   —*The Oregonian*

"Natalie pulls us along happily into her wide world of wine—you are right there with her at the table or in an underground cellar. The conversations are lively and the wine flows. And when a winemaker pours a glass for her, you might look around wondering, 'Where's mine?' She made me itchy to get on a plane and hit the wine route myself."

—**Kermit Lynch, award-winning wine merchant and author of** *Adventures on the Wine Route*

"Today's top culinary gift pick. . . . Natalie writes with such a refreshingly straightforward manner that she makes the reader feel as though they are being transported into each environment and tasting room right along with her. . . . Educational and enlightening."   —*Minneapolis Examiner*

"A book for people who like to get lost in good stories (and pick up some bargain wine-hunting tips along the way)."   —*Chicago Sun-Times*

"MacLean offers up her personal winery tasting experiences followed by tips for seeking out wine bargains in various regions. You know, the typical practical wine advice setup. Only these wines, and the prose, are good."

—LAWeekly.com

"There is plenty to take away from her inspired recommendations, food pairings, list of her favorite value wines and wineries, plus plenty of pointers that will deepen the reader's drinking pleasure." —WinesWorld.com

"MacLean has an engaging style that makes the book fun to read."

—*The San Jose Mercury News*

"Natalie knows whereof she speaks, and does so eloquently. Her tone is both playful and illuminating and liberally sprinkled with humor. *Unquenchable!* is most highly recommended." —*Albuquerque Wine Examiner*

"One of the most gifted, entertaining, and downright funny wine writers to put pen to paper." —*Dayton Daily News*

"Natalie MacLean's *Unquenchable* is one of this year's most entertaining—and genuinely useful—wine books." —*The Louisville Courier-Journal*

"Natalie's prose is passionate, witty, honest, and informative. This entertaining read is a must for wine lovers." —VintageCellars.com

"Natalie generously brings us into her fun-filled world of great discoveries and fascinating travels; in fact, this book doubles as a beautifully written novel."

—**Rose Levy Beranbaum**

"With fully extracted prose that lingers on the palate, Natalie MacLean has wisely headed off the beaten path to get at the essence of wine. As she probes the elusive intersection of quality and value, we are lucky sidekicks on her well-observed journey through the landscapes, people, stories, and—let's just say it—buzzes that make wine so wonderful."

—**Benjamin Wallace, author of** *The Billionaire's Vinegar*

UNQUENCHABLE!

A TIPSY QUEST
FOR THE WORLD'S BEST
BARGAIN WINES

Natalie MacLean

A PERIGEE BOOK

A PERIGEE BOOK
Published by the Penguin Group
Penguin Group (USA) Inc.
375 Hudson Street, New York, New York 10014, USA
Penguin Group (Canada), 90 Eglinton Avenue East, Suite 700, Toronto, Ontario M4P 2Y3, Canada
(a division of Pearson Penguin Canada Inc.) • Penguin Books Ltd., 80 Strand, London WC2R 0RL,
England • Penguin Group Ireland, 25 St. Stephen's Green, Dublin 2, Ireland (a division of Penguin
Books Ltd.) • Penguin Group (Australia), 250 Camberwell Road, Camberwell, Victoria 3124, Australia
(a division of Pearson Australia Group Pty. Ltd.) • Penguin Books India Pvt. Ltd., 11 Community
Centre, Panchsheel Park, New Delhi—110 017, India • Penguin Group (NZ), 67 Apollo Drive,
Rosedale, Auckland 0632, New Zealand (a division of Pearson New Zealand Ltd.) • Penguin Books
(South Africa) (Pty.) Ltd., 24 Sturdee Avenue, Rosebank, Johannesburg 2196, South Africa

Penguin Books Ltd., Registered Offices: 80 Strand, London WC2R 0RL, England

While the author has made every effort to provide accurate telephone numbers, Internet addresses, and
other contact information at the time of publication, neither the publisher nor the author assumes any
responsibility for errors, or for changes that occur after publication. Further, the publisher does not have
any control over and does not assume any responsibility for author or third-party websites or their content.

PUBLISHING HISTORY
Perigee hardcover edition / November 2011
Perigee trade paperback edition / September 2012

Perigee trade paperback ISBN: 978-0-399-53780-6

The Library of Congress has cataloged the Perigee hardcover edition as follows:

MacLean, Natalie.
Unquenchable : a tipsy quest for the world's best bargain wines / Natalie Maclean.
p.   cm.
"A Perigee Book."
Includes index.
ISBN 978-0-399-53707-3 (hardback)
1. Wine and wine making.   I. Title.
TP548.M1953   2011
641.2'1—dc23   2011024632

PRINTED IN THE UNITED STATES OF AMERICA

10 9 8 7 6 5 4 3 2 1

Most Perigee books are available at special quantity discounts for bulk purchases for sales
promotions, premiums, fund-raising, or educational use. Special books, or book excerpts, can also
be created to fit specific needs. For details, write: Special Markets, Penguin
Group (USA) Inc., 375 Hudson Street, New York, New York 10014.

For my mother, Ann;
my husband, Andrew; and my son, Rian:
I raise my glass to you all.

CONTENTS

A NOSE FOR A BARGAIN

Opening Thoughts

THE QUESTION I'M asked most often: "What's your favorite wine?" My answer: "The one someone else pays for." The second question I'm asked is, "Can you recommend a great wine that costs less than $5?" Answer: "Not unless all you want is a wet tongue."

When I'm not in a smart-ass mood, my answer to the first question depends on what I'm eating, who I'm with, and what the occasion is. But I never forget price. The reality is that wine from regions such as Tuscany, Bordeaux, and Napa Valley have become too expensive for most of us. Yet we still want that fleshy fruit pleasure that wine gives us rather than settling for tasteless plonk.

Tasteless plonk, of course, brings to mind memories of homemade wine. When I was a student, I eagerly dipped a boy-band mug into a bathtub filled with "shablie." After I graduated, I covertly doused the already well-watered fern at a friend's house with her "True Love Chardonnay." Years later, after I became a wine writer, I thought that my Château de Haute House Hooch days were over. Alas, they were not.

Occasionally, dinner hosts serve their own homemade concoctions and lock eyes with me expectantly. I usually try to escape with half-spoken comments such as, "This is a delightful wine" out loud, and then under my breath, "if I were shackled in Kingston Penitentiary." Or I might say, "This has a smooth texture," mentally adding, "making it an acceptable antiseptic to clean a chest wound before knife surgery in the Brazilian rain forest." Had I written a fancy-pants tasting note, it would have been: Under an initial layer of rotting roadside tomatoes, I detect nuances of a burning Fiat tire floating on a lake of rancid olive oil. Pair this wine with nasty divorce settlements or grand jury appearances.

Somewhere between Super Tuscans and vinous Tang crystals, there are delicious wines that we can still afford. But while most people believe that they can taste the difference between a wine priced at $5 and one at $50, it gets trickier when the difference is between $15 and $30. And since most of us would prefer to shell out $15 rather than $30, one of the missions of this book is to demystify wine pricing in relation to quality. Some regions have natural advantages that make winemaking inexpensive, whether that's climate or cheap land and labor. Other regions are still establishing their reputations and must keep their prices low to be competitive with better-known wines.

So why even bother searching for today's great cheap wines? Why not just be happy with whatever glass of vino is in front of you? Well, most of us don't drink just for the buzz: we want better taste experiences. Many nostalgic hedonists recall our first good wines; their taste can transport us back to a beach, a first apartment, a small bistro. Some people spend their lives trying to re-create the intensity of that first taste. But because our palates mature as they age, the wine has to be much better as we get older to achieve a peak experience.

My nose for a bargain was honed early in life. I grew up on the

East Coast with my mother, who separated from my alcoholic father when I was two. Money was tight, and we moved from one town to another frequently as she took up teaching posts at various elementary schools. We lived in rented trailers and basement apartments. I wore bread bags in my leaking boots, and we rummaged through the piles of secondhand clothing at a store called Frenchies, delighted when we found something our size. At night, we joked that we were going "to mattress" since our beds didn't have box springs or legs. Our weekly treat was to walk down to the local bowling alley on Friday evening and buy a chocolate sponge cake. In the morning, I'd look for lost change on the sidewalk.

So I know there are good deals and great experiences to be had if you're willing to search for them. As a mongrel taster, I know that even inexpensive wine is one of the most complex natural substances we consume, with more than a thousand compounds that contribute to its fragrance. The human nose can smell more than two thousand aromas, some at minute concentrations (think of a single drop in the equivalent of three Olympic-sized swimming pools). So with all the varying smells and their intensities, there are millions of unique combinations. In wine, such complexity is a stunning triumph of diversity, but like music, all the elements have to work together or the result is just cacophony.

Rich, layered experiences hold our attention, whether they're books, paintings, or wines. Our minds grapple to understand them as our senses play along their touch points. But who says that only expensive wines can be complex? I've tasted many inexpensive wines with flavors and aromas that lingered long after I swallowed, giving my mind time to wheel back and forth over my sensory impressions. It's simply snobbery to suggest that only pricey bottles have the unexplained magic that leaves us reaching for the words to express what we're smelling, tasting, feeling.

As I discuss these issues in this book, my views will be influenced by the type of writer (and drinker) I am. Some critics pride themselves on their "objectivity" and don't use first-person narrative. Not me. I'm neurotically personal, prone to tangential digressions and Bridget Jones–like overreactions. I fall in love too easily with people, places, and wines.

While some wine critics are afraid of vulnerability and intimacy with their readers, for me, these are the foundations of trust. I openly admit that I like to drink wine—and I like the buzz. I have personal preferences, and I make mistakes. In these ways, I am like my readers, and I don't hold myself at a professional distance from them. We all share a glass around the kitchen table, even if it is virtual. That's how today's "experts" operate: with candor and closeness that's as informal as your next tweet on Twitter or post on Facebook. That's also why I get about two hundred emails a day from my website readers at www.nataliemaclean.com.

My goal isn't to dumb down wine, because I think it's endlessly fascinating. I believe that it can be complex without being complicated. But some people misinterpret my approach. One website of male critics invited me to join as an afterthought just before launch, thinking that they needed some estrogen balance. I remember the mock-up screen they emailed to me. The men were described as respected, thoughtful, analytical. My description? I was fun and lively; in other words, the good-time wine gal there to provide blond relief in a sea of black stubble.

I was a competitive Highland dancer for fifteen years, placing fifth in the world championships behind four men from Scotland. Highland dancing is one of the few sports in which men and women compete with each other without restrictions. Traditionally, these dances were the preserve of military men who performed them as physical training drills to prepare for battle. The names of these dances still speak to that legacy: Sword Dance, Sailor's Hornpipe, Highland Laddie, and Wilt Thou Go to the Barracks, Johnnie.

Years later, my MBA class was more than 80 percent men. When I graduated, I joined a computer company as the marketing manager. At techie trade shows, I was sometimes mistaken for one of the "booth babes," models hired to draw prospective male buyers into the demo area. And now here I am writing about wine. That said, many of my strongest supporters have been men, not least my husband, Andrew, and my son, Rian. And I've never regretted being one of the few women in the room—it's a competitive advantage to be underestimated.

I guess I'm drawn to these fields because I've always been a geek of one sort or another, which goes along with being socially awkward and shy. I bond with other geeks who share the same passion; it helps me make connections that don't come to me naturally. That obsessive-compulsive hunger for one thing also keeps me from rusting.

Still, I have a terrible tendency to interrupt other people's thoughts (even my own). I often say awkward things that just hang in the air like moldy laundry. I frequently trip over my own cleverness and have to recalibrate back to humility. My sense of adventure and my short attention span combine to make me vilely allergic to the comprehensive, encyclopedia-style approach to wine. I'm a sucker for a good glass of vino—and an even bigger fool for a great story about it. I just think that you should know what you're getting into with this book.

We wine writers tend to be obsessive souls. How else can a person stay fascinated throughout a career with just one drink? Compare us to food writers: Over their lives, they'll encounter thousands of ingredients and ways of combining and cooking them. Wine, by contrast, is just fermented grapes. But it engages our primary senses—smell, taste, touch—in a way that is both hedonistic and cerebral.

That's why I've spent the past several years traipsing around the world, visiting wineries, tasting their offerings, and searching for the world's best cheap wines: one terrific bottle for each night of the week, plus an extra one for Sunday lunch. It's been an unquenchable journey to learn about new people, new places, and new wines. The narrative is as familiar as Arthur's quest for the grail and as naive as the little bird's plaintive search for the affirmative in *Are You My Mother?*

Inevitably, the emails will flood my inbox demanding how I could possibly leave out this region or that producer. But somehow, the subtitle "147 Cheap Wines to Drink Before You Die" just didn't seem as catchy. In each of the eight regions I explored, I visited between thirty and forty wineries, and I've tasted thousands more wines from each place. Still, I don't claim to have found all of the world's best value wines; I've just selected a handful that I heartily recommend. I hope you'll also find, as I did, that the search is as pleasurable as the answer—and that just a taste will leave you thirsting for more.

BEYOND THE ADVENTURES

THIS BOOK EXPLORES the subject of wine in a way that's relatively timeless, a whirlwind tour of the history, geography, and people who make it and drink it. It's as much a travelogue and memoir as it is a guide to wine. For those of us with a pragmatic bent, I've also added a takeaway section at the end of each chapter under the title "Field Notes from a Wine Cheapskate" in which I include the following:

- **INSIDER TIPS:** A summary of some interesting (and obscure) bits of wisdom that I gleaned from my travels.

- **WINERIES VISITED:** I feature about three wineries per region, sometimes fewer. These generally represent only the highlights of my visits to each country, but are selected based on where I found the most fascinating places and characters along with the best value wines.

- **BEST VALUE WINES:** The list of "value" wines that I tasted on this trip doesn't include the vintages for each wine, since they may no longer be available. However, these wineries are consistently good producers, so the odds are that their latest vintages will be as tasty as those I enjoyed. While I also tried a number of pricey bottles to get the full scope of each region and to anchor the value range, I haven't included them in this list. Rather, this is a brief guide to good labels from producers you can trust. Although it's impossible to select just one winner from so many terrific wines in each region, I have put an asterisk (*) next to the wine that I'd pick first for my own dinner each night.

- **Top Value Producers:** This list comprises more great value producers from the region, beyond those I visited for the book. Some producers have other brands or labels that I've listed separately.

- **Terrific Pairings:** I've included only a few highlights of what I consider good pairings for selected wines in each chapter. (If these whet your appetite, I also offer thousands of wine and food pairings in my Drinks Matcher tool, www.nataliemaclean .com/matcher.)

- **Resources and Related Reading:** I've included a short list of books, websites, and blogs, both of specific relevance to the wines discussed and to the region visited.

The world of wine is constantly changing, with new vintages, techniques, and producers coming onto the scene every year. So rather than trying to update this book as rapidly as things change, I publish a website that covers, among other topics, reviews of bottles in stores now, updates on the latest news in the wine world, and what your fellow drinkers think of the wines they've tried recently. Read the book for the adventure stories and then visit these web pages:

- My picks of top-value wines from each region in liquor stores now, including my tasting notes, scores, bottle shots, and food matches. You can create your own shopping list: www.nataliemaclean.com/winepicks.

- The website addresses, contact information, pictures, and other information for the wineries in this book, including my list of top-value producers at the end of each chapter, in this Worldwide Winery Directory: www.nataliemaclean.com/wineries.

- Recipes for the dishes I enjoyed along the journey, contributed by the winemakers and winery chefs, all paired with the local wines: www.nataliemaclean.com/food.

- A food-and-wine matching tool that you can use to find pairings for any dish. You can also post it on your own website or blog: www.nataliemaclean.com/matcher.

- A photo album of pictures from each chapter of the landscape, winemakers, and food: www.nataliemaclean.com/book.

- Suggested questions and discussion points for book clubs, along with tips on organizing an informal wine tasting for your group: www.nataliemaclean.com/book.

- My blog (www.nataliemaclean.com/blog), Facebook (www.facebook.com/natdecants), and Twitter (www.twitter.com/nataliemaclean), where I post updates on my latest travels, wine-tasting events, and other news.

- Mobile apps for iPhone, iPod Touch, BlackBerry, Droid, and other smartphones, with all of the information above: www.nataliemaclean.com/mobileapp.

I'd love to hear from you. Please email me at natdecants@natalie maclean.com when you have a moment, and we'll raise a virtual glass together.

Cheers,
Natalie

UNQUENCHABLE!

ONE

SUNDAY

The Wine Wizards of Oz

"WATCH OUT FOR the snakes," my friend Robyn said when she heard I was going to Australia.

The what?

"Nine of the ten deadliest snakes in the world are in Australia," she replied, proud as a quiz show contestant.

I changed the subject to our dinner plans.

Now, as I fly over the Barossa Valley, Robyn's comment comes back to me. I squint down at the vast dry biscuit of russet earth but don't see anything slithering on the ground, and I comfort myself with my usual self-delusions that snakes don't eat grapes.

The Barossa Valley is just forty-five minutes northeast of the city of Adelaide, located on the south coast. It's Australia's best-known wine region, and produces its most iconic wine: shiraz. The grape actually originated in the Rhône Valley of France, where it's called syrah and has been growing since 500 BCE. It's usually the leading grape in the blends of wines such as hermitage and Côte Rôtie. Although shiraz and syrah are the same grape, various wine-producing regions have chosen one name or the other. Australians went with shiraz, a variation on the original name they had for these vines—scyras—that was easier to pronounce, whereas California tends to use syrah because many feel their style is more European.

Shiraz thrives here on the planet's most arid continent because the vine is so vigorous that it needs hardship to produce concentrated wine. What little rain falls in the Barossa evaporates quickly, and temperatures can average in the high nineties for weeks on end. Shiraz transforms these dry furnace conditions into the lyrical, liquid voice of this sun-drenched land.

This "overnight sensation" began in 1832, when a progressive governor, James Busby, planted the first scyras (shiraz) vines in the country in the Hunter Valley near Sydney. He believed that local wine would be less intoxicating than the rum that the early settlers, mostly convicts and gold rush speculators, brought with them.

However, the Barossa Valley was mostly settled by Lutheran families, led by their pastors who had fled religious persecution in Silesia, in what is now part of Poland. Each family received a grant of thirty acres, and many started planting shiraz vines around 1842. Ownership was stable through the generations, and so these are among the oldest shiraz vines in the world.

Winemaking in Australia has continued uninterrupted ever since, thanks to several factors. Unlike North America, the Aussies never implemented Prohibition, and the continent's isolation spared most Oz vintners from having to replant acres of vineyards lost to the vine louse phylloxera that destroyed both North American and European vineyards in the 1800s and 1900s. However, Down Under wines weren't always popular or even good. Between the 1960s and the 1980s, they were mostly sweet and fortified—connoisseurs described them as tasting like alcoholic jam in an oak box. Their dubious quality was parodied in a Monty Python skit that featured Eric Idle, surrounded by men in cork-fringed hats, describing the "Château Nuits St. Wagga-Wagga" as smelling like a "kangaroo's aahmpit."

Today, however, with modern refrigeration and other advances, Australia has harnessed the heat and makes spectacularly tasty wines at incredibly low prices. Producers there don't have to fight cold and mildew as they do in cool climates. They're also incredibly free from the government regulation that restricts many European countries, such as France and Italy, from using certain grapes or making different blends. That allows Australian winemakers to use the grapes from the region that fared best in a particular vintage so that their wines are consistently good and low priced. Even most New World countries don't draw on grapes as far afield as do the Australians—it would be like labeling a wine as coming from "Western North America."

As a result, these wines have jumped to the number one or two market position in many countries. As a Scot who comes from generations of hard-drinking penny-pinchers, this pleases me immensely. It means that I can buy four bottles rather than one. It also means that I can pass off these wines as being much more expensive than they really are when giving them as gifts or serving them at dinner parties. Let me be clear: being cheap is in my DNA, but I'm also a hedonist after great taste. These are usually opposing forces, but that's easily solved if you travel around the world for five years and taste 15,267 wines. (I've done that so you don't have to.)

I'm also starting with Australian wines in this book, especially the robust shiraz, because it's ideal for a Sunday dinner of roast beef or meat lovers' pizza: comfort wine for comfort food. If you're like me and skip the introduction in books, let me say quickly that this is how I'm organizing these chapters: I start with a wine for Sunday dinner, progress through each day of the week, and end with one for Sunday lunch. The Barossa Valley is home to many of Australia's best producers fit for the Sunday table: Peter Lehmann, Grant Burge, Yalumba, Penfolds, Wolf Blass—and yes, those friggin' snakes, I remind myself as I jump into my rental car and, absurdly, lock the door.

A few hours later, as I cross the manicured lawn of the Wolf Blass winery, it occurs to me that many people don't realize there actually is a man after whom the winery is named. They think of Wolf Blass as another brand character, like Duncan Hines or Betty Crocker. But just as there is a Calvin Klein and Ralph Lauren, there's also a Wolf Blass—and no marketing team could ever invent a man so colorful.

He's barreling toward me now, trailed by an entourage of paid optimists. "Aren't you a supreme cookie!" he exclaims, beaming up at me as he grabs my hand and forearm with both of his. Well into his seventies, Wolf's a trim five-foot-three with mischievous dark eyes and pepper gray hair. He has the energy of a man half his age and twice his height. He wears one of his trademark bow ties (and has seven hundred of them, I'm told): a fire-engine red number that matches his banker's suspenders and arm band. He doesn't let go of my arm as he steers me over to the Wolf Blass museum, his worried PR people in tow. (Their boss is known for his stream of unedited thoughts about wine, money, business, friendship, sex, and success.)

Wolfgang Franz Otto Blass was born on the move. In 1934, in the German state of Saxony, his mother barely made it through the hospital doors before he arrived. Even as a child, "Wolfie" was a natural performer, though much of his childhood was grim. Inside the museum, Wolf stops in front of a black-and-white photo of three stone-faced children—himself and his two brothers. Growing up in postwar East Germany was "a bloody nightmare," he tells me. There were few jobs and less money.

"People were so desperate, they traded their watches for bread,"

Wolf explains, adjusting his Rolex. "I became a street fighter whose main concern was getting tucker." That's Australian for *food*, and I'm starting to tune into his carefree mangling of German and Australian, which comes out as a matey drawl in the middle and ends with a militant clip. Germany produced him, but Australia made him.

"Mother told me, 'Go into agriculture; at least you'll get something to eat,'" he says. "So I started to apprentice at the winery of a friend—he was a tyrant, you know, a real Nazi! But I learned inch by inch. Took me three years, very slow. Best terrible experience of my life."

Working with wine was his ticket out of Germany. "I wanted to get away, overseas, anywhere. So I went to France. I don't like the French." (One publicist looks uncomfortably at another one.) "But I learned how to make sparkling wine in Champagne."

In 1961, he jumped at a job offer from Penfolds and immigrated to Australia with a few hundred dollars in his pocket. "I was a bad employee because I always thought I could do things better than management could." After a few years, he became a traveling consultant to a number of wineries before opening his own in 1973.

"In those days, I did it all: I made the wine, I sold the wine," he says, as we look at a photo of Wolf in his early twenties, with a slicked-back ducktail haircut, sitting on the hood of a convertible. He became known as much for the way he sold his wine as for the way he made it. At baseball games, for instance, he'd chat with the television cameramen, telling them he'd be in the crowd with his winery sign. Every time they focused on the sign, there was a case of wine for them.

"So the ball is hit out of the park. It's a home run—up, up, up . . . everyone's watching it except the cameraman because he's found my sign. Bloody cunning!" he says approvingly at the memory.

He also used to have himself paged over the intercom system at airports so that shoppers in the duty-free stores would hear the name Wolf Blass, and he'd conduct impromptu wine tastings on planes with captive audiences. He was one of the first in the industry to realize that the winemaker is integral to the marketing of the product, the human face of the wine.

"People do business with people, not products. They want to put a face on the bottle. I went to every bloomin' state, every black-tie dinner, every bloody radio station," he says, his eyes twinkling like stage lights. "In one speech, I told them I didn't think Australian wine was worth more than $10. I told them, 'I'm going back home: you don't deserve good wine!'" But his chronic dissatisfaction for the status quo made him stay and create his first namesake wine priced at $15.

"I can't stand to lose," he says, as we walk over to a large glass cabinet filled with his trophies from wine competitions. Critics of Australian wine shows say that just about every wine gets a medal, and the heftiest ones win these sensory weight-lifting contests. However, Wolf believes that the competitions have raised the overall quality of Australian wine. Winemakers often share their knowledge at the gatherings, allowing the industry to fix faults and improve techniques.

In the early 1970s, Wolf was frustrated by a losing streak with his wines. A friend advised him to ask the judge's advice (rather than punching him out). The judge taught Wolf how to adjust his palate to "the winning formula." His new approach helped him win the country's top winemaking prize, the Jimmy Watson Trophy, three years in a row, in 1974, 1975, and 1976—a record never equaled before or since.

In his acceptance speech, Wolf declared that his wine could "make strong women weak and weak men strong. It's a bloody aphrodisiac: I can prove it because I'm testing it on myself!" His comments were in the newspapers the next day. After his third Jimmy Watson Trophy, he and winemaker Chris Hatcher celebrated late into the night and woke up together in the same hotel room the next day, much to their manly chagrin, even though they were fully clothed.

"Without proof of success at the wine shows, I would have been a nobody. No medals, no job," he says, clearly moved by his own words. He has little patience for producers who don't enter their wines into competitions, but complain about them. "That's like having a racehorse in the paddock and never racing it. If you're not in the competition, you shouldn't comment on those who are."

In his private tasting room, he's now pouring us a sample of that "winning formula": a blend of cabernet sauvignon and shiraz. Power and elegance dance in the glass: Fred Astaire shiraz and Ginger Rogers cabernet. Wolf believes that blending is a large part of Australia's success in the international wine market, since it offers the flexibility to choose the best ingredients. Australia is also famous for its "GSM" blends: grenache for lift and fruitiness, shiraz for body and flesh, and mourvèdre for spice and structure.

"We are consistent year after year. Consistency is quality. It's like the signature dish of a restaurant: you want it to be the same every time you go. It creates loyalty. We make wines the consumer likes to drink—they buy the brand. Maybe the wines aren't for fanatics; they might find them too . . . symmetrical. But we are an extremely safe brand, consumers depend on us. It's a big responsibility when there's seventy million bottles with your bloody name on them."

I can tell that this is a spiel Wolf has delivered many times to many audiences as he rolls on enthusiastically. "I'm proud of our success: we get down people's throats! Too many precious winemakers think commercial success means the wine is no good. But what's no good is to be a loser. Manchester United: seventeen times champions. Bloody beautiful!

"Shiraz is all about full, fat flavor. You can't have high-acid wines that are a commercial success: people won't drink the bloody stuff. The everyday punter doesn't understand it," he says with a significant rise of his eyebrows, as though we've come to a mutual unspoken agreement.

"Shit. Don't write that."

The senior PR woman gives me an apologetic what-can-you-do smile. I return her smile as sweetly as I can.

Wolf changes the subject as quickly as a river finds a path around a boulder, moving on to his marketing innovations, such as his different label colors to distinguish each wine. "Most people didn't know their bloody grapes, and they didn't go into the wine store describing the grapes they wanted. They'd say I want the Wolf Blass yellow label or gray or whatever." The yellow label was inspired by the yellow jerseys of the Australian football team; gray was for the wolf; red came from a trip to China, where it's a lucky color; and green was "for the Irish." Black is reserved for the company's best blended wines, and platinum is for its flagship Barossa shiraz.

Consumers responded enthusiastically: his $17 Yellow Label Cabernet became the bestselling red wine in North America, at least until Casella Wines' $12 Yellow Tail Shiraz hopped onto the scene in 2001. It became the most successful wine launch in North American history, selling more than a million cases in the first year. Today, annual global sales of Yellow Tail are about twelve million cases compared to six million for Wolf Blass.

Yellow Tail was part of the "critter craze": cuddly creatures on wine labels designed to make wine more accessible and fun, such as Crocodile Rock, Little Penguin, and Cat Amongst the Pigeons. Other countries also launched their own brands: French Rabbit, France; Monkey Bay, New Zealand; and Wolftrap, South Africa, among many others. Such labels are easy to remember when you want to buy that delicious purple lizard wine again. More important, they appeal to women, who buy most wine—and who, apparently, are suckers for a cuddly little creature.

"Yellow Tail did a great job of soaking up the oversupply of grapes in Australia," Wolf observes. "If it gets people into the wine category, then it's a good thing. But they pinched my yellow!" he adds teasingly.

The idea of color coding is based on Wolf's close observations of the female mind: "My marketing was always driven toward women because I love women—I married four smashing crackers! The beer companies ignored women, the puffs," he says cheerfully, pouring a glass of his Red Label Shiraz Cabernet Sauvignon.

"I call this wine the leg opener," he says with a sly grin.

I look down at my notebook.

"Well don't bloody write that down!"

As I divert my eyes to the wine I'm sipping, it's clear that his wine does have a loosening effect, even though my legs remain firmly crossed. His blend, dominated by shiraz, is full and lush on the mid-palate, with a mocha-coffee character that backs off the spice and pepper. I can just taste the blackberry hint of cabernet at the tip of my tongue, which is quickly flooded by fleshy plums before I swallow. Clearly, Wolf's outsized personality is not solely responsible for his success: the broadsides are backed up by wines that are pretty damn good.

Shiraz, Wolf claims, shouldn't have a dominating flavor: "It's a winemaker's wine, like chardonnay. It can be whatever you bloody well want it to be. But it's also powerful and needs American oak because it's creamier and sweeter than French oak. Putting shiraz into French oak is like stuffing a fat man into a lace corset. American oak is also half the price of French oak—the bloody French!—which is important when you have to compete on price. My motto is 'no wood, no good.' But you need to know what you're doing; you need to be a timber expert. I'm going to buy wood from forests near Chernobyl so I can make glow-label wines.

"Shit! Don't you print that now."

I smile. The PR woman smiles.

"Leave that out."

I smile again.

"These wines have great drinkability. They take the mickey out of the French," he says, pounding his fist on the table, then leaning toward me to push his words in. "If you're paying $2,000 for a bloody bottle of bordeaux, you need to get your head shrunk."

Wolf takes another sip of the wine and turns more reflective: "The boom we experienced in the last decade only happens once in the history of an industry. Now we have to fight to hold on to that leadership. We don't have competitors on quality, only on price. Germany paid the price for selling cheap wine in the 1970s. We have to be careful not to turn into style merchants who want to make wine into liquid fast food. We wouldn't survive the bulk market . . . tall poppy syndrome . . . someone will eat our tucker!"

Wolf Blass took his winery public in 1984, and then it subsequently merged with several others, increasing in size and value until the beer giant Fosters bought the company in 1989. Fosters's wine division is now called Treasury Wine Estates. Today, Wolf Blass winery exports 70 percent of what it produces. Wolf himself, no longer running the company, is now its brand ambassador. What's his official title these days?

"Troublemaker," he says, grinning. "I can say anything I want now because I can't get sacked. My job is to go around the world and sell my Australia. This wine is Australia."

And after all these decades of experience, what does he think the industry needs to do? "We need to go to Asia . . . they're very thirsty over there. There are too many wineries in Australia, too many amalgamations; 60 percent is controlled by five companies. We need more boutique wineries, more small operators, more cellar-door sales.

"And we need to use our natural advantages: we need to convince people around the world that Australia is a great place for a vacation. It's not ripping overcrowded, like Napa Valley, and you don't need a bloomin' letter of introduction to get into the wineries, like France. You can speak English, the wines are cheap, the food is great, the land is beautiful."

And for Wolf personally? "When we do bottle signings, I get mobbed," he says, winking at me over the rim of his glass. "Yeah, I'm a bloody legend, but I'm not dead yet. I'm fit, my mind still works, lots of sex—it's all good."

PERHAPS THE ONLY thing more mind-boggling than meeting Wolf Blass is driving in Australia. Not only am I on the "wrong" side of the road, but the steering wheel is on the passenger side. I keep signaling with my windshield wipers. In Adelaide, I could follow the car ahead of me; but after an hour of driving out here to wine country, I'm disoriented. I turn a corner hidden by eucalyptus and gum trees, and find myself head-on with a tractor. Fortunately, it's going so slowly that I can swerve out of its path and continue on my way to Penfolds.

There I meet Peter Gago on a ramp in front of the barrel cellar— a slim man in his early fifties in an understated gray tunic and designer pants. He looks more like an art gallery owner than Penfolds's chief winemaker, whom I'd expected to be in wine-splattered overalls. Peter's title is actually "custodian," embracing a wider role than simply winemaking. His off-season road trips would leave a rock band exhausted—a recent tour involved twenty-six cities over ten weeks.

Penfolds was founded in 1844, making it older than many European wineries. The original vine cuttings from southern France were planted for medicinal purposes: a physician who had emigrated from England, Dr. Christopher Rawson Penfold, wanted to make wine for his patients. Predictably, more and more locals sought the "wine cure" for an increasingly wide range of ailments. Demand soon outpaced production, and Dr. Penfold decided to give up medicine and make wine full-time.

The business prospered for decades, and after the good doctor's death in 1870, his widow, Mary, ran the business for another fourteen years. Penfolds remained in the family until part of its stock was sold in 1970. Then, in 2005, the winery was bought by Fosters, which also owns Wolf Blass.

Peter joined the company twenty-two years ago, after graduating from oenology at the prestigious Roseworthy College of Agriculture at the University of Adelaide. He invites me to tour the cellar before we taste the wines, opening the large door with balletic grace. Inside are long rows of massive dark oak barrels, twelve high and fifteen feet in diameter. "We are the world's largest boutique winery," he says in a soft Australian accent with polished finishing-school diction. The winery produces 2.5 million cases a year and is one of the country's largest exporters.

There's a small plate on one of the barrels, bearing the name of Helen Keller. "When she visited the winery in 1948, she was fascinated by the texture and girth of this vat," Peter explains, brushing his fingers against it. "Someone told her its height, and she took less than a minute to correctly calculate that it held 10,774 gallons of wine."

A previous Penfolds winemaker pioneered the use of oak in Australia. Max Schubert joined the company as a messenger boy in the early 1930s and over two decades rose to become winemaker. In 1949, he went to Spain for a month to learn sherry-making techniques, since at the time, Australians who didn't drink beer mostly drank fortified wines. On his way home, he stopped in Bordeaux, tasted the local wines, and noticed that producers there aged their wines in oak barrels. He realized that oak was the ideal cradle for unfortified wines to develop the structure they needed for aging.

When he got back to Australia, he experimented with a small batch of red wine. Since he hadn't planted any bordeaux-style grapes, such as cabernet sauvignon or merlot, he used the local shiraz, then mostly the base for port-styled wine. After the wine had fermented, he didn't have any French oak, so he used American casks. He positioned the wax-coated wooden closures called bungs at the twelve o'clock position and topped the barrels up regularly so that the wine wouldn't oxidize. A small percentage of the wine slowly evaporates through the wood—it's whimsically called the angel's share.

Max drained the clear wine from the sediment that had settled out of it at the bottom of the barrel to a new barrel, a process called racking. He then aged the wine another eighteen to twenty-four months in oak for a tight-weave flavor and structure—a warp and woof of tannin and fruit. He named the wine Grange Hermitage, in honor of Grange Cottage (Mary Penfolds's home in England) and the French wine syrah (known as hermitage in the Rhône region).

However, at that point, the wine was merely his personal project. When he unveiled his creation to the senior management at Penfolds in the early 1950s, they were less than impressed. The dry style of wine, with a hint of oak, didn't suit their taste or that of their customers, they believed. They didn't understand that the wine would soak up the oak over time and that they wouldn't taste it directly, just as you don't notice the structural beams in a beautiful house when it's finished.

Grange became proof that senior management often doesn't know what they're doing. They issued Max a direct order on company letterhead to cease production, or he would be fired. Fortunately, Max was convinced of the wine's potential, didn't listen to his bosses, and kept making the wine in secret from 1957 to 1959. These are now called the Hidden Granges and are coveted by collectors around the world.

Grange is also proof that wine critics often don't know what they're talking about. When the wine was first launched, they said it tasted like crushed ants. But in 1962, Max entered his 1955 Grange into the Sydney Wine Show, where it won the gold medal. Penfolds senior management relented and asked Max to restart production (unaware that he had never stopped).

A decade later, more and more winemakers adopted Max's approach and started using oak and creating a dry style of wine. Today, Grange is the world's most expensive shiraz. (The Hermitage part of the name was dropped in 1990 before the French could protest that the name belonged to them, as much as names like Champagne and Bordeaux do.) The starting price of Grange is $500 a bottle when it's released every May 1. One bottle from 1951 recently sold at auction for more than $50,000.

Hang on, this doesn't sound like a wine for a cheapskate, even a choosy one. Well, the brilliance of Penfolds is that they established their reputation at the high end of the price scale. Then, over time, the company diversified into a wide range of wines with lower price tags, though they still had the signature flavors of the flagship wine.

The entry-level wine, Penfolds Rawson's Retreat, starts at about $12, followed by the $15 Koonunga Hill, the $20 Thomas Hyland, and then the pricier Bin numbered wines (128, 138, 28, 407, 150, 389, 707), the St. Henri, the Magill Estate, the RWT, and finally, Grange. The Penfolds style trickles down through all the tiers. Other Australian brands, such as Rosemount and Hardys, also use "ladder brands" to move their customers up the product line. Personally, I'm happy to stay on the lower rungs, where the price-quality ratio of these wines is terrific.

Like Wolf Blass, Peter believes that American oak is well suited to shiraz because the wood's wider grain can support the rich flavors of the grape. Still, not all American oak is the same. Peter explains that its character differs depending on how it's seasoned. When oak staves are first cut, the wood is still green and full of tree resin, so the barrels made from it would impart green, dill pickle flavors to the wine. Many barrel coopers leave their wood slats outside for several years, allowing the rain and sun to naturally leach out the resin and dry the wood before making them into casks.

The wood staves are set around a small fire, but not touching it, in order to make them pliable enough to be shaped into a barrel. A high-temperature toasting releases estuary compounds in the wood—notes such as coconut and vanilla—whereas lower temperatures may impart aromas of chocolate and coffee. Whatever the technique, Peter says, the essence of the flavor should be "oak-derived" but not quite oak. "It's interesting that many Americans didn't like the taste of their own oak until they tried Australian wine" he observes.

When tannin is balanced with the fruit of the wine, it acts like acidity, as a mouth scrubber with its drying astringency. This leaves your palate refreshed for the next bite of food rather than fatiguing with the same taste. Tannin is terrific with fatty foods, cutting through their richness, and in turn, the food smoothes out the wine. The combination is exhilarating: the food brings down the roughness of the wine, and the wine brings up the different flavors in the food.

As the only animals who cook our food, we humans have grown to love a broad range of foods and flavors. Many of us have also developed a liking for the smoky flavors derived from the hardwood originally used to cook our food, especially oak. In wine, oak adds complexity with non-fruit flavors, such as vanilla, smoke, caramel, and cedar.

However, too much oak in a number of other Australian wines I've tasted obliterates the taste of the wine, much like dousing everything you eat with ketchup or salt. These "termite specials" club your palate until it's numb, assaulting you with flavors and tannins. If the death of elegance had a taste, this would be it. They don't even pair well with food except perhaps wild buffalo—if it's still alive.

"At Penfolds, we blend most of our wines, both the grapes and the regions," Peter explains. The signature Grange, for instance, is a multiregion blend in American oak, but it's protected stylistically in the market by RWT, a shiraz that's from a single region, the Barossa, and finished in French oak. "Blending diminishes the troughs, so the style isn't on a roller-coaster ride from year to year," he says. "Winemaking is a culture of renegades—we love a difficult year! But we don't want our customers to have to deal with it. We want our wines to be dependable for investors, collectors, and everyday drinkers."

Consistency is a controversial benchmark for wine quality: many vintners feel a wine should reflect the individual vintage. It's also at odds with the efforts of the industry group, Wine Australia, to market the differences between the country's more than sixty wine regions. It's a thin red line to walk because some drinkers don't want wine that's indistinguishable from one region to the next, while others don't want French-styled complexities imported to the country that's made wine so accessible.

Peter is less concerned with such philosophical debates and more focused on creating good wines at Penfolds—he's most comfortable when talking about that. "Aiming for ripeness is like confusing information with intelligence," he asserts. "We don't chase flavor: we create structure first; then flavor follows and fills in the structure.

For us, cabernet is usually the bridesmaid to shiraz. When you taste cabernet on its own, it's long and lean because of those drying tannins. However, when those structural tannins are fleshed out with shiraz flavor, the wine becomes full and balanced. After the richness of shiraz on the mid-palate, you feel that fresh lift of cabernet just before you swallow. This gives our wine longevity—it's why the 1953 Grange is drinking so beautifully now. Just because the tannins feel silkier in our wines doesn't mean that they can't age."

The famed Penfolds longevity is also the result of another of Max Schubert's innovations. He realized that the heat of Australia's climate in many of its regions ripened the grapes to such a degree that their sugar was high and their acidity low. Acidity protects them from bacterial infection. Without this natural protection, Australian winemakers often had to throw out up to a third of their production every year. Max realized that if he could stabilize the wine to the right level of acidity and pH, it could have the potential to age for decades. His solution was to "correct" the finished wine by adding a small amount of tartaric acid, a substance that's already naturally in grapes.

This move attracted the criticism that Max was manipulating the process too much and making a "chemist's wine." In France, the corresponding controversial activity is chaptalizing, which means adding a little natural grape sugar to the fermenting wine to increase its body and alcohol. This is done mainly in cool climates, such as northern European countries, where the grapes don't get sufficient warmth to fully ripen in some years. Obviously, that's never the issue in Australia's warm regions, like the Barossa. Increasingly, though, winemakers on both sides of the ocean are learning how to best work with their grapes in the vineyard to get enough sugar and acidity rather than having to add them afterward.

Peter shows me around several large open vats made of concrete. They're empty now because the harvest took place about two months ago in April, so the new wine is already in barrels. Australia is in the Southern Hemisphere, so its seasons are the opposite of those in the North. The open vats are a highly aerobic method of winemaking, which doesn't simply refer to how hard the winemakers work (they do) but to exposing the wine to oxygen. Several times a day during fermentation, Peter does what he calls "rack-and-return": the juice is drained from the bottom of one tank into another tank and then splashed back over a grate to aerate it. The skins sink to the bottom of the tank as the must is drained, and then the must is pumped back over the skins. The skins gradually rise to the top again as the juice extracts more flavor and color from them, conditioning the wine for long-term aging.

The culture of innovation remains widespread in Australia: the country publishes more research papers on technology than any other country, led by scientists at Roseworthy. Penfolds's own history of innovation didn't end with Max Schubert. In the early 1960s, winemaker Don Ditter named the newest wine Bin 707 after the Boeing 707, one of the most advanced aircraft of the time. In 1997, the vintner before Peter, John Duval, created RWT, which stood for Red Winemaking Trial—the name was supposed to be a temporary one for an experiment with aging Barossa shiraz in French oak. When the trial turned out to be successful, the name stuck. Peter also experiments on a variety of winemaking aspects, including his 2011 launch of the Coonawarra Bin 169 Cabernet Sauvignon matured in French barrels, as the stylistic foil to the American oak-aged Bin 707. However, he is wary of depending on either oak or technology too much.

"Technology can make your wines too squeaky clean," he cautions, as we walk out of the cellar. "They can be pasteurized beyond personality. We need to have technology in Australia to drive down our costs because we're too distant from cheap labor to help pick the grapes and make the wine, the way that California and Europe can.

But technology can't tell you what to do—just how to do it more efficiently. Tradition influences us just as much."

Peter's never far from the tradition of Penfolds: his office is in the old Magill Cottage, the Penfolds's original home, which still stands beside the cellar. Inside the timbered cottage are sepia-toned photos of Mary, Christopher, their children, and their grandchildren. There are yellowing deeds and land certificates and leather-bound books. Peter takes me to a small room where we taste the wines. It's fascinating to taste both history and modernity as a gathering essence in the glass. The modestly priced Rawson's Retreat, Koonunga Hill, and Thomas Hyland are all exceptionally well-made for the price. There's a sheen to the fruit that seduces you, and a lusciousness in the taste that makes good on the promise.

The St. Henri is lighter bodied than the Grange, but with the same fruit intensity. It's fermented in large 385-gallon vats that are fifty-five years or older, so it has little oak character or oak tannin. The flavors unfold in my mouth like a peacock tail, growing wider and more varied as I taste.

Peter pours me the higher-end offerings. RWT offers concentric circles of pleasure: fleshy blackberries roll around the outer circles of flavor, deepening to a dark, concentrated core of hedonism. There's an elemental interplay of liquid, air, and wood that's built for aging. By contrast, Grange is an expansive darkness of licorice, black olive, and graphite depths. The first sip is big, and then it builds in your mouth. It's a cumulative wine that swells and engulfs your senses like the musical signature of Ravel's *Bolero*, becoming more pronounced, more exciting, the more you taste it.

As we taste the wines, Peter and I chat about the winery's recorking clinics, constituting what must be the best after-sales service in the wine world. Penfolds invites customers to bring their Penfolds bottles older than fifteen years to selected venues in cities around the world. Peter opens the wines under argon, a protective inert gas cover, then samples a tiny amount to determine if the wine is as it should be and without faults. If it is good, the bottle is topped up with a few ounces of the same wine but from the latest vintage, which isn't enough to change the taste or the wine's integrity for resale. Then it's resealed with a stamped cork and a new capsule, and Peter signs a certification label on the back. This seal of approval boosts the wine's value: bottles sold at auction often fetch more than they otherwise would with this updated guarantee of quality.

"The clinics are a great way to meet our customers, and almost every bottle has a story," Peter says. "One man found a bottle of Grange behind a park bench in the city. Another customer took a bottle with him when he climbed up Kilimanjaro. Recently, a young woman brought in a bottle from 1951 that she had inherited. But when we opened it, we found that it was filled with tea! Her grandfather must have enjoyed the wine decades ago, then recorked it."

Over the past twenty years, more than a hundred thousand bottles have been checked for their quality. "We've found less than 2 percent have been faulty. Still, we do advise many people to drink the wine soon," Peter says. "That's the biggest mistake people make with all wines: keeping them too long in the cellar."

I enjoyed attending a recorking clinic in Toronto; it was like a wine version of the *Antiques Roadshow*, with lots of surprised and happy customers. As I watched Peter listen attentively to an elderly woman, both of their hands on a bottle with a yellowing label, I couldn't imagine a better title for him than custodian.

As I DRIVE along an old dirt road, through the gaps in the wattle and gum trees, I spot some kangaroos hopping through the brush. A few of them stop and stare at me curiously, looking as soft and unreal as stuffed toys. This magnificently strange country makes me feel like *Alice in Wonderland*—and not just because of the Down Under notion of falling through the rabbit hole and finding everything reversed. It's the sensory playfulness and abandon here that I love: the odd, joyful jumble of color and flavor and aroma.

My mind wanders back to my favorite part of the Lewis Carroll story: "She found a little bottle . . . and round its neck a paper label with the words 'Drink Me' beautifully printed in large letters. . . . Alice ventured to taste it, and finding it very nice (it had a sort of mixed flavor of cherry-tart, custard, pineapple, roast turkey, toffee, and hot buttered toast), she very soon finished it off."

I wish Alice were with me now—we'd share a bottle of shiraz. She'd describe it perfectly but not take the tasting too seriously. We'd laugh when she'd recall how the Red Queen and her guests "put their glasses upon their heads like extinguishers, and drank all that trickled down their faces; others upset the decanters and drank the wine as it ran off the edges of the table."

I swim back up to reality when I spot the old stone Henschke winery nestled amid a tangle of trees and bushes. True, Henschke wines are not cheap, but they do offer great value compared to many other wines of their quality. And I can't resist going off the path occasionally for the sake of a tasty nip. I'm prone to tangential digressions, but I've never regretted being remarkably inconsistent: it's led me to fascinating people and interesting stories. If you're looking for consistency, try the *Oxford Companion to Wine*. If you want adventure, let's go . . .

I'm here to meet Stephen Henschke, the great-great-grandson of the original founder. He's a compact, scholarly looking man, dressed in an Oxford shirt and Dockers. His quiet, serious manner amid this wild plant life reminds me of a botany professor on a remote expedition. He meets me in the winery's small reception area and gives me a brief history of the family business. Its founder, Johann Christian Henschke, was a buggy maker and farmer when he came over from Silesia on a ship of Lutheran farmers in 1868 with his wife and five children. Only he and two of his children survived the journey. But he worked hard on his grant of land, saved money, planted vines, married again, and had eight more children.

The Henschke winery has stayed in the family over the generations. Johann's great-grandson, Cyril Henschke, went to Oxford University as a Churchill Fellow, and then worked with Max Schubert at Penfolds during his viticultural training. Like Max, Cyril was also an early proponent of dry table wines in the 1950s. He had the foresight to develop his vineyards and bottle his wine rather than sell his grapes in bulk to larger companies, as most growers did. Stephen, Cyril's middle child, studied botany and biochemistry at Roseworthy. There he met Prue Weir, who was studying zoology and botany. Ten days after they graduated, they got married and moved to Germany. Stephen enrolled in the renowned Geisenheim Wine Institute, while Prue audited classes and worked at the Geisenheim Grape Breeding Institute.

When the couple returned to Australia in 1978, they started making wine on the family farm, which they inherited when Cyril died. However, they had a huge inheritance tax to pay to the government. "We were penniless," Stephen recalls. "Those were long days and nights. Most winemakers know that you're only as good as your current release. But it was very motivating to be fighting for your home as well as your business."

Their big break came one day when a major British importer dropped into the winery and asked for more of their wines. He thought their style was more French than Australian and would sell well in the U.K.—provided they left the word *shiraz* off the label. They did, relying instead on their vineyard names, and sales built steadily. Today they produce forty thousand cases a year.

Stephen takes me to the back office to meet Prue, who's sitting at a large oak desk covered with stacks of papers, books, envelopes, and charts. Her pencil moves rapidly down a long list of numbers that looks like the ledger of a 1950s general store. She glances up when Stephen introduces me, says hello in a whisper, then goes back to her numbers. She has the same dazzling sapphire blue eyes of the late Princess Diana, as well as her shy manner.

"It's going to be a cracking afternoon," Stephen comments.

"It should be raining," Prue replies.

Indeed, there hasn't been rain for four months. Dry weather was ideal for the harvest, but now the vines need rain to develop their leaves and shoots in preparation for the growth cycle. There's also the Murray River to worry about, since it's the main source of water for many wineries here. I stand there awkwardly for several moments until I think to ask Prue what's happening with the river. She lights up at the question, clearly more comfortable with science talk than with small talk. "The river is almost dry," she says. "Not quite the drought we had in 2007 but dangerously close."

She explains the environmental problem: "In the 1970s, thousands of trees around were pulled out to make way for vineyards and farmlands. Those deep roots were natural desalinators; their constant absorption of moisture kept the water table low. Without them, the water table rose, pushing up layers of salt and saline water that had been distributed lower down through the soil strata. This sterilized the topsoil, turning vegetated areas into sand bowls and making the groundwater too salty for the vines to thrive. Most Henschke vines are dry-farmed rather than irrigated. This forces the roots to search deeper for moisture, thereby exposing them to a wider and deeper soil volume, as well as making them less vulnerable to droughts."

Prue is active in a number of land preservation groups in the country, and water conservation is at the top of their agenda. All wineries today need licenses to get a water allocation from the Murray River or any other water catchment, but these are a lower priority than drinking water. Back in 2007, the river fell so low there was no water left for the wineries, and the region's crop was down by about 70 percent over the previous year. One solution that's been proposed is to build a desalination plant in Adelaide, but that will cost $1.2 billion, so it will be some time before that happens.

"When you have a basic knowledge of plants and agriculture, you can see what the land will be like in ten, twenty years," Prue tells me. "I feel a responsibility to use that knowledge to convince others of what we need to do now."

Prue and Stephen have replanted 30 percent of their land with indigenous vegetation to try to reestablish the natural balance and water table. They've planted native grasses and cover crops between the vine rows; these grasses harbor beneficial insects, such as ladybugs and wasps, that feed on the insects that eat the grapes, such as vine moths.

"The cover crops are also helpful because vines can't draw up flavors from the rock," Prue says. "The clover and lichen allow a healthy mycorrhiza fungi to grow around the roots of the vines. These break down the minerals in the soil into micronutrients so that the plants can absorb them and produce sugars and carbohydrates for healthy fruit. It's a natural system of viticulture."

The grasses don't take much moisture from the vines because they're sparse and have shallow roots. The couple also protect their vineyard's precious moisture by putting down a straw mulch, which has the added benefit of keeping the worms active, those natural tillers of the soil.

After Prue explains this, she goes back to her figures, and Stephen takes me on a quick tour of the winery. It's clean and orderly, though tiny compared to Wolf Blass and Penfolds. It's much older, too: the last renovation seems to have been done around 1870. Large blackened wood beams span the ceiling over rough-hewn concrete vats that show years of pockmarks.

At Stephen's suggestion, we leave for the vineyard. I follow him out to his truck, open the door, and find myself about to sit on his lap—I'm still not used to the driver-passenger seat switch here. As we drive down the bumpy road, I comment on the fragrant light blue haze in the air. Stephen explains that it's eucalyptus oil from the trees. Researchers at the Australian Wine Research Institute have found that the airborne compounds in this oil settle on and seep into the skins and leaves of red grapes and are responsible for that faint mint flavor that's often in Australian red wines. These compounds don't affect white wines as much because they're made with little to no skin contact.

Stephen stops the truck and pulls a leaf from a wattle tree as gently as a parent removes a Band-Aid from a child's elbow. He crushes it between his fingers and hands it to me. It smells like a forest of green flowers. He stops the truck several more times to show me different leaves and berries, rattling off the Latin names of half a dozen species. These plants are lucky to have such a good friend.

As we trundle along, the fiery evening sun is on the horizon ahead of us. Slowly, a black spire comes into view, trying to pierce the red balloon above it. This turns out to be the community's original Lutheran church, built in 1860 and called Gnadenberg—German for "Hill of Grace," after which the Henschke vineyard surrounding it is named. Stephen pulls up in front of the church, with its chipped headstones and a stone angel that looks sad to have lost her arms. This is all that's left of what was once a thriving village, apart from some ruins of a few former homes and an old schoolhouse. After the last teacher moved away a century ago, the town couldn't persuade another one to come to such an isolated spot. So the families moved away one by one, and eventually the town was no more.

The vineyard is a thin slice of eight acres at the confluence of two dried-up creeks that have contributed an astonishing variety of soil types. The red-brown earth gives a fruity character to the grapes, the sandy loam adds a perfume lift, and the heavy black soil and tight red clay impart a robust, masculine character. These vines have become scavengers here, sinewy but strong, and always in survival mode, working hard for their nutrients and water. Against the surrounding countryside, they look like a small island of green in a sea of red dust.

These vines have grown here since the settlers planted them before phylloxera destroyed most European vineyards in 1856, more than 150 years ago, and I wonder how many hands have touched and tended these vines since then. Stephen calls them "the grandfathers." They are the reason that he asked me to stand in a tray of antibacterial solution before we left the winery, to ensure I didn't bring any diseases into the vineyard on my shoes. It reminded me of the same reasonable precaution they took at the Louvre when the Mona Lisa was finally put behind glass.

"These vines were planted before the motor car was invented; they've seen two world wars, a global depression, and many droughts. They can take whatever nature throws at them. We don't have any old châteaux here, but we do have living history."

Stephen and Prue's single-vineyard approach is the antithesis of Australia's multiregion blending but not at odds with it. To me, it seems more in tune with what the medieval philosopher Duns Scotus called *haecceitas*, or "thisness." The fashionable term in the wine industry today is "somewhereness," essentially the English translation for the traditional French concept of terroir. It refers to the specific place where the wine is grown and made because it's particularly suited to that place. This wine couldn't be made anywhere else because the memory of the land hasn't been erased.

Age is a virtue in grapevines, Stephen explains. Larger trunks mean better management of sugars and carbohydrates. "The spindly young ones are always in a hurry to ripen their fruit, but they're all talk—they can't keep their acids up," he says. "It's only when a vine hits twenty that something changes: the taste and texture of the grapes become more balanced, and the wine they produce throws you more texture. The old vines take their time and let the flavor rise and develop slowly in the grapes. Less talk, more wisdom."

As I watch the red fingers of the setting sun touch the gnarled crevices on these vines that have weathered so much, I think of the stoic Lutheran doctrine: "Here I stand. I cannot do otherwise." We walk deeper into the rows, and some of the vines start to lean toward each other, like old men holding each other up on a park bench. They look so wizened that it's hard to believe there's something still alive in their core. Stephen calls this the vineyard within the vineyard. These vines aren't vigorous, and they produce less fruit every year, perhaps only a bottle per vine compared to three to four bottles per vine for the younger ones. But what glorious wine that one bottle is! Later, when I try some of it over dinner, I can taste the subtly spiced fruit, which that has the texture and zing of acidity but is more nuanced. The pepper and wintergreen notes are gone, replaced with rich, dark blackberry-mulberry aromas.

"Controlled neglect is how we keep the plants strong," Stephen says. Every year, one vine in a hundred dies of natural causes, old soldiers dropping out of the annual veterans' march. However, in the truest sense of estate planning, Prue has a fifty-year succession plan that involves taking the best genetic material from the vines and propagating it in her nursery before replanting. She no longer buys any outside plant material. While she and Stephen now have the scientific proof that these old vines produce extraordinary wine, it was simply Cyril's good intuition that kept him from pulling them up in the early 1970s when the government paid growers to replant more marketable cabernet.

Off in the distance, I can hear the soft lowing of cattle between the tinkling of their bells. Surprisingly, I can also hear someone laughing a few rows over—I thought Stephen and I were alone in the vineyard. When I ask him about this, he laughs, too, and explains that I'm actually hearing a kookaburra, the Australian kingfisher bird. Unlike the North American loon, whose haunting call sounds like a lunatic (hence the name), the kookaburra's sound is a dead ringer for human laughter. It makes the vineyard a happy place to be.

A more familiar bird, a magpie, lights on a post near us and warbles with all its might from its tiny chest. "They're beautiful creatures," Stephen says. "They eat the grubs and insects that would damage the vines." As the sun sets, the magpie flits on from post to post, until it's lost from sight against the black shapes of the gum trees and the vines that seem to huddle closer together in the darkness.

Suddenly, after a day of feeling too hot, I get a cold shudder up my back. The nights here along the mountain ranges of the Barossa, a thousand feet up from the valley, have a piercing freshness to them, with a risk of frost in the winter. That's why the vineyard is dotted with several large electric windmills that go into action whenever the nighttime temperature dips toward freezing. Their rotating blades create a circular wind that can reach up to twenty miles an hour, and inverts the layer of warm air that sits above the cold air. This brings warmth closer to the ground, helping to melt the frost.

As Stephen and I get back into the truck, he explains, "Our climate sets the intensity of our wine. In the 1970s, we tried to make European wine with lower levels of alcohol, but it just ended up being wishy-washy. We have to accept that our style means a lot of color, flavor, and richness. Barossa wines are always slow to mature because in the extreme heat, the vine shuts down to protect itself. But that's a good thing because it results in a greater depth of flavor in the fruit."

After a quiet period, he says something that surprises me, given how hard he and Prue work. "Wine makes itself if you let it," he observes. "A winery is not about fixing things. You can only make the wine that the land will give you."

The night is clear and crisp, the moonlit sky marbled with a few wispy clouds as we drive to dinner at a small resort called the Louise. Its outstanding restaurant, Appellation, is unapologetically wine-centric. When we get there, Prue has already arrived, and we join her at a table for a delicious meal to showcase the local cuisine and the Henschke wines.

For our first course, we enjoy a creamy chowder of oysters, accented with spring onions and chervil. The Henschke Eden Valley Riesling is a perfect foil for the soup: it starts with floral grace and then fills out with aromas of grapeseed and lemon-lanolin. The Eden Valley is only an hour away from the Barossa, yet its climate is dramatically cooler. Although Australia is best known for its reds, the country also produces spectacularly refreshing white wines in the cool climate regions, such as Eden Valley, Mornington Peninsula, Victoria, Yarra Valley, and Tasmania. Neighboring New Zealand is known for its zesty sauvignon blanc, but Australia's white specialties are riesling and chardonnay.

As we eat, I love listening to the catch-and-release play of Stephen and Prue's conversation, reminding me of the poet Rilke's "deep calling to deep." The world of science and plants brought them together; now theirs is a marriage of two fine intellects. They're interested in everything; they wrap themselves in curiosity. Out the window, we see clusters of stars dancing, and they debate which constellation it is.

They seem to have experimented with every aspect of winemaking: vine genetics, grape types, yeast strains, barrel woods, toasting methods, maturation periods, tannin structures, and soil compositions. "We take one sliver of a subject and do minute variations on the same experiment every year, such as a small change in harvest temperature or a drainage elevation," Stephen says. "We are microwinemakers."

A prime example is Prue being one of the first in Australia to use Scott Henry trellising, a method of training the vines so that the grapes get more sun exposure. This results in fewer herbal and green notes in the wine. I ask Prue why she doesn't graft some of the dying old vines with the new phylloxera-resistant stock to save them. "Grafting on rootstock can save a vine's life, but it can shorten it, too, like an elderly person who gets a hip replacement," she explains. "We have to understand the vineyard health and energy forces to foster the best of its precious genetic material."

Our second course arrives: a dish of juicy local corn-fed chicken, with thin slices of *lachsschinken*—cold-smoked loin of pork—tucked in the middle. Pork has long been a staple in the Barossa, ever since the settlers brought with them their love of sausages and schnitzel. The locals say that the only bit of the pig that escapes the pot is the squeal. The pork gives the chicken a wonderful smoky note, which is enhanced by the glaze of fried butter, diced garlic, and fresh sage leaves. It's perfect with the white wine blend in the Henschke Tilly's Vineyard Semillon, Chardonnay, and Sauvignon Blanc. The wine is a sun field of aromas: clover blossom, daisies, and green apples.

Both wines we've enjoyed so far have a screw cap. As no-nonsense scientists, Stephen and Prue hold no romantic notions about corks. They were among Australia's earliest adopters of screw caps. Wine corks, made from the bark of cork trees in Spain and Portugal, have been the traditional closure for wine bottles since the 1600s. They were a great improvement on the previous method of a cloth and rope around the bottle opening. However, natural bark corks can contain a chemical compound that can taint the wine. Even a mild case of cork taint strips wine of its expressive aromas, and a severe one makes it smell like moldy cardboard. Screw caps, however, don't have that problem.

"Often, you need to drop your suspicions and just try something," Prue says. Stephen explains that wine ages better under a screw cap than a cork, letting very little oxygen into the bottle. It's the same principle as a large-format bottle, such as a magnum: the lower wine-to-oxygen ratio helps it age more slowly, which helps to better integrate the elements, such as fruit flavor, acidity, and tannin.

Screw caps are also up to a thousand times less likely than corks to allow the wine to become tainted. Still, the Henschkes acknowledge that many consumers prefer the traditional option, so they're experimenting with Vino-Lok glass stoppers, which have the same benefits as screw caps. "They're a great placebo for cork," Stephen says. "They look gorgeous and let you play with elegance, yet they're easy to open and won't ruin your wine."

Ah, here comes our first red wine of the evening, their Mount Edelstone Shiraz. The name is derived from the German word *edelstein*, meaning "gemstone." Made from ninety-year-old vines, Edelstone is full of fruit with just-squeezed juiciness that tapers into fine tannins, like the tinkling top notes of a piano concerto. It finishes with just the right sweep of acidity to prevent its lushness from becoming too heavy. It's that lift at the end that makes you return to this wine.

Some say that you should "eat" shiraz with a fork because it's so hefty, but Prue doesn't think that wine should be a meal on its own. Shiraz is a succulent wine, she believes, that goes best with tender meat dishes. That's why we're drinking it now as our third course arrives: a croquette of lamb with a salad of curly endive and Barossa bacon. The lamb comes from Hutton Vale, which abuts one of the Henschke vineyards. The animal is a cross-breed between Merino (grown for wool) and Suffolk (grown for meat). It has a richer flavor than the lamb I've had in Europe, America, or even New Zealand because of the pasture grasses the sheep eat here.

Our endive salad is garnished with strongly smoked bacon—yet another tribute to the ethnic heritage of the Barossa. Smoked foods are a cornerstone of the cuisine, though with a distinctly Australian twist. Unlike German meats that are smoked over European hard-woods, the woods here are from red gum and acacia trees. The result is spectacular, and the smoky bacon fills every corner of my mouth with flavor. It pairs beautifully with the wine's lashings of dark plums and fleshy berries. I drink lustily, giving myself permission to love shiraz again and all its fleshy goodness after a streak of drinking mainly Burgundian pinot noir. Saturated fruit flavors flood my mouth and pool around my taste buds before slipping down to deeper pleasure centers.

The Henschke shiraz would pair well with other hearty fare: I imagine that it would encase rare roast beef, then pierce and soak Yorkshire pudding. My rule of thumb is that when the weather is cold, drink wines from warm regions, like Barossa shiraz or Argen-tine malbec: they produce full-bodied, high-alcohol wines that pair well with robust dishes and warm you up when it's chilly. When it's hot, drink wines from cool climates, such as German or Canadian riesling. These regions produce lean, more acidic, lighter-alcohol wines that are great refreshment when it's warm and pair well with lighter dishes.

"Shiraz is a gorgeous freak of nature; it's our signature," Stephen says. I couldn't agree more, but my mouth is full. "The North American palate has an affinity for shiraz, with its sweet, spicy, lush flavors. Compare that with cabernet, which is far more astringent and drying, a chalky sensation that often has a strong oak component," he adds. "You can only drink so much of it. By contrast, shiraz has an incredible generosity of flavor and vivacity because we lead with fruit, not forests. You want to drink something from a grape, not a tree."

Next we try the 1986 Hill of Grace, and I recall the ghost village around the vineyard. Drinking it makes me feel like a tourist of time. The silky tannins make it taste sensuously slippery. It also has a lengthened lingering; it tastes like more. Stephen says it's also delicious when young. "Never believe anyone who says a wine doesn't taste good now but will in ten years," he warns. "They're conning you. A good wine should taste great when you open it and even better ten years on."

As we enjoy our next course of a breast of Eden Valley pigeon in a semolina and pea puree with their shiraz, Prue and Stephen reflect on their industry: "We did a great job of convincing people that Australian wine is cheap and cheerful," Stephen says. "We made consumers comfortable with our category. But the dangerous thing is that people get used to you being one thing and then they don't want you to change.

"Big brands like Jacob's Creek spill more wine in a year than we make," he comments wryly. "They're good anchors for the category, like a department store in a mall, but we need to personalize our wine now. We need more midsized boutique wineries like Peter Lehmann, Brown Brothers, Yalumba, and Henschke to tell the story of Australia at the grassroots level. A place gives you a sense of belonging; a story gives you a sense of familiarity."

In Stephen's opinion, the biggest threat to the future of Australian wine is not other New World countries like Chile and Argentina.

It's actually the traditional winemaking countries like Italy, Portugal, and Spain. "They've got the distribution channels, the cheap labor, the developed vineyards—and, above all, a strong history of place."

As our waiter brings us our dessert, a Riverland lime and lemon tart, Prue expands on Stephen's vision with a more personal note: "More than anything else, we need to complete the cycle of the previous generation and prepare for the next one," she says. The Henschkes have three children: their eldest, Johann, twenty-six, is already a qualified winemaker; Justine is studying marketing at the University of Adelaide and helps with public relations at the winery; and the youngest, Andreas, studying engineering at the university, helps in the vineyard during his vacations. "Sometimes, it seems like an enormous task," she adds. "But making wine teaches you that the end is always the beginning."

Field Notes from a
Wine Cheapskate

So you've breezed through the first chapter, and now you ask: "How's this going to help me find a good bottle of value-priced wine for Sunday dinner?" This is probably because you skipped the section entitled "Beyond the Adventures" near the beginning, but no matter. Although most of the wines I discuss in this book are widely available, I know that you won't be able to find every one of them at your local liquor store.

So at the end of each chapter, I'll give you my cheat sheet of tips that I've picked up from my travels to help you find great wines from each region, as well as other terrific producers. Visit my website at www.nataliemaclean.com to get the latest reviews of wines in stores now.

INSIDER TIPS

* Look for wines from warm regions, like the Barossa Valley. Often the cost of production is cheaper because winemakers aren't battling disease, rot, and weather as much as cool-climate producers do. Therefore, there's less crop loss and lower costs for production. It's no coincidence that six of the eight regions in this book are warm climates. (Niagara and Germany are cool climates.)

* When it's cold outside, drink wine from warm regions, and when it's warm, go for those from cooler climates. You'll drink the full-bodied, soul-warming styles that are comforting in the winter and the lighter, more refreshing ones in the summer. The bonus is that these wines also complement the dishes we eat in the different seasons.

* Twist and shout when you see a bottle closed with a screw cap! No longer does a screw cap necessarily mean that the wine is plonk. Many good producers are using this effective closure to protect their wine. The bonus is that no special equipment is needed to open your bottle.

WINERIES VISITED

Henschke: www.henschke.com.au
Penfolds: www.penfolds.com.au
Wolf Blass: www.wolfblass.com.au

BEST VALUE WINES

Henschke Eden Valley Riesling

Henschke Tilly's Vineyard Semillon, Chardonnay, and Sauvignon Blanc

Penfolds Koonunga Hill

Penfolds Rawson's Retreat

Penfolds Thomas Hyland

Wolf Blass Red Label Shiraz Cabernet Sauvignon*

Wolf Blass Shiraz

Wolf Blass Yellow Label Cabernet Sauvignon

My first pick for my own Sunday dinner.

TOP VALUE PRODUCERS

The following list comprises more great value producers for the region, beyond those I visited for the book. Some producers have other brands or labels that I'll list separately. For example, Clancy's is made by Peter Lehmann Wines. You can find the website addresses for all of these wineries in my online Worldwide Winery Directory at www.nataliemaclean.com/wineries.

You can also find my most current reviews of these wines on the site, with prices, scores, tasting notes, food matches, recipes, and bottle shots at www.nataliemaclean.com/winepicks.

Angove	d'Arenberg
Banrock Station	Elderton
Brokenwood	Evans & Tate
Clancy's	Gemtree

Grant Burge

Kilikanoon

Leasingham

Lindemans

McGuigan

McWilliams

Mitolo

Peter Lehmann Wines

Pirramimma

Robert Oatley

Rosemount

Saltram

Shingleback

St. Hallet

Thorn-Clarke

Tyrrell's Wines

Wakefield

Wyndham Estate

Xanadu

Yalumba

Yering Station

SUNDAY DINNER FOR A WINE CHEAPSKATE

I've posted recipes for the dishes that we enjoyed at Appellation, the restaurant at the Louise resort, as prepared by executive chef Mark McNamara, at www.nataliemaclean.com/food.

*Barossa Corn-Fed Chicken and Smoked
Pork in a Garlic and Sage Glaze*

Butter-Poached Chicken

Chicken with Fennel Bulb and Sunchokes

Creamy Oyster Chowder and Scallions

*Striped Bass or Tilapia with Red Wine
and Thyme-Infused Glaze*

*Breast of Pigeon or Squab with
Semolina Gnocchi and Pea Puree*

Lamb Croquette

Lime and Lemon Tart

TERRIFIC PAIRINGS

Shiraz and syrah both create rich, robust wines with a smooth texture and signature aromas of spice, pepper, clove, and licorice leading, followed by dark fruit such as raspberry, plum, and black cherry, as well as truffle, earth, violets, vanilla, smoke, sandalwood, cedar, cigar box, earth, and leather.

Shiraz and syrah pair well with many meaty, robust dishes.

Aged cheddar	Meat lovers' pizza
Barbecued beef ribs	Meat or game casseroles
Beef or chicken fajitas	Peppercorn steak
Bison steak	Roast beef
Brisket	Roast goose
Grilled or braised lamb	Smoked pork chops
Grilled vegetables	Spicy sausage
Hamburgers	Squab
Meat loaf	Venison stew

RESOURCES

To learn more about Australian wines and shiraz:

James Halliday Australian Wine Companion by James Halliday
Heart and Soul: Australia's First Families of Wine by Graeme
    Lofts and James Halliday
Crushed by Women: Women and Wine by Jeni Port

Wineries of Australia: www.nataliemaclean.com/wineries
Wine Australia: www.wineaustralia.com/australia
Wine Australia USA: www.wineaustralia.com/usa
Australian Wine Society Ottawa: www.awsottawa.com
Australian Wine Society Toronto: www.aws.ca
Australian Wine Society Calgary: www.members.shaw
    .ca/auswinecgy
Australian Wine Appreciation Society Vancouver: www.awas.ca
South World Wine Society Vancouver: www.southworldwine
    .com/aboutus.html

RELATED READING

The following books, while seemingly unrelated to the main subject matter of this chapter, provided some enjoyable reading before, during, and after my travels:

Alice's Adventures in Wonderland by Lewis Carroll
The Selected Poetry of Rainer Maria Rilke by Rainer Maria Rilke
Oscar and Lucinda by Peter Carey

TWO

MONDAY

The Unbearable Lightness of German Riesling

BELOW THE MOUNTAIN road on my left, the slope plunges down a half mile to the river. Grapevines cling to the weathered rock with white-knuckled nerve. As I drive through Germany's Mosel Valley on this honeyed September morning, I can see the medieval homes and churches of Wehlen. The village's watercolor reflection on the river slowly divides on either side of a barge and re-forms behind it. Here, at the world's northern edge of viticulture, they create a wine with the weightless intensity of white lightning: riesling.

For thousands of years, the Moselle River has shaped this valley, first in one direction and then in another, unable to make up its meandering mind. Its three-hundred-mile journey starts in the Vosges Mountains of Alsace, flowing into Germany via Luxembourg and then joining the Rhine to the west. While the Mosel area is only the fourth largest of Germany's thirteen wine regions, more than half the country's riesling grapes are planted here. And while several other areas are also famous for riesling, those from the Mosel float above them all in their ethereal blend of aroma, delicacy, and steely concentration.

That's what makes German riesling ideal for Monday night dinner: it's low in alcohol, so it's a gentle way to start the week after indulging on Saturday and Sunday; the bonus is that you won't fall asleep on the sofa at seven p.m. when you're trying to catch up on email. Plus, the wine goes well with the less fussy dishes we have after a busy day at work, such as grilled chicken or fish, creamy pasta, Indian or Asian takeout, or a simple salad.

Riesling is a tough-skinned little berry that likes to fume all day, then calm down in the chilly nights. So it loves the confluence of climate and geology here in the Mosel. Its vines can withstand winter freezes as low as –13°F, cold enough to kill less-hardy plants between growing seasons. The precipitous rock walls cradle the vines from the coldest winds racing overhead. As the ancient river wore down this valley over millions of years, it deposited minerals and uncovered the Devon blue slate. Slate is a rock that fractures easily with extreme variations in temperature; it covers the ground here like thousands of discarded arrowheads. That makes it excellent for drainage—essential for growing flavorful grapes in a wet climate. The unyielding rock challenges the vines to survive. Their roots often have to slither aboveground until they can fight their way down through craggy fissures, often groping ten feet or more in the stony layers to find sustenance. Riesling thrives on suffering. I like that in a plant.

Slate also slows vegetative growth. Even the trees planted along the ridge have a tighter grain than those in less acidic soils. So the grapes accumulate their flavors slowly. (In warmer regions, riesling hurtles headlong into ripening, and the resulting wine tastes like watered-down chardonnay.) But here the grapes' depth of taste is akin to small, wild tomatoes rather than those bland, supersized, fertilizer-fed ones. In fruit, as in people, complexity is built under difficulty. The rock's porous crystalline structure helps it to trap heat in the day and release just enough to the vines at night. The result is a barely possible wine from a small indent on the planet that's on the same fiftieth parallel as Krakow, Winnipeg, and Mongolia.

Over the centuries, vintners have discovered how to extract the best from this harsh land. They've planted the vines angled to soak up warmth from the low northern sun and light reflected from the water. The river also circulates warm air up between the vines like a balmy tide. The vines, two-thirds of the way up on the mountain, get just the right amount of warmth to make wines of prickling excitement. They're part of a thirty-mile stretch through the heart of the region, known as the Mittelmosel (middle Mosel). The vines lower down get too much heat, while those at the top don't get enough to make the finest rieslings. And yet even these wines are priced at a fraction of those benchmark wines in other great regions, such as Bordeaux and Tuscany. Both history and fashion have kept riesling's prices in the bargain range.

Some of the best rieslings here, and throughout Germany, are made by a family named Prüm, which has lived in Wehlen since 1156. I start with this winery to calibrate my palate for the less-expensive wines I'll taste later in the trip. In my opinion, bargain wines aren't worth drinking if they're completely blown away by the top producers. I am choosy even if I don't want to pay for it. And as a true cheapskate, I wouldn't miss the opportunity to taste these wines for free.

The winery that Johann Josef Prüm founded in 1911 is now run by his grandson, Manfred Prüm. A lawyer by training, eccentric winemaker by choice, Manfred is also famously private. No one outside the business has ever descended into his cellars. I've pestered in vain to be permitted the privilege, but at least Katharina Prüm, the eldest of his three daughters, has agreed to meet with me.

The family's Victorian manor house is tucked into a narrow strip of land between the river and the mountainside. Looking up at the emerald hillside across the river, I can see the ten-foot sundial that Manfred's great-great-uncle built into the rock face in 1842. It gave workers a strong sense of the time—and presumably all the work they had to finish before going home. The German word for "sundial" is *sonnenuhr*, and this vineyard, Wehlener Sonnenuhr, is named after it.

Walking around the Prüm house in search of the front door, I almost run into an elderly man with a thick shock of white hair and ruddy cheeks. An old family vineyard hand, I think, as he doesn't seem to understand when I ask him for directions. Then he smiles, gently takes my arm, and guides me to the entrance. I ring the bell and turn to thank him, but he's gone.

Katharina Prüm looks like a young Jane Seymour, dressed in a cashmere turtleneck, tweed jacket, riding jodhpurs, and leather boots. I follow her past the mounted antlers and tusks in the hallway—relics of Manfred's successful hunting of wild boar and deer—and into a dark-paneled drawing room. The sun streams through the tall windows, burnishing the gold frame on the portrait of her great-grandfather Johann Josef Prüm, known to wine fanatics as JJ.

Katharina is the fourth generation in her family to make wine, and she's expected to succeed her father and her uncle Wolfgang. "As a child, I didn't want to become a winemaker, but I loved being with my father in the vineyards," she reminisces. "My deepest wish was always to be with him, to smell the grapes, to walk beside him tasting them."

Like her father, Katharina studied law, completing a doctorate at Münster University as well as a certificate in American law. Her focus on the United States landed her an internship in Tulsa, Oklahoma. While there, she hosted tastings of her family's wines for American importers and retailers. Although her father had been forced to leave school to run the family business when his own father died, it was Katharina's choice to return to the winery when she graduated.

"It's helpful to leave your home and your village for a few years to see the world," she says. "The backgrounds of the people who go into the wine business are so varied: artists, lawyers, doctors, real estate agents, and so on—this industry collects people who love life. After a while, I knew I'd come back. I think about all the previous generations who gave their energy and time to these vines. Their memory lives in them."

After a meditative moment, she suddenly perks up, grins, and reaches into the cooler at her side. "Now, let's have some fun!" she says, pulling out a bagged bottle and pouring some wine into two glasses. Oh hooray, a blind tasting. There's no better way for a vintner to expose self-proclaimed wine experts than to play guessing games with them using their own wines.

When I raise the glass to my nose, my heart drops. This wine reeks of rotten eggs, burned matches, and animal sweat. How on earth can this be wine from one of Germany's most coveted estates? Why does it earn scores of 99 and 100 from the critics? And what do I say now? Katharina's eyes are locked expectantly on mine.

"Hmmm," I say, closing my eyes and breathing deeply. I'm wondering which animal's sweat I smell. "I'm not quite sure I can put my finger on exactly what I'm getting here," I murmur, playing for time.

"Well, I hope you *don't* like it—at least not yet," Katharina says, laughing. "This is from last year; we just bottled it, so what you're probably getting is the sulfur. I wanted you to taste our whole range, though, so you could see how the wines develop."

I laugh, releasing my usual nervousness. The young Prüm wines are tightly wound, feral creatures, with forbidding aromas of yeast and sulfur. They're often described as "backwards" because they don't reveal their rich fruit and finesse until after at least five years of aging. The family favors longevity over accessibility, tradition over innovation.

Katharina and I move on to sampling the next riesling, which shimmers like a gold leaf. This wine reels me in with an electric interplay between fleshy fruit and racy acidity. Prüm wines, while never the boldest, are among the most exciting in their ephemeral vibrancy. I lick my lips, savoring its tangerine fragrance. It's refreshing in a world awash with vanilla, oak, and jam. (In life and in wine: too much foreplay is frustrating and too quick satiation is boring.) We often confuse light body with lack of taste.

"It is fascinating to live with wine," Katharina observes softly. "Every day, the wines become a little more expressive. To work on one thing for months, you must have discipline, but it is also peaceful, meditative work. After fermentation, we work hard to do nothing," she says, smiling. "We just try to keep the wine stable."

Every time wine is moved, even for filtration or pumping, it loses some of its freshness and purity. So the Prüm bottling line is a mobile unit that's brought to the wine, rather than the other way around. The wine is further coddled with a gravity-flow system rather than a mechanized one. All these measures, plus the use of wild yeasts, which create sulfur by-products as they metabolize, as well as the sulfur the winemaker adds, help the wine retain its acrid smell. That's a good thing for wines designed to age, since sulfur, like the tarry tannins in young red wine, allows the wines to mature slowly, though it makes them a bitter mouthful when young.

The Prüm's famously frigid cellars slow fermentation from the usual two to four weeks to three months or more. The chill also gives the wine a light spritz because a little carbon dioxide remains in them. The wine ferments in stainless steel tanks rather than in oak, which works better for vines grown on stone. The grapes move from rock to metal; both preserve freshness. Barrels are better for wine from heavy soils, such as the clay in Chile and California. The open-grained wood allows a little oxygen in, giving the wine more texture and heft. But riesling doesn't need power any more than angels need muscle.

Riesling has a robust longevity that goes back almost two millennia. Like all vines, riesling is a weed, originating in Germany during the Middle Ages. Well before that, the ancient Romans first cultivated vines here for some 450 years. The remains of their pressing houses are scattered along the Moselle. In 371 CE, the poet Ausonius wrote about winemaking in this valley in his poem "Mosella." In medieval times, the monks tended the vineyards, and then the aristocracy took them over when Napoleon secularized the holdings in the early 1800s.

During this time, exports were steadily increasing throughout Europe. In 1845, Queen Victoria, who was married to a German, her beloved Prince Albert, coined the term *hock* for riesling, which became her favorite wine after she drank it in the Hockenheim region on the Rhine River. ("A glass of hock keeps away the doc.") Soon after, hock became *the* white wine of aristocratic British dinners, joining the select company of bordeaux, the red also known as claret, and port, the postprandial drink.

Although generations of winemakers have cultivated riesling, it remains the most naked of wines, never blended with other grapes or wines in Germany, and rarely combined with riesling from neighboring vineyards. In some other countries, wines labeled as single varietal are still allowed to have other grapes in the blend. A Californian cabernet sauvignon, for example, can actually contain as much as 25 percent merlot in the bottle. And unlike nonvintage champagne, riesling from different years isn't blended, so there's no compensating for one bad year with a few good ones. It's also not aged in wood to add oaky flavors, nor does it undergo malolactic fermentation, in which harsh malo acids naturally present in the wine are converted into softer lactic acids. That's why riesling is considered a wine of purity, a liquid mirror of the vineyard—and of winemaking mistakes. Small flaws are magnified in the bottle. That's why more and more producers are now using screw caps to avoid the taint that corks can easily impart to such a transparent wine.

Like Prüm, many leading estates focus exclusively on riesling. However, they may make ten or more of them from different vineyards, different parts of the same vineyard, different styles, or different quality levels. Prüm's pickers sometimes make fifteen or more passes through their vines in the fall, combing them to select only fruit at peak ripeness and sorting them by hand. The grapes are fermented in small batches to preserve subtle differences. In fact, the eight-gallon tanks often used for riesling look like milk cans in comparison to the gleaming fifty-foot ones in other regions that are always part of a tour (even though when you've seen one tank, you really have seen them all).

"Some vintners have an image of the wine they want to create, but we just take the wines nature gives us," Katharina explains. She pours me another glass, her large brown eyes alive with mischief. "So what is this?" she asks.

Since our last glass was her most basic wine, a riesling kabinett, it's not a terribly astute guess that she's gone one step up. "Riesling spätlese?" I ask tentatively.

"Yes, but what year?"

The fruit aromas are still fresh in this one, but without the heavy sulfur residue. "Could it be 2002?"

"It's 2004. It has a good line," she says simply. "Clear and elegant."

We taste through a range of vintages and styles as the sun shafts through the emerald bottles on the table. (Mosel bottles are green glass; those from the neighboring region of the Rheingau are brown.) Katharina uncorks a bottle of Wehlener Sonnenuhr Riesling Auslese Long Gold Capsule. It delivers a mouth-shock of ripe apricots, finishing with a haunting lemon smoke. There's also the elusive exhilaration of a dream about running a marathon that makes your heart pound, even though you haven't left your bed.

"This reminds me of the wonderful 1893 vintage," she says, as though she remembers picking the grapes. I love the way she can telescope time—a hundred years is nothing when your family has been making wine for centuries.

"We can't rest on our history, but you should still taste it in the wine," she says as we say good-bye.

Leaving the house, I look up at the high windows and spot the man I met earlier. Before I can wave to him, he's gone. Later in my trip, paging through a book on German wines, I find his photo and realize that I did meet Manfred Prüm.

No one could be less elusive or more vocal than Ernst Loosen of the Dr. Loosen wine estate, the next vintner I meet. Ernie loves to enthuse about German wines and to rail against the country's restrictive wine laws, which are among the toughest in the world. Compared to the Prüms, he and his family are relative parvenus: they've owned their Mosel estate for only two hundred years. Also unlike them, Ernie isn't shy. He's part of a small international cadre of winemaker rock stars that includes California's Randall Grahm and Italy's Angelo Gaja—men known as much for their opinions as for their wines. The British wine writer Hugh Johnson observed, "Ernie Loosen has brought the Mosel and its rieslings into the twenty-first century with a bang. He thinks worldwide, as few German vintners have done."

Ernie studied viticulture at Germany's renowned Geisenheim University, but he had no intention of taking over the family business. He was just there to appease his father, even though Loosen senior had treated the winery as a sideline to his real work as a lawyer and politician. At Geisenheim, Ernie and his roommates "didn't get up before noon" and skipped most of the lectures. Still, he managed to graduate in 1981 and then went on to pursue his true passion at the University of Mainz: archaeology.

When his father fell ill a few years later, his mother talked about selling the winery. Ernie decided that he would run it. Before doing so, he embarked on a self-directed tour of some of the best estates in Europe and North America to understand what makes a wine great. The journey taught him to respect local traditions as it broadened his perspective globally. One of the most important things that he learned was from Olivier Humbrecht in Alsace, who showed him whole-cluster pressing—the grapes are pressed in full bunches, not crushed individually—to retain fresh fruit flavors. Ernie, in turn, introduced this technique in the Mosel.

When he started managing the winery in 1987, Ernie realized that his family's benign neglect of their vineyards had actually been a bonus. Back in the 1970s, they had ignored the fashion to rip out old riesling vines for more productive, less flavorful grapes. As a result, his mature vines, some now 120 years old, produced tiny amounts of concentrated fruit. They were still on their original rootstocks, having escaped the phylloxera blight that ravaged so many of Europe's vineyards in the late 1800s. The destructive aphid can't survive in much of the Mosel's rugged terrain. Ernie had the two things he needed most: old vines and great dirt.

He made some radical decisions, one of which was to hire his college classmate Bernhard "Bernie" Schug as winemaker. He also decided to slash yields, to use organic fertilizers instead of chemicals, to let the grapes ripen longer on the vines, to hand-select them at harvest, and to treat the wine gently in the cellar. In these matters he was ahead of his time, but his employees weren't happy with the new hands-on approach: it meant more work for them. They walked out in the middle of the 1987 vintage.

"I could either apologize to them so that they'd return, but I'd never be able to control them," he tells me later. "Or I could just ignore them. If I fired them, I'd have to pay expensive severance fees. So I called their bluff. Best decision I made."

After this hurdle, he had to identify which vines he owned, since the family holdings were fragmented into more than 160 parcels of land scattered among other producers' vines. A consummate prag-matist, Ernie decided to simply wait until everyone else had finished picking so he could tell which grapes were his. His tactical decision turned out to be a brilliant strategy. That November was warm and dry, perfect for ripening 67 percent of his late-hanging grapes to the highest quality, while most other estates had only 1 percent at that level that year. He still picks later than most producers, hoping that even after bloating September rains, the weather will warm and ripen the grapes just that little bit further.

Ernie's next big obstacle was his own father, who was reluctant to give him credit or control of the winery. Several months after they agreed on a lease, his father wanted to increase the payments that he received from Ernie because the doctor on the label referred to him, not to his son. Ernie reminded him that his new wife had graduated from medical school: "She's the doctor on the label."

I'm meeting Ernie at the pretasting for the Grosser Ring Auction in Trier, Germany's oldest city. Founded in 16 CE, it still has the noble ruins of Roman amphitheaters and imperial baths. The annual auction, which attracts serious collectors from all over the world who buy the Mosel's rarest wines, helps set the prices for all the rest. This free-market approach would probably have been scorned by Trier's most famous native son, Karl Marx. However, he did write sympathetically about the difficulties facing local producers in the 1800s. Grape pickers unite!

As I make my way through the chattering, clinking crowd, I spot his hand first, stabbing the air enthusiastically above the cluster of people around him. Then I catch sight of the tousled gray curls, gold-rimmed glasses, and waistcoat. He reminds me of a radical classics professor I once knew: irreverent, witty, outrageous, and still on fire with his subject, especially when he finds attentive students.

"A great wine begins in your head," Ernie says to the group. "But of course, the measure of a great wine isn't where it begins but where it ends—in your glass!"

The man is still a tornado of energy, whose vortex is propelled by travel, talk, and drink. The group doesn't disband until the bell rings for the auction to begin, and I finally get the chance to introduce myself. "Ah, Natalie, good!" he exclaims. "We'll talk after the auction. Lots to discuss!"

Four hours later, it's a relief when the auction is over. Ernie has invited me to taste his wines at his home this afternoon. As we walk to the parking lot, he launches into his manifesto: "Many wines are big and fat and that's it, you know, but riesling is strong and delicate at the same time. It has many facets, like a diamond, depending on when and where you taste it and what you're looking for."

As we jump into his burgundy Porsche SUV, its interior all spotless cream leather with bird's-eye-maple woodwork, he doesn't pause in his dissertation. "When cabernet and chardonnay grapes get riper, the wines get more flavorful," he says as he peels out of the garage. "But riesling isn't like that. Quick ripening just makes it awkward. It demands spot-on viticulture."

As we hit the Autobahn, his explanations—and the Porsche— accelerate. "There are thirteen distinct regions in this country, you know, so we don't talk about German wine, we talk about Mosel riesling," he says, hitting the steering wheel, making the SUV swerve a little into the opposite lane. "I am fascinated with the differences!"

I am fascinated with the oncoming traffic. Fortunately, another passionate gesture gets us back over the line into safety.

"When I drink Mosel riesling, I want to *smell* the blue slate soil that formed the fruit. I want to *taste* the memory of the old vines, and I want to *feel* the rain and the sun that year," he declares. "Without all of this, wine is just another drink."

Mosel rieslings are sculpted from acidity rather than from alcohol, so they need some sweetness to soften their taut lines and to flesh out the fruit flavors. Producers stop fermentation when it's only about two-thirds complete to preserve the grape's natural sweetness, which also results in a relatively low alcohol level of 7 to 8 percent.

In fact, riesling's versatility from puckeringly dry to succulently sweet can be a handicap. The wine can surprise novices who open a bottle expecting a dry taste and instead discover a dessert wine. By contrast, chardonnay is always made in a dependable dry style, so drinkers have a better idea of what they're getting. Dependable, of course, doesn't mean good, just consistent.

Ernie shifts gears literally and figuratively: "We understand the difference that soils make because we can see them: slate, quartz, limestone, clay, and so on. But it's hard for most people to imagine the microclimate around the vines or the drainage conditions below them. Yet these factors have a profound effect on wine. Technical analysis doesn't tell you those things, only tasting does."

Ernie doesn't seem to be a man who lacks marketing savvy; his wines are now sold in fifty-nine countries. Other Mosel vintners might wonder why he bothers with tiny islands in the South Pacific or outposts in the frozen north, but he views global distribution as a sound sales strategy. He jokingly refers to his missionary work as "The Rocky Horror Riesling Show." He is also one of the organizers of the Riesling Rendezvous, an annual summit in Washington State that draws vintners, wine lovers, and writers from around the world.

"When others gave up, I kept going, giving tastings even when it was just for two old ladies in a hotel ballroom," he says, laughing. He believes that these grassroots efforts are the only way to return riesling to its rightful place as the queen of white wines. But don't get him started on the marketing success of liebfraumilch in the 1970s.

"It almost destroyed Germany's image," Ernie growls, knocking the rearview mirror askew with a dismissive wave. The wine had a harmless genesis back in the 1800s. *Liebfraumilch*, medieval German for "blessed mother's milk" or "milk of Our Lady," was first made on former convent grounds near Wittenberg, where Martin Luther was purported to have nailed his manifesto to a cathedral door to start the Protestant Reformation. Back then, liebfraumilch was a high-quality wine of limited distribution made by the Valckenberg family. But the quality declined over the years, helped by the infamous German Wine Law of 1971.

The bright idea was to introduce *grosslagen* (large or collective wine-growing sites) to simplify wine labels. The plan was to expand the definitions of the most prestigious vineyard and village names from precise boundaries to areas of hundreds of miles. This would give a commercial boost to many wine cooperatives and small growers. The rules were open to abuse because high quality was equated only with ripeness. Suddenly, it was all about sugar, so these wines simply increased their sweetness without balancing acidity or flavor. The obscure hybrid grapes used were so vigorous they often collapsed the vines under their weight.

Liebfraumilch brands such as Blue Nun and Black Tower killed riesling's reputation just as Mateus killed dry rosé, Beaujolais nouveau the age-worthy Beaujolais crus, and white zinfandel the red kind. Decades later, top German producers are still trying to shake that cheap-and-sweet image from the drugged-out 1970s.

"Blue Nun and Black Tower don't represent a region or a style," Ernie mutters. "They're Coca-Cola brands. Even *cru bourgeois* wines are still typical of Bordeaux—the French never gutted their reputation as we did."

However, these wines fed on the zeitgeist of North Americans who were new to wine and wanted something sweet to wean themselves from martinis and spirits. The wines were perfect with shrimp cocktails and hot-dog canapés. In the late 1980s, a backlash against cheap, sweet wines began and has continued ever since, as North Americans developed a taste for drier, more complex wines. Drinkers moved on to wines made in Australia, Chile, and California, and began asking for their wines by grape name.

"No one wanted to hear about riesling when I started. It was all chardonnay, you know?" Ernie says, looking at me and shrugging. I shake my head vehemently, hoping he'll watch the road again.

At its peak in the 1970s, Blue Nun was selling more than 35 million bottles a year worldwide, and Black Tower around 12 million. By the late 1980s, sales had fallen to less than half of that. Sales have since recovered, and the two brands remain Germany's top-selling wines. Like specters emerging from the Black Forest, they both have assumed a new form. The companies now use riesling grapes, and their sugar content has dropped, though they're still more "fruity" than average. (That's the term wine companies prefer today rather than the S-word, which is bad for sales.) They've also started to make red wines. Black Tower blends pinot noir with the German hybrid grape dornfelder. The red version of Blue Nun (Purple Novice?) uses merlot grapes from the southwest of France.

They've updated their look as well. The iconic stone-crock-style Black Tower bottle, a re-creation of a Roman wine vessel, has been slimmed down and the label simplified. Both the Blue Nun's robe and her bottle have been changed from brown to blue. The old girl herself got a makeover, too, going from frumpy to fit—less Sister Wendy, more Julie Andrews. And unlike traditional German wines with long, difficult names, Blue Nun and Black Tower are easy to say in a liquor store or restaurant.

"Why do we have to throw *all* those damn terms on our labels?" Ernie exclaims.

With their indecipherable gothic script and nomenclature, interpreting most German labels is a Wagnerian exercise. Hugh Johnson once commented that he was surprised that no one had ever endowed a university chair in German wine labels. Ernie's own view is that basic wines should print only the estate name on the front label, and all other information should go on the back.

He also thinks that marketing-driven brands, with no connection to a particular grape, style, or place, do nothing to help Germany. In his view, more and more people "don't want to drink anonymously anymore. They want to know about the wine, where it came from, who made it. The specific is knowable, but the generic is not. One is artisanal, the other is mass culture."

In pursuit of that goal, he believes that the top German estates should follow France's example and produce second labels—a more economical version of their best wines. Château Mouton-Rothschild, for example, produces Le Petit Mouton and the even lower-priced Mouton Cadet. This top-down philosophy makes a lot of sense.

"For years, we led with the cheap wines, and now we need to focus on the best estates to reestablish our reputation," he tells me. "Look at France: Château Margaux sets the image, and the basic wines benefit. Most people can't afford the great estates, but they can still buy a small piece of the Bordeaux prestige with the bourgeois wines."

At last, we pull in front of his vine-covered home, high on the bank of the Moselle River just outside the town of Bernkastel. Inside, the library overlooking the river is lined with sagging bookshelves, photographs, maps, and awards. A pitted oak desk in one corner is strewn with papers, notebooks, and old vine cuttings. We sit at the dining table and he pours me a glass of Dr. L Riesling. Even his wines—gutsy and opulent—are a stark contrast to the delicacy of J. J. Prüm's, yet both have a crystalline clarity. This one begins with wild field flower aromas, then offers the snap-and-attack of limes and green apples.

The next wine he pours, his Ürziger Würzgarten Riesling Spätlese, glides to the back of my mouth so quickly that it brings to mind the term *seamless integration*—one that some critics use to describe such wines. To me, it's just slippery-good. *Würzgarten* means "spice garden," and I can smell the faint notes of nutmeg and cloves that give the wine its name. These vines grow in red volcanic soil that gives even white wines exotic aromas of red berries rather than the green apple and lime notes associated with blue slate.

In fact, most Mosel rieslings tend to have citrus aromas, such as lemon, lime, and grapefruit, whereas wines from the neighboring Rheingau are chiseled from yellow stone-fruit notes, like apricot, peach, and Anjou pear. In the warmer region of the Pfalz, rieslings have aromas of dark yellow fruit, like mango and papaya. However, all those flavors can change with the temperature of the growing season. In cooler years, they all lean toward tart citrus fruit and green apples; in warmer vintages, they achieve riper tropical-fruit notes.

As we continue tasting, he brings out his Wehlener Sonnenuhr Auslese, which, like Prüm's interpretation of this vineyard, fills my senses with tangerine radiance. Although the wine is sweet, its filigreed acidity gives it a clean, refreshing taste. It finishes like a sunset that throws slashes of purple, red, and amber across the sky.

"We need riesling back on stage," Ernie says as we sip the wine. "But single estates are too small to carry the message alone." Like Burgundy, most producers here are small because the inheritance laws are based on the Napoleonic code, introduced in the early 1800s. When a father died, the estate was divided equally among male offspring. The result, over two hundred years, was that vineyards were divided among ever-greater numbers of descendants, becoming ever-smaller parcels of land. Today, the average vineyard size is just seven acres. Many winemakers view themselves as gardeners, tending their tiny plots with the attention usually paid to roses and hollyhocks. In contrast, Bordeaux châteaux often own thousands of acres because inheritance passed solely to the eldest son under the law of primogeniture.

While Ernie explains this to me, we taste his Erdener Prälat Riesling Auslese Long Gold Capsule from his most prized vineyard. He owns less than four acres of this treasured plot, nestled into a curve of the Moselle where the warmth of the sun and river are concentrated. The grapes for this voluptuous riesling are picked last, giving the wine a heady richness and length that chardonnay can only dream of. It's also a subtle wine, with a finesse that occurs to you only after the second or third glass. It reminds me of evenings when I settle into a good book, race through the rolling narrative, and then look up at the end to realize that it's morning.

I ask about the story behind its unusual name. Prälat refers to a Christian prelate in 1066 who was captured and held for ransom by robber barons in a castle on the hill. Like many entrepreneurs, the villains misjudged their market: no one was willing to pay the ransom. So they dumped the goods, throwing the abbot off the steep cliff to his death into what is now the Prälat vineyard. Local legend says that the soil is still stained with his blood. In fact, the earth is naturally rust colored from the underlying red slate. But as Ernie tells me poker-faced, it does produce "a bloody good wine."

Many believe that the resurgence of riesling began in 2001, spurred by one of the greatest vintages in a quarter century. Those wines were heralded by sommeliers, retailers, and writers around the world. The famous American critic Robert Parker published his first big report on German riesling that year. Since then, North American sales of riesling have jumped 49 percent, making it one of the fastest-growing categories of wine, along with the other fresh, unoaked white wine from Italy, pinot grigio.

Despite this, riesling remains an insider's wine. Wine drinkers love to ignore the writers who keep recommending it. Of the 19.5 million acres of all vineyards worldwide, riesling is just half a percent.

Ernie sighs and looks out at the glittering river. "This riesling renaissance everyone talks about isn't going to start in Germany. The New World will lead it. But once people are hooked on the wine, they'll come back to us. We are riesling's spiritual home."

* * *

LATER THAT EVENING, after saying good-bye to Ernie, I'm driving along a country road through an ancient forest. As my stomach grumbles, my mind turns to the questions about food-and-wine pairings that my readers often email me.

"What should I drink with Pacific salmon?"

Try a crisp riesling, I usually reply.

"How about an Indian curry?"

Have you thought about a slightly off-dry riesling to balance the heat of the spices?

"What goes well with fresh salad greens and a lemon vinaigrette?"

A citrusy riesling would be perfect.

"Herb-rubbed chicken?"

You can't go wrong with a riesling.

Did I mention that riesling is incredibly versatile? The wine is like the foam cuisine: an ethereal essence of flavor. We drink it with some of the foods that are toughest on wine, such as sauerkraut, bratwurst, and Wienerschnitzel. (Maybe the Germans *had* to invent such a resilient wine just to match their traditional cuisine.)

Riesling doesn't get clobbered by rich dishes because of its steely acidity, but it also pairs well with delicate dishes because of its low alcohol and subtle flavors. In our modern health-conscious society, more and more people are turning away from the problems plaguing meat production, such as unsanitary and inhumane factories, steroids, animal diseases, and fear of cancer. Instead, we're eating lighter foods, like salads, vegetables, and seafood, and we prefer spices and herbs for flavoring rather than butter and salt. All these choices are natural partners for riesling.

The magic ingredient that enables riesling to be such a vinous chameleon is acidity. I avoid using the word *acid* in my tasting notes because of its unfortunate connotations of drinking battery acid or sucking on lemons. But the natural acidity in riesling is both harmless and beneficial. It gives the wine lift and refreshment; it's the cool wind that tempers the heat of alcohol. If alcohol in wine is depth, richness, and power, acidity is zest, vitality, and youth. Acidity is the prickling excitement that gets your juices running, your mind wheeling. Imagine a salmon steak from the grill with no lemon juice to brighten the smoky char. Whenever you squeeze lemon juice on food, drink riesling with it. (But if you slather butter on the dish, try chardonnay instead.)

As I round the last forest bend in the road, I see the lights of Rüssels Landhaus St. Urban, the companion restaurant of St. Urbans-Hof winery, glowing in a clearing. I've been dying to visit this bistro for its modern German cuisine that has evolved well past the heavy dishes I mentioned earlier. In fact, this country is now second only to France in its number of Michelin-starred restaurants. Yet because there are very few German restaurants in other countries compared to the number of French and Italian establishments, we're not as familiar with this country's cuisine and wine. As well, many people travel to France and Italy on culinary holidays, but far fewer choose Germany.

This evening, I'm looking forward to chatting with Nikolaus Weis, the third generation of his family to run the winery originally founded in 1947 by his grandfather. Before taking over the family business in 1997, Nik studied at Geisenheim, then apprenticed in California, Champagne, and Niagara. His winery, St. Urbans-Hof, is named after the patron saint of wine producers, the third-century St. Urban, also known as Pope Urban I. The restaurant is run by Nik's sister, Ruth, and her husband, Harald Rüssel, who are mâitre d' and chef, respectively. As I enter the warm, cozy restaurant that smells of simmering sauces, I'm greeted by Nik, a handsome thirty-five-year-old, who clearly enjoys a good meal.

"Shall we start with a glass of riesling?" he asks playfully, as we sit down at a table with two chilled glasses of St. Urbans-Hof Kabinett. "It's a peerless aperitif, the only wine to drink in the morning," he adds. "It satisfies your blood sugar without making you drunk."

Wine in the morning? Nik is my kind of man. But he's not the first to propose such a civilized start to the day. Thomas Jefferson, who visited Germany in 1775 before going home to pen America's Declaration of Independence, described the rieslings as the "best breakfast wines."

I'm loving this riesling, a bewitching bouquet of freesia and lilacs. It's a slender wine but incredibly flavorful, with just 7 percent alcohol. I comment on this, and Nik agrees. "We are happy with each percentage of alcohol that we *don't* have to put in the bottle. People no longer drink aperitifs and ports in restaurants because they're concerned about the calories and the drive home."

Ruth and Harald, an attractive couple in their thirties, come out to greet us. If I don't mind, they say, they'd like to prepare a surprise menu this evening of local game and fish, homemade breads, fresh vegetables, and fruit from their garden. I don't mind.

Our aperitif riesling goes beautifully with the first course: breast of wild duck with poached duck liver, sautéed figs, and a sherry-vinegar jelly. "Riesling cuts through the fat in the duck and lifts up a heavy dish," Nik says, moistening his lips.

The wine works just as well with savory game birds and braised meats, which are often accompanied by a sweet garnish like jelly, chutney, or berries. Riesling's own sweetness, Nik explains, adds piquancy rather than heaviness, making the wine taste more alive.

The natural sugar amplifies the wine's fruity ripeness. Sweetness is as much the signature of riesling as bubbles are of champagne.

The next kabinett Nik and I drink comes from the famous Ock-fener Bockstein vineyard, another steep, rocky slope, with slate that leaves a bluish powder on your fingers. Nik still uses viticultural techniques introduced by the Romans two thousand years ago, like trellising his vines on single poles rather than on horizontal wires between posts, as is done in other countries. The vine canes are tied to the pole in the shape of a heart, which gives the grapes more exposure to the sun and makes them easier to pick. These leafy hearts look like rows of Irish valentines. Grapes are then handpicked into shoulder-mounted baskets so they're not damaged.

Our next wine, the Piesporter Goldtröpfchen Riesling Spätlese, is a bit sweeter and dances with our second course: belly of pork and goose liver on noodles, with nuts and apple-vinegar sauce. Nik starts to talk about sugar and riesling, a subject that provokes debate and frustration for many vintners here.

"We're the only country in the world to put our sweetness front and center on the label," he says. "Château d'Yquem doesn't list the grams of sugar on its label. We created our own problems by focusing on that aspect. Describing a wine solely in terms of its sweetness is like describing a woman just by her height and weight—it doesn't give you a sense of the complete person."

Sweetness, like acidity, is necessary for complexity. The main source of sweetness in wine is the natural sugar in ripening grapes, which increases with more warmth and hang time. Grapes for the best wines are picked over a six-week period to capture just the right degree of ripeness for each particular wine style. The second source of sweetness is when the vintner adds süssreserve (unfermented grape juice). This process, permitted only for the most basic wines, is used when grapes fail to ripen enough to balance their acidity. Top estates, such as St. Urbans-Hof, Loosen, and Prüm, rarely use this method, or don't at all. That's because sugar, like oak, can mask faults or lack of taste in inferior wine.

German rieslings often get an unfair rap for cloying sweetness, even though many "dry" New World wines actually taste sweeter. Take Californian chardonnays, for example. Some of the more popular brands don't have the acidity to balance their residual sugar, ripe fruit, and creamy oak notes. The same applies to high-alcohol wines, which taste sweeter than they really are because alcohol gives the impression of sweetness even though it actually has no flavor. So, we talk dry and drink sweet.

"With riesling, sweet can be good, dry can be good," Nik observes. "But completely dry chardonnay sucks."

Riesling, with all its complexities, is often overshadowed by the more obvious charms of chardonnay, the world's most popular white wine. Chardonnay is the pliable good-girl of the wine world, adapting to the winemaker's hand and absorbing the barrel's flavor. Oak is the sensory counterpoint in wines that don't have much acidity. Just as many people who eat hot-buttered popcorn actually like the taste of butter more than the corn, many of those who love chardonnay actually love the taste of oak, butter, cream, vanilla, and smoke.

"It's just mean to put a California chardonnay beside a German riesling in a blind tasting," Nik says. "Their robust flavors overwhelm rieslings. We call them U-boats."

For me, the difference between the two wines is their comparative ranges. Riesling is a quivering wine of potential energy that reminds me of opera diva Sarah Brightman singing pop tunes. She barely pushes her voice, yet what thrills me is knowing that her range stretches far beyond what I hear. Conversely, many chardonnays remind me of breathy pop stars who have to whisper the high notes.

That's why there's been a growing pendulum swing against chardonnay called ABC (Anything But Chardonnay). Of course, not all chardonnays fall into this stylistic camp. Chablis, unoaked chardonnay from northern Burgundy, shares riesling's nervy vivacity.

However, it's not just the unaffordable benchmark wines that should be considered great, whether it's riesling, chablis, or pinot noir. As Nik points out, "Relevance is an aspect of greatness. It's important to have a wine that you can make a part of your daily life rather than having to save it for special occasions. Affordability is part of that."

Entry-level German wines are labeled QbA (*Qualitätswein bestimmter Anbaugebiete*), meaning a quality wine that has enough character to taste like its growing area. The best rieslings are labeled QmP (*Qualitätswein mit Prädikat*), meaning a quality wine of special distinction. Like it or not, the Germans categorize their finest wines not by vineyard or region, like the French and Italians, but according to the grape's sweetness when picked. So prädikat wines are "predicated" on six levels: *kabinett, spätlese, auslese, beerenauslese, trockenbeerenauslese*, and *eiswein*.

The greater the ripeness, the higher the wine is ranked. But this designation only refers to how sweet the grapes were at harvest, not necessarily how sweet the wine will eventually taste. Vintners can still ferment their grapes to complete dryness. You need to learn your prädikats to understand German wine the way you learned your multiplication tables for basic math. Quit moaning; just do it.

Kabinett (*kah-bee-NEHT*) rieslings, like the delicate, dry one that Nik and I started with this evening, are made from fully ripened grapes. "Kabinett" originally referred to the locked cabinets in which the most valuable wines were cellared. These wines go well with light dishes, such as sole, trout, sushi, salads, smoked salmon, and mild curries.

The next level up is spätlese (*SHPAYT-lay-zuh*), meaning "late harvest." These grapes are picked at least a week after the main harvest is finished, so the wines have a hint of sweetness and are more full-bodied than kabinetts. Legend has it that the spätlese style was created by accident in 1775. Back then, a courier on a fast horse took an annual sample of the grapes to the Prince Abbot of Fulda to get his approval to begin the harvest. But that year the prince was late in giving his consent. By the time the "Spätlese Rider" returned, the grapes had overripened.

So rather than lose both the harvest and their heads, the vintners decided to pick the grapes anyway. To their delight, these sublimely rotten grapes created a new luscious style of wine that was a hit at court. In subsequent harvests, they experimented with leaving some grapes on the vines for longer and longer periods. Goethe, author of *Faust* and a man who surely knew how easy it is to sell one's soul for greatness, was an avid fan of these sweeter styles. In 1814, he wrote in his diary, "The excellence of the wine depends upon the site, but also upon the late harvesting."

Nik and I are now enjoying our third course of codfish in a potato-pumpkin broth with white onions and mushrooms. His Piesporter Goldtröpfchen Riesling Spätlese goes beautifully with the dish. We also drink this wine with the next two courses: pikeperch with chin of pork, bacon-mashed potatoes and chicory with orange-cardamom gravy, and then (you didn't think you were done yet, did you?) red mullet with chickpeas, polenta, and beans in a carrot-thyme sauce.

Our sixth course—sweetbreads on fig couscous—dances with our third wine, Ockfener Bockstein Riesling Auslese, redolent of ripe apricots. Auslese (*OWS-lay-zuh*), German for "select," are rieslings made from selected bunches of late-harvested grapes. Often, they've started to overripen, becoming affected by the desirable mold

Botrytis cinerea, or noble rot (*edelfäule* in German). The mold attacks the grape skins, dehydrates the fruit, and concentrates its sugar and flavor. This natural chemical transformation in the grape gives the final wine a lovely orange-tinged honey flavor. Germany's most famous dessert wines are touched by botrytis, as are Bordeaux sauternes (like Château d'Yquem) and Hungary's tokaji.

"The ugliest grapes give the best juice," Nik says, showing me a bunch he's brought from the vineyard. The leathery, furry berries don't look good enough for horse feed, but he tells me that the fruit will yield five different wines. The bitter botrytis taste finds its balance in the wine's honeyed notes, creating a savory character that works with hearty meat dishes, like the one we have next: a nut-encrusted saddle of deer, accompanied by dumplings and quince in a pepper gravy. Savory dishes like venison demand mature rieslings, since the sweet and sour element of the meat and plum or raspberry sauce requires a wine that has intensity of flavor but isn't obviously sweet. That's why mature rieslings also pair with hearty meat dishes. It's easier to match a white wine like riesling with most meats than it is to pair most robust red wines with fish.

When we get to beerenauslese (*BEAR-rehn-OWS-lay-zuh*), or BA for short, we're into the dessert wines. These are made from individually selected grapes (*beeren*) that are shriveled and fully affected by botrytis. Nik's Leiwener Laurentiuslay Riesling Beerenauslese pairs well with the Dawson apricots in aspic with Guanaja-chocolate cream and Tahitian-vanilla ice cream.

Balancing the wine's luscious texture is less a flavor than a faint tingling sensation, like I used to get as a child from Lick-a-Maid powder. Winemakers call it minerality, a trait imparted by the slate and other rocks in which the vines grow. It's as much a texture as it is a taste, but it shouldn't be confused with the aroma in mature riesling called petrol. Plants don't metabolize minerals as they do organic material, so grapes grown near roads, for example, don't produce wines with lead in them despite all the gasoline fumes they're exposed to. However, put white roses in blue-colored water and they absorb the color pigments that tinge their petals blue. The minerals in slate also dissolve in water. That's why mineral water has a more distinctive taste than filtered water. Think of it like drinking water that's gushing fresh in a mountain stream and running over the rocks.

Nevertheless, some people confuse minerality and petrol, despite the fact that most winemakers here despise the latter. The P-word is almost as verboten as the S-word. Others use the descriptors kerosene, motor oil, or gasoline. I wondered at first if these nuances were imparted from the country's famous Autobahn. And after this morning's drive, I was convinced.

Nik certainly doesn't look happy when I ask him about it. "Petrol says oxidation at best, contamination at worst," he observes. "Who wants to drink either one?"

While some drinkers and critics think petrol is a good aroma, many consider it a flaw. The aroma often develops when certain compounds in the wine oxidize, usually the result of a short, hot growing season with too little water and too much nitrogen fertilizer. As the grape tries to protect itself against environmental stress, it produces organic compounds that smell like linseed oil. Other critics say that gasoline aroma is just a matter of perception: drinkers also confuse it with dried fruit notes or the butterscotch-toffee character of mature residual sugar.

Riesling's ability to age is another aspect of its greatness. The British wine writer Jancis Robinson called them "whites for eternity." Riesling's acidity survives on its residual sugar, enabling the wines to live longer than most whites and even many reds. They can easily age for five to ten years; and the great ones, for twenty-five years or more. Chemically, riesling's molecules bind together to become longer flanking chains. New ones are created and others are destroyed in a gloriously silent battle within every bottle. The result is a long, smooth, open wine.

"The things that last have greatness, whether it's a novel that still reads well after a hundred years or a wine that drinks well after thirty," Nik says. "We all want the secret of youth, but the real secret is how to age well."

During a brief respite between courses (gasp), we enjoy a small glass of Nik's icewine. Eiswein (*ICE-vine*) is made from grapes of beerenauslese sweetness that are left on the vine in winter until frozen and picked at 18°F or colder. What little water the grapes still have in them is left on the press, so what's extracted is highly concentrated fruit flavor.

Icewine was actually discovered in Germany, by accident, in 1794. Vintners were preparing for the harvest when an unexpected early frost froze the grapes on the vine. The vintners pressed them anyway and were delighted to learn that the resulting wine was not only drinkable but exceptionally sweet and delicious—thanks to the concentration of sugar in the frozen dehydrated grapes.

Trockenbeerenauslese (*TROK-ehn-BEAR-rehn-OWS-lay-zuh*), or TBA, means "dry berry selection," for the individually selected grapes in this wine that have completely shriveled to raisins from botrytis. This wine encases our last course, an exquisite dessert of wine-poached vineyard peaches with a verbena-mousse ice cream. TBA wines are the richest, rarest dessert wines of nectared depth.

Mentally, I compare this wine with Château d'Yquem, also made from 100 percent botrytis-affected grapes, but the sauterne has more alcohol and less acidity than TBA wines. For the true hedonist who wants to prolong pleasure, TBA is your wine. You don't tire of it quickly. That's why many people enjoy it with foie gras at the beginning of a meal; it's lighter than the traditional sauternes and, hence, less filling and less inebriating. In fact, through extensive research, I've discovered that the only dishes that clash with riesling are rare steaks (the wine lacks tannin for the meat's juicy proteins to latch on to) and cotton candy (for pete's sake, you're at the fair so have a beer).

Now that dinner's over, Nik and I keep ourselves from falling asleep at the table with a spirited discussion on how the country's wine labels are a metaphor for the German soul. "Why should our labels be easy to read when our wine was so hard to make?" Nik jokes. "Should Thomas Mann's *Magic Mountain* be condensed to make it more accessible? We Germans love complexity."

I can tell. Unlike France's relatively stable bordeaux classification of 1855, the changes to Germany's prädikat system since 1971 would bring a senate inquiry to its knees. The problem was that the new classifications were both too vague and too generous (political) in awarding top status. They also didn't replace the existing system but simply added more layers of confusion.

However, Nik makes a good point: "Burgundy is even more complex, but wine lovers make an effort to understand it because the wines are so great. Germany deserves the same effort." At least riesling is labeled with the grape, whereas Burgundy's pinot noir isn't. And often there are many owners of one Burgundian vineyard whereas there are more German estates owned by just one family.

Today, the best riesling producers agree that a national classification of vineyards is the only way to escape the chaos of the sugar cult. However, they're not waiting for the country's wine laws to change. Many have started to brand-name their own wines to guarantee quality, such as Loosen's Dr. L Riesling and Nik's Urban Riesling.

The International Riesling Foundation, formed in Washington State in 2007, has proposed an even simpler Riesling Taste Scale. It designates wines as one of the following: dry, off-dry, medium dry, medium sweet, and sweet. The power of such voluntary guidelines is not only that they're easier for consumers to understand but also that they can be universally applied to rieslings from many regions and countries.

Closer to home, Nik feels that riesling should be the only wine made in the Mosel. Until 1988, making red wine here was actually illegal, but now the government allows up to 10 percent of production to be red. He also believes that wine should be made on only the south-facing sites, and yields should come down. The poor-quality growers get three times as much wine from a vine as the better-quality ones do.

"I have riesling in my blood," Nik says, smiling. "Every generation reinvents winemaking from the way their parents did it—we just do what our grandfathers did. We're trying to get back to where we were, but it might take another generation to do that—or a century."

A FEW DAYS later, I'm driving beside the Moselle as dazzling shafts of sun burn through the morning fog. I've tasted an impressive array of wines this week, both from the Mosel and from other regions: Fritz Haag, Willi Schaefer, Egon Müller, Zilliken, Christoffel, Dr. Pauly-Bergweiler, Dr. Bürklin-Wolf, Selbach-Oster, Schloss Vollrads, and Robert Weil. All were remarkable in their own way but share an effortless vitality.

Now I'm on my way to visit Bernkasteler Doctor, one of the

country's best vineyards and certainly its most storied. Founded in 1291, Bernkastel is an opera-set village of half-timbered houses, window ledges filled with flowers, narrow cobbled streets, courtyard fountains, and a medieval clock tower. High above the town, a crumbling castle is a black shadow against the sky.

Nine vineyards can put Bernkastel's prestigious name on their label, but the most famous is the Doctor. This tiny vineyard clings to the cliff that soars up behind the village, where eight acres are sheltered from cold winds by the Hunsrück Mountains. The south-facing vines soak up reflected warmth from the sun, the river, and the town's slate roofs.

The Bernkasteler Doctor vineyard earned its name in 1630, when the Prince of Trier, Archbishop Bohemund II, fell gravely ill while visiting the village. He declared that the person who saved his life would be granted any wish. A local winemaker gave the cleric a flask of his wine, which resulted in a miraculous recovery. The archbishop granted the man's wish to call the vineyard "the Doktor" for its curative properties. The wily vintner knew that its value would soar with such a name.

A few decades later in 1650, Christoph von Söetern, the owner of the vineyard, decided to create a storage vault for his wine inside the mountain. There were no machines or explosives back then; the 210 feet of slate rock was all dug out by hand. Today, the cave still has 90 percent natural humidity and a temperature that stays at 50°F in summer and winter. It's perfect for wine storage.

The vineyard passed from owner to owner until 1900, when local brothers Carl and Julius Wegeler bought the largest parcel of it for an astronomical sum. For every single vine, they paid roughly the price of a horse—some one hundred goldmarks, or $29. But their enormous investment paid off. The vineyard's wines have long commanded Germany's highest prices. The 1959 Wegeler Doctor Spätlese, for instance, sold for $10.25, whereas the 1959 Pétrus went for just $7.95. Such was the wine's prestige that Dr. Konrad Adenauer, a chancellor of Germany, gave fifty bottles to President Eisenhower during his state visit in 1962. Today, the Doctor vineyard is the highest-priced piece of agricultural land in Germany, and its grapes cost three times as much as those from vineyards on either side of it.

In 1957, Carl Wegeler's great-grandson Rolf retired and handed over the family's 148 acres of vineyards, including the Doctor, to his oldest daughter, Anja. Until then, her interests lay more in commerce. She had taken a master's of business administration at the University of Trier. There she had met her future husband, Tom Drieseberg, while he was completing his PhD with a thesis on the rituals of eating and drinking as cultural indicators. They married, both worked briefly in the consumer products industry, and then Rolf suggested that they take over the estate.

I meet Tom in front of the Wegeler home. He's six-foot-three with laughing periwinkle blue eyes and a friendly manner. He claps me on the shoulder as we shake hands. With him is winemaker Norbret Breit, a shorter, more compact man who looks down shyly when I say hello. I follow them into a long, rectangular room above the wine cellar, its arched ceiling made of blackened old-barrel staves. The large open window is filled with the green sunlit hill, and children's voices drift up from the courtyard below.

We all sit down at a long oak table, and Norbret brings out glasses and several bottles. Tom pours the Bernkasteler Doctor Kabinett Riesling. "This wine challenges you to pay attention to it," he tells me. I don't find it a challenge to pay attention to this wine at all. A citrus zing runs up the sides of my mouth, softened by a spring drizzle of ripe peaches. The wine opens my senses, first making my mouth water. Then as I breathe in deeply, its aromas travel upward, lifting my eyebrows and perfuming my mind.

"You must come out to meet this wine," he says. I'm already there, in the glass.

Next we try the spätlese, which has the fragile intensity of Chagall stained glass. Its flamboyant fruitiness suffuses the room the way the jeweled light from the artist's pane does a church. As *Slate* editor Fareed Zakaria once observed, "This is what God drinks at five o'clock in the summer."

For Tom, the wine calls to mind a dinner in the Caribbean. "It was perfect with the marinated mahi-mahi I had on the beach in the Grand Caymans once," he recalls. "But maybe that had less to do with my wine and more to do with being on a beach in the Grand Caymans."

The next wine Norbert pours is his beerenauslese. The room fills with nectarine, peach, and honeysuckle. Then we taste the trocken-beerenauslese, a smoldering wine of honey and clementines. It has a disturbingly attractive aroma, like a field of flowers with a snarling undergrowth. The wine's luscious texture seeps into all the crevices of my mouth and coats the back of my throat.

Distractedly, I confirm if I heard them correctly: do they make 110 cases of this wine a year? Both men look at each other and burst into laughter, slapping the table. Apparently, I've told a good one.

This is the Doctor's most expensive wine; a half-bottle sells for $400 (though mature vintages at auction command thousands). They produce just ten cases in a good year. To make a mere half bottle, it takes one worker a full day to pick ten pounds of these grapes, which have to be the ripest and most succulent.

Tom recalls a memorable moment with this wine while he and Rudi Wiest, his American importer, were dining in Las Vegas. The two men enjoyed challenging each other, and that evening Tom offered to eat a spoonful of wasabi without bursting into flames or tears. Sushi fans know that wasabi, the bitter flavoring herb often called Japanese horseradish, is much hotter than jalapeño peppers. Its heat is generated by compounds called isothiocyanates, which create intensely hot nasal vapors. Rudi took him up on the dare, expecting fireworks. Then he watched in disbelief as Tom ate the wasabi without batting an eyelash, following it with a mouthful of his riesling.

What Rudi didn't know was Tom's secret weapon: osmosis. Riesling, a thicker, higher-density liquid, enveloped the wasabi and mixed with a thinner liquid, his saliva, generating more of it. It effectively protected his palate because the heat compounds weren't able to attach to his tongue and throat. The key, Tom emphasizes, is not waiting more than a second or two after eating the wasabi to drink the wine. "You don't want to miss that deadline," he says, smiling.

Although employees were initially wary of the "son-in-law who has a PhD," the winery thrived under the young couple's management. The family invested more than $3 million to modernize the cellars. And in 1993, Tom hired Norbert, whom Tom describes as "a fantastic sparring partner."

Now the two seem to finish each other's sentences. Tom observes, "It's the German love of precision that makes us work with a grape that creates so many styles. We want to know exactly what we can produce depending on what we do with it." Norbert agrees. "You can trim riesling to the essence you want from it. It's such a personal wine that where it grows and who makes it matter deeply."

Are there any tricks to working with riesling? I ask.

"Time," Norbert says. His placid farmer's features give away nothing and take in everything. "You can tell people a lot about riesling, but finally they just have to taste it."

As we sit silently smelling our glasses, the open window reminds me of the May morning after a party in my first apartment. I woke up to a slender-sloped bottle of riesling, half full, on the window ledge. The lace curtain brushed over it and back again in the breeze. Its aroma of lime and nectarine mingled with the white cherry blossoms outside and drifted over the sheets.

"Let's go see the vineyard," Tom suggests. The three of us pile into his old van and drive up a steep path that would tire a mountain goat. At the top of the vineyard, the air is crisp and cool. From up here at the curve of the Moselle River, you can see the grandest sweep of vineyards in Europe. As far as you can throw open your arms to fill your lungs with mountain air, there are vine-draped slopes to the south and to the west.

However, just looking straight down at the rows of vines almost gives me vertigo. I try to imagine what it's like for the Polish immigrants who work here. Flatland vineyards can use machines to harvest the grapes and need only about two hundred hours of labor per acre a year. But growing cliff-face riesling demands thirty-five hundred or more grueling hours hiking up and down carrying a hundred-pound basket of grapes while strapped to cables. As Tom notes, "We practice sustainable viticulture, but to be organic would require slaves."

So what's the first thing you do in the spring, I ask him?

"We remove the bones of the workers who didn't make it through the fall harvest," he quips.

From the back of the van, Norbert takes a chilled bottle of the 1982 Bernkasteler Doctor Riesling Spätlese. The glasses mist over as he pours the wine. We clink them together and look out at the green shadows across the hillsides. The wine opens with expansive aromas of lemon and honeysuckle edged by a streak of smoke. The valley opens beneath the fog, which rolls up like a sleeping blanket to reveal the silver braid of water.

I'm infused with a desire to tell someone how beautiful this valley is, how glorious the wines are, but I don't want to move. Fortunately, I don't have to. Wine is the voice of the soil; without it, the land would be silent. Norbert's soft voice breaks in on my reverie, as though he's read my thoughts.

"I love this place," he says quietly.

Field Notes from a
Wine Cheapskate

INSIDER TIPS

• Look for labels that have illegible gothic script and impossibly long names that are difficult to pronounce in the liquor store (or anywhere else). Few people can read them, so they don't buy the wines, and demand doesn't push up prices.

• Wines that had a bad reputation several decades ago are behind the eight ball in trying to reposition themselves as good quality producers at reasonable prices.

• Low-alcohol wines are often your most versatile food-wise because they can go with so many lighter dishes that we enjoy today without overwhelming their flavors.

WINERIES VISITED

Dr. Loosen: www.drloosen.com
Johann Josef Prüm: www.jjpruem.com

St. Urbans-Hof: www.urbans-hof.de
Wegeler: www.wegeler.com

BEST VALUE WINES

Dr. Loosen's Dr. L Riesling*
St. Urbans-Hof Kabinett Riesling
St. Urbans-Hof Riesling
St. Urbans-Hof Urban Riesling

*My first pick for my own Monday dinner.

TOP VALUE PRODUCERS

Anselmann
August Kesseler
Balbach
Balthasar Ress
Becker-Steinhauer
Black Slate
Carl Reh
Darting
Dr. Fischer
Dr. Hermann
Dr. Pauly-Bergweiler
Geil
Josef Kollmann

Karl Erbes
Kloster Eberbach
Kruger-Rumpf
Lingenfelder
Pfeffingen
Reichsgraf von Kesselstatt
Reinhold Haart
Schloss Johannisberg
Schloss Reinhartshausen
Schloss Schönborn
St. Antony
Studert Prüm
Zilliken

MONDAY DINNER FOR A WINE CHEAPSKATE

You'll find Ruth and Harald Rüssel's recipes for the meal that's similar to the one that Nik and I shared at www.nataliemaclean .com/food.

Pork with Sweet Potato Salad, Lentils, Smoked Salmon, and Crawfish

Terrine of Beef

Pike Perch (Zander) in an Orange Cumin Broth

Sauté of Veal Kidneys and Heart Sweetbreads

Wrapped Venison Knuckles and Nut Escalope

Potato Ravioli and Sweetheart Cabbage

Semolina Gratin

TERRIFIC PAIRINGS

Riesling is a light, vibrant white wine that often has aromas of apricot, peach, wet slate, minerals, and flowers. It's incredibly versatile with food because its styles range from bone-dry to intensely sweet. Here are some of my favorite pairings:

Dry, Kabinett, and Spätlese Riesling

Cheese: Brie, Camembert   Chicken: fried
Chicken korma   Chicken: lemon or citrus sauce

Curries: mild or medium
Duck liver pâté
Fish: barbecued or
  planked
Indian and Thai dishes
Pizza: cheese, vegetarian,
  Hawaiian
Planked salmon

Risotto with butternut squash
Salad: Caesar or green
Shellfish: crab, lobster,
  mussels, oysters
Smoked trout
Turkey: roast, soup
Vegetarian dishes

Auslese, Beerenauslese, Eiswein/Icewine, and Trockenbeere-nauslese Riesling

Biscotti
Cheese: Stilton, Muenster, Gorgonzola
Curries and spices: medium or hot
Fruit-based desserts: flan, tart, cobbler
Toffee pudding

RESOURCES

For more information about German wines and riesling:

The Wines of Germany by Stephen Brook
Riesling Renaissance by Freddie and Janet Price
Wineries of Germany: www.nataliemaclean.com/wineries
Wines of Germany-Canada: www.germanwinecanada.org
Wines of Germany USA: www.germanwineusa.com
International Riesling Foundation: www.drinkriesling.com
Riesling Rendezvous: www.ste-michelle.com/winery/
  rieslingRendezvous
The Germany Wine Society: www.germanwinesociety.org

RELATED READING

The following books, while seemingly unrelated to the main subject matter of this chapter, provided some enjoyable reading before, during, and after my travels:

The Magic Mountain by Thomas Mann
The Tin Drum by Günter Grass
Faust Part One by Johann Wolfgang Von Goethe

THREE

TUESDAY

Helicopters, Hawks, and Hellacious Ladybugs

UNDER HEAVY GUNFIRE, we run for the chopper. Gray clouds roil overhead as the wind whips our faces. The ground man signals us to scramble in but then stops and waves for us to turn around. As we do, we're blinded by white flashes.

We're not being fired at, though: it's just the smiling tour guide snapping photos of us. The shotgun blasts are automatic "bird bangers" to scare birds away from the fields of Niagara grapevines around us.

This isn't Baghdad, but it is war.

The enemy—massive in numbers, cunning, and beady-eyed— weigh less than two ounces each: the European starling. These birds travel in black clouds of peckish delight, swooping down to strip vineyards clean of the fruit in a few hours. They're especially partial to grapes at this time of year, just before harvest, when they're sweet. Hence the bird bangers, which work like an exploding barbecue on a pole. A propane tank inside the cannon-shaped drainpipe ignites a tiny spark plug at odd intervals, firing the gas out through a long barrel that amplifies the sound. This works for a while, until the birds get used to the sound. I've seen them perched saucily on top of a cannon, barely fluttering as it goes off.

"The other choppers have left; let's get out of here," I yell for no apparent reason, other than having watched *Black Hawk Down* too many times. I'm about to take an aerial tour of Niagara with Martin Malivoire, whose pinot noir is a favorite of both starlings and wine lovers. Pinot noir is also my favorite red wine; I often give pinot noirs from various producers the highest scores, even though wine critics aren't supposed to allow their personal preferences to influence their "objective" analysis—hogwash. I stopped being objective the day I was born.

Pinot noir is difficult and expensive to make. That's why it's often pricey, with benchmark wines from Burgundy, France, starting at $60 a bottle and going up to several thousand dollars for legends such as Domaine de la Romanée-Conti. However, pinot noir from Niagara is a relative steal, often just $25 to $35 a bottle. It's a gorgeous wine that packs a lot of flavor yet isn't heavy and alcoholic—I think of it as riesling's red twin, though they're completely different grapes. But this makes pinot noir perfect for Tuesday night dinner.

My thoughts are jolted back to the chopper as we lift a hundred feet straight up into the air, then zoom like a crazed bumblebee over the patchwork of farm fields below. At one point, the chopper tilts almost onto its side, and I wonder if the ground man remembered to lock the full-sized window—all that's between me and the ground below.

Flying over Niagara is a meditation on landscape: horizon-reaching rows of vines, weather-scarred farmhouses, wispy peach trees, antiques stores, roadside fruit stands, and limestone bluffs that plunge down to the shimmering waters of Lake Ontario. By now, in mid-October, most vineyards have turned shades of yellow and brown, like a spice cabinet, but some are still summer green. I ask Martin about this, and he grins. "Bright green at this time of the year isn't natural," he explains. "Those vineyards have had a little chemical help."

The chemical help comes in the form of fertilizers, fungicides, pesticides, and other applications. Farming in Ontario is tough; growing wine grapes is even harder. Vintners battle mildew, leaf disease, and pests. Martin doesn't use any synthetic chemical treatments on his vineyard; Malivoire Winery was the first commercial organic winery in the region.

As we bank over the Niagara Peninsula, I can see almost all the triangular arm of land where the Great Lakes meet. The name Niagara comes from the Iroquois word *Ongniaahra*, meaning "point of land cut in two." Niagara is defined northward by Lake Ontario, southward by Lake Erie, and eastward by the Niagara River, reflecting silver and gray below us. We scout up the river until we reach Niagara Falls, the raw power of unstoppable nature. More than six million cubic feet of water a minute plummet 180 feet over the cliff edge, the equivalent of 85 million bathtubs full of water. Its rising spray is shot through with rainbows.

The falls sit on the Niagara Escarpment, a massive ridge of fractured limestone, dolomite, shale, and sandstone that stretches for a thousand miles south to New York and on to Wisconsin and north to the Canadian Shield. This particular section is where the escarpment shifted and lifted up between Lake Erie and Lake Ontario, creating the faster water flow.

This shrugging shoulder of land is actually the upthrust shoreline of the Jurassic sea that retreated eighty-three million years ago, long before the Ice Age. Now the ridge divides the Niagara

Peninsula, creating a series of protected slopes and nooks that trap the moderating airflow from Lake Ontario. The lake, eight hundred feet deep in some places, acts like a giant water bottle, slowly releasing stored summer warmth in the fall to help ripen the grapes and in the winter to help protect the vines from icy death. The moderating effect of the lake and escarpment is limited to the Niagara Peninsula.

More than twenty million people a year visit Niagara Falls, so why do comparatively few of them drive twenty minutes north to Niagara-on-the-Lake? Granted, it doesn't have the gold-trimmed souvenir ashtrays, wax museum, and casino gambling, but it does offer beauty, history, and culture. British Loyalists settled here at the end of the American Revolution. The last battle between Canadians and Americans, during the War of 1812, was fought at Fort George. Today they stage battles and mock displays there. The internationally acclaimed Shaw Festival features the works of Irish playwright George Bernard Shaw and his contemporaries.

I recalled Shaw's wit as I considered the challenges for local vintners. He once observed: "The reasonable man adapts himself to the world; the unreasonable one persists in trying to adapt the world to himself. Therefore all progress depends on the unreasonable man." Winemakers here must be exceptionally unreasonable, not to mention unusually stubborn, to brave the climate: humid summers that can cause rot and mildew, rain right before harvest that can bloat the grapes and dilute their flavor, and winters that can kill the vines. As one vintner told me, "You can lose the whole field—and a year's work—in an afternoon."

What doesn't kill you makes you stronger, right? True for humans, maybe. For grapes, no. Grapes thicken their skins to protect themselves from winter cold. This can mean too much tannin without enough balancing fruit ripeness. For years, Ontario wines were made from winter-hardy Labrusca grapes, like concord and white Niagara. They produced nasty little wines that were then fortified with brandy to make them drinkable. Their alcoholic strength earned them the nickname "block and tackle" wines because after drinking them, you could tackle anyone. In the sixties and seventies, Canadian wine went through a grim cheap-and-sweet zoological period, featuring wines named Baby Duck, Gimli Goose, Fuddle Duck, Pussycat, and so on. Bright's wine, founded by pioneer Thomas Bright, was uncharitably dubbed Bright's Disease.

Things started to improve with the 1988 Ontario Wine Content Act, which banned Labrusca grapes in table wines. That same year, the Vintners Quality Alliance (VQA), an appellation system for Ontario wines similar to France's AOC and Italy's DOC, was founded. The VQA designation guarantees that wines are grown and produced in Canada to certain standards. Another spur to better winemaking was the 1989 Canada-U.S. Free Trade Agreement, followed by the 1994 North American Free Trade Agreement. These initiatives prompted a renewal of the wine industry: the government phased out protectionist taxes on foreign wines and gave vintners subsidies to plant better-quality European grapes.

Today, the Niagara region is home to some of North America's most exciting wineries, such as Malivoire, Tawse, Flat Rock, Coyote's Run, Le Clos Jordanne, Featherstone, Lailey Vineyard, and Inniskillin—the first commercial winery to open after Prohibition. Founders Karl Kaiser and Donald Ziraldo are credited with bringing international recognition to Canadian wine, after their vidal icewine won France's 1991 Grand Prix d'Honneur in a blind tasting against more than four thousand of the world's best wines.

The icewine story is a particularly Canadian one, associated with this country as much as snow, ice rinks, hockey, parkas, and maple syrup. Other countries make it, too, but Canada, with its consistently cold weather, has long since surpassed them in both volume and consumer awareness. At its best, icewine tastes like an incoming tide of pleasure. Vibrant notes of apricot, mango, peach, clementines, honeysuckle, baked apples, and quince are all suspended in a gossamer haze of sweetness.

Canada now sells some $45 million of icewine a year, accounting for more than half the country's wine exports. Seventy-five percent of it is made in Ontario, and the rest in British Columbia, Quebec, and Nova Scotia. Half bottles sell for $50 to $80. The high price tag is because it's an expensive and risky wine to make. Most icewine is made from the vidal grape, which has winter-hardy skin and aromatic intensity. Some vintners also use the more elegant riesling, with its lovely tension between acidity and sweetness. Harvesting in January can mean losing up to 60 percent of the crop compared to the fall, as the grapes are more prone to damage from both weather and pests. The surviving grapes are picked at temperatures of 17°F or colder, usually at night. When these frozen vinous pellets are pressed, they yield only 15 to 20 percent of the juice of unfrozen grapes. One year, this icy fruit broke a two-ton wine press at Inniskillin.

The largest buyer of Canada's icewine is Asia, where it's considered a luxury—which may be why most fakes come from Asia. Some of the knockoff wine labels are creative with both geography and spelling, such as "Chilliwacko, Ontario" (inspired perhaps by Chilliwack, British Columbia), "Snow White," and "Elixir of the Gods from Torontow"—the latter bears a picture of Whistler, a British Columbia ski resort more than five thousand miles west of Toronto.

That Inniskillin icewine win turned Canada's snowy image into both a boon and a bane. It helped the reputation of Canadian wine change from plonk to quality. This, in turn, encouraged the growth of Ontario wineries, which have jumped from 18 in 1989 to 140 today. The wine and grape industries are now worth $550 million and provide some seven thousand jobs. However, the international triumph was for a niche dessert wine, and the country has been struggling to shake that typecast role ever since. That's why I've decided to focus on pinot noir while I'm in Niagara. It's the wine that I believe is the most exciting for this region, and it will change the world's perceptions of the Grape White North. As one winemaker remarked, God made cabernet sauvignon, but the devil made pinot noir. I'm here to drink some black magic.

When the helicopter drops Martin and me at Malivoire Winery, I'm relieved to be on terra firma again, even though my stomach is still circling above Lake Ontario. As we came in to land, I was curious about a series of giant tin canisters lying on their sides. It turns out that's actually the winery: they're buildings made from large semicircular sheets of corrugated steel, like the Quonset huts the British built in World War I as barracks.

"We built this winery out of found objects," Martin explains with gee-whiz enthusiasm. "Some of the corrugated steel sheets came from a local building that was being torn down. They're light and fast to assemble, and the design mimics the curves of the hills." It also follows the gravity-flow design of the winery: as the cylinders descend down the hillside, the juice flows through them for various stages of the winemaking process. This treatment is gentler than mechanical pumping, and it results in better wine.

The other parts of the structure were scavenged, too: the rocks and pediments are "blaster's mistakes" from a local quarry, and the wood beams are telephone poles rejected by Ontario Hydro. "We need to think more about our energy footprint," Martin says. "Thinking about human time and energy ultimately leads to thinking about how you spend your life."

In his case, the answer is very productively. Martin recently retired from a successful career as a movie special-effects producer. Some of his best-known films are *Quest for Fire*, *Porky's*, *My Big Fat Greek Wedding*, *Hairspray*, and *Fly Away Home*. A native of Oakville, Ontario, it was while filming *Trapped in Paradise* in 1993 that he fell in love with the Niagara region. In 1996, he and his partner, Moira Saganski, an investment banker, built a home here and bought eighty-six acres of vineyards. At first, they sold their grapes to local winemakers. But when Martin tasted one of the resulting wines, he wasn't impressed. That prompted him to try making wine himself, though the experiment was short-lived.

"I followed a winemaking book step-by-step—and that was the first and last time I ever made wine," he says, laughing. "The next year, I hired a winemaker." But even Martin's failures seem to succeed: his wine won a gold medal in an amateur competition. After that, he and Moira built the winery in 1998 and devoted themselves to serious winemaking.

I'm keen to talk to Martin because he's one of Niagara's best producers of pinot noir. Known as the "heartbreak grape" for its racy taste and finicky nature, its siren call lures winemakers into its rocky shoals when they'd be safer on the shores of chardonnay, cabernet, and merlot. Niagara is heartbreak central when it comes to this wine. The grape got its name for its tight bunches shaped like pinecones (*pineau* in French). This reduces air circulation around the grapes, which increases their susceptibility to rot and mildew. So you'd think that it would be the last choice for Niagara with its cool, wet climate. In the winery, it's susceptible to bacterial spoilage called *Brettanomyces*, euphemistically described as smelling like a barnyard.

However, winemakers keep going back to it like a bad boyfriend who is dangerously exciting. Pinot noir loves living on the edge: regions right at the last margin for growing grapes often excel because the grapes don't overripen and become alcoholic and flabby from too much sun. Still, the fruit has incredible depth of flavor. The escarpment is loaded with the fossils of ancient microscopic marine animals and seashells, giving it a calcium-rich composition similar to the famous soils of Burgundy and Champagne. As a result, Niagara pinot noir has a mid-Atlantic style that combines the fleshy fruitiness of Oregon with the brooding earthiness of Burgundy.

Given these challenges, I'm surprised that Martin farms organically, without even a little chemical help. Partly, that's a reaction to having tried it once: during his first harvest, he sprayed his crop with a commonly used chemical. Its airborne drift into his winery caused him heart palpitations for several months. "There was no question about our approach after that," Martin says.

Until the 1950s, there was no such distinction: most crops, including wine grapes, were grown without synthetic pesticides and fertilizers. Crops were at the mercy of diseases and pests, so farmers had no choice but to wait until nature recalibrated itself after the blight died out with its food source, the crop.

Then along came the so-called green revolution, with chemicals perceived as the modern way to farm. This was aided by the phosphorus and nitrogen left over from World War II. These chemicals seemed to offer problem-free fields, and for two decades, they ruled agriculture in North America and many other countries.

In the 1970s, the backlash started. Consumers began to worry about the domination of big agribusiness, the harm to the environment, and the long-term effects of chemical dependency. A growing back-to-the-land movement, along with the hippie culture's yearning for self-sufficiency, strengthened public desire for "natural" food. Ever since, modern concerns—genetically modified foods, mercury poisoning, mad cow disease, and fast food—have all contributed to the organic momentum.

What does *organic* actually mean when applied to wine? There are two answers to that because making wine is a two-step process: first you grow the grapes, and then you make the wine. There's a distinction between "wine from organically grown grapes" and "organic wine." Organically grown grapes must not have any synthetic fertilizers, pesticides, herbicides, fungicides, or soil fumigants used on them.

However, organic farmers can still use chemicals that are derived from naturally occurring substances. Some of these organic chemicals also come with worker protection warnings. And which is more virtuous: organic sulfur, which is mined and consumes a lot of energy, or synthetic sulfur, which is a by-product of petroleum distillation? The issue isn't simple, even though our desire for "natural" farming is. As Martin points out, how far do you want to go with organic? Should the winemaker wash his hands with organic soap?

Organically made wine takes this a step further; not only were the grapes grown organically, but the wine itself must also not contain any of the five hundred or so additives available to winemakers. That includes not having more than ten parts per million sulfites— the salts of sulfuric acid—a common food preservative that prevents the wine from spoiling after fermentation.

Sulfites are harmless to most people, though some asthmatics are allergic to them. More important, there's no avoiding sulfites, because they're a natural by-product of fermentation. They exist naturally in many fruits and vegetables as well as in fruit juices, jams, baked goods, salad bars, and bottled mineral water. A single glass of orange juice has more sulfites than a whole bottle of nonorganic wine. Organic wine tends not to travel well or keep long because it doesn't have much sulfur. Therefore, it's wine made from organically grown grapes that you see in the organic section of most liquor stores.

For wine lovers, there's no evidence that organic wine is any better for you than nonorganic, or that it will reduce your risk of cancer, heart disease, or other illnesses. In blind taste tests, many experts perceive no difference between well-made organic and nonorganic wines. (And no, drinking organic wine won't reduce your hangover.) Having said that, though, my instinct is that farming methods do make a difference. Wine is an expression of the earth where the vines grow. If that earth is rich and alive with microorganisms and insects, rather than being a chemical wasteland, that's got to affect the health of the vines, the taste of the fruit, and the quality of the resulting wine, even though the difference may be subtle.

Martin agrees. He also believes that organic farming is not just more sustainable but also cheaper in the long run, with its lower dependence on fossil fuels and expensive synthetic chemicals. He thinks that many farmers, including winemakers, will eventually be forced to maintain their prices, even if the cost of oil goes up, in order to compete with organic producers. Plus, he says the organic approach is part of an overall commitment to quality. It requires a deeper understanding of the vineyard and a greater vigilance. Problems must be detected early because organic fixes take longer to work.

"The world will become healthier out of sheer necessity because organic foods will become the cheaper choice," he observes. "The simpler we make our business, the easier it is to run."

Organic also fits with the new fashion for fresh and local with the popularity of the hundred-mile diet and sustainable agriculture. Why not the hundred-mile cellar? Organic wine sales have been growing at 20 percent a year compared to about 5 percent for nonorganic-certified wines. "It's like the peach industry," Martin explains. "Years ago, they had to change from canned to fresh peaches because no one was eating canned fruit anymore."

Malivoire met the stringent requirements for an organic designation from the Canadian Food Inspection Agency in 2004; however, he still doesn't put that fact on any of his labels. I ask him why not. In a word, he says, consumer perception. Most drinkers already think of wine as a natural product, though they're likely less influenced by knowledge of the winemaking approach and more by those leafy pictures of vineyards on labels and in ads. So although they may seek out organic versions of lettuce, tomatoes, or beef, they don't think to do so for wine.

Martin isn't alone in his caution; many wineries hesitate to promote their organic designation. Most consumers buy wine for its taste and quality; the organic part is just a bonus. As well, organic wines have an unfortunate history. In the past, they were perceived (often correctly) as being poorly made and prone to going bad quickly because they lacked preservatives. More important, many vintners don't want to lock themselves into one mode of production—just in case there's an unexpected attack of pests or rot that requires emergency chemical treatment. If a winery had to remove the organic designation from its label, it would be awkward to explain why to its customers. And if a winery produces several wines, and not all are organic, that declaration on one label could reflect poorly on the others. For all these reasons, only a small percentage of wineries that are certified organic actually market that fact.

One of my favorite parts of Martin's organic approach is his ladybug strategy, which is why many of his bottles feature a cheerful little red beetle crawling across the label. To combat destructive insects that have a taste for grape leaves, Martin releases thousands of ladybugs into his vineyards. The ladybugs are selective about what they eat, whereas insecticides destroy every bug in their path and leave a vineyard more vulnerable to pest attacks the next year.

But wait, didn't ladybugs taint Niagara wines a few years ago? After wines were barreled or bottled for the 2001 harvest, many winemakers noticed an odd smell of rancid peanut butter. A number of wineries, including Malivoire, pulled their affected wines from store shelves that year.

Eventually, they traced the problem to an Asian species of ladybug, quite different from the indigenous five-spotted ladybugs. Farmers in the southern United States had introduced the bug to feed on the aphids that were plaguing their pecan trees and soybeans. The problem began when these ladybugs migrated north, following the aphids, and became a seasonal pest in wine country. Swarms of these beetles amass whenever a cold snap is followed by an Indian summer. They hibernate in the grapevines, which offer both food and warmth as winter approaches.

When the affected grapes were picked and crushed, these stowaway ladybugs emitted a foul fluid called pyrazine that smelled like rancid peanut butter. The smell also has a dampening effect on the wine's natural fruit aromas, similar to mild cork taint. Wine tolerance for this type of beetle is low; more than four beetles per four-ton bin can ruin the entire harvest. Martin, though, is philosophical about the problem: "It's just Mother Nature doing her thing, and we're the ones who have to adapt."

The good news is that early-ripening grapes, such as sauvignon blanc, provided the first warning about the problem. Martin and other vintners largely addressed the issue before it affected pinot noir and other later-ripening grapes. Vintners have also learned how to deal with the pests: spraying the vines with certain chemicals, harvesting at night when the beetles aren't active, shaking them out by hand when picking the grapes, and sorting the grapes before crushing them. The sorting table at Malivoire starts with a heat blower to blow off intruders; then the grapes travel along a vibrating belt to shake them off, with workers picking them out; and then the grapes go past a final heat blower.

Martin has invited me back to his home for lunch. The house is a modern glass-and-concrete affair, designed by the late architect Andrew Volgyesi, that somehow fits in this forest setting. Large glass doors open onto a wraparound porch and bamboo garden. Inside is open concept, with big wooden beams supporting a twenty-four-foot-high ceiling and three fireplaces with sitting areas. In the center is a large open kitchen with a marble counter, a Wolf gas oven, and cabinets full of pots and wine glasses. Pumpkin soup is simmering on the stove, its spicy aroma warming the house.

"I started cooking in my filmmaking days to help me relax after a long day of blowing things up and killing people," Martin says, smiling as he stirs the soup. "With such a superficial job, I loved the reality of cooking: fresh ingredients, a glass of wine. It changes your whole focus."

He's an intuitive, shoot-from-the-hip cook, with a passion for cookbooks; more than five hundred of them line the shelves around the house. "Every recipe is a story," he says. "I'm not a classically trained cook, so I try to understand what the author is saying with the flavors in the dish."

He hands me a large cleaver to chop new potatoes in half, showing me how to make an even slice with a quick flick of his wrist. I am the world's slowest chopper, if you don't count also slicing your own fingers. But it feels natural to be working beside him as the conversation continues.

From the fridge, Martin takes out a tray of deboned quails that have marinated overnight in maple syrup. They were raised on a local farm. "I know the farmer, and that's important to me," he says. "They ran free and were happy. The ingredients on my plate are personal."

He salts the quails and takes them outside to the barbecue, where eleven cats circle and meow. Most of them are adopted strays; the oldest one jumped inside the filming truck ten years ago. The cats and I watch Martin hungrily as he slides the small birds on the barbecue, the flames leaping and sizzling around them.

"Entertaining in the country usually means sharing more of yourself with guests," he says. "When you have dinner together, you're likely staying overnight—it's not the drive-through visiting of the city."

When the quails are cooked, we go back inside. Martin ladles the steaming soup into freshly cut pumpkins for bowls. He's added chicken stock and chestnut puree to give it more savory richness. The soup tastes wonderful with several vintages of his Courtney Gamay, which offers superb instant gratification with its peppered raspberry and black currant notes. The fiery reflections in the wine are an antidote to the chilly fall air.

Gamay is a little lower down on the wine social scale, but Martin believes Niagara needs it to support the more aristocratic pinot noir. It's winter hardy and disease resistant and can be priced lower to fill out a product portfolio. "You need a dependable and affordable wine to make up for all the money you'll waste on pinot," he observes. He's even tried blending pinot noir with gamay. "We're too hung up on varietal purity," he says. "Pinot noir brings the complexity and silky texture, and gamay punches up the fruit and makes the wine more vibrant. As a winemaker, you need to keep your ego in your back pocket."

Alongside the juicy quails with their seared barbecue notes, we enjoy three vintages of Moira's Vineyard Pinot Noir. They flood the senses with fleshy aromas of damson plums and a core of stone-fruit acidity. Their smoky finish is a lovely match with the charred gamey notes of the quail. We also sample his estate pinot noir, which has a creamy texture and is pleasingly mouth-filling. "I don't want people to hit those tannins; it should have a velvet texture," Martin says.

As we finish the meal sipping on pinot, Martin grows reflective about his second career. "There are lots of times when I don't want to be in this business," he confesses. "We're trying to grow finicky fruit from a hostile land. But when someone tastes my wine and smiles or says they like it, that's all I need to keep going."

THE NEXT DAY, approaching Featherstone Winery, I can see a pepper storm of starlings flying over the vineyard. Husband-and-wife team David Johnson and Louise Engel have a passion for all things fowl. Before they became winemakers, they ran a gourmet poultry shop, selling tasty birds, from turkeys to quails. (That's where the "feather" comes from; the "stone" is the Niagara Escarpment.)

However, those hungry starlings that feed on the ripening grapes are no friends of David and Louise. That's why I'm going to meet their latest avian associate today, a Harris hawk that's trained to hunt those pesky birds.

In 1989, David started making wine as a hobby and won awards in amateur competitions. He began to spend less time at the shop and more in the cellar, eventually becoming certified with the Amateur Winemakers of Ontario judging program. In 1999, he and Louise sold the poultry shop and bought a farmhouse surrounded by twenty-three acres of vines on the Niagara Escarpment. The vineyard's lovely contours and rolling hills dip down to a small creek running between them. To the east is a rich stand of pine trees, and to the west looms the rugged rock face of the escarpment.

Louise Engel could be Peter Pan's sister, with her pixie haircut, impish grin, and compact frame that would be perfect for flying. I ask her about the harvest. "We *just* managed to pull this one out of the moat," she says. "After such a wet summer, we really needed those twenty-six days of sunshine. Could be a sleeper year, like 2008."

David comes out of the barn, taking off his heavy gloves to shake my hand. He looks more like an English professor than a winemaker, with steel-framed glasses and a serious expression. Louise tells him she's taking me to see the lambs—vital team members in maintaining the Featherstone vineyards.

David got the idea when he worked at Sileni Estates winery in New Zealand, where many wineries use sheep to nibble down the grass and unwanted vine leaves. ("This may have something to do with the fact that there are thirty-five million sheep and three million people in the country.") For larger wineries, the savings add up, especially since there isn't a ready source of cheap farm labor there. One New Zealand vintner, Peter Yealands, calculated that without sheep, he'd have to have seven tractors mowing his two thousand miles of vineyards a dozen times a year—at a cost of about $35,000.

"When I got back, we tried a few 'lambmowers' here," David says. The experiment was such a success that now about forty lambs arrive every July. Once they finish with the grass, they start eating the tender, young grape leaves that grow low on the vines. In the fruiting zone, where the grapes will eventually grow, the leaves must be thinned to give the bunches more sun exposure to ripen and better ventilation to avoid mold.

"Sheep are ideally suited to the job," David observes. "They can't reach high enough to damage the vine, and they're not interested in eating the unripe grapes. They graze 24/7, don't complain about the weather, and don't ask for days off. They also cultivate the soil, not just with their natural fertilizer of digested nutrient-rich grass but also with their hooves, which till the earth. That means less chemical fertilizer. Their environmental hoofprint is quite small."

There's even a vineyard tool called a sheep's foot for when the woolly kind isn't available. They eliminate the need for tractor mowing, which compacts the soil and reduces the biodiversity of the earth's natural microorganisms.

Raising vineyard-friendly lambs is now a niche market for some farmers, such as Cindy Deserioux, from whom David and Louise buy their lambs. Louise takes me to visit her postcard-charming farmhouse, where two dozen adult ewes run away to the pasture when they see us coming. Only the breeding ram, twice as large as the others, stands his ground and stares us down. "He's from Alberta and thinks he's hot stuff," Cindy comments.

The sheep are a low-slung breed descended from an ancient British mountain stock called Olde English Babydoll Southdowns. They're rugged, short-legged creatures that only grow two feet high at the shoulder, the perfect range for thinning vine leaves. Most are bred to be born in February and ready for work in July. Right now, in October, there are only two out-of-season lambs frolicking far out in the field, one black and one white. These babydolls are so damn cute, like bowlegged granny wigs. They're skittish around Louise and me, eyeing us with suspicion.

"Come here, girls!" Cindy calls in her sweet, motherly voice. If I were a lamb, I'd follow her anywhere. We move back and eventually they come bounding to the barn, where she feeds them.

At Featherstone, the lambs stay until the end of August, just before harvest. Where do they go then? ("Do you hear the lambs, Clarice?") David and Louise sell them to restaurants, where they finish their happy lives on plates matched with local wines. (Hey, it's the circle of life.) That's why Louise never names any of the sheep: "I'm never here when the truck comes for them."

Every fall, Treadwell Restaurant in the nearby town of St. Catherine's hosts a Featherstone Lamb Dinner. The menu celebrates the animals from snout to tail, featuring dishes like pickled tongue with lobster knuckles and celery root remoulade paired with Featherstone's Blacksheep Riesling, and then pan-seared liver with caramelized shallots and brown butter matched with the winery's Canadian Oak Chardonnay.

This is followed by a savory "odds and ends" (don't ask) shepherd's pie with whipped mashed potatoes and parsley bread crumbs served with the Cabernet Franc, stout-braised shank ravioli with confit shoulder and autumn ratatouille paired with the Gamay Noir, and a saddle of roasted lamb and garlic dauphinoise potatoes in truffled pan juices served with the Onyx Cabernet Franc Merlot. A selection of Ontario sheep's milk cheeses and homemade preserves paired with the Late Harvest Cabernet Franc caps the meal.

Back at the winery, Louise fills me in on the biggest problem she and other vintners face in this region: bird predation. It's estimated that North American farmers lose about $1.6 billion a year from birds and other crop predators. The Niagara grape growers association estimates that starlings destroy $15 million or 5 percent of wine crops a year. A flock of birds can strip clean several tons of grapes in a couple days, with a vintner's entire year's work sliding down those beaky little gullets. The fruit they don't eat they peck at and leave to rot on the vine.

Louise dislikes starlings. They're not even a native species but an import from England. In the 1870s, some idiot who was enraptured with Shakespeare decided to collect all the songbirds mentioned in the sonnets and release them in New York City's Central Park. The starlings fared best as opportunistic feeders and prolific breeders, and muscled their way into habitats across North America.

"They have no redeeming features," Louise says, her personal enmity showing. "They are parasitic rats with wings." She remembers

Thanksgiving 1999 with particular venom because "the friggin' starlings ate *all* our crop. That was when I became determined to do something about it."

Modern technology has given vintners an arsenal of weapons to fight the avian menace. Among the tools are advanced computerized versions of the bird bangers that explode at random intervals so that the birds don't get used to a pattern. Other wineries use "screamers," modified starting pistols that shoot firecrackers, and biosonic technology known as "squawk boxes," which broadcast distressed bird calls. Then there are "terror eyes," balloons painted with the eyes of predators; foil-glittering Mylar ribbons; reflective windmills; flapping windsocks; and automatic guns that spray the vineyard with pebble pellets. Some vintners (or their teenaged offspring) ride all-terrain vehicles through the rows, dragging cans.

The problem with all of these approaches is that the birds quickly adjust to most of the attempts used to scare them. For instance, they learn exactly how far the automatic pellet spray reaches and stay just outside its range, like an enemy outside the castle walls taunting the besieged.

The most effective way to protect vineyards from birds is to drape the whole property in nets. That works, though it's an expensive solution, and they need to be replaced every five years. The nets also make tending the vines more time-consuming. They can also cause other headaches: after some birds became accidentally ensnared in one local winemaker's nets, the provincial ministry of natural resources fined him for "trapping birds out of season." (Fortunately, the charges were dropped.) Most wineries use nets just for icewine grapes, which are more vulnerable to birds because they must stay on the vines until December or January. The precious (and pricey) dessert nectar they produce justifies the expense.

However, Louise is about to demonstrate the one starling-repellent that really works. She introduces me to Amadeus, a Harris hawk with gorgeously sleek saffron plumage. She puts on a big leather glove and gently lifts him out of his wire pen in the yard. Louise is a licensed falconer who owns several hawks, though she's not required to have a license to own Amadeus (he's not an indigenous species). But she chose to get the qualification, enrolling in a two-year study program, to better understand him.

"Owning a hawk is a substantial year-round commitment," Louise says. "It's on par with owning and training a horse. They're not pets."

We start walking through the vineyard, Amadeus flitting ahead of us, from one trellis post to the next. I haven't been paying much attention to the background birdsong, but I notice that as we stroll along with Amadeus, the vineyard suddenly goes eerily quiet, as though every living thing has frozen into silence at the sight of a predator.

Hawks are trained entirely by the reward of food. Punishment is ineffective; unlike dogs, raptors couldn't care less about pleasing their owners and won't respond to a gruff tone of voice. Louise describes Harris hawks as the Ford pickup trucks of the raptor world: durable, dependable, and open to tailgating.

What about those little thieves that are his prey? Louise explains that the flocks that damage vineyards include both resident and migratory birds. The migrating birds start arriving in mid-August en route to their winter homes in corn and soybean fields in the southern United States. For those grackles, sparrows, crows, waxwings, and orioles, the Niagara vineyards make a lovely roadside diner. To encourage them to keep moving, Featherstone uses four propane bird bangers and a battery-powered squawk box, which sounds to me like a screeching bird hell. The bangers' only drawback is their effect on some tourists, who are convinced that the winery must be on prime hunting grounds and ask eagerly what's in season. (On the plus side, Louise quips, it's great cover if you ever want to get rid of someone during the fall.)

Niagara's year-round resident birds are mostly robins, starlings, and mourning doves that live in the woods bordering the farm's fields. Because the birds become accustomed to the bird bangers, Louise tries to prevent them from settling in, since they're much harder to remove once they establish themselves. That's why Amadeus is such a powerful "there goes the neighborhood" deterrent: his mere presence in the twenty-three-acre vineyard discourages them from settling in. Even if the hawk flies for just a few hours each day, he can establish dominance over the vineyard. However, when she doesn't fly him for a few days because of the weather or other projects, she notices that the bird activity increases again.

Some birds, such as robins, starlings, and mourning doves, are protected by federal law, so Louise needs a permit to hunt them even on her own property. She also needs a hunting license because a falcon is considered a weapon and must be registered like a firearm. Louise took the same course designed for hunters who shoot moose or deer with rifles. Hunting with falcons is a blood sport, which may be why only 10 percent of licensed falconers are women.

Louise tells me that when Amadeus does catch a songbird, he carries it to a tree branch, where he's hidden from other predators who might steal his lunch. He'll "mantle" his food, covering it with his wings while he eats. He plucks off the large feathers, then eats the whole bird—bones, cartilage, small feathers—in about twenty minutes. After eating, his crop (throat) swells visibly, and about twelve hours later, he casts up the indigestible feathers and bones.

Although he could snack on a starling a day, it's more natural for raptors to gorge three to four times a week and not eat in between. Captive raptors have their diets monitored vigilantly. Managing the bird's weight is critical: if he's too heavy, he won't bother hunting; if he's too light, he gets weak and unhealthy. Amadeus is weighed daily, and the result is recorded along with his food intake and weather. (When it's cold, he needs more food.) In the summer, his ideal flying weight is twenty-two ounces: if he gets just one ounce heavier than that, he loses interest in hunting, akin to the demotivational principle, such as too-high unemployment benefits.

Amadeus is part of David and Louise's commitment to both sustainable and organic farming. "We're not tofu-and-granola people, but this approach makes sense," Louise says. "I read a warning on a bag of synthetic fertilizer that said, 'Do not enter the vineyard for seven days after applying.' Well, we live here!" Instead, David spreads mushroom compost on the vineyard to help aerate the soil and improve its moisture retention during dry periods. This compost helps control weeds as well and reduces the need for herbicides. David plants cover crops of rye grass and radish to help control erosion and to enrich the clay with organic matter.

The couple also tries to minimize the winery's impact on the environment, using all of their resources efficiently, such as water and energy, and to use recycled and nonpolluting materials wherever possible. David stopped using insecticides in 1999. Instead, like Malivoire, he releases ladybugs and lacewings into the vineyard to control aphids. He releases pheromones to disrupt the mating cycle of the grape berry moth. By avoiding insecticides, the farm fosters beneficial insects.

While she's telling me this, Louise leads me into the tasting room. David joins us and pours us a glass of their Black Sheep Riesling, a medium-bodied wine with mouthwatering notes of melon, pear, peach, honeysuckle, lime, and tangerine zest. It would marry beautifully with spiced Thai cuisine, grilled salmon, and vegetarian dishes.

Next we try their chardonnay. Featherstone was one of the first wineries to use Canadian oak barrels to age wine. The trees are grown, harvested, air-dried, and milled near Ancaster, Ontario. Then the wood slats are shipped to California for coopers to make the barrels. It's the same species as American oak but with a tighter grain that supposedly imparts less oak flavor. Using Canadian oak on Canadian wines may make sense conceptually, but I find that the wood imparts a funky aroma, with an odd fennel aftertaste. Maybe it's just a matter of working out the toasting and cooperage methods.

We move on to several vintages of their pinot noir, my favorite wines. These bright young things wake up your mouth and enliven your senses. Pleasingly tart cherries dance across your palate, followed by a dazzling weave of truffles, rose petals, and spices. This wine would be perfect with a starling stew. (Four and twenty blackbirds baked in a pie would be better with their icewine.)

Next we try their cabernet franc, which dispels the misperception that Niagara can't make this wine without it tasting of bell pepper. Their rich version is loaded with ripe dark berries and mocha notes. A full-bodied, balanced flavor gives way to dried tobacco leaves and blackberries on the finish. This would be perfect with lamb and mint sauce—or perhaps with liver and fava beans.

As our wing-and-hoof visit draws to a close, I almost expect to hear the theme music from *Born Free* swelling behind us. However, the hawks and sheep are not some sort of stealth PR strategy; they're an integral part of the couple's approach to winemaking. Growing grapes can be a monoculture, so they like having the animals around to make the winery feel like a working farm.

"We want to get wine off a pedestal," Louise says. "That starts with our visitors seeing the vineyard for what it is: a grape farm."

* * *

IT WAS THE pop of a cork heard around the world. The results made headlines even outside the wine industry, with newspapers proclaiming "Chardonnay Shocker," "Transatlantic Upset," and "Tempest in a Wine Glass."

In 2009, an expert panel of fourteen sommeliers and wine critics gathered in Montreal to blind-taste and rank sixteen top Burgundian and Californian chardonnays—and, slipped into the lineup as a ringer by the organizers, one unknown from a Canadian winery. It was audacious even to contemplate a comparison. But when the results were announced, Le Clos Jordanne's 2005 Claystone Terrace Chardonnay from Niagara had bested all of the wines.

Journalists dubbed it "the Judgment of Montreal," after the similarly upsetting 1976 Judgment of Paris tasting in which French critics chose California's Chateau Montelena Chardonnay and Stag's Leap Cabernet Sauvignon over top French wines. This win helped to debunk the myth that Old World wines were inherently superior to New World ones. The story was later made into a film called *Bottle Shock*, featuring the splendid Alan Rickman who was ill-served with a mediocre script.

This morning, I'm on my way to visit the winery that put dry Canadian table wine on the map, just as Inniskillin had two decades earlier with dessert wine. However, finding Le Clos Jordanne is proving difficult. I drive up and down the Niagara highway several times before realizing that it's a large, green, windowless building—no iron-wrought gates, no cherub fountains, no scripted winery name.

Why is Canada's flagship winery hiding in an industrial warehouse? I get the full story later: the plans for the proposed temple of wine are still gathering dust in the offices of superstar Canadian architect Frank Gehry, whose builds have been described by the *New York Times* as "powerful essays in primal geometric form."

In 2000, Le Clos Jordanne's owner, Vincor—the Canadian company that also owns wineries such as Inniskillin, Jackson-Triggs, and Sumac Ridge—commissioned Gehry to design a building that would be part of the contoured landscape—not an easy task when buildings have hard edges. They hoped Gehry would do for Niagara what he had done for a Spanish winery, the iconic Marqués de Riscal, with its undulating rooflines that evoke the movements of a flamenco dancer.

Gehry's design for Le Clos Jordanne included a roof of billowing titanium ribbons to give the feeling of a cloud floating across the vineyards. Inside, floor-to-ceiling glass columns would reveal all aspects of winemaking. The goal was to capture the energy of the entire process in one visual sweep: sorting grapes, pressing them, fermenting the juice, racking the wine into barrels, aging the wine, and bottling it. It was the most ambitious project in Canadian winemaking history, a breathtaking concept—and so was the projected price of $30 million. That may be why the project came to a full stop in 2004, when steel and titanium costs started to soar.

Feeling like the guy who's come to read the meter, I pull open a metal door on the side of a building—and almost get forklifted into the air. I jump back as the driver reverses, the metal prongs sliding from under my feet to pick up the wine boxes instead. Inside the warehouse looks like Santa's workshop on Christmas Eve: people scurry in different directions, someone's climbing a ladder up a wine tank, trolleys whiz past, workers sort grapes at conveyor belts, engines rev and beep.

And look, there's Santa in the middle of it all! His hair is pepper-gray rather than white, and at six-foot-five, this jolly old elf is taller and leaner than the North Pole version. But with his merry red cheeks, brown button eyes, and warm smile, I know he's the man I'm looking for. Le Clos Jordanne's winemaker, Thomas Bachelder, comes striding across the room to say hello.

"Let's start in the vineyards," he says above the noise, as I follow him outside to the parking lot, where I hope to find his sleigh and reindeer. Instead, we climb into his standard-issue, mud-splattered winemaker's pickup truck. As we drive along the Niagara back roads, Thomas explains his winemaking approach.

"We're searching for the geography of flavor," Thomas says. "Let the vineyards express themselves. To do that, you need to get out of the way of your vines and just let them do their thing. You still have to watch them closely, but keep your paws off. We are trying to make small preserves of the land."

He also tells me about his own background. A former Montreal wine journalist, he had his first taste of winemaking in 1985, when his brother gave him a Beaujolais home kit for Christmas. "That's when I became more interested in making wine than in describing it," he explains. Thomas became a successful amateur winemaker, winning competitions. However, it was only when he and his wife, Mary, took a honeymoon trip to Burgundy four years later that he decided to make wine professionally. As honeymoons are wont to do, the trip revealed the depth of his true passion.

Thomas realized he needed to strengthen his winemaking education; his degree from Concordia University was in communication studies. So he enrolled in Burgundy's prestigious school of oenology and obtained the agricultural diploma in viticulture and oenology, becoming only the second Canadian to do so. While studying, Thomas apprenticed at two Burgundian wineries, where he met Pascal Marchand, the first Canadian to have studied at the school and his future boss. (The Quebec bench strength should come as no surprise: the province has a strong wine culture and a consumption rate that's 50 percent higher than Ontario's.)

After graduation, his classmate Luisa Ponzi helped him get a job with her father, Dick, considered one of Oregon's pioneer winemakers. Thomas worked for two years at Ponzi Vineyards in Oregon, then returned to Burgundy in 1995 as head winemaker at the two-hundred-year-old Château Génot-Boulanger in Meursault. He returned to Oregon as chief winemaker at Lemelson Vineyards for four years. During this "wine gypsy" period, he was gradually honing his skills as a specialist in chardonnay and pinot noir.

In 2003, Pascal Marchand, then an executive director of Le Clos Jordanne for Boisset, Vincor's joint-venture partner, convinced Thomas to join the winery. The Burgundian-based Boisset owns famous pinot producers such as Bouchard Aîné et Fils, Jaffelin, and Mommessin. Jean-Charles Boisset, the second generation to run the company, grew up near the Clos de Vougeot, the famous Burgundian vineyard. Boisset has created a global portfolio of wineries through joint ventures and other types of mergers. (In 2009, he married Gina Gallo, heir to the Californian wine dynasty.)

Thomas was drawn to Le Clos Jordanne's strong Burgundian culture of winemaking. Still, it was his native terroir that brought him back to Canada. "I didn't come home out of a dumb sense of national pride; I came because the potential flavors excited me."

He thinks back to those first days at his new winery. "When I arrived, there were no vines, no winery, just little sticks in the ground. I wondered if I'd made a mistake," he admits. "But the contours of the Clos were so beautiful that I just put my head down, took a deep breath, and went to work. I made the first vintage in one-ton plastic bins on the Jackson-Triggs loading dock."

With 130 acres planted, Thomas sought to identify the local flavor in each of the winery's four vineyards and express it in the finished wine—a highly site-specific Burgundian method. He tackled his project with a Jesuitical zeal that took an intellectual's approach to hard labor. He tested and selected the best Burgundian grapes to suit each vineyard, combining them with local natural yeasts. He tended and hand-pruned each vine as painstakingly as a medieval monk illuminating a manuscript.

Nothing Thomas did was revolutionary. It was just the first time someone in Niagara combined all of the classical and modern techniques—tightly spacing the vines; pruning, harvesting, and sorting by hand; keeping the yields low; fermenting in long, unhurried stretches; gravity-flow handling the juice—with the business and viticultural know-how of a Burgundian wine powerhouse.

The winery's most prestigious vineyard is called Le Clos Jordanne. The best grapes from its western side go into the winery's flagship wine, Le Grand Clos. The rest of the grapes from the eastern side are bottled as the Clos Jordanne Single Vineyard. The remaining three vineyards—Claystone Terrace, La Petite, and Talon Ridge—each have a single vineyard bottling from which only the best, most distinctive vineyard pinot noir grapes are used. The rest of the grapes from these three vineyards are blended into the Village Reserve wine. All of the vineyards except La Petite have both chardonnay and pinot noir grapes.

Le Clos Jordanne Vineyard is perched on a natural plateau of limestone soils and rich sediments on the escarpment. The Claystone Terrace Vineyard has heavier, darker clay soils that retain more moisture. This makes its wines more robust and masculine, with fleshy black-fruit flavors wound tightly around a core of minerality, acidity, and tannin. Talon Ridge Vineyard—at seventy-four acres, the largest of the vineyards—is located at the top of the escarpment rather than at its base. It has a southerly orientation, so it's influenced less by Lake Ontario's warming effect and more by the natural sunshine of the slope. With its cooler temperatures and stonier soils, the vineyard's wines are lighter and fruitier than the others. La Petite Vineyard is the smallest and most easterly. The combination of warmer temperatures and sandier soil with better drainage results in leaner but highly perfumed wines.

"No two vineyards are alike here," Thomas says, as we get out at Talon Ridge. "The glaciers pushed the limestone to the Canadian Shield in a heterogeneous way. But they all have a heady mix of glacial till that imbues the wines with outrageous perfume and a strong sense of place."

As we walk through the vineyard, I can just make out the sprawl of Toronto, hovering on the horizon across Lake Ontario like a moveable city pinned down by the CN Tower. Looking around, I see that the vineyard is draped in lacey white nets, as though dressed for a fall wedding. (It cost $300,000 to install them on 130 acres.) As the nets flutter in the breeze, the vines seem to be walking in a procession up the gentle incline of the hill. However, their feet are firmly planted in the limestone below us. Pinot noir, chardonnay, and riesling vines all love rock loaded with calcium, which manifests itself as nervy acidity in the wine.

"The idea is to liberate the trace elements in the soil," Thomas says, going down on one knee to dig a little around the base of a vine. "That means understanding the mineralization cycle in the earth so that when we plow the wild-grass cover crops back under, we make their nitrogen available to the vine roots."

As you might guess, Le Clos Jordanne grows its grapes organically. "With that approach, we're looking for *le juste milieu*—the happy medium," Thomas says. "We want to help the vines just enough to do their thing. Organic treatments sit on top of the soil, whereas synthetic chemicals penetrate the vines and get into their 'bloodstream.' Those chemicals standardize the vineyard."

Niagara's growing season, though short, is still one to two weeks longer than Burgundy's and starts later in the season due to the heat-sink effect of Lake Ontario in the fall. This gives the wines great fruit depth, with exuberance of pure pinot and chardonnay expression. To further focus their flavors, Thomas keeps yields down to just two tons per acre. That concentration shows in his wines, which have classic proportions and textural polish.

When I ask Thomas about the Judgment of Montreal tasting, he says, "It came out of the blue for us. We didn't even know our chardonnay was entered into the tasting." Even more surprising was the fact that the 2005 vintage was only the second for Claystone Terrace. Most Burgundian vintners wait until the vines are ten years old before making their finest wines from them. The lineup of sixteen white wines included Burgundian heavyweights such as the 2005 Hubert Lamy Clos du Meix, which placed second, and the 2006 Joseph Drouhin Clos des Mouches. Among the sixteen red wines tasted, the 2004 Château Mouton Rothschild from Bordeaux placed first.

The judges weren't permitted to talk among themselves as they tasted, in case they influenced one another's assessment. "The tasting room was like a monastery," said Marc Chapleau, the Quebec magazine editor who organized the competition. The judges had to guess the origins of each wine, and most assumed that Le Clos Jordanne was French.

The announcement of the winners was followed by the usual accusations of judging bias, a rigged competition, and statistically meaningless results. Of course, blind tastings can be overread or misinterpreted. One wine can be at its peak drinkability while another is going through a dumb stage, aromas and flavors muted or not yet developed. Some wines require years of aging before they taste good, while others are terrific right after bottling. The wines selected for the tasting may not represent the best from the region. As well, certain characteristics, such as big oak, alcohol, and fruit flavor, can make a wine stand out in a tasting, even though it may not be the one you want to drink with dinner. But even with all of these faults, consumers still love a side-by-side comparison, whether it's of pinot noir, Pepsi versus Coke, or Tide and the "other leading brand." We feel they reveal some sort of naked truth.

That may be why so many articles about Canadian wine still start with Inniskillin's icewine several decades ago, and why insider sour grapes didn't dampen the enthusiastic headlines or the cultural impact of encouraging wine drinkers to give Canadian wines a try. I can't help wondering, though, why it's even still news when a Canadian wine wins in competition. After all, New World wines from Argentina, Australia, New Zealand, and California have been besting the French for years where it matters most: in the market.

Thomas is a rising-tide-lifts-all-boats kind of guy and turns the victory into a win for all Ontario wines. "Any number of wines could have been in our place: Flat Rock, Tawse, Lailey, Inniskillin, Hidden Bench," he declares. "It just so happened it was our wine the organizers put into the tasting. It's gratifying, of course, but we need the Céline Dion–Shania Twain phenomenon in the wine world."

I think he's right; Canada needs cult wines that are famous outside of Canada. We think of Italy's Sassicaia, France's Château Margaux, and Pétrus, Australia's Penfolds Grange. They're the $10,000 haute couture dresses on the runway. Few of us can afford them, but we still try to buy a piece of their mystique with overpriced perfume, scarves, and handbags. Le Clos Jordanne is positioned to do just that with pinot noir.

After Thomas shows me the other vineyards, we return to the winery. The fresh wood of the barrels smells like caramel and pine. Thomas has arranged them to mirror the geography of the vineyards: those from southernmost Talon Ridge Vineyard are closest to the door, followed by the others by vineyard subparcel across the cellar floor. "So much of life is intent and visualization," he explains, drawing a sample of the Village Reserve pinot from a cask with a pipette and pouring it into my glass. This wine wraps the finesse of Burgundy around the power of the New World. The black cherry and cedar forest aromas unfurl, rising and sliding out of the glass, like one silky garment after another tossed into the air.

"Don't use too much oak but do use Burgundian wood," Thomas says, knocking on one of the barrels. "It has a tighter grain, so there's less interference from the vanilla and butterscotch notes that it can impart. Oak should oxygenate the wines slowly." He likes to blend barrels that are one, two, and three years old for a nuanced effect. "It's the averaging of the whole that matters.

"I love racy wines that ally finesse, perfume, and power—the kind that frustrate you as a winemaker and excite you as a drinker," he tells me. "In Burgundy, that's Chambolle, Vosne-Romanée, Volnay, Chassagne, Santenay, and Nuits-Saint-Georges. They're the sort of wines you love to distraction: you love them with your mind first, then your senses. I want wines that I still smell after the meal is over and the glass is empty."

I'm still sniffing at my glass even though I've long since emptied it. (I didn't "forget" to spit; I meant to drink it all.) Thomas refills my glass with some La Petite Vineyard pinot. Hundreds of fruit flies swarm around, taking kamikaze dives into my glass. I don't blame them; the wine has a plush, generous body, with a sheen of polished cherries. The small, shimmering pool of ruby in my glass is bewitching.

"The truth of the land is starting to emerge," Thomas says thoughtfully, as we sip. "We will make Ontario sing out of the glass."

The Claystone Terrace pinot is a butch wine that's powerful and masculine up front, followed by a floral finish that runs wild with macerated black cherries. A vein of violets and truffles rippling through it gives me gooseflesh. Nothing could top that, except maybe Le Grand Clos. Its towering structure and massively concentrated black fruit, dark spices, and deep minerality open the core of the wine like a sunlit glade in the middle of a forest. As I taste it, the winery noises fade away and I am alone with this wine.

"Niagara is blessed and damned by being so close to Toronto and Buffalo," Thomas says, bringing me back from my vinous reverie to commercial realities. "Having those large urban markets right on our doorstep has kept us from lifting our eyes to the world stage. We have remained provincial and unfocused in our grape choices." He believes that the region's wineries need to pull together to market their products and to decide on the flagship reds and whites—pinot noir and chardonnay, in his opinion.

How can the Vintner's Quality Alliance (VQA) support this varietal focus, I wonder. Certainly, this quality designation tells consumers which wines are made from Canadian grapes. However, a number of winemakers I spoke to believe that such appellation systems, with their regulations and fees, have no place in developing wine regions; they stifle experimental vineyards, technological innovation, marketing creativity, outside investment, and industry growth. Such systems, they believe, are better suited to mature wine regions (such as Champagne and Chianti), where it's important to protect established names, wine styles, and viticultural techniques. Their main goal is to prevent anyone else from using the names (and brand equity) for commercial gain. That's why the Champagne region of France has fought vigorously and successfully to prevent other sparkling wines from calling themselves Champagne or even having "made in the Champagne method" on the label.

I can't help wondering, then: is Canada an emerging region or an established one? I think it teeters on the edge. Wine grapes have been grown here since 1811. Children born the year of Inniskillin's big win are now of legal drinking age. A vibrant industry can't just be based on a niche wine like icewine. It makes a great gift and a special treat, but it's not what people put on the dinner table every night. A strong wine industry needs to produce good dry whites and reds—both premium wines, such as pinot noir and chardonnay, and more modestly priced workhorses, like vidal, cabernet franc, baco noir, and gamay.

The challenge for Niagara, and for Canada, is to establish an identity that is broader but still regional. Yet I'm not worried. There's a gorgeousness to these wines that will eventually draw people to them. And just as the little town of Niagara-on-the-Lake nestles quietly, almost hidden, near the noise and crowds of Niagara Falls, these wonderful regional wines are waiting here for anyone willing to travel the back roads of the wine world.

Field Notes from a
Wine Cheapskate

INSIDER TIPS

- While $25 to $40 a bottle may not seem like an inexpensive wine, value is relative. Pinot noir is expensive to grow and make.

Niagara pinots are a bargain compared to those in Burgundy, which easily top $50 a bottle as a starting price.

• When a region is stereotyped for one kind of wine—in Niagara's case, icewine—look for what else it does well, such as pinot noir and riesling. These are the best supporting actors, which often offer stellar performances in the glass.

• Organically grown grapes don't guarantee you a better or more healthful wine, but it does mean that the producer is paying close attention to the vine health and the winemaking process. That increases your odds of getting a better quality wine.

WINERIES VISITED

Featherstone Estate Winery: www.featherstonewinery.ca
Le Clos Jordanne: www.leclosjordanne.com
Malivoire Winery: www.malivoirewineco.com

BEST VALUE WINES

Featherstone Winery Black Sheep Riesling
Featherstone Winery Cabernet Franc
Featherstone Winery Pinot Noir
Le Clos Jordanne Claystone Terrace Chardonnay
Le Clos Jordanne Claystone Terrace Pinot Noir
Le Clos Jordanne Village Reserve Pinot Noir*
Malivoire Courtney Gamay
Malivoire Estate Pinot Noir

*My first pick for my own Tuesday dinner.

TOP VALUE PRODUCERS

Cave Spring Cellars
Château des Charmes
Creekside Estate
Fielding Estate
Flat Rock
Henry of Pelham/
    Sibling Rivalry
Hillebrand Trius
Inniskillin
Jackson-Triggs/Open
Kacaba Vineyards
Konzelmann Estate
    Winery

Legends Estates
Mike Weir Wine
Niagara College
    Teaching Winery
Peller Estates
Reif Estate
Rosewood Estates
Southbrook Vineyards
Tawse
Thirteenth Street Winery
Union Wines
Vineland Estates
Wayne Gretzky Estate

TUESDAY DINNER FOR A WINE CHEAPSKATE

You'll find Martin Malivoire's recipes for a delicious fall meal at www.nataliemaclean.com/food.

Marinated Quail or Chicken Thighs

Foil Potatoes

Pumpkin Soup

*Baked Upper Canada Comfort Cream with
Grilled Peaches and Icewine Reduction*

TERRIFIC PAIRINGS

Pinot noir is a wine of great sensuality, silky texture, and seductive aromas, such as black cherries, raspberries, violets, sassafras, mushrooms, truffles, and fresh earth. It pairs with a wide variety of dishes because it is flavorful but not heavy in alcohol, oak, or tannin. My favorite pairings include:

Beef bourguignon
Cheese: goat, Brie,
    Camembert, Swiss,
    Gouda, Gruyère
Chicken with pancetta
    and herbs
Chicken, turkey, goose:
    roasted
Coq au vin
Cornish hen, squab, quail
Curries: mild
Duck in port reduction
    or cranberries
Halibut: grilled
    with rosemary

Matzo balls
Mushroom risotto
Osso buco
Pasta with herbed tomato sauce
Pizza: vegetarian, cheese,
    mushroom, Margherita
Planked salmon
Pork chops or tenderloin
Prime rib or rare roast beef
Tuna: grilled or seared with
    pepper crust
Veal: breaded cutlets
Vegetables: grilled

RESOURCES

For information about Niagara wines and pinot noir:

Niagara's Wine Visionaries by Linda Bramble
Icewine: The Complete Story by John Schreiner

A Pocket Guide to Ontario Wines, Wineries, Vineyards, and Vines
    by Konrad Ejbich
Ontario Wine Society: www.ontariowinesociety.com
Wine Country Ontario: www.winesofontario.org
Vintners Quality Alliance Ontario: www.vqaontario.com
Ontario Travel: www.ontariotravel.net
World of Pinot Noir: www.worldofpinotnoir.com

RELATED READING

The following books, while seemingly unrelated to the main subject matter of this chapter, provided some enjoyable reading before, during, and after my travels:

A Fool and Forty Acres: Conjuring a Vineyard Three Thousand Miles from Burgundy by Geoff Heinricks
The Heartbreak Grape: A Journey in Search of the Perfect Pinot Noir by Marq de Villiers
Silence of the Lambs by Thomas Harris

FOUR

WEDNESDAY

The Cape Crusaders of Africa

I CAN'T BELIEVE how many teeth this shark has. Two rows of pearly knife tips rim the top and bottom of his gaping maw. I can't see well enough to count them, though, since I'm several feet below the surface of the choppy Atlantic, off the coast of South Africa. The twenty-foot great white shark now circling me will replace his three hundred teeth every three months—over a lifetime that can span more than a hundred years.

Even when his dorsal fin slices through the water, his attacks are a terrifying surprise to seals, dolphins, porpoises, and other prey—a category in which I now find myself. As he comes in for his final attack, I lean forward to get a better look—I am always distracted by trivia. Luckily, I remember to pull my fingers inside the steel bars of my cage just before he slams into them. I almost feel sorry for the shark; he seems bewildered by the tamper-proof meat packaging. After a few seconds, he swims away to look for an easier meal. In these waters, it's eat lunch or be lunch.

Of course, thinking about lunch makes me wonder which South African wine would pair best with a juicy shark steak? This is the urgent question I put to Bevan Johnson, winemaker at Newton Johnson Winery, as he hauls me back into the boat after our bait-and-switch expedition.

"I'm not really sure," Bevan says as we dry off. "I haven't tasted a shark before, but then again, a shark hasn't tasted me, either, so I guess we're even."

Bevan, thirty-seven, with tousled blond hair and a love of surfing, could be mistaken for a Californian—except for his South African accent, which sounds like a cross between British and Australian. As we drive down the Hemel en Aarde Valley in his jeep, I look up at the avalanche of white clouds sliding slowly down the mountains. Rows of emerald vineyards stretch out to the ocean on this glorious March morning. It surprises me just how lovely the Cape wine region is. (Then again, most wine regions are scenic. This is why I don't write about plumbing fixtures and go on world tours of damp basements and smoggy factories.)

This is the only wine region in the world influenced by two oceans: the icy Atlantic and the warmer Indian Ocean, which meet at the continent's most southern tip, the Cape of Good Hope. Although South Africa's wine region is just thirty-five degrees south of the equator, at the same latitude as southern Australia, its climate is more Mediterranean than tropical, much like Italy. That's because the Atlantic ushers in cool air from Antarctica to counteract the African heat.

The Cape is the smallest of the world's nine floral kingdoms, with an area of only fifty-five thousand square miles. Despite this, it's also the most diverse, with more than ten thousand species of plants—more than the entire Northern Hemisphere. Seventy percent of plants here can't be found anywhere else on the planet. The indigenous shrubbery, called *fynbos* ("fine bush" in Afrikaans), is a collection of low-lying plant species that are critical to South Africa's ecosystem. The countryside is stitched in their jeweled colors: yellow and white orchids, red disa, fuchsia king protea, and orange pincushions.

You may be wondering what flowers have to do with wine. They're all part of the same complex interaction of weather, rock, and soil. The Cape has more than fifty soil types, ranging from granite and loam to sandstone and shale; they're the most ancient soils in the world, some as much as a million years old. No wonder, then, that a region that produces such a diversity of plants also produces such an incredible variety of wine styles.

This is my first trip to South Africa. For years, I confused the country of South Africa with the whole continent of Africa, based entirely on watching *Wild Kingdom* as a kid. See cheetah, see gazelle, see cheetah chase gazelle, see gazelle dash left, see cheetah almost get gazelle, cut to commercial. For more culturally aware individuals, South Africa may bring to mind Nelson Mandela, lions, apartheid, Archbishop Desmond Tutu, diamonds, slavery, cinnamon sands, famine, Charlize Theron, cardboard shantytowns, and Jane Goodall. Wine, however, usually isn't on the list.

I'd never associated Africa with wine myself until one evening as I sat sipping on a lime-fresh Mulderbosch sauvignon blanc by the crackling fire under a navy sky of starry pinpoints. Low growls came from rustling bushes nearby, but they didn't concern me. Okay, so maybe it was a wood-burning oven under glitter-glued ceiling with the piped-in soundtrack from *The Lion King*. I suppose it was only natural that my first taste of good South African wine would be at Disney World's African-themed restaurant Jiko (Swahili for "cooking place"), where they also specialize in prepackaged culture.

Did I mention that I'm a woman who enjoys the great indoors? I am not even a camping person, let alone a safari person. Those down-filled vests from L.L. Bean still hang in my closet with the price tags on them. Would I like to portage with a canoe and backpack through the wilderness, you ask? How about I'll meet you at the rustic Holiday Inn, where I'll be playing the loon CD and enjoying the minibar. However, the electrifying icy heart of the Mulderbosch sauvignon blanc was wildly different from anything I had tasted from South Africa—it made me curious (and thirsty) to learn more.

Winemaking in this region is nothing new. Five hundred years ago, European sailors would follow the coast of Africa south to the Cape, then turn northeast across the open Pacific to India to buy spices. Back then, instead of Good Hope, the Spanish named the headland *Cabo Tormentoso*—Cape of Storms. Still, it became a port of call for ships to restock supplies, especially fresh citrus fruit. The British ate limes to prevent scurvy, earning themselves the nickname "limeys." The Dutch, however, preferred wine, which is also loaded with antioxidants.

In 1655, Jan van Riebeeck, a doctor employed by the Dutch East India Company, planted "palliative vines." Four years later, he wrote in his diary: "Today, praise be to God, wine was made for the first time from Cape grapes." (A neighbor was less enthusiastic, noting in his own journal that the wine was only good for "irritating the bowels.")

The first governor, Simon van der Stel, gave his name to the settlement of Stellenbosch (Stel's Bush), today a charming university town in the heart of South Africa's wine country. The evening sun casts a reddish halo around the gabled rooflines of Cape Dutch manor homes and their sprawling verandas, which have the *Gone-with-the-Wind* grace of the Old South.

Simon van der Stel planted vines on his Groot Constantia estate, about forty-five miles from Stellenbosch. In 1688, the Dutch colony swelled with the arrival of the Huguenots, French Protestants fleeing Louis XIV's religious persecution. With the French expertise to guide production, the quality of the wines improved dramatically. They made Constantia's magnificent muscat wines, which at that time cost more than Bordeaux's famed Château d'Yquem. They achieved a concentrated sweetness by twisting the stems of the grape bunches on the vines just before they were fully ripened. This stopped the flow of sap to the fruit and resulted in grapes that were shriveled and raisined with concentrated sugars and flavors. Pickers dubbed them *oumensgesiggies*, or "old people's faces."

This dessert elixir was exported back to Europe, where it became wildly popular. Frederick the Great, Baudelaire, Longfellow, Charles Dickens, and Jane Austen were all among its fans. Napoleon demanded a steady supply for his exile on St. Helena. Thomas Jefferson shipped many cases to his Virginia home. German Chancellor Otto von Bismarck preferred it to his own Rhine rieslings. King Louis Philippe of France bought an entire vintage. Constantia eventually fell out of favor with European courts, replaced by more reasonably priced Hungarian tokaji. Recently, however, the Constantia estate has been revived and is again producing dessert wines of magnificent concentration and popularity.

The South African wine industry developed slowly for the next two hundred years and then suffered the same 1886 blight as the rest of Europe: the vine-killing root louse phylloxera. Growers replanted grapes that were more robust and high yielding, such as cinsault. They produced low-quality wine and were used mostly for distilled brandy. That industry flourished under apartheid, the government system of racial segregation, which also drew economic sanctions from major trading partners in the 1980s. As a result, South Africa's wine was poor or nonexistent for several decades—long enough for a generation of drinkers (like me) to be largely unaware of it.

Happily, more open international markets with the end of apartheid has fostered a winemaking revolution in South Africa. Today a new winery opens here every nineteen days. The industry employs more than three hundred thousand people and produces a billion bottles a year worth more than $3 billion, making it the seventh-largest producer in the world. Some of the largest and most inexpensive wine brands in the liquor store are from South Africa: Two Oceans, Sebeka, Nederburg, Simonsig, Fish Hoek, and Obikwa.

Of all the country's agricultural businesses, wine is the fastest growing and most profitable—despite searing droughts, fierce cyclones, bloody revolutions, and failing infrastructure. As the British writer Auberon Waugh observed, "The world is divided into the reckless, the brave, the amiable—and the rest. The wine community of South Africa is on the A-list. Even in this exasperating, least tamed (but most beautiful) of countries, it renders almost everything easier, funnier, profounder."

This brings me back to the adventurous Bevan Johnson, who's sitting beside me on the terrace at his winery. As we look out at the rolling gray Atlantic, we sip his syrah—liquid black plums roll down a velvet carpet of violets. It strikes me as a perfect transition wine to enjoy on a Wednesday between the lighter riesling and pinot noir early in the week and the more robust wines to come on the weekend. Rosemary and lavender perfume the salty breeze that blows off the water. I'm filled with a quiet happiness. I've found another pocket of like-minded obsessive personalities.

THE NEXT MORNING I drive up the green slopes of Paarl Mountain north of Cape Town to visit Charles Back, a winemaker who loves to butt heads with French authorities. He's named some of his wines Goats do Roam and Goat-Roti—puns on France's famous wine regions, Côtes-du-Rhône and Côte Rôtie. But there's a lot more to Charles Back than a flair for tweaking French sensibilities.

He produces some of South Africa's most coveted premium wines under the labels of Fairview and the Spice Route Company. He also founded one of the most successful black empowerment labels, Fairvalley. Charles was an early practitioner of many of the principles now formalized in the government-funded policy of Black Economic Empowerment. This aims to bring more black employees into management and winemaking roles, as well as improve labor practices, skills development, and employment security.

The Wine Industry Transformation Charter works within this framework and has the ambitious goal for blacks and women to own and manage more of the country's wineries by buying and redistributing land. However, grape farming requires highly specialized agricultural, technological, and marketing skills, which take years to acquire. It's also a capital-intensive business, with low profit margins—not an industry that attracts anyone who isn't already passionate about making wine. As a result, simply turning land over to new black owners doesn't work. Skills transfer partnerships, like Charles Back's at Fairvalley, are crucial.

Even Charles's Goat line of wines is no joke: he exports 65 percent of them to forty countries, and they account for 25 percent of South Africa's independently owned wine exports. Goats do Roam is the bestselling South African label in North America. In front of the Fairview winery is a twenty-five-foot-tall stone tower. Its most famous resident looks down at us from an open window at the top—an old billy goat with long gray whiskers. I learn later that he's a retired member of a herd of a thousand or so hoofers from whose milk Fairview produces a hundred tons of cheese every month. Charles's father, Cyril Back, started the herd back in the 1980s. Charles's grandfather, a self-taught winemaker who emigrated from Lithuania, bought this estate.

Charles approaches me while I'm still looking up at the tower. I jump a little, startled by this compact man with curly white hair and a bushy white mustache. His mischievous eyes seem to scan the area for something to climb up or nibble on.

"Natalie, I see you've met the bearded elder," he says warmly. "The first resident escaped and headed straight for the vineyards. As we chased him, we noticed he was eating only the Rhône grapes: shiraz, mourvèdre, grenache. So we made a blend based on what he nibbled," he explains, smiling, as we walk into the winery.

Inside, I notice the gourmet food shop to the left that sells his wines, cheeses, artisanal breads, and other comestibles. The whimsical names play here, too, such as Paarlesan, a Parmesan-style cheese. On the back of the package, a goat nibbles its way across the top of the bar code that looks like wispy grass.

"For some reason, the French get all twitchy when they see their place names on other wine labels," Charles says, as we walk through the busy tasting room, lit by twinkling lights on goat-horn chandeliers. Drinkers cluster around three tasting bars; the room is abuzz with French, German, Dutch, Japanese, and other languages. (I love the spittoons: gray milking pails.)

Charles's puns are a cheeky riposte to stiff French tradition. There's also Goat Door, a chardonnay wink at Burgundy's Côte d'Or, and the Goatfather, a blend of Italian barbera and sangiovese. My favorite label is from a cabernet blend: it has a rather blasé-looking female goat in front of a French château. The name: Bored Doe.

"The wines originally took off because of the critter-label craze, even though we weren't trying to be part of that," he recalls. "The anti-French sentiment in America over the Iraq war also helped, as some consumers saw these wines as a playful alternative.

"Eventually, I had to separate two lines because Fairview is serious and the goats are frivolous," he explains. "I didn't want to be known only as the guy who makes Goat wines."

Charles reminds me of Randall Grahm, the owner of Bonny Doon Vineyards in California, who also has an irresistible love of wordplay and Rhône wines. Randall's red wine named Le Cigare Volant is a mocking tribute to a Rhône town's ordinance passed in 1954 at the peak of the Cold War forbidding flying saucers—or "flying cigars," as the French call them—from landing in vineyards. His label in the traditional French sepia tones shows a cigar hovering over a vineyard.

Randall and Charles both embroider humor in unexpected places to deftly deflate wine snobbery. However, as Charles points out, the product still has to be good. "People bought the wines as a joke, but then came back for more. The first sale is based on the label; the second sale is based on what's in the bottle."

It certainly helps that the wines are value-priced under $13. Pricing wine is always tricky: too expensive and you exclude most of the market and get eaten by the competition. Too cheap and you suffer the fate of Hungarian, Chilean, and other wines that enter a market with rock-bottom prices and then never get out of that vinous ghetto.

As consumers, most of us like deals, but we don't like the word *cheap*, given its association with *trashy* and *worthless*. The notions of "inexpensive" and "inferior" are deeply entwined in our shopping culture, but it's a false assumption that price always equates with quality. A cheap wine isn't always a bad one, just as an expensive wine isn't always a great one. That's why my quest for good wine value is also a journey into good taste and authenticity. Those qualities aren't found exclusively in pricey wines.

"The consumer perception is that we have cheap labor and low costs in South Africa, and therefore we can produce cheap wines," Charles explains. "But that's not true. With the new post-apartheid laws to avoid further exploitation, labor is expensive. Land costs more per acre here than in the Languedoc. We need to charge more for our wines to stay competitive internationally. Cheap is strictly about price; value is about expectations and over-delivering on them."

Evidently consumers agree that the Goat wines delivered on their promises. The line grew so quickly that Charles created a new company for it and built two new winemaking facilities. His brilliant marketing is backed by solidly made wines. I find the reds, in particular, exceptionally well-made for the money: full-bodied with ripe black fruit flavors, eminently gulpable. If I were a French vintner, I'd lie awake at night worrying about these wines—not for their names but for their quality.

When France threatened to sue for trademark infringement, Charles took a busload of his farm workers to the French consulate in Cape Town. They sang traditional black struggle songs and presented the French attaché with a vacuum-sealed package of goat droppings for his garden.

"I have no idea how CNN heard about it, but they showed up with a camera crew," Charles says, grinning. "We got more from the publicity than we paid in legal fees. Unfortunately, the French backed off, and the story faded. I'd appreciate whatever you could do to stir up the controversy again."

I suggest he launch a new brand called Get Your Goat, with a label featuring French wine legislators and strategically placed ram's horns. He smiles and says, "Well, that would require some hands-on market research. Want to milk a goat?"

"Ah . . ." I hesitate, sensing a test. "You'll show me how to do it?"

"Oh no," he says, laughing. "My days of milking goats are *udderly* over. Let me call my chief goatherder," he says, flipping open his cell phone.

"Yes, she wants the full farm experience," he says into the phone. Then he calls his chief goat-to guy, Chris Bryant, the winery's webmaster, who meets us in the tasting room. Charles tells him: "Take pictures—and be sure to post them everywhere: the blog, Twitter, Facebook. Take this thing international."

We walk to the pasture, where small white kids frolic, kicking up their hooves behind them like children pleased with new sneakers. Others poke their curious pink noses between the slats of the wooden fence. In front of the barn, I meet Donald Mouton, whose last name really is the French word for *sheep*. He has a kind, weathered face and holds the leash of a large white nanny goat that stands docilely beside him, her udder swollen with milk.

"Oh, she's lovely!" I say. "What do you call her?"

"Um, we don't give them names, ma'am, because eventually they . . . have to move on to greener pastures," Donald explains. To cover the awkward moment, he demonstrates how to grasp the teat and pull it down. Milk squirts into the pail. It looks easy enough. He stands and gestures toward the goat, which seems to be looking at me with mild amusement.

I squat down beside the goat, leaning my cheek against her warm belly for balance. Donald, Chris, and a group of strapping lads in grass-stained overalls gather around to watch. I grab one of the teats and pull. Nothing. I try again. Nothing. My cheeks start to burn.

"Start higher up on the teat," Donald advises.

I do, and it works: a long stream of milk sprays at me and then into the pail. I feel Rebecca-of-Sunnybrook-Farm pleased. After I half-fill the bucket, Donald pours some of the milk into a plastic cup and offers it to me. I'm squeamish at first but then drink it. The milk is warm and summer-meadow fresh. I'm curious to see if I'll be able to taste the essence of this milk in the Fairview cheeses back at the winery.

When we're finished, Chris and I walk back to the winery. Charles meets us and asks with a devilish smirk, "What's that smell?"

As Chris leaves to write his blog post, Charles and I go into the Goatshed, the winery's restaurant. It's a busy place, alive with chatter, clinking glasses, laughter, and more milk pails. A young server brings us several bottles of wine and a plate of cheeses.

"Thanks, Victoria," he says, and she smiles warmly back at him. He knows every employee by name, and they respond as though they'd like to share a glass of wine (or beer) with him after hours.

"This restaurant alone has created twenty-nine jobs for people from here—we didn't bring in anyone," he says. "It's all about the right training. We have all the resources we need to do everything for ourselves." He seems to be referring more broadly to the South African wine industry and perhaps even to the country itself.

We taste his Roydon Camembert, with its earthy barnyard flavors, which is beautifully complemented by his Fairview Riesling, an off-dry white with notes of field flowers and white peach. I ask why he makes both cheese and wine.

"Cheese gratifies my impatience: if I have an idea for a new recipe, I make it, and three weeks later, it's ready," he says. "Wine is longer term, but it satisfies a deeper need."

Cheese, Charles explains, ripens and deepens in flavor from the outside in toward the center. His Pont-l'Évêque, an Alsatian-style cheese, has a washed rind that's been bathed in salted water and wine. This breaks down the curd and helps make it part of the cheese, rather than just the skin, intensifying the cheese flavor. Its wild pungency tastes civilized with his Fairview Viognier.

The wine is also surprisingly good with his Blue Tower cheese, which has more holes than a typical blue cheese. This allows the mold more room to grow, so the result is a stronger flavor. I had thought such a strong cheese would overwhelm such a delicate wine, but the wine's floral notes and perky acidity are up to the task.

His Fairview Chenin Blanc is terrific with Le Berle Blanc cheese, which has been aged on straw mats for three weeks to intensify its flavors. Chenin blanc, also known as steen, is the most widely planted grape in South Africa, accounting for a quarter of all vineyards. Sadly, much of it is still used for those cheap brandies and wines that come in two styles: paint-stripper strong or dishwater light. This marvelous wine is far removed from those liquid abominations. It's made from the oldest bush vines, whose grapes produce wines of extraordinary concentration and crisp citrus flavors that rival the best chenins from France's Loire Valley.

Almost three-quarters of South African grapes are white, another hangover from the brandy days. That needs to change, Charles believes. The country needs to focus on red wines, though not the best-known ones, such as cabernet sauvignon and merlot.

"With our climate, we should be looking to the Rhône or Spain or Portugal, not Bordeaux," he says. "When it comes to Bordeaux varieties, we have delusions of grandeur. Instead, we should take risks: plant new red grapes to see what works."

The man knows what he's talking about. Charles was the first in the country to plant varieties like mourvèdre, tannat, petite sirah, tempranillo, and souza, a Portuguese grape. His specialty, though, is shiraz. Plantings of that grape have increased sevenfold since 1990 and now comprise 7 percent of South Africa's vineyards. Shiraz may be best known as an Australian wine, but South Africa actually gave Australia its first vine cuttings.

Charles opens a bottle of shiraz, a smoky black-fruited wonder, from his Spice Route estate on the blustery Atlantic coast. He cofounded that winery in 1997 with three partners whom he's since bought out. The winery, housed in an old tobacco-drying barn, now produces ten thousand cases a year of Rhône varietal wines, which regularly achieve scores of 90 and above from critics.

We try another Spice Route wine, Chakalaka, which takes its name from the traditional, spicy South African relish. Made from low-yielding bush vines, it's imbued with vanilla smoke and fleshy plums with a midnight depth of crushed blackberries and cloves. It's delicious with the steaming plate of grilled springbok that Victoria sets in front of me. The dark meat of this gazellelike creature is tender and savory. The country's popular rugby team, the Springboks, won the 1995 World Cup match against New Zealand, made famous in the movie *Invictus*, starring Matt Damon and Morgan Freeman.

The springbok dish reminds me to ask about baboons, which I've heard make a dinner special of wine grapes. I had already noticed a few crafty baboons sitting by the road waiting for any edibles to fall off trucks. Charles tells me that marauding baboon troupes occasionally raid a vineyard, grabbing bunches of grapes and running back up the mountain. Efforts to deter them haven't worked, from erecting fences to scattering lion dung. Most vintners just write off the 10 percent loss each year to nature.

Wildlife aside, Charles believes in working with the people who are native to this land. In 1997, he donated sixteen acres of land adjacent to Fairview to sixty-three black employees and their families, who created the wine label Fairvalley. The government built the workers' homes. Charles helped with skills training and lent space in his winery to make the wine.

"You can't just throw money at these projects," he explains. "Affirmative action can't come at the expense of profitability because it's not sustainable. Labor laws are strict, land purchase is difficult, and falsely raising people's expectations is worse than doing nothing at all. Just transferring land is not going to change lives; you must transfer skills.

"True empowerment also can't be a marketing gimmick to gain consumer sympathy—politics in wine leaves a bad aftertaste. We have a good story here, and the legitimacy of that story is important—we have to be able to show the goods in terms of both the workers' lives and the quality of the wine."

To prove his point, he pours a glass of Fairvalley sauvignon blanc. It has the vibrant lime freshness of New Zealand, without the grassiness, and the lanolin-soaked richness of the Loire Valley. It sweeps across my mind like a spring rainstorm, carrying aromas of fresh-awakened earth and wild alpine flowers.

Charles's cousin, Michael Back, who owns Backsberg Winery, also worked with a group of black employees to create the Freedom Road label named after Mandela's biography, *Long Walk to Freedom*. Profits from the sale of the wine go to building the workers' homes. Still, less than 1 percent of the country's wineries are currently owned by blacks, despite the best efforts of businessmen like Charles and Michael. What inspired them to lend a hand?

"We always had two or three runaway or orphaned children living with my family when I was growing up, so my parents set a good example," he says. "But Fairvalley is not a charity. Charity is short-term and isn't based on economic value. This is a business proposition with a social dimension. I've been farming since 1978, and I know how much this land means to me. And all of these people worked the land with me, but none of them owned a piece of it."

It seems to me that few other winemaking regions have such historic moral obligations. Charles agrees. "Success, not legislation, is the greatest lever for change here," he asserts. "Other wineries see that you can do it and still make money. Something as simple as selling a good bottle of wine can change many lives. Three hundred workers make it, and they all have families—that's two thousand people."

Today, Fairvalley produces 150,000 cases of wine and exports to both the United States and the U.K. The original workers' homes are being converted into cottages for tourists to finance building new homes and winemaking facilities.

"Our industry has been playing catch-up for ten years," Charles muses. "Apartheid isolated us entirely from modern techniques of grape growing, winemaking, and marketing. We were denied outside capital investment for years, and so we were left in a time warp. We thought we could just pick up where we left off, but now we're paying the price. We could only watch as Chile, Australia, and California flooded the international market with decent, inexpensive wines."

Academics at Stellenbosch University devised the structure of apartheid (separateness)—the legal racial segregation of whites and blacks—which the National Party government introduced as law in 1948 and which lasted until 1994. In the late 1980s, twenty-three nations, including Canada, the United States, and the U.K., imposed economic sanctions against South Africa to protest apartheid, stopping all commercial trade with the country. This was just as the wine boom in North America was beginning: the CBS television show

60 Minutes announced the health benefits of red wine, and North Americans turned from hard liquors to wines and started ordering them by the grape.

Those forty years of isolation also took their toll internally. Most of South Africa's wine industry was controlled by the government-backed KWV (Kooperatiewe Wijnbouwers Vereeniging), the cooperative wine growers association that dictated prices, yields, production quotas, and varieties. It was geared to producing large volumes of cheap grapes for brandy distillation. Winemakers weren't permitted to travel abroad to get experience in other regions. The quarantine system made it impossible to import good vine stock. Chardonnay, for example, was illegal.

Then, in 1990, President Frederik Willem de Klerk began negotiations to end apartheid and freed black activist Nelson Mandela, who had spent twenty-seven years in prison. In 1994, Mandela's African National Congress (ANC) won the first democratic elections in which blacks were able to vote. Observers compared the end of apartheid to the fall of the Berlin Wall. They celebrated the planned revitalization of the country's wine industry—though at the time, they toasted the new democracy with truly terrible wine.

"Back then, we were exporting wines that were so bad we didn't even drink them ourselves," Charles observes. "That didn't help our image. After the Mandela effect faded, our wines had to compete on taste."

The real strides have come in the last decade; millions of people who moved away during apartheid have returned home, bringing with them an influx of talent. The average age of winemakers in the country has decreased by ten years, and this new generation has a more global perspective and training. Even the basic infrastructure now supports the industry. Under apartheid, only 30 percent of townships had electricity and running water; now, 80 percent do. The next step is for South African wine to reinvent itself, as Argentinean and Chilean wines have done. Early growth—replacing cheap bad wine with cheap good wine—is easy. The real challenge is sustaining that momentum as competition increases and as your wines move up-market in quality and price.

"One of the few good aspects of our isolation is that it kept us from developing a homogeneous international style," Charles says. "We're neither Australia nor France. We're the oldest New World country and the newest Old World country. So we can focus on making wines that are a different interpretation of what others are doing—wines that are uniquely South African.

THE STORIES OF Fairvalley and Freedom Road make me curious about other black brands in the country, such as Thandi, Tukulu, New Beginnings, Winds of Change, M'hudi, and Seven Sisters. A recent book titled *Ithemba* ("hope" in Nguni, the language of a pastoral South African clan) profiles more than thirty black vintners. It's partly an inspirational business story and partly an exploration of the industry's socioeconomic and racial transformation since the end of apartheid. It's filled with words like "righting historical wrongs" and "social upliftment" that hint at how deep and old the rifts are and how much work still remains to be done.

On the book's cover is a photograph of a beautiful woman in her late thirties who could be Halle Berry's sister. Carmen Stevens's head is cocked to one side, her lips curved in a just-watch-me smile. She's described as South Africa's first female winemaker "of color," a term that includes not just blacks but many other races in the country that Mandela described as a "rainbow nation."

This morning I'm meeting Carmen at her winery, Amani Vineyards, on the southern slope of Kanonkop, near Stellenbosch. Off to the west, I can see Table Mountain, its long, flat top draped with a tablecloth of white mist. It towers over the Capelands, a constant presence. Last night a fiery sunset drenched its granite dominance in Technicolor reds and oranges.

Amani is the Swahili word for "peace"; a metal medallion is affixed by hand to every bottle the winery produces. The winery is the physical expression of its name: the vineyard rows look as though they've been trimmed with fingernail clippers. Canna lilies frame the doorway. South African artwork—tribal masks, spears, and colorful paintings—adorns the walls inside the tasting room. On the floor is a large zebra rug. That's why I'm surprised to be greeted by a broadly smiling barrel-chested white man in his fifties.

"Howdy, you must be Natalie," he says with a deep southern U.S. drawl and an unhinging handshake. "I'm Rusty Myers. I own the place . . . Carmen will be right with ya."

We sit at an oak table by the tasting bar, and Rusty fills me in on his own history. He and his wife, Lynde, moved from Oklahoma to South Africa in 2002 to join Lynde's father, Jim, who had bought the farm the year before as a quick turnaround investment. Rusty had been a financial adviser and Lynde an ultrasound diagnostician, so they brought with them a passion for wine but no experience in making it. They decided to stay in South Africa and have since taken over the ownership of the winery. Rusty met Carmen in 2004 while she was working at another winery.

"I didn't hire her because I wanted her picture on my brochure; I hired her because she was good. Damn good. There she is now," he says, looking up.

Carmen stands at the doorway to the tasting room, haloed by the brilliant afternoon sun. She looks like a winemaking saint—with hellfire in her eyes. She's not what I expected at five-foot-one and maybe a hundred pounds. Then again, Carmen Stevens has spent her life not being what anyone expected.

"My mother worked at a clothing factory for sixteen hours a day to support her three young children," Carmen explains when I ask how she became interested in wine. "She didn't have time to help us with our homework, and I had trouble reading. But one day I found one of her romance novels on her bedside table. The book was set in a winery, and I was fascinated with the young heroine who tasted wines in a dark, mysterious cellar. I read all the books in the series and made up my mind to work in the wine industry."

After finishing high school, Carmen worked as a waitress to save money for the country's top oenology program at Stellenbosch University. She was told she required several courses in agriculture as prerequisites. She completed these, then applied again. This time she was flatly denied entrance. It was the early 1990s, and the entire student body of the university was white.

So she applied to Elsenburg College, another respected viticultural school in Stellenbosch. She was refused twice before finally gaining entrance in 1993, one year before Mandela's election.

"I was twenty-two when I stepped into a wine cellar for the first time, at Elsenburg," Carmen says, her eyes shining with the memory. "It was just like the novels described it, right down to those underground smells of oak and earth hanging in the air. I knew this was what I must do!

"There were only five women that year, the first time they also let women into the program. A lot of the guys thought we wouldn't make it," she recalls.

Her story resonates with me. When I started writing about wine, one of the most widely published wine critics in the country, a man of considerable experience, advised me to "treat it as a weekend hobby, sweetheart." I found that extremely motivational—to prove him wrong.

After all that initial rejection, Carmen was understandably nervous when she finished at Elsenburg. "I thought I was going to drown, I was so scared," she confesses. "I never expected to be welcomed into the industry."

However, luck was with her, or rather, her newly acquired skills and determination. She wanted to get international experience first and worked in California at Simi Winery with Paul Hobbs. She respected him most for how closely he watched his vines: "He'd say, 'This grape must come in at three o'clock tomorrow.' He knew that was the right time for that grape to be picked. That's the way I want to make wine."

In 1998, Carmen returned home to take a job as an assistant winemaker at Stellenbosch Farmers Winery, South Africa's largest wine producer. (It's since been renamed Distell.) The company created Tukulu, a joint venture with a group of black liquor retailers.

"The first year I made wine here, I spent hours at the tank just watching it," she says, laughing. "I was so captivated that I'd even come at night just to have another look. It was the most exciting thing I'd ever done."

When I ask Carmen about her favorite part of the process, she seems equally keen on it all. "I love the personal contact I have with the vines, and I love the link between eating the grapes and drinking the wine," she enthuses. "I taste every day; it's incredible how the wine changes in just a few hours. There's a secret code of communication when you taste someone else's wine. You may never meet them, yet you feel you know them through every bottle they make."

At Tukulu, Carmen worked with Paul Pontallier, the director of Bordeaux's first growth Château Margaux, who had been hired as a consultant. He taught her the master art of blending, the heart of all great wines. "It's one thing to pick up a glass and say 'that's nice' or 'it smells like dark fruit,' but the real trick for a winemaker is to isolate the components that create a great wine. You make your intentions real through blending," she says.

Carmen remembers Pontallier tasting her pinotage, looking up in surprise, and asking, "Did you make this?" She thought she'd done something wrong, but it turned out that he loved it.

She was all the more pleased because she believes that pinotage is the greatest challenge for a winemaker in this country. "You must make the exact right decisions at the exact right time," she explains, pouring us each a glass of it. "Pinotage, like one of its parents, pinot noir, is so fussy at every step in the process. And the longer it stays in wood, the darker it becomes—it'll run to black if you let it."

Carmen's pinotage has a luxurious palate weight, with layers of peppered raspberries, black cherry, licorice, and mocha spice. A smoky, velvet plum heart slowly emerges. We also taste some of her older vintages. As the wine ages, its aromas become less fruity and more like the leather, violets, and cigar box of mature bordeaux.

The story of pinotage is uniquely South African. In 1925, Abraham Perold, the first professor of viticulture at the University of Stellenbosch, crossed Burgundy's pinot noir with what he thought was Rhône Valley hermitage (syrah or shiraz). However, it was really cinsault, a more rustic French grape. He brushed their flowers against each other and the result was four precious seeds. He planted these in the garden of his home on the university's experimental farm.

Pinot noir, known as the heartbreak grape, is notoriously difficult to grow, susceptible to disease and rot. When handled well, it produces wines of great elegance and flavor. Conversely, cinsault is a hardy and prolific producer but usually only results in ordinary, tannic wines. Perold wanted to create a vine that produced flavorful grapes but could survive South Africa's climate and diseases. He evidently wasn't impressed with the results, though: two years later, when he left the university to work for KWV, he didn't take the new vines with him.

After his departure, the university hired a team of workers to clear his overgrown garden. By chance, Charles Niehaus, a young lecturer and former student of Perold, happened to be cycling past just as they were about to rip out Perold's pinotage vines. Niehaus recalled the experimental plantings and asked the workers if he could take them to a nursery. They let him, and he continued tinkering with the new breed.

The first commercial plantings didn't happen until 1943 when the name was changed from Perold's Hermitage x Pinot to the catchier pinotage. Herminot and a few other monikers were also considered. My suggestion for a name based on the tannic monsters that assaulted my mouth with flavors of varnished banana and cold fireplace? Pinosault.

Those early wines were dreadful. At one of the first wine shows I ever attended in 1998, I made the mistake of asking the man pouring the pinotage how a wine could be both jammy and bitter at the same time.

"They can't," the snippy wine booth guy told me. "You just don't understand the style."

Apparently neither did the head of the wine department for Christie's wine auction house, Michael Broadbent. In 1977, he led a group of British Masters of Wine around the Cape. He described pinotage as "hot and horrible," reeking of "rusty nails." The late wine writer David Wolfe described it as the "taste of apartheid."

Pinotage has long been the punching bag of wine critics who

often describe it as smelling like burned rubber. Think smoking skid marks on a hot tarmac. Of course, this imprecision isn't helpful: Were the skids from Michelin or Firestone tires? Steel-belted or radial? Was the tarmac on a small airport or a large commercial one? Nuance is everything in wine.

That description caught the attention of Florian Bauer, a biotechnology professor at Stellenbosch University. He and his research team grappled with the problem of defining the smell and its cause. He tried using gas chromatography to separate the various chemical compounds of pinotage to identify the culprit at a molecular level.

The professor and his research team flew to London to taste sixty South African wines alongside such critics as Jane MacQuitty, formerly the wine columnist for the *London Times* and a vocal critic of pinotage. They nailed nine wines as having the burned-rubber smell. The scientists took the wines back to Stellenbosch for another tasting and singled out two that were the most pungent. Those two wines were used to train tasters to recognize that particular aroma.

Part of the problem, as Bauer admits, is that smell and taste are such subjective experiences. The research was, in his words, "a response to an ill-defined description in a newspaper." Initially, his team was "not even sure what smell we were looking for," he wrote to me in an email. "Each person's perception of taste is different. One man's burned rubber may be another's sun-dried tomatoes. As well, people's descriptions of smells are imprecise. If you don't like a wine, you come up with your own set of terms: dry, medicinal, cat urine."

Back at Stellenbosch, the researchers examined possible causes: rootstock, soils, vintage, storage, and bottling. One popular theory was the leaf-roll virus, which prevents grapes from fully ripening: the virus makes the leaves roll up and die before the grapes can absorb enough nutrients from the sun. In the 1980s, almost every vine in the country was affected, and the Cape's late, hot summer exacerbated the problem. If vintners pick the grapes too early, they're still green and bitter, like a chicory rubber; if they leave them too long, the wine tastes jammy. The only cure for leaf-roll virus was aggressive replanting, which solved the problem for most fine wines that could handle the expense. The virus still flourishes in many bulk wine vineyards.

Still, the team couldn't identify the culprit, and they also found the burned-rubber smell in wines from other countries. The conclusion? Bad winemaking, particularly when fermentation is allowed to run too fast and too hot. Sulfur compounds that come into contact with bacteria can double. The result is a cooked character in the wine that can taste burned and bitter, almost like rubber. Regardless of the cause, South African winemakers were accused of denial and worse: cellar palate—they had become so accustomed to the smell of rubber, they no longer noticed it. Among good quality wines, the rubber smell isn't nearly as prevalent today, though I still find it occasionally.

All that controversy makes pinotage a hard wine to sell: it still comprises less than 3 percent of vines planted in South Africa. Many believe that pinotage is South Africa's viticultural flag, the equivalent of California's zinfandel. But I think that California's best wines are cabernet-based, not zinfandel. Cabernet is a noble variety, with great structure, complexity, and longevity. It's the reason bordeaux is a world benchmark.

In my opinion, pinotage, like zinfandel, can make good wines but not great ones. It works best when blended with cabernet sauvignon, merlot, or syrah—adding a dash of pepper and dark berries. It will always be a niche wine, loved by a small group of people and misunderstood by everyone else.

Among those devoted to pinotage are the judges of the prestigious ABSA Cape Epic competition. In 2000, they selected Carmen's 1999 pinotage as one of the country's top ten wines. She was the first woman to achieve such an honor. More commercial honors followed; the wine became part of the list for first-class Lufthansa passengers. The only downside was some sour-grapes mutterings attributing her success to being a token woman of color. Considering how hard she's had to work, that rumor makes her impatient that her wines don't stand on their own merits.

"Those are the same wrong-headed notions about why a black-made wine sells: because it's made by a black person? No, because it's a bloody good wine!" she says, pounding her fist on the table. "I remember an early advertising campaign with pictures of black people holding wine bottles. Who were these people? They were models! It's so important to show real people for our story to have merit."

That said, she acknowledges that she'll probably be known as South Africa's first woman of color winemaker for a while yet. "But I hope the adjectives eventually go away, and I'm just known as a good winemaker."

Carmen's life sounds like it's been ripped from the pages of a novel: the thrilling story of a young woman who defies odds and follows her heart to international success. The recognition from the competition brought Carmen offers to work at other wineries. Although she was reluctant to leave Tukulu, she accepted the position of head winemaker at Welmoed Winery because she wanted more responsibility at a smaller operation.

Her tough-minded capacity for unflinching hard work and focus also helped her through her divorce several years ago. During the proceedings, she heard about the Master of Wine (MW) program.

The most coveted designation in the industry, it's also the most difficult, requiring five years of intensive study. There are only 288 MWs in the world, and only 84 of them are women. The pass rate is just 10 percent. The odds were again against her, but as she said, "I needed something to take my mind off the divorce, so I applied." She was accepted as a candidate with a full scholarship.

"It opened up my world: the seminars, the travel, meeting people from different countries, tasting their wines. The Australians, in particular, are so generous—they'll tell you all their secrets," she says, laughing. "The program forces you to read more, to understand better, to dig deeper. I have more ideas now about what I want to do. If you stick to one formula, you've lost the plot. The mind is the best winemaking instrument."

We taste her Chardonnay Viognier, a lovely floral wine infused with green apple and apricot notes. There's a Condrieu aspect to it, a hint of ginger and white pepper. Mouthwatering acidity folds all the flavors together and magnifies them. This wine would be perfect with smoke-cured ostrich carpaccio.

"Acidity in wine helps with longevity because it's a preservative," Carmen explains. "But it also helps in your glass right now. After the big rollover of fruit on your palate, you want a clean, dry, refreshing finish. That's where acidity does its job."

Next we sip on her blend of cabernet franc and merlot that's a savory mix of blueberries, coffee, and graphite. The nose is on the move, changing now from blackberries to darker, tarry notes. Cabernet franc gives tannin weight and structure; merlot imparts plushness and fleshiness to the wine. "We give it a touch of oak to bold the palate, but the essence of the grape must remain."

Carmen's rich, concentrated cabernet franc reminds me of the observations of Herman Charles Bosman, one of South Africa's best-known short-story writers: "If you write for the press, why can't it be for a wine press? Your words will then all come out with thick purple sunshine on them. Your words will be like grapes and your thoughts will be like gold, rich with the splendid intoxication of the summer."

Call me shallow, but I agree. I'm just not interested in the technical minutiae of wine. I know that fermentation produces both alcohol and carbon dioxide, but for me, the by-product of wine is contentment.

We walk to the winery cellar, glasses in hand. Carmen tells me some stories from her time at Amani so far. Spotting a stack of barrels in one corner, she says that despite her diminutive size, she's actually "a very physical person. When I started here, I asked two muscular young men to stack some empty barrels. They weren't doing it correctly, so I stacked them myself, twenty-seven barrels in five rows, no machinery. I told them, 'This is how I want you to do it.' They just nodded and stared, but they did it that way every time after that."

As we walk farther along in the cellar, Carmen recalls another story. One of the cellar workers saw Carmen's pay slip on her desk and told all the other employees what she earned. Carmen gathered all the employees together. "I told them, 'Now you all know my salary. Well, my mother was a factory worker, and she earned the same as you do. So make sure your kids go to school, check their homework every night, and someday they can earn what I earn.'

"I believe that we must start with the children; put them in schools, give them at least one good meal a day, select the most talented, send them to university. You ask the children of the workers, 'What do you want to do when you grow up?' They'll all tell you they want to move to the city. They don't want to work on the farm like their parents because they have no idea that they could ever own the farm or be a winemaker."

The legacy of slavery and apartheid isn't just short-sighted career ambitions; it's also generational alcoholism. From 1928 to 1961, labor laws allowed farmers to partially pay their workers with cheap wine. The system known as *dop* (Afrikaans for "drink") only really declined in the 1990s and still continues clandestinely on a smaller scale. As a result, not only is alcoholism endemic among adults, but many children also suffered from the effects of fetal alcohol syndrome. A recent study of a thousand children in the Wellington wine region showed that almost 9 percent of them were affected, up from 5 percent in 1997.

Despite this, South Africa now offers the most guilt-free wine on the market for those who purchase with their conscience. The country is the world's largest producer of Fair Trade wines, made by companies that pay their workers fair wages and meet health and safety standards. As well, there are the black empowerment brands and those that are sustainably farmed, environmentally sensitive, and biodiversity conserving.

As Carmen says good-bye to me, she looks out over the vineyards. "In a previous life, I was a winemaker—and I'm coming back as a winemaker in the next one. In this life, I will own my own winery. It is inevitable because I must pass it on to my daughters."

MEETING ANTHONY HAMILTON Russell, the forty-seven-year-old owner of Hamilton Russell Vineyards, didn't strike me in advance as an unnerving prospect. It's only when the handsome, six-foot-four vintner walks up to me in front of his winery that I realize my mistake.

"Such a pleasure to meet you, Natalie—I've heard so much about you," he says with European elegance and a George Clooney smile.

"Huh, huh, ha-hi," I splutter with North American neuroses and a sardine handshake.

With merciful sensitivity, Anthony pretends not to notice my anxiety as he shows me in to the tasting room, a stone cottage with the vineyard plots of his 420-acre estate painted on the walls. He pours me a glass of his sauvignon blanc, and in the absence of any questions from this intrepid journalist, he launches into a presentation of soils and elevations. I nod vigorously until I regain myself, then wonder about questioning him on something he may have already said. I take a chance and ask him about the history of his family and the property.

Anthony's father, Tim Hamilton Russell, chairman of the South African arm of the advertising agency J. Walter Thompson in the mid-seventies, was an amateur wine enthusiast. In 1976, he planted a few vines in his Johannesburg garden and made a batch of wine in his sauna. He was so pleasantly surprised with the results that he decided to start a winery.

Tim had studied climatology at Oxford University, so he knew how critical climate was. He decided against building in Stellenbosch itself; all the country's wineries were there, so property was very expensive. He also wanted a cooler climate to experiment with pinot noir. In the end, he bought land on the tip of chilly, foggy Walker Bay, an hour southeast of Stellenbosch. His vineyard became the first in the region and the most southerly in South Africa.

Tim's wines were a success, and in 1989 he retired from advertising to devote himself full-time to the winery. Unfortunately, his winemaker and manager were used to an absentee boss and didn't welcome closer supervision. They resigned, and without their support or his executive advertising income, the farm went into a tailspin.

Things were looking grim in 1991 when Anthony, who was then a management consultant at Bain & Company in London, suggested that he come home to help run the winery. Tim agreed, surprised by his son's interest; until then, Anthony's only experience with wine had been, as he laughingly puts it, "drinking down his collection of bordeaux." But Tim thought him quite capable, as Anthony, too, had gone to Oxford, studying geography, and then had completed an MBA from the Wharton School of Business before becoming a consultant.

Indeed, Anthony exudes the confidence of a colonial baron. He brings to mind Cecil John Rhodes, the British industrialist who established a worldwide diamond monopoly when he bought all South Africa's diamond mines in 1880 and formed the De Beers Mining Company. Rhodes believed that "to be born an Englishman, is to win first place in the lottery of life." He established the coveted Rhodes Scholarships to Oxford University for colonial white boys not lucky enough to be born British. (It wasn't until 1977 that women were eligible for the scholarships. Even in 1989 when I and a few other women went for the finalist interviews, it still felt odd—like admitting women was a magnanimous indulgence.)

Like any good consultant, Anthony did his research: an in-depth analysis of the estate's soils. He discovered that clay and shale produced the best wines, so he narrowed the product line, focusing just on chardonnay and pinot noir—the two grapes that thrive in such soils and a cool climate. His efforts paid off; within several years, the winery grew tenfold, and Tim was able to retire from actively running the winery.

"It's a broadminded father who allows his son to take control," Anthony observes, handing me into his battered Jeep. "It's very male, territorial, chest-beating stuff, tied up with a sense of home and domain—it's not easy to give up."

As we drive up the curving gravel road, I see ahead of us the graceful manor house that Anthony built on the hilltop in 1996. He named it Braemar after the name of the original winery. It had been owned by a Scottish woman; the hills reminded her of the heathery moors near Braemar, Scotland. He chose that spot because it was where he would always stop to admire the view when riding his motorbike around the property. "There's an appealing balance between the mountains and the rolling vineyards," he says.

The house is built in a style that Anthony describes as Cape Georgian: simple and symmetrical, precise in scale and proportion. He worked closely with the architect to use local materials, even trying to bake his own roof tiles from clay mined on the farm, but there were too many breakages, so he ended up buying them.

As we get out of the Jeep, I notice three giant turtles on the lawn. Anthony tells me that these fifty-pound Leopard tortoises, more than seventy years old, are ex-pets, whose owners didn't want them anymore and set them loose. They turned up here one day, took a liking to the place, and have never ventured off the lawn in four years. "Ha, I think Sheldon just made a move on Agatha!" Anthony remarks, as one tortoise moves half an inch toward another.

They're not the only animal life around. As the front door opens, an enormous black Great Dane bounds out of the house and comes straight at me—as all dogs instinctively do, knowing that I am both allergic to and petrified of them.

"Horrocks, here, boy," Anthony calls, and the horse-dog skids away from me and gallops over to its owner. Horrocks is named for the large disheveled butler in *Vanity Fair*, which does absolutely nothing to redeem him. He's quickly joined by more household members, both canine and human. Next out of the house scampers a Great Dane puppy named Ophelia (after Hamlet's love interest);

then two golden retrievers, Como and Hendrix (after Perry Como and Jimi Hendrix); and finally, a lovely woman with long dark hair: Olive, Anthony's wife.

In the house, an airy dining room opens directly onto a pillared veranda with large sofas and chairs. Anthony incorporated this Italianate *loggia* to bring together the interior of the home with the rolling green hills it looks out over. The home is ideal for entertaining—and for wishing you could move into it. At the end of the manicured lawn is a grove of olive trees that meets the vineyards. Beyond them, I can see the fishing village of Hermanus, the calm blue expanse of Walker Bay, and the frothy Atlantic.

I still feel nervous, but I realize that writing about wine gives me an excuse to be invited into a beautiful home like this; to ask these successful, glamorous people bold questions; and in a sense, to invade their privacy. Writers are spies, nosing our way into other peoples' lives, making notes in our mental breast pocket to be analyzed in private, then revealed elsewhere. After reading my story about them, a number of winemakers have commented that I sucked in an incredible amount of information while I was with them. Yes. I'm always listening; nothing's off my radar or the record.

The pursuit of beauty runs through almost everything Anthony does. As he puts it, "Making wine isn't a business as much as it's an aesthetic pursuit." Every year, he makes dozens of visual improvements to the estate, from planting avenues of poplar trees to installing garden sculptures. For the last project, he hired a mason from the local funeral home. Every vineyard block is named after women related to the Hamilton Russell family, either directly or by marriage. When Anthony asked the mason to inscribe the four granite headstones with the women's names, "he thought we'd had a terrible number of deaths in the family," he recalls, smiling.

We sit in the dining room, and Anthony pours his 2006 Ashbourne Sandstone, a crisp blend of sauvignon blanc and chardonnay. The wine is named partly after his great-great-grandfather, Lord Ashbourne, who was Ireland's lord chancellor in the late 1800s, and partly for the sandstone soil in which sauvignon blanc absorbs a mineral-marine depth. The chardonnay in the blend was fermented in clay amphora, which oxygenates the wine like oak barrels do, fattening and rounding its texture. We sip the wine while nibbling on Olive's homemade pine-nut focaccia bread and a Klein River Gruyère cheese. The creamy Gruyère folds into the richness of the chardonnay; the woodsy pine nuts dance with the sauvignon blanc.

"The wine is a sympathetic food partner, wouldn't you say?" Olive asks. I nod, feeling myself a sympathetic partner to the wine. I ask about the paintings on the walls.

"They're all by South African artists—Pierneef, Sekoto, Naude, Van Heerden, Boonzaier, Coetzer," Anthony says. "I started collecting them when I was eighteen, and they've gone up in value so much that I couldn't afford to buy most of them now. I never find that photographs of landscapes are as evocative as a good painting—it expresses so much more than just what's there."

That's his belief about wine, too: it's the distilled essence of place. Anthony talks about the "Hamilton Russellness" of his wines, their somewhereness. "They bear the unmistakable signature of the place. Even from year to year, you recognize them as you would different books by the same author. The story changes, but the style remains— the style is the soul of the land. I'm really more interested in place than in wine."

He's actually interested in a lot of things, and with great relief, the three of us chat about art, books, politics, and anything but wine for the next hour. Anthony loves to chew on an issue, peppering his conversation with witticisms and wide references. He pours us his Hamilton Russell Vineyards Chardonnay; the 1993 vintage was served to Nelson Mandela at a state banquet in Buckingham Palace when he became South Africa's new president.

The chardonnay is a pliant partner with Olive's gnocchi dish, with tender baby shrimp in a mayo-tomato sauce and slivers of avocado marinated in lime juice and lemon-infused olive oil—all topped with lightly toasted almond flakes. The wine's white pear and lime notes cut through the satiny avocado, and the vanilla-smoke finish weaves in with the toasted almonds. Like many chardonnays, this one is aged in oak barrels. Anthony imports the wood from the French forests of Alliers, Vosges, and Tronçais, and lets it air-dry on the estate to infuse it with the icy winds of the Atlantic.

I ask Anthony about the self-medicating sauvignon blanc I'd gulped down at the tasting cottage, having no recollection what it was called. All I remembered was the tree-top foliage freshness and the spine-chill of ice melting on granite. It turns out this wine was from a special project that Anthony started in 2005, on a thousand acres that adjoined the Hamilton Russell estate to the west.

"I wanted to protect the lands and stop more condo development, so I started a new winery focusing just on sauvignon blanc and pinotage. I named it Southern Right in honor of the southern right whales that come into Walker Bay every year to birth their calves. We make a donation to their conservation from every bottle we sell."

Olive brings out a fillet of beef in a creamy mushroom sauce, and some dishes of mushroom risotto, bright green beans, and baby beets. She believes that the best-stocked pantry is mother nature: she's a forager for food on the estate, and a curious cook who searches for new flavors behind a stone or a tree. She found the porcini and oyster mushrooms for the sauce in the pine forest beside the winery. They're oven-dried and mixed with some finely chopped jalapeño peppers for a hint of heat.

The mushroom sauce and risotto are earthy echoes of the pinot noirs that Anthony pours to accompany them. They're from the 2007, 2008, and 2009 vintages, along with the 2005 Ashbourne Pinotage. The slight charred quality of the pan-fried beef is hugged by the wrap-around velvet tannin in the wines.

I'd love to drink them all; always a good sign. For me, quality is always in the second half of the bottle, or even the second bottle. It's whether you want to finish the wine or you've become exhausted by too much. Anthony describes those who buy his wines as aesthetes with a global perspective. I'd describe them as lucky. Even though pinot noir, notoriously difficult to make, is the benchmark wine here, he senses a greater challenge.

"I don't want my tombstone to read, 'He made great copies of burgundy,'" he declares. "I want to add something to the world of wine. Our chance to do that in South Africa is pinotage." Like Carmen Stevens, he's passionate about the wine. Anthony's whole reason for being is pinotage: site expressive, age-worthy, benchmark wine to show the world what South Africa can do. He blends in some other red grapes for complexity. The wine telescopes aromas of dark berries and open-fire wood smoke.

"South Africa is a hard country to place on the wine map; we're neither Europe nor the New World," he says. "We need to build more meaning into that middle place rather than trying to be a mini-Australia. Making wine is an expression of place, a gamble with nature, an accident in time. It's not that we're clever winemakers; it's just that we happen to live on an interesting plot of earth."

Earth and time also merged when Anthony did his soil analysis. He discovered that his estate is littered with prehistoric stone tools.

He now has more than a thousand specimens, which he invites me to see in his wood-paneled study. A large cabinet with glass shelves contains the collection: rough-hewn stones of various shapes and sizes. The centerpiece is a pear-shaped Acheulean hand axe made by *Homo erectus* 1.5 million years ago.

"The larger, cruder hand axes are usually older than the smaller, more intricate ones," Anthony explains with the enthusiasm of a gentleman paleontologist. "The tools themselves cannot be dated, but surrounding material in deposits where they're found can be. It astounds me that humans have lived on this very land for 1.5 million years." He takes a spearlike rock out of the cabinet and hands it to me. "When I found this tool in the garden, it looked like it had been dropped there the day before. I'm not a mystic, but these tools make me feel a deep connection to this valley's past."

Last year, he deepened that connection by starting to build a stone chapel beside the family burial plot, in a remote spot on the estate. Around it, he planted olive trees grown from cuttings from the Garden of Gethsemane. "I'm not religious, but I am spiritual," Anthony says. "I was inspired to build the chapel after I saw one of the vineyard workers praying under a tree here."

Looking to the future, he hopes one day to leave the estate to one of his four daughters, as his father did to him. "I wouldn't want the winery to be fragmented or sold in pieces, so I hope that the most interested or capable daughter will take over. I'm not worried—think of all the formidable women running the great wine estates of the world," he says.

Back in the dining room, Olive has set out malva pudding, a traditional Cape dessert: warm sponge cake with apricot jam and a hint of ginger. Over it is poured a melting custard with gooseberries, whose piquant tartness lifts the sweet warmth of the custard and cake. The dessert is a lovely contrast to the Muscat d'Alexandrie from

Aan De Doorns winery—Hamilton Russell doesn't make a dessert wine. With crumbs and empty glasses in front of us, we retire to the veranda tipsy and full.

"Mind if I smoke?" Anthony asks. I abhor cigarettes but love the smell of wafting cigar smoke; it reminds me of a mature bordeaux. From a wooden case he takes out a Cuban cigar, a Hoyo de Monterrey Epicure, and from his back pocket, surprisingly, he pulls out a ten-inch knife to cut the tip. The knife, he tells me, is his favorite from a collection of Mediterranean knives and has traveled with him to nine countries. The steel blade was made in the Italian town of Berti, just north of Florence, and its blonde ox-horn handle was crafted in central Africa.

The cigar lit, he takes long, slow puffs, arms folded, looking out over the hills. He's the benevolent feudal lord and the Hemingway man of action, yet there's also the Anthonyness of him. I am more interested in people than in wine.

"If you're lucky and you work hard, a winery can pay for itself," he says. "But it's everything around the winery—the people, travel, food, conversation—that are the real rewards. I live and work in nature—I don't spend two hours stuck in traffic every day to get to a cement tower." He gazes across the hills of his estate. "South Africa offers the possibility of an extraordinary life to those who are open to it."

Field Notes from a
Wine Cheapskate

INSIDER TIPS

- International trade bans are tough on any country, but it can motivate domestic industries to be more competitive afterward. South African wine has made amazing progress quickly following the end of apartheid.

- Check your perceptions about which regions can make wine. South Africa benefits from the confluence of the oceans as well as the cooling breeze of the Antarctic. Who would have thought that this created ideal conditions for growing wine? Now you know.

- There are so many terrific South African wines on the shelves these days. Start out with the familiar grapes, such as sauvignon blanc, shiraz, or cabernet sauvignon. Then, as you discover the producers you like best, branch out into their chenin blanc and pinotage wines.

WINERIES VISITED

Amani Vineyards: www.amani.co.za
Fairview: www.fairview.co.za
Hamilton Russell Vineyards: www.hamiltonrussellvineyards
   .co.za

BEST VALUE WINES

Amani Vineyards Cabernet Franc Merlot
Amani Vineyards Chardonnay Viognier
Fairvalley Sauvignon Blanc
Fairview Chenin Blanc
Fairview Shiraz*
Fairview Viognier
Goats do Roam Pinotage
Goats do Roam Shiraz
Hamilton Russell Vineyards Chardonnay
Hamilton Russell Vineyards Pinot Noir
Newton Johnson Winery Syrah
Southern Right Sauvignon Blanc (Hamilton Russell)
Spice Route Chakalaka

My first pick for my own Wednesday dinner.

TOP VALUE PRODUCERS

Bellingham	Graham Beck
Boekenhoutskloof	Ken Forrester
Bon Cap	Le Bonheur
Boschendal	Meerlust
Cathedral Cellars	Mulderbosch
Delheim	Nederburg
Diemersfontein	Obikwa
Drostdy-Hof	Porcupine Ridge
Durbanville Hills	Robertson Winery
Fairvalley	Rustenberg
Flagstone Wines	Rust en Vrede

Sebeka

Simonsig

Spier

Stark Conde

Two Oceans

The Winery of Good Hope

Wolf Trap

WEDNESDAY DINNER FOR A WINE CHEAPSKATE

You'll find Olive Hamilton Russell's recipes for the dinner we shared with Anthony in their home at www.nataliemaclean.com/food.

Olive's Homemade Focaccia

Fillet of Beef with Mushroom Sauce

Mushroom Risotto

French Beans

Gnocchi-Avocado Ritz Style

Malva Pudding

TERRIFIC PAIRINGS

I find that many of the pairings that work for Australian shiraz also do well with South African shiraz. So in this section, I'll focus instead on pairings for South African's refreshing sauvignon blanc, with its signature aromas of freshly mown grass, lemongrass, gooseberry, green bell pepper, green melon, grapefruit, canned peas, asparagus, lime, nettle, acacia, hawthorn, and herbal notes.

Asian dishes

Avocado dishes,
  guacamole

Ceviche

Cheese: goat, Brie,
  Camembert, Gouda

Chicken and feta tostadas
Coquilles Saint Jacques
Corned beef and cabbage
Curry: green Thai
Lamb: Irish stew
Lasagna: vegetable
Mushrooms: Portobello
Pasta with cream or
    pesto sauce
Pizza: Hawaiian, vegetarian
Quiche: spinach and
    cheese, asparagus

Salads: green, Cobb, chef
Sauerkraut
Shellfish: crab, lobster, mussels,
    oysters, scallops
Shrimp cocktail
Spring rolls
Sushi
Swordfish
Turkey: roast
Vegetables: green, especially
    asparagus, peas

RESOURCES

For more information about South African wines and sauvignon blanc:

Africa Uncorked by John Platter
John Platter South African Wine Guide by John Platter
Sour Grapes by Neil Pendock
Wineries of South Africa: www.nataliemaclean.com/wineries
Wines of South Africa: www.wosa.co.za
Wines of South Africa USA: www.wosa.co.za/usa
Wines of South Africa Canada: www.wosa.co.za/canada
South Africa Wine Society: www.southafricanwinesociety.ca
Neil Pendock, wine columnist, South Africa's *Sunday Times*
    blog: www.blogs.timeslive.co.za/pendock

RELATED READING

The following books, while seemingly unrelated to the main subject matter of this chapter, provided some enjoyable reading before, during, and after my travels:

Mafeking Road and Other Stories by Herman Charles Bosman
Long Walk to Freedom: The Autobiography of Nelson Mandela by
    Nelson Mandela
Conservationist by Nadine Gordimer
Jaws by Peter Benchley

FIVE

THURSDAY

Vino Under the Volcano

I EXPECTED SOMETHING a little more dramatic: the sizzle of a lava river oozing down the volcano, the rumble of the earth as it split between my feet, the screams of villagers running for their lives. Instead, all I hear are the clicks of tourist cameras as we look up at Mount Etna, its white tip puffing peacefully against the blue sky.

"To have seen Italy without having seen Sicily is not to have seen Italy at all," Goethe wrote. "For Sicily is the clue to everything." That's why I'm here on this island of dazzling sunshine and menacing shadows, with its barely controlled wilderness and passionate personalities. I've heard that the people here have fiery tempers, forming friendships over lunch and falling out by dinner. No one does vendettas like the Sicilians.

I like my wines with a little hellfire in them; volcanic viticulture fascinates me. Making wine from water is so BCE, but making wine from lava—now that fires the imagination. I also believe that just as Sicily is the clue to Italy, today's winemaking unlocks the country's vinous past. The ancient Greeks believed that Sicily was the birthplace of wine. One of their legends describes the journey that Bacchus made from Mount Olympus to the island, carrying a tiny vine in a hollowed-out bird bone. As he traveled, the plant kept growing, so he moved it to a lion's bone and then into a donkey's bone. When he got to Sicily, he planted the vine; and from the grapes it bore, he made the world's first wine. The symbolic message is that a little wine will make you as light as a bird, a little more will make you as brave as a lion, and a lot more will make you as dumb as an ass.

The Greeks called Sicily Oenotria, meaning "land of vines," from the Greek *oinos* for "wine." The Athenians invaded the island in 415 BCE, according to the historian Thucydides in his *History of the Peloponnesian Wars*, determined to spread Hellenic culture and government. Greek city-states such as Siracusa (Syracuse) had been long established on Sicily, along with the cultivation of grapevines. Homer described Sicilian vineyards as "watered by Zeus, yielding wine of strength in which ambrosia and nectar flowed in abundance." Odysseus used that robust local wine to intoxicate the Cyclops, so that he and his crew could escape from the island. The boulders strewn along the coastline are supposedly the ones that the Cyclops hurled after the departing ship.

By 404 BCE, the Spartans and Persians had helped the Sicilians to oust the Athenians, and they in turn were ousted by the Romans, who were eventually kicked out themselves by the locals. The island's strategic position in the middle of the Mediterranean meant that someone was usually invading it. You can see the successive conquering influences in the architecture of the capital city, Palermo: a Greek temple, a Norman church, a Roman theater, a Moorish roofline, Arab flourishes on a balcony and window, a Bourbon archway. Stairs between buildings tilt right and left like a game of snakes and ladders. The markets feel ancient and mysterious, bustling with colorful people and produce but edged with dark, shadowed alleyways. Palermo is an open-air museum: a boisterous blend of narrow streets, piazzas lined with multicolored mosaic tiles, fashionable wine bars and bistros, grand opera houses, and soaring cathedrals.

On this sixteen-thousand-square-mile island, a tiny football a mile off the toe of mainland Italy, there are about three hundred thousand acres under vine, more than in Bordeaux and Chile combined. It produces 185 million gallons a year, more than all of Australia. If Sicily were a country, it would be the fifth-largest wine producer in the world. Producers here refer to the island as a continent of wine for both its production and diversity.

As one of the world's oldest and youngest winemaking regions, Sicily is trying to resolve the conflict between ancient local traditions and modern international style. For years, southern vintners had no incentive to make fine wine for export. Grape prices were so low that producers earned more money making workhorse wines for local consumption and low-end export. Most wine made here was sold by the tanker-load to beef up prestigious but anemic wines in northern Italy and France, where it was often delivered to the estates' back entrances at night.

Sicily also has a cultural divide with the rest of Italy, especially the north, which produces some of the most beautifully designed clothing, cars, and wine in the world. The brand names roll luxuriously off a consumption-loving tongue: Ferragamo, Ferrari, Tignanello. In fact, few countries have such a contrast between an industrious north, with its sleek fashions, fast cars, and 4 percent unemployment; and a languid, lawless south, with its agrarian focus, slower pace, and 20 percent joblessness. There's even a divide between southern Italy and Sicily. The islanders refuse to build a bridge to the mainland just a mile away, even though it would help with commerce and tourism. No wonder Sicilians are often considered the most Italian of Italians: fierce, loyal, stubborn, passionate.

That divide in Italian culture extends to winemaking, which the rest of the world has long perceived as either cheap and cheerful or costly and confusing. Think of those squat, straw-wrapped chianti bottles (candle is optional) that epitomized the sixties and seventies. Now think of the sleek, gold-embossed labels of Super Tuscans, such as Sassicaia and Tignanello, that represented the greed-is-good eighties and nineties. There's never been much of a middle ground for consumers who just want good quality, reasonably priced Italian wines.

However, since the 1980s, the market for low-end wines has been drying up. The only way Sicilian producers could survive was to improve quality. And frankly, there was plenty of room for improvement. Unfortunately even today, Sicily's best-known wine is also its worst-regarded: marsala, a fortified dessert wine. Historically, it was hard to swallow, with its oxidized, burned flavors.

In 1773, when the British merchant John Woodhouse (stranded on Sicily for several days during a storm) tasted the wine at a local tavern, he realized that it would keep on a long sea journey if it were fortified with brandy. Marsala eventually replaced port as the British sailor's drink of choice, Nelson's navy drank it up, and Woodhouse retired a rich and groggily happy man.

Marsala is still unfairly tagged as plonk. This wine has the potential to be a divine after-dinner drink—a fact foreseen perhaps by the Arabs, who originally named the town *Marsa el Allah*, meaning "port of God." It's a mystical watery world between land and sea on the island's western shore, where the setting sun plays off the salt flats, sending shafts of red and purple light up through the clouds. Like sherry, marsala uses the solera method of aging: wine from the current vintage goes into the first barrel and is gradually siphoned from one barrel to another, year after year. Wine from the last barrel is drawn off to be consumed, and that barrel is then topped up with wine from the second oldest. This fractional blending preserves the flavor signature of the wine over years because, in theory, a little wine from the first vintage, and from all others since then, is in every bottle.

However, in the 1940s, marsala fell from grace, no longer suiting the taste of the times. Shoddy winemaking, such as adding egg yolks, almonds, and other unmentionable ingredients, hastened its demise. This syrupy wine was relegated to cooking sauces, no longer considered a digestif like port or brandy. Soon most Sicilian wines were described as *marmalata* because they were so jammy-overripe— hardly surprising when temperatures in Sicily can soar to 115°F during the harvest.

Even though Sicilian winemaking has improved considerably over the past decade, marsala's former image still sticks to it. Poorly made wines are like a crime-ridden neighborhood, tarnishing the reputation of an entire city. However, marsala is worth trying. It's graded according to color, sugar, alcoholic strength, and length of aging. The best types are Vergine (five years aging) and Stravecchio (ten years). Some of the most reputable producers today include Florio, De Bortoli, Martinez, and Lombardo.

One of my favorite Italian authors is Giuseppe Tomasi di Lampedusa, whose brilliant novel *The Leopard* chronicled the decline of the nineteenth-century aristocracy in Sicily. The author could have been describing the local wine industry when he observed: "If things are to stay as they are, then something has to change."

The setting of his book is now a winery called Donnafugata, meaning "fugitive woman." It was named for Queen Maria Carolina of Naples, who fled to the estate when Napoleon's army invaded her city at the end of the eighteenth century. My favorite wine from Donnafugata also has a romantic, windswept name: Mille e Una Notte—a thousand and one nights.

When the market for marsala collapsed in the 1960s, the local government created winemaking cooperatives that bought 80 percent of the harvest, mostly from small farmers. These co-ops still exist; the largest, Settesoli, is now the size of an oil refinery, capable of crushing more than 110 million tons of grapes. The company occupies much of the village of Menfi on the western shore, employs more than twenty thousand people, and owns more than 5 percent of the island's vineyards.

By the late 1980s, the market for bulk wine started to tank as well. Europe had become a wine lake, producing much more than it could drink or distill into spirits such as vermouth or even turn into ethanol for automobiles. Government subsidies dried up, and the big co-ops had to change their strategy. One of the most prescient executives was Diego Planeta, president of Settesoli, who started the drive to improve quality. With the help of oenologist Giacomo Tachis, who had just retired from the respected Super Tuscan winery Sassicaia, Diego planted experimental vineyards with a wide variety of grapes to determine which best suited Sicily's climate and soils.

The winner? Nero d'avola, the black (nero) grape from the town of Avola in eastern Sicily. Apart from small plantings in Calabria, on the toe of the mainland, it's only grown in Sicily today. Nero d'avola produces a wine packed with distinctive flavor, reminding me of the quirky Italian actor Roberto Benigni in *Life Is Beautiful*. This inky wine with a tightwire streak of acidity is as plush and quaffable as merlot, but it also has the darker, peppered-violet character of syrah. It shares the chameleon nature of Tuscany's sangiovese grape, which makes chianti such a round, generous wine, but becomes austere and structured in brunello di montalcino. It's a perfect complement to our Thursday night pasta meals.

Even within Sicily, the style of nero d'avola varies according to climate and soil. It can be spicy and taut like Rhône syrah in the limestone soils near Noto, or fleshy and fruity like Australian shiraz in the clay soils near Menfi. The thin-skinned, late-ripening grape is susceptible to rot, like merlot, and so it thrives in Sicily's hot, dry climate. The island is on the same latitude as Tunis, North Africa, and gets an average of 130 days of sunshine a year. A hot, stinging, sand-laden wind called the scirocco often blows north across the Mediterranean from the Sahara Desert, sometimes reaching hurricane speeds of eighty miles an hour. It ripples the horizon, whips up dust clouds, burns off excess moisture. The few raindrops that fall on Sicily acquire a sandy coating before reaching the earth.

Working a Mediterranean vineyard means tending a scorched garden under an apocalyptic sun. Until the sun sets, that is. Of evenings on the Sicilian coastline, Colombian novelist Gabriel García Márquez wrote that "the sea on windless nights reflects the beams of African lighthouses, while on the bottom of the sea lies a sleeping wine amphora."

When it comes to winemaking, nero d'avola is best when yields are kept low to focus the vine's nutrients in fewer grapes, which produces more concentrated flavors. It likes a slow, temperature-controlled maceration and fermentation to extract more flavor, color, and tannin compounds from the grape skins and seeds. These compounds give it structure, balance, and the ability to age. It also has the ability to blend; nero d'avola is a grape swinger, mating easily with merlot, cabernet sauvignon, syrah, and the local red grape frappato. On its own or blended, it's a wine with a robust love of flavor that's not heavy, making it an excellent house wine: it's charm-on-the-cheap.

Like most Italian wines, nero d'avola has a vibrant acidity that makes it taste fresh and clean. This helps it to pair well with the savory profusion of Sicilian food. The island's rustic cuisine is complemented by the flavors of many cultures: capers, olives, garlic, peppers, mint, fennel, almonds, raisins, citrus, and dried herbs. The

Arabs introduced spices, mint, fennel, saffron, eggplant, almonds, lemons, limes, oranges, raisins, capers, pine nuts, anchovies, pasta, pastries, and couscous (which they adapted to make a dish based on fish rather than lamb). The Greeks made honey, olive oil, and wine; the Romans grew wheat, vines, and beans; the Normans brought salt cod; the Spanish made rich tomato sauces. The food and wine here speak of history, terrain, identity, and people. You can devour Sicily's history on your plate.

The white wine grape that thrived in Diego's Planeta vineyards was insolia, a grape also known as inzolia or ansonica. It's the backbone of marsala, which never helped the grape's reputation. But by keeping yields down and using temperature-controlled fermentation, insolia produces a wine that's a wonderful jumble of white peach, mango, lime zest, and coconut sliver aromas. It reminds me of excellent dry riesling and makes my mouth water to think how well it would go with the island's seafood, especially fresh grilled swordfish with olives, tomatoes, and capers.

Diego was impressed with the results of his vineyard experiments, which included clonal selection, trellising, and irrigation methods. (Sicilian wine regulations forbid irrigation except by an emergency ruling, but there seems to be an emergency every year.) In 1995, he started his own boutique winery, Planeta, on the hillside village of Sambuca di Sicilia. Planeta's flagship nero d'avola, Santa Cecilia, is a heady aroma cloud of blackberries, sage, and dark chocolate. A potent core of dark, fleshy flavors roll over your tongue, finishing with a blast of black raspberries and anise. Dare I liken it to the smoldering, dark bride in *The Godfather*? Slap me twice if I try to weave *The Sopranos* into this chapter.

Still, it was Diego's chardonnay that first gained worldwide attention, receiving rave reviews in the 1990s. Critics compared it to the California cult chardonnay from Kistler, though some criticized it for having too much oak and butter. Like many vines in Sicily, though, his are more than eighty years old and produce grapes with enough depth of flavor to absorb the oak. In fact, some Sicilian chardonnays rival the elegance and length of good burgundy.

Soon other producers followed Diego, entering the world wine market with recognized, brand-name grapes. Some bemoaned the "cabernetization" of their wine industry and the loss of local identity. The international style has such market power today that it can trample eccentricity, the vinous equivalent of big, blond Texan hair and too much makeup that leaves little room for local, unadorned, odd-ball wines. By the late 1990s, Sicilian producers were blending international and local grapes to offer more interesting flavors yet keep the safety of brand-name grapes on the label. Since then, grape and wine prices have risen, fostering the growth of modern boutique wineries.

Even today, only one-quarter of Sicilian wine is bottled on the island, and just 2 percent is labeled DOC (*Denominazione di Origine Controllata*), the quality-control designation that specifies the approved grapes and winemaking methods. Maybe that shouldn't surprise us, since the Italians aren't exactly noted for following authority. Another 8 percent of wine is labeled IGT (*Indicazione Geografica Tipica*), which is like France's *Vin de Pays* (country wine) designation. What Diego would like to see is more family names on the labels to dispel the anonymity of Sicilian wine.

The Planeta family now owns a thousand acres of vineyards in three locations on the island, and the winery produces two hundred thousand cases. Six cousins work in the business; Diego's daughter, Francesca, is in charge of marketing; nephew Alessio is the wine-maker; and another nephew, Santi, oversees domestic sales. Family is all-important in Sicily; everyone seems suspicious of everyone to whom they're not related. Did I mention that this is the birthplace of the Cosa Nostra? Palermo's Falcone Borsellino Airport is named after the two anti-mafia judges who were murdered in 1992. I'm afraid that's all I can say.

In 2008, the Planeta family started planting vines on Mount Etna to complete their "rainbow of Sicilian soil colors," as Alessio says. He believes the black volcanic earth produces wines of unparalleled depth and complexity. The soil, a mix of slivered rock, pumice, lava, and ash, has a low acidity that keeps the grapes' natural acidity from getting too high. It has many fissures, so it drains well. Another plus: the root louse phylloxera, which devastated the rest of Europe's old root stock, can't survive on volcanic rock, so many vines here are old and ungrafted or, as they say, *pied frau*, which sounds delightfully footloose and fancy-free.

So I've come to the volcano to taste the wines borne from these fractured rocks and fiery depths. The name Etna comes from the ancient Greek word *aitho*, meaning "I burn." At thirty-three hundred feet above sea level and covering 750 square miles, it's Europe's largest and most active volcano—almost three times larger than Vesuvius, which destroyed the city of Pompeii in 79 BCE. *La Montagna*, as the locals reverently call it, is supposedly the home of Vulcan, the Roman god of fire and smithery. The ancient philosopher Empedocles leapt into the crater in 430 BCE to prove he was immortal. (He wasn't.)

When there's an eruption, locals say *"scassau a muntagna"* ("the mountain has broken"). A 1669 eruption destroyed the hillside village of Catania and most of its twenty thousand inhabitants. Although the volcano has been fairly quiet since then, just a few decades ago, in 1985, Etna sprayed its fiery discourse across the sea for miles around. When it hardened, it left a lunar landscape onshore and daggers of black rock piercing the turquoise sea. The lava came *proprio vicinissima* (really close) to the vineyards. So far, the solidified rivers of black rock have stopped just a few meters above the vines. In such places, the locals erect white statues of the Madonna, her arms held out from side to side, as if to say, "Stop!"

In 2002, a major eruption closed the Palermo airport for two days of ashfall—islanders used umbrellas when they went outside. Etna still sends out smoky reminders of her presence, like a whispered "I'm still here." On this crisp April morning, though, she seems more prim than menacing: a fulsome Victorian lady wearing a snow lace collar above the folds of her black dress.

Leaving the tourist stop, I fold myself back into my five-inch Fiat. It takes about ten hours to drive to the top of the volcano, though I'm not going that far today. Still, with every twist and turn in the road that takes me higher up the mountain, my ears pop and my heart beats faster, as I wonder whether I'll come head-on with a tour bus barreling downward. Out of the corner of my eye, I see vineyards tucked between the medieval villages, chunks of volcanic stone in marvelously strange shapes crouching between the vines.

I'm on my way to meet Giuseppe Benanti, of Vinicola Benanti, a vineyard that's been in his family for eleven generations. I finally arrive, shaken but safe, in front of the stone winery that clings to the hillside like a small gray boat on a rolling ocean of green. The land has belonged to the family since 1734, when King Vittorio Amadeo II granted 320 hectares in the village of Catania to his faithful servant Antonio Benanti. The Benanti family were knights for the king, and he wanted to establish a large and loyal clan in southern Italy.

I learn this family history from Lisa Sapienza, the winery's export sales director, a beautifully coiffed woman with red-polished nails. She also outlines the business goals to merge science and tradition, which usually translates to: *We're using fancy technology to improve profits, but we keep our historical look in the brochures for branding purposes.* She leads me into the oak-paneled hall to meet Giuseppe Benanti, great-

great-grandson of Antonio. He looks just like the successful pharma-
ceutical executive he is: mid-sixties, silver-framed glasses, Armani suit,
quizzical expression. His features resemble those of his ancestors, who
seem to be watching us from the gold-framed portraits along the walls.

Giuseppe sits at the head of the oak table to my right, while Lisa
sits across from me to translate, since apparently Giuseppe's English
is not strong. Giuseppe's father, Lisa explains, taught cataract surgery
at the University of Catania, preferring the sterile environment of
the operating room to the family business. He didn't want muddy
shoes, Lisa explains. He died in 1958, and the vineyards sat dormant
for four decades, until Giuseppe decided to revive the winery in 1988.

As Lisa translates, Giuseppe watches me with his head cocked to
one side and a faint smile. I nod and smile too much at both of them,
unnerved by this conversation, which makes me feel like Alice with
the Queen of Hearts and the Cheshire Cat in the tree.

Although he had followed in his father's footsteps, earning a doctorate in chemistry and pharmacy, Giuseppe remembered harvests
with his grandfather: the grapes that smelled so sweet, the workers
who sang the old songs, the outdoor feasts with everyone gathered
around the table. His first challenge was buying back the estate,
which had been divided among seventeen cousins. ("The first sixteen
were no problem—it was the seventeenth who gave all the trouble.")

Next, he hired local winemaker Salvo Foti, who was working just
a few miles down the road, making wine for Mick Hucknall, lead
singer of Simply Red. After centuries of assaults from various countries, the latest invaders of the island are celebrities: Hucknall,
Madonna, and Gérard Depardieu all own wineries here. Hucknall
called his wine Il Cantante, "the singer." Though why he didn't use
Simply Red and Simply White is a mystery—and a lost cobranding
opportunity.

Unlike Diego Planeta, Giuseppe decided not to plant any international grapes. ("When in Rome, why eat at McDonald's?") Nor did he choose nero d'avola, which doesn't grow well in volcanic soil. Instead, he focused on Etna's two specialty red varieties: nerello mascalese and nerello cappuccio. These grapes are variations of the nerello mother vine, one of the oldest on the planet. They don't grow well anywhere else but thrive on Etna's ashen slopes, producing incredibly complex wines.

Mascalese is planted more widely than cappuccio; it's a slow ripener planted higher up the mountain, so it's often not picked until late October. The grape knows how to hold its acids and tannins, and yields wines with long aging potential. Cappuccio ripens earlier and is picked in September; it's fleshier and rounder, with very little tannin. The two grapes are often blended: mascalese has a cabernet character; cappuccio is considered more merlot-like. Rumor has it that almost a century ago, when Bordeaux suffered a vineyard blight, nerello was sold there as the local wine, and few people noticed the difference.

As Lisa is explaining Giuseppe's 150 trials on fermentation methods, he takes a small camera from his coat pocket and starts taking pictures of me. For the first few shots, I turn to smile at the camera, as if this is, of course, an expected part of an interview for any journalist. But when he starts tilting the camera this way and that, moving closer across the table and then pulling back for different angles, I become fascinated with Lisa's explanation of the fourteen yeasts that were tested.

"Dr. Benanti is a true visionary," Lisa says. I also suspect that he may be a lonely visionary, as the white flashes continue to my right. "He has brought forth the wines that best express the indigenous soil and the indigenous mind. He believes there is a difference between wines merely produced on Etna, and Etna wines made by Etna people."

Mano Uona Etna," Giuseppe says, setting down the camera.

"Etna Man," Lisa translates. The door opens with the welcome distraction of an assistant carrying several bottles and three glasses.

"*Si, i vini*, they speak for themselves," Giuseppe says with surprisingly good English. "They speak better than we do, so let's taste!"

He pours his Rovittello, a blend of nerello mascalese and nerello cappuccio, from eighty-year-old vines. The wine has aromas of fresh-turned earth, dried tobacco, and blackberries. As the wine matures, the oak notes will recede as the tertiary nuances—aromas that develop from bottle age—emerge, such as leather and violets.

"We are pursuing the ancient fragrances," Giuseppe says as we savor the wine.

Next we try his Serra della Contessa. Drinking it is like plunging headfirst into a vat of fleshy plums. There's a mild tingling in the mouth from the dark spices, then a mouthwatering acidity that washes it away on soft layers of ripe blackberries that roll over each other. This makes you wonder if your first impression of the wine was correct. Naturally, you must take another drink to confirm. Giuseppe and I are confirming many impressions, while Lisa is now absorbed in her BlackBerry email.

"White wines must be young and fresh," Giuseppe says, smiling slyly, "but reds just get better with age."

Although Sicily is better known for its red wines, being more climatically suited to making them, two-thirds of the island's grapes are white. Most were originally selected for their resilience to extreme heat and drought. Obscure varieties such as grillo, grecanico, carricante, catarratto, damaschino, and insolia delivered large yields and were fermented at high temperatures, which resulted in whites that were tired and oxidized.

Today, though, improved techniques, such as night harvesting and temperature-controlled fermentation, prevent premature fermentation and allow the fresh fruit character to come through. Modern

Sicilian whites are crisp, clean, and zesty. Sadly, few of them travel well, so they're often not sold abroad. These lovely local wines are best consumed in Sicily, preferably on a sun-drenched terrace over-looking the dazzling Mediterranean. Sipping them is like staying at a small family-run inn rather than a big chain hotel.

Giuseppe pours me his Benanti Bianco di Caselle, a zesty white made from the carricante grape, with an apricot-lemon core. Tasting these strange and wonderful wines is like discovering an island of gem-colored butterflies when you've been living among moths.

"When I taste the wine, I see the vineyard," Giuseppe says enthu-siastically. "You must see the vineyards, come!" As I marvel at how quickly he has become fully bilingual, we leave Lisa at the table, clicking away at her email, and head out into the fresh morning air.

Giuseppe's vines are cultivated using the ancient *alberello* method: low freestanding bushes tied to wooden stakes. The volcanic soil extends down a good thirty-five feet, giving the vines a longer life— many are more than a hundred years old. Vines of this age, Giuseppe believes, are best tended by people of the same age: "They understand each other." Walking through this forest of gnarled stumps makes me feel like a giant stomping through a magical forest where the trees might come alive any moment and wrap their limbs around my legs.

Giuseppe possesses each vine with his eyes. There is a fierce, vis-ceral attachment to the land here; some families have owned their vineyards for generations, even if they've let them grow wild. Family-run operations have usually long since paid off their property and capital costs, so their wine prices don't have to account for these costs. Many of them are more interested in preserving the family name on the label than in making an overpriced "badge wine." There's another reason why wine is so affordable here: it's an intrin-sic part of the culture. The diversity of the industry in terms of grapes, styles, prices, and quality is the result of a strong domestic market.

As we walk, Giuseppe plucks a stray leaf here and a dead branch there. "Winegrowers don't like things to come to an end; we are perpetual tinkerers," he tells me. "We know our vines personally and individually. When we prune one, we know exactly where to put our shears without thinking—like a lover when you put your hand on her waist."

His next question takes me by surprise: "Have you ever suffered from cenosilicaphobia?"

Huh?

When I ask him what that means, he shakes his finger at me with a conspiratorial smile: "Ah, only a crafty wine journalist would pretend she didn't know what cenosilicaphobia is. Very disarming, brilliant!"

"No, I can assure you that I'm just an ignorant wine journalist," I say, hugging my embarrassment. "I'm really just a highly functioning liver with a few superfluous organs attached."

Giuseppe laughs dismissively, refusing to believe me—or perhaps refusing to believe that he's spending so much time with someone who hasn't heard of cenosilicaphobia. So I admit reluctantly to having felt it once or twice, but not recently, still wondering what on earth he's referring to. Later when I check online, I discover that it means "fear of an empty glass." *Ceno* comes from the Greek word for "empty" (as in *cenotaph*, an empty tomb), and *silica* is the Roman word for "glass." Occupational hazard for those in the wine biz, I guess.

"Would you like to see my chapel?" Giuseppe asks me next, spider cunning in his eyes. "We are no longer *sconosciuti* (strangers)," he says, wrapping his forearm in mine. It's an offer from a Sicilian vintner I can't refuse. We walk down the cobblestoned path through the vineyards to a small white building, nestled amid silvery olive trees. The late-morning light burnishes the stained-glass windows and the golden pointed spire.

Inside, a twenty-five-foot ceiling invites my eyes upward. Large oil paintings of biblical scenes hang on the walls along with wooden crosses. Giuseppe takes me up to the tiny choir loft that overlooks two pews facing the small alter below. As we lean over the balcony, light streaming in through the windows like a Vermeer painting, he starts singing a Latin hymn. His rich, baritone voice fills the chapel. Then he stops, we smile in the silence, and we walk downstairs.

It is a contemplative end to the visit. As we say good-bye, Giuseppe says something to Lisa in Italian; his English has mysteriously vanished again. He looks away shyly as she translates: "Dr. Benanti says you ask questions with your heart. He hopes there is a good man at your side."

I smile at Giuseppe as we kiss on both cheeks, twice. When I climb back into my Fiat, Lisa walks back into the winery. Giuseppe stands in front of the chapel, waving.

SICILY IS ALSO known as *mezzogiorno*, "the land of the midday sun"—and of the midday nap. This May afternoon is so warm that I decide to take *la pausa* before my next visit. I love that notion of an afternoon pause: it doesn't sound lazy, just meditative. I retreat to my dark hotel room and flop on the cool bedsheets, mesmerized by my ceiling fan as its breeze evaporates the sweat on my arms and legs. Outside, a dog barks, someone laughs, a door slams. Then quiet.

After several hours of drugged sleep, I head out again along a rutted road farther up the mountain. The land on either side still seems wild, reminding me of Lampedusa's observation in *The Leopard*: "'Countryside' implies soil transformed by labor; but the scrub clinging to the slopes was still in the very same state of scented tangle in which it had been found by the Phoenicians, Dorians, and Ionians when they disembarked in Sicily."

I'm on my way to a small trattoria to meet Marco de Grazia for dinner. I spot him at a small table in the corner, a stocky, ebullient man with brown velvet eyes. A former wine importer in the United States, he recently started his own winery. "I had sold the most remarkable wines to dozens of countries for thirty years," he tells me, as he pours me a glass of his rosé open on the table. "But I have never sold a wine that everyone wanted as much as these. It's the power of Etna."

Marco's grandparents lived just southwest of Etna, where his mother, a successful Italian painter, was born. His father, Sebastian de Grazia, was a professor of political philosophy at Rutgers as well as an author; his book *Machiavelli in Hell* won the Pulitzer Prize. They met while Marco's father was on a fellowship in Italy, then moved to the United States, where Marco was born. They returned to Italy when Marco was just eight months old. Marco was also academically gifted, studying at the University of Florence, the Sorbonne, Rutgers, and Berkeley, earning degrees in philosophy and comparative literature.

"I guess the ineffable paradoxes of Etna draw unusual characters to it," he says, pushing back a red beret that gives him a Che Guevara look. "I suppose I must belong in that category as well."

Marco got his first taste of winemaking at sixteen, when he helped his best friend, Sandro, at his family's nearby farm. He recalls the first bottle that they shared one weekend when Sandro's father was away.

"I'll never forget that gentle beauty," he reminisces of that youthful escapade. "We had intended to drink it with a dish of snails—we had captured hundreds of them and kept them in the cellar, feeding them lettuce. But we discovered that they had escaped and were crawling all over the veranda, inching toward a getaway. We just sat on the steps drinking the wine, watching them and laughing."

A server brings us freshly baked bread with warm ricotta cheese.

It melts on my tongue with a tangy bite. I cup my hands around an earthenware bowl, steaming with fresh chunks of glistening pink tuna in a broth of herbs, garlic, and cognac. The evocative flavors of the ancient south waft up from the bowl, thick with flavor and memory. Marco's Feudo di Mezzo Il Quadro delle Rosé, with its aromas of field berries, goes beautifully with them.

Sicilian food, with its honest, rustic flavors, is a cuisine of the senses, with the fragrances of the fresh and local. The waters teem with fish; lemon, orange, and olive trees hang heavy with fruit; and the hillsides ripple with wheat for pasta. This natural bounty is perfumed with the flavors of many cultures.

"Sicily is a layered civilization, so many tribes and nations have contributed to what Etna is today," Marco says, his eyes closed as he breathes out the wine's finish. "Hands from around the world have worked this soil. Invaders come and go, but the land stays. Winemakers come and go, but the vineyard stays."

Despite his evident passion, Marco didn't think of wine as a profession until he was an undergraduate at Berkeley. He wandered into a local wine shop that had a decent selection of Italian wines but told the owner that he could do better. The owner didn't believe him, so Marco invited him to dinner at his apartment. They got sloshed on Marco's stash of wines from Italy, and the merchant offered him a job. Eventually, he became a full-time, independent importer.

Marco describes Etna as the Burgundy of the Mediterranean because its climate and soils also produce wines with an obsessive-compulsive edge. Like Burgundian producers, he doesn't blend grapes. "It's a difference in philosophy: burgundy versus bordeaux, Plato versus Aristotle, the ideal form versus moderation in many things," he muses. "Just as philosophy is the struggle to impose order on thought, winemaking is the struggle to impose order on nature. My goal is to express the classical ideal of wine."

Marco raises his glass. "We drink with the angels," he says as we clink tumblers.

The server sets down a platter of deep-fried calamari and a wooden board covered with *spinchone*, a traditional Sicilian pizza made with diced tomatoes and fresh basil. The calamari's crisp batter gives way to buttery richness in my mouth, and the tomatoes on the pizza dance with the tangy Etna Rosso, Marco's basic red made from nerello mascalese. The early evening light streams down from the high windows in the trattoria, catching the jeweled colors of the food and wine and illuminating our ghostly hands and faces like a Caravaggio painting.

"Sicily has the ancient recipe for producing great wines," Marco says. He pours his Calderara Sottana, also a nerello mascalese but made from the lower terraces in the vineyard, which produce more full-bodied wines. I'm entranced by its edgy eccentricity. It's a wine that teleports you to a place in your mind: I've disappeared into a grove of olive trees.

"The Mediterranean climate concentrates flavor, and an active volcano keeps everyone on their toes." But does he worry about the volcano erupting?

"The volcano gives so much that if, once in a while, it takes something back, no one seems to really mind," Marco observes with a volcanic mentality—that fatalistic happiness shared by those who live with other natural time bombs, like tornados and earthquakes. "Etna will devastate you and then give you everything. The more she betrays me, the more I love her.

"There's a certain edge to making wine when, at any minute, you could be buried under molten lava. Etna is the goddess of fertility, but she's six hundred thousand years old. Anyone can get cranky at that age."

Next we try his Santo Spirito Rosso, radiating the freshness of the mountain air and the power of the Sicilian sun. Its mineral core is wrapped in fleshy berry fruit flavors that pair beautifully with our entrée: a meaty red mullet baked in a pistachio crust. The bushlike pistachio trees are planted all over the island, and their green nuts are used in many local dishes.

"We need to stand out from New World wines flooding the market," Marco observes. "Even more, though, we need to cling to our heritage as we find a new way to do that." I have to agree: Sicilian wines strike me as an intriguing application of new methods on ancient grapes. The result is distinctly Sicilian yet also newer than *nuovo*. A good example is his Guardiola, a towering, tightly woven wine with a stone heart. The layers of blackberries and plums finish with a spicy slap of licorice.

After that, we enjoy a traditional dessert of cannoli: pastry tubes filled with ricotta cheese, candied fruit, and slivers of dark chocolate. It belongs to a category of desserts called *agrodolce*, with their contrasting flavors of sweet and sour. Cannoli supposedly originated in the city Caltanissetta (Kalat Annisa), where sultans locked up their harems in great castles. These women, bored out of their minds, made cannoli to pass the time. Another Arab creation popular in Sicily is granita, an ice dessert infused with the flavors of jasmine and rose petals.

Dinner over, we leave the trattoria as the lengthening light of evening drapes itself across the hills. Marco has suggested that we visit his winery, Tenuta delle Terre Nere (Black Earth Estate), nestled on the northern slopes of Etna, just a few minutes away. We climb into his VW van, which bears the scars of brushing against many vines and an argument or two with some larger branches. When we arrive, I breathe in the heady scents of fuchsia and oleander and wonder if there's an extra room, so I can move in.

"The challenge is to coax from this traditional grape my interpretations of these different patches of land," Marco says as we walk. "If I can do that, people will recognize these wines the way they recognize the sentences of certain writers. This is what we mean by terroir."

His hillside concave amphitheater has some thirty terraced rows, each edged with a low moss-covered black stone wall. Some of his vines are more than 140 years old, their green narrative punctuated by black commas of lava stone. The gnarled gray stumps lining each row look like grumpy old men waiting for the show to start.

"The more transparent I am as a winemaker, the better—I'm the least important link between the vineyard and the bottle." He waves away my protestations about his role in this wine. "My job is just to remove anything that might damage the vines and then stay out of the way." To him, that means gentle tilling of the soil so the roots can breathe, and a gravity flow in the winery so the juice isn't bruised. "I extract what's beautiful and leave the dross behind."

A light evening wind called *et alaria* makes the leaves tremble. I notice that they're planted in such a way that no vine covers another. This keeps the ventilation in the vineyard constant, which prevents mildew and rot. The vineyard style is said to be *a lada all'aria*, "in the air."

"There's a rhythm to this work and a joy in working with the seasons. I remember as a child spending October afternoons picking grapes, lathered in sweat, then plunging into the lake, the cold water shocking us.

"History takes a long time," he says, his smile not quite reaching his eyes. "You're making decisions today based on what you think the wine will be in twenty years. Yet making wine happens just once a year, so it takes a long time to become good at it." In his opinion, winemaking school gives you the technical skill to create correct wines but not exciting wines. "You need a palate that can distinguish good from great. Tough vintages are for the pleasure and interest of great winemakers; they seek and achieve the beautiful year after year."

Marco opens the door to his winery. Despite the late hour, the bottling line is in full swing, and the sound of clashing and clinking bottles rushes out at us. A half dozen employees are working the line, making sure the bottles are in place and taking the filled boxes over to the towering white stacks of cases. It's a gray mechanical whir, with a few human hands darting in and out.

In another area stands a stack of brightly colored boxes adorned with crayon drawings. They're the work of Marco's three-year-old daughter, Elena, after whom the wine is named. She produces a new set every year, so they graphically follow her development. (The profits from this wine go to the local children's hospital in her honor.)

We retire to his kitchen, where we sit at a rough wood table. Bronze pots hang on the walls, in between mesh bags of onions, garlic, and herbs. Marco seasons a nine-pound piece of steak on a wooden plank and slides it into the blazing wood-fired oven. Dried vines crackle and hiss, infusing the meat with a smoky flavor that curls around the kitchen. He's hosting a gathering of local winemakers later tonight.

"In Sicily, few things are what they seem," Marco observes as we drink his La Vigna di Don Peppino, made from pre-phylloxera vines that are 140 years old. There's nothing earthy about this wine: it tastes like clouds. We watch the sun wash the hills in greens and golds as it sets. "But once you come to terms with this most complex of places, learn to respect its profound identity—and work like a dog to express it—it will reward you with wines that rival the finest in the world."

THE NEXT MORNING, I drive farther up the mountain along a narrow, vertiginous lane called Passopisciaro, or "fishmonger's road." It was originally named after a seaman who used to sell his catch here on sunny afternoons. He charmed his female customers, generously offering them his services in addition to the seafood. Eventually, their husbands banded together and killed him.

Most of Andrea Franchetti's wines are labeled Passopisciaro, but his customers are safely scattered around the world. In 2001, having spent ten years in Tuscany making wines that received rave reviews, Andrea decided to buy land here. His nineteenth-century stone winery sits on a rock terrace as though it's barely glued to the ledge. His vineyards stretch their long green fingers around the mountain, trying to hold it.

When I pull up in front of his villa, Andrea Franchetti strides out to meet me. In his mid-fifties, six-foot-six, and looking like a successful Parisian architect, he sports square black glasses, a cashmere sweater tied carelessly around his shoulders, and highly polished Ferragamo loafers. He greets me, encasing my hand in a firm shake, and gets right to the point. (I'd heard he hates small talk.)

"I started making wine on Etna just to have an excuse to live here," he explains, unprompted, as we start an almost straight-up ascent of the mountain. "This is an authoritative land, the Orient of Italy—exotic colors, shapes, seasons, people. I came here not just because it's the best place for making wine but also for what it suggests to my imagination."

Andrea's family tree blooms with eccentric imagination on every branch. In 1530, his ancestor Giuditta Franchetti was burned as a heretic after she took to the streets, screaming and railing against the church. ("She was a polemicist and had a collection of books that the Vatican didn't like.") In 1894, his great-grandfather Giorgio Franchetti bought the famed Ca' d'Oro (the golden house), considered one of the most beautiful palaces on Venice's Grand Canal. The palazzo, with its ornate gothic style and lavish gold finishes, was originally built in 1428 by the Contarini family, which produced eight Venetian doges. Giorgio Franchetti helped to add some dazzling mosaics to the house. When he was finished, he committed suicide, donating the palace and his vast art collection to the city, where it is now displayed in the Museo Franchetti alla Ca' d'Oro.

Giorgio's brother was the composer Alberto Franchetti, who wrote widely acclaimed operas for the Belle Époque, such as *Asrael*, *Cristoforo Colombo*, *Germania*, and *Notte di Leggenda*. Alberto's mother, Luisa, had learned to play the piano from Franz Liszt. Andrea calls Alberto's son Raimondo Franchetti "the Italian Lawrence of Arabia," noting that he explored Borneo, Ethiopia, and the Sudan. "He was a quintessential Italian explorer—he crossed the Abruzzo Park at night alone, when it was full of wolves." Raimondo died in 1935, when his small plane crashed in Africa's Great Rift Valley. He later became the inspiration for the dashing adventurer *Corto Maltese* in Italian comic books. Raimondo's son Nanuk was an ichthyologist, mountain climber, speleologist, and friend of Ernest Hemingway—Hemingway often hunted ducks in his marshes.

In the early 1950s, the Franchetti family ran a circus that traveled around Europe. Andrea recalls his father's gypsy soul and his love of dressing in circus clothing. While in the United States, his father met his American mother, heiress to a South Carolina textile fortune. She moved to Rome with her new husband but didn't trust Italian hospitals, so Andrea was born in New York. She returned to Rome, where Andrea grew up. His mother made him sing in the choir of the Sistine Chapel until his voice broke at thirteen.

When he turned seventeen, he jumped on his bicycle and pedaled from Italy to Afghanistan via Brindisi, Istanbul, Tehran, and Kabul. Then he sold his bike in Afghanistan and went home by train. "It was the best trip of my life," he says now. "I was fanatical, frightened, and alone."

When Andrea returned to Rome, he started writing for the Italian magazine *L'Espresso*, made two avant-garde films, and acted as an extra in several movies. When he got restless again, in 1982, he moved to the United States to become an importer of Italian wine. That, too, failed to hold his interest after four years. In 1986, he moved back to Italy and bought a Tuscan villa. "When I woke up the first morning, I decided to make wine," he says. "I could not go back to city life, even with its exuberance of people coming and going."

As he strides up the mountain and I pant to keep up with him, Andrea sweeps his hand to indicate a broad swath of land. "All this was a tangle of weeds and thorns. I had to use a pickax to clear it away. But it was worth it, just for the light. When I arrived, I was struck by it." He pauses to look around as I start to sink onto one of the low rock walls.

"A sash of light lay along the mountainside, through hidden carpets of broom and wild roses, inviting restoration. The sea reflects shadows and light up to the sky, which throws them down into the vineyard. It's a saturating light that illuminates my vines on every side. Luminosity, yes, but even more: limpidity, a crystalline light that comes from how close we are to the sun," he says, answering the question I haven't asked, and starts back up the mountain.

"I am inspired by the way the light changes about around me throughout the year, with its days of green and red and gold, the white mornings and violet nights. The weather swirls round us. The powerful process of photosynthesis affects both the vines and the owner. The transformation of berries into wine is a shade of nature's essence, hidden, then caught by surprise in the turmoil of fermentation, captured in a thick, red mirror."

While he's talking, I notice the lava stone terraces encircling Etna, following the slope's steep decline. They look as though Vulcan had absentmindedly traced a finger around and around the mountain. The walls were actually built by peasants a thousand years ago, without a bulldozer or drill. I think about how their fingers must have bled.

Today, it's difficult to hire vineyard workers, since climbing the slopes is exhausting. It's a world of clouds and stones. "I had a team of swearing Frenchmen who were accustomed to the light soils of Médoc," he tells me. "Still, they came back, year after year. They accept that you're a foreigner, so you're already crazy."

We're standing at thirty-three-hundred feet, and the deliciously cool air lines my lungs with mint. Andrea's vines are planted at the highest possible elevation on Etna, where the difference between day and night temperatures can vary greatly. This diurnal dip extends the growing season a month or so longer than on the rest of the island. It also creates polished wines of superb depth, acidity, and minerality.

While Giuseppe Benanti and Marco di Grazia are traditionalists, Andrea is a modernist. He plants and blends both international and local varieties, and has little patience for those who scorn this. "The wine itself is more important than the grapes that go into it," he says. "What you taste isn't just an expression of nature, it's also an expression of thought." Like many modernists, he thinks that nature is overrated. "Nature buffets the imagination, prods it to create, but we are the greatest mystery."

Andrea learned how to make wine in Bordeaux and has planted those varieties here: cabernet franc, cabernet sauvignon, merlot, and petit verdot. Those vine cuttings came from old parcels of vineyards that had produced some of the best wines in Graves and Saint-Émilion.

"For the French, making wine is like breathing. They're generous and will tell you everything you need to know. Bordeaux winemakers have selected and discarded for generations and have gathered a number of grapes that are exceptional both by themselves and in their capacity to be blended with others."

Those plants, Andrea explains, had it too easy in Bordeaux: he had to thin 60 percent of their crop late in their first summer when they started to lose their vigor. He believes that small berries are the secret of good red wines: more concentrated flavor and better air flow between bunches so that mold doesn't set in. These small stressed grapes thicken their skins to protect themselves and concentrate on maturing their fruit. It's also best, he believes, to make wine from at least three types of grape, each maturing at a different time. Then, ideally, at least one grape every year will fit its particular cycle to the weather changes of that vintage.

"We interpret this place and create terroir where none existed before," he says. "Etna wines harness the lush fruitiness of the grapes with the acidity of the volcanic soil in an ineffable combination of contrary impulses." This creates a concentrated wine, he says, that is more recognizable and imprints itself in your memory. "Every year that passes increases the wine's identity, its ability to become more itself. That is terroir: a taste that says, 'Ah! *There.*'"

Understanding terroir involves understanding the times we live in, he explains. The vineyard changes with changes in taste. When wines meant to be consumed after the softening of long aging are in vogue, a vineyard is starved, production reduced to a quarter to concentrate the wines.

"Our image of wine is as capricious as our views on architecture, fashion, and automobile design," he continues. "Right now, our idea of viticulture is the restoration of nature. That image is stressed. Once we considered ourselves titans ruling over the earth, exaggerating our interventions. So now it's time for us to be humble and follow nature."

However, he does listen to nature to time the harvest, the most important and difficult part of what he does. "People get too damn poetic about harvest time. You work your ass off all year long, and then you can lose it all in an hour. It's wet and cold and discouraging.

What's romantic about that?" he says, his voice growing hard and enameled.

"Viticulture may be the Hollywood of farming, but it's lost its way and is too caught up in the glamour. We are farmers. Every year, you think you've lived through it, but you haven't; you suffer horribly. You should *never* talk to me during harvest," he says, tightening his eyes on someone in the past who made that mistake.

Got it.

Once harvest is over, he assembles the wines that have emerged from more than fifty fermentations. Slowly a style forms, he says, from discarding and choosing and mixing. His resulting wine receives the full I-don't-need-to-earn-a-profit treatment that comes from starting a winery with family wealth: barrels made from the finest French forests and rigorous declassification of any less-than-perfect wine into a second label. His top wine is left on its lees for a year to develop in a crescendo of flavor.

At last we sit down on the rock wall, and Andrea reaches into a tuft of wild grasses behind it and pulls out several bottles and a couple of glasses. The first one he opens is his petit verdot. As he pours me a glass, he observes, "A vein of tar sneaks into the taste of all the wines of this area; we must take care not to lose it." As I sip, I'm not getting the tar, but I do taste that lovely Italianate bitter-fresh, dark-savory flavor of chiseled darkness, with two opposing forces holding tension down through its center. I feel as though I'm invading the private history of the grapes in this wine.

As we drink, he continues. "I don't want to make fruity wine; I'd rather eat fresh fruit. I want to make an earthy wine because I want to taste this place. Vines have such a long vegetative cycle that they really show the territory in their fruit. The ground under our feet was once the ancient ocean floor. The crushed fossils of prehistoric creatures are in the sediment of this wine."

I nod in agreement, my mind more on the warm Mediterranean light moving across the slopes. I think of D. H. Lawrence's observation of Etna: "Anyone who has once known this land can never be quite free from the nostalgia for it." Then I think of the volcano again. Does Andrea worry about it?

"Not at all. We are gladiator winemakers here: all or nothing," he says, smiling as he pours me his cabernet franc. "The danger gives your work a knife-edge focus. This is an insane way to make wine." This dark-berried wine is insanely good. It seeps through my pores and along my veins until I'm running warm and flush with its flavor.

"You need to discover what is too much, to cross that line and then come back. The mountain draws stubborn people to it. It gives us something to struggle against—ourselves."

Looking around, I spot a few blackened patches of earth to our right. Andrea tells me that the local shepherds burn the grass because tasty and nutritious plants sprout up afterward that are good for their flocks. Unfortunately, several times these uncontrolled fires reached his vines. The twisted dark stumps look like dead hands reaching out of their graves.

"Oh, that's such a shame," I say, consoling myself with more wine.

"Everything dies, Natalie," Andrea says, his eyes settling on me. "There's something joyfully self-destructive about Etna. Nature throws an element of desperation at you, and you respond. You can't change nature, only your response to it. The value of life is defined by death. Here we live on top of a symbol of death—and enjoy life more because of it."

Field Notes from a
Wine Cheapskate

INSIDER TIPS

- Ultra-fashionable wine regions often get all the attention for any particular country, as do Italy's Tuscany and Piedmont and France's Bordeaux and Burgundy. Look for the lesser-known regions for your best value bottle, like Sicily in Italy and southern France's Languedoc-Rousillon.

- Some of the most ancient wine-producing regions are now the "newest" ones in that they've revitalized their techniques and styles. The advantage is that they have a deep knowledge of their soils and grapes, and often, family-run operations aren't paying high capital costs, since these have been paid off long ago.

- Regional food and wine matches often make sense, since the food and wine "grew up" together in the same soils and climatic conditions. It's not a rigid rule but a great starting point when you're looking for pairings.

WINERIES VISITED

Passopisciaro: www.passopisciaro.com
Tenuta delle Terre Nere: www.marcdegrazia.com
Vinicola Benanti: www.vinicolabenanti.it

BEST VALUE WINES

Planeta Insolia
Planeta Nero d'Avola
Tenuta delle Terre Nere Etna Rosso*
Vinicola Benanti Bianco di Caselle
Vinicola Benanti Rovittello

My first pick for my own Thursday dinner.

TOP VALUE PRODUCERS

Ajello Majus	Feudo Arancio
Canaletto	Feudo Montoni
Cantine Colosi	Firriato
Cantine Francesco Minini	Girelli/Lamura
Caruso & Minini	Lagaria
Cusumano	Morgante
Donna di Coppe/	Pellegrino
Nativo/Picciotto	Planeta
Donnafugata	Podere Castorani Picciò
Duca Di Castelmonte/	Rizzuto
Cent'are/Cavallina	Spadina
Fazio/Torre Dei Venti	

THURSDAY DINNER FOR A WINE CHEAPSKATE

You'll find delicious Sicilian recipes that are similar to the meal Marco and I shared at www.nataliemaclean.com/food.

Fresh Tagliolini with Cuttlefish Sauce and Olives

Deep-Fried Prawns and Squid

Red Mullet in Pistachio Crust and Oregano Sauce

Redfish and Broken Spaghetti Soup

Cassata of Ricotta Cheese

TERRIFIC PAIRINGS

Beef roast or stew
Cheese: bianco sardo, cheddar, smoked, Swiss
Chicken: herb-rubbed roasted
Pasta alla norma or tomato sauce
Pizza: ambrosia, meat lovers, neopolitan
Red mullet
Sausage
Shepherd's pie

RESOURCES

For more information about Sicilian wines and nero d'avola:

Journey Among the Great Wines of Sicily by Andrea Zanfi
Wines of Sicily by Kate Singleton
Palmento: A Sicilian Wine Odyssey by Robert Camuto
Association of Sicilian Wines: www.assovinisicilia.it
Made in Italy: www.italtrade.com

RELATED READING

The following books, while seemingly unrelated to the main subject matter of this chapter, provided some enjoyable reading before, during, and after my travels:

The Leopard by Giuseppe Tomasi di Lampedusa
Machiavelli in Hell by Sebastian de Grazia
The Godfather by Mario Puzo

SIX

FRIDAY

A Smoldering Liquid Tango

MY HORSE REFUSES to budge. Her name, Briosa, probably translates to "one who despises gringo wine writers." As I look up at the snow-capped Andes, I feel very Ralph Lauren—even without *bombachos*, the traditional Argentine riding trousers. I breathe in the crystalline mountain air to the bottom of my lungs.

The region of Mendoza, 650 miles northwest of Buenos Aires, has a big-sky, Wild West feeling. In fact, I'm hankering to mosey over to a campfire and whittle me a stick. But I decide to clutch the reins more tightly as Briosa turns her silky black head to snuffle at me. After a seven-minute standoff, 967 pounds of horseflesh grudgingly starts clopping behind her bemused trainer, Carlos Fernando, riding in front of me.

As we move through the vineyard rows, the few words that Carlos and I exchange are absorbed in the mountain quiet. The suede-smooth folds of the foothills beg to be touched.

I'm visiting the aptly named Cheval des Andes (Horse of the

Andes) winery, a joint venture between Bordeaux's Château Cheval Blanc and the Argentine estate Terrazas de los Andes. Cheval des Andes makes spectacular malbec–cabernet sauvignon blends—and owns a polo team. The thirtysomething winemaker Nicolas Audebert is an avid player on the team. As he tells me later, "We make wine in Argentina like we play polo: passionately."

Polo is one of many national obsessions here, along with Evita, tango, and soccer—recall Diego Maradona's "hand of God" goal that beat England in the 1986 World Cup quarterfinals. Some of us remember the country's 1982 Falklands War with Britain, described by Argentine writer Jorge Luis Borges as "two bald men fighting over a comb."

The country's capital, Buenos Aires, is often called the Paris of South America. I spent a few days there before heading out to wine country, and was surprised at its beauty and cosmopolitan feel as I walked the streets, carrying the short stories of Jorge Luis Borges, who was born there in 1899. In his miniature fictions, he captured the intensity of feeling and color in this bustling city of twelve million people and forty-seven barrios, or neighborhoods: the smart cafés and designer boutiques, the flea markets and brothels, the Belle Époque architecture and the black granite vault of Evita's tomb, the taxis who treat driving as blood sport, the chatter of people and parrots, the expansive tree-lined avenues and the darkened cobblestone alleyways. Buenos Aires doesn't close: light and people spill out of tango bars at four a.m., just as the cafés start making fresh brioche for early risers.

However, I had only a vague notion of this South American country that's five times the size of Spain. It spans more than a million square miles, from the subtropical jungles and parrots in the north, near the equatorial Tropic of Capricorn, to the Antarctic ice fields and penguins of Patagonia in the south. In the east lie the expansive cattle-grazing grass fields of the pampas; in the west, the country rises to the crescendo peaks of the Andes.

I knew even less about the country's wines, often lumping them together with next-door neighbor Chile's vino. Both countries hug the Andes—the mountain range that runs down the spine of South America, with valleys and plains thrown to either side, as though Bacchus had cleaned out his topography drawer. Both have evolved from dictatorships to democracies. Both are Spanish-speaking with Latino flair.

Both countries also produce wines that are incredibly well-priced for the quality. The reason is that they share some natural advantages: a warm climate that produces consistently ripe grapes, so there's less crop loss, as well as cheap land and labor costs. This translates into comparable wines that are often less than a quarter of the price of those from Napa, Tuscany, and Bordeaux.

While Chile and Argentina are terrific bargains, stylistically, the wines are quite different. Chile, situated to the west of the mountains beside the Pacific Ocean, has a cooler, more humid climate than Argentina on the eastern side. The Andes block the cooling Pacific breezes and trap rain clouds on their snowy peaks, making Argentina's climate dry and hot.

What kinds of wines does such a climate produce? Traditionally, not very good ones. When I first tasted Argentine wine twelve years ago, I spat it out immediately. (This would have been fine had I not been in a restaurant.) The wine tasted of scorched prunes speared on lacquered toothpicks. Face-sucking tannins squeezed it into a tight, rusty package. However, in the last five years, I've discovered that Argentina has started producing wines of ravishing vivacity. They're perfect for Friday night barbecues at the end of a long week, when you want something hearty but don't have the energy to cook a big meal. So I'm here to find out how they coax such fresh, vibrant wine from this hostile land at such ridiculously low prices.

Meanwhile, as we return to the polo clubhouse at Cheval des Andes, the tingling menace I felt from Briosa is fading. (I later learn that her name means "high-spirited.") She seems to have settled into a companionable tolerance. As I slide off her with one foot still stuck in a stirrup, she rolls her eyes—fondly, I think.

NEXT MORNING, I abandon equine transport for the motorized kind and drive to the Bodega Catena Zapata winery, one of the country's largest wine producers. Catena is also the wine that changed my opinion of Argentine wine: I remember drinking it one night at a friend's house and guessing that it was Australian shiraz. My body hummed with contentment as I let myself down into its berry decadence. I was pleasantly surprised to find out what it was and started buying more malbec.

Now, as I follow the long gravel road, a space-age stone temple rises from the vines, framed against the silver peaks of the Andes. This extravagant architectural statement is the concrete gesture of one man's desire to revolutionize his country's wine industry. As owner Nicolás Catena later explains, "We could not build a French château or an Italian palazzo here. We had to tell the world that we are doing something different in Argentina."

The artistic inspiration for the building came from the ancient Mayan civilization, despite the fact that Mayans never ventured beyond Central America. However, they were great architects, fascinated with mathematical symmetry and the sacred geometry of pyramids. This winery is built according to the same philosophy: every angle at exactly the same inclination toward the sun. Although it looks like a temple of molecular displacement, the beige stone gives it an earthy warmth.

Inside the sixteen-foot doors of burnished copper, I meet Catena's export manager, Jorge Crotta, who takes me on a tour of the tank room and cellar, while giving me the winery's background. It now produces about 3.6 million bottles of wine a year, exporting 85 percent of it. Seventy percent of the wines are red, with malbec accounting for 55 percent of production. The wines include Alamos, Catena, Catena Alta, and the flagship, Catena Zapata, as well as a joint venture with Bordeaux's Château Lafite-Rothschild called Caro.

Afterward, he leads me up to the top level of the winery, to a quiet study filled with books and big leather chairs. Sunlight streams in through large open windows that look to the Andes. I'm to be granted a rare audience with Dr. Nicolás Catena. As I wait, my stomach flip-flops. I recall thinking how what a coup it would be to interview Argentina's most brilliant and insightful winemaker. Now I'm wondering how I can carry on a conversation with a man whose IQ is in a range that I'll never see, except maybe on the bathroom scale. I'm not prepared to defend any thesis to this professor.

A few minutes later, the door opens and a silver-haired, bespectacled man enters. He looks every inch the distinguished scholar in a navy corduroy jacket and crisp white shirt. This takes me right back to one-on-one tutorials at Oxford University; I can feel the sweat between my fingers and down my back. His blue eyes radiate from a tanned, weathered face as he greets me in a soft Spanish-accented voice, "Please, call me Nicolás." As he pours me a glass of his brooding, blackberry-rich Catena Malbec, he tells me about his life as an academic and a vintner.

Nicolás Catena has lived among the grapevines for all of his seven decades. He was even born in the vineyard, since his mother didn't make it to the hospital in time for the birth of the last of her five sons. At age six, he was already walking the family horses out to their pasture several hours before school in the mornings, and then bringing them back home again at the end of the day.

That robust work ethic has been in the Catena family for generations. In 1898, his grandfather Nicola left a small village in Sicily for Argentina. He started planting vines in 1902 and raised a family. His eldest son, Domingo, married Angelica Zapata, a daughter of a large landowner, increasing the family's holdings. By 1973, the winery had become the country's largest producer of cheap wines, pumping out 240 million bottles a year.

Nicolás, the son of Domingo and Angelica, was a brilliant boy and finished high school at fifteen. At the request of his father, he delayed university to work in the vineyard. After several years, he continued his education, eventually earning a PhD in agricultural economics from Argentina's University of Cuyo and then a master's degree in economics from Columbia University. But sadly, in 1963, his mother and grandfather were killed in a car crash. Nicolás returned home to help his father run the winery, postponing a doctorate at the University of Chicago.

"I worked side by side with my father. I was too young and too arrogant then to learn anything—but at least I knew I was arrogant," he says, smiling.

Eventually, when the winery stabilized, young Nicolás longed to go back to academia, despite his love for the family business and making wine. "The pull of the intellectual life has always been as strong as the entrepreneurial for me. I have tried all my life to resolve that. Perhaps this is why I've always felt like two people."

In 1982, he accepted a post as visiting professor of agricultural economics at the University of California at Berkeley. The academic environment was stimulating: his colleagues won six Nobel prizes while he was there. He also enjoyed discussing wine matters with professors in the viticultural program. One weekend, he and his wife, Elaina, drove up to Napa Valley and toured the Robert Mondavi winery. Much later, he learned that his grandfather and Mondavi's father had lived only fifteen miles apart in Sicily, though they never knew each other.

Nicolás admired both the quality of the wines and the energy of the Mondavi people. "I remember the shock of the freshness and the fruit in the wine, its balance and complexity," he says, tilting his head slowly to one side and then the other, as though considering the visit from different angles. "I thought, there's no reason we can't do this in Mendoza. That visit opened my eyes to the fact that a New World country could compete with Europe."

After that, Nicolás and Elaina spent most weekends visiting Californian wineries. When they returned to Argentina in 1992, he took over the winery and sold all the family's vineyards except for the original Bodega Esmeralda, planted by his grandfather. He invested in advanced computer and robot technology as well as stainless-steel tanks and French oak barrels. He also convinced Paul Hobbs, a respected Sonoma winemaker, to work with him during the harvest. Since Argentina lies south of the equator, the grapes are picked from January to April, conveniently off-season for Hobbs.

Nicolás planted chardonnay and cabernet sauvignon, believing (like many others) that these two grapes alone defined wine quality internationally. "I made the same mistake as the Californians: I tried to imitate France in order to beat them," he admits quietly.

It was his father who convinced him to consider malbec, which the senior Catena believed to be the country's patriotic grape, making it in the popular oxidized style that Nicolás calls the "sherry approach to winemaking." Malbec got no respect in fine-wine circles, the stunt double of brute strength but no subtlety. Its only role was to beef up the color, alcohol, and tannin in more aristocratic cabernet blends.

"I loved my father very much, so in order to please him, I started a little project on malbec," he recalls.

That "little project" lasted fifteen years and involved planting 145 malbec "clones"—the same grape but from different parent vines—to see which would do best in different sites. ("Wine caters to obsessive personalities; it makes you worse," Nicolás observes with a sigh.) He knew that until the late 1800s, when phylloxera destroyed most European vineyards, malbec had been one of the most planted grapes in Bordeaux, whereas today, it's less than 10 percent of vineyards there.

Malbec still thrives in the warm region of southwest France called Cahors, which makes a tannic, deeply colored, palate-whacking "black wine." This may be why the name malbec is believed to be derived from the French *mal bouche*—"bad mouth," referring to this rustic style. Thankfully, Argentine malbec is a much friendlier, cuddlier creature than the inky monsters of Cahors. (I recall drinking Cahors for the first time and thinking that I could use it to restain the front deck.)

Ever the scientist, Nicolás narrowed down all those clones to the five best, a process he says married his bookish and business interests. "As a theoretical economist, I'm trained to develop a hypothesis and then to use a methodical approach to prove or disprove it," he explains, taking off his glasses and rubbing his eyes.

He was aided in this quest by a friend, Bordeaux winemaker Jacques Lurton, who also has wineries in both Chile and Argentina. Lurton convinced Nicolás to plant at higher altitudes, which further improved the grape quality. ("Jacques has a genius for climate.") In gratitude, Nicolás had a thousand pounds of prime Argentina grass-fed beef delivered to Lurton in Bordeaux.

Like many artists, Nicolás is fascinated with light: its luminosity, its diffusion, its interplay among the vine leaves. "It's all about funneling that extraordinary intensity of sunlight here into the wine."

His scientific mind is also engaged with light, studying its effect on the health benefits of red wine. Intense sunlight doesn't mean hotter temperatures, just more intense rays. The intense ultraviolet light at higher elevations speeds photosynthesis, making it more efficient, so the plants are healthier.

It also causes the grape skins to thicken in an attempt to protect themselves from the increased radiation. This accelerates the development of natural compounds, such as polyphenols, flavonoids, and anthocyanins, which give wine its color, tannin, and flavor. These compounds, or phenolics, in grapes grown at over fifteen hundred feet are three times higher than in grapes grown at sea level.

The phenolics help to inhibit the development of endothelin-1, the nasty enzyme that blocks arteries and contributes to heart disease. Since only red grape skins are fermented with the grape juice, these benefits are mostly in red wines. (I love it when I can rationalize my alcoholic intake with medicinal benefits. And at my rate of consumption, I should live forever—or at least be well preserved [completely pickled] by the time I make my exit.)

The result is wine of extraordinary elegance, with a rare combination when young: solid structure and silky texture. Argentine wine isn't just bottled sunshine; it's the liquid expression of solar energy. When I drink malbec, I feel voluptuous and expansive—that's probably why I'm also often wearing my buffet pants with the elasticized waistline. I like to indulge my thirst and my hunger to just this side of plump.

The Catena Alta Malbec Cabernet we're drinking smolders in the glass. Its sultry edge is more enticing than the sweet, soupy international style of many brand-name grapes. Nicolás believes that drinkers are shifting away from the herbal flavors of cabernet and turning more toward wines like malbec (and syrah, tempranillo, and grenache) that have fleshy dark red fruit and violet flavors. Blending malbec and cabernet grapes is still traditional. "These blends give us

French elegance and Latin passion," as Nicolás explains. However, he no longer believes that malbec needs cabernet sauvignon—or any other grape—to make great wine.

Nicolás is aided in his research by his daughter, Laura, who also has both a scientific mind and a bent for commerce. While she was pursuing her medical degrees at Harvard and Stanford universities, her father gave her a credit card.

"I told her that she could spend as much as she wanted, but it had to be on wine," Nicolás says, a playful glint in his eyes.

Laura now divides her time between San Francisco—where she, her husband, and their three young children live, and where she works as an emergency room doctor—and Argentina, where she's export director for the winery. She's conducting fifteen hundred experiments on different variables that contribute to wine quality, such as vine exposure to the sun, pruning at different times of the year, irrigation methods, and fermentation temperatures. Every season, she applies the successful methods to next year's vintage and adds more variables.

Laura and her father believe that there is no one optimum moment in the vineyard, as other producers do; rather, there are many captured in the glass by harvesting the grapes as many as eight different times. Their view is that one harvest with one vinification (fermentation) is a one-dimensional wine, which is why they have more than three thousand separate vinifications. That may sound iconoclastic, but as Nicolás observes, "We can innovate because the consumer has no history for us; we are creating that now. The French have a five-hundred-year lead on us, but every year, we jump a decade in learning."

Argentina may be new in consumer memory, but it has a long history of winemaking. It's another country that doesn't fit neatly into either the Old World or the New World categories, but is more Middle Earth. In 1541, Spanish conquistadors in search of silver (the

Latin "argentum," after which the country is named) planted tempranillo grapes here to make wine for religious services (and for thirsty invaders).

For three centuries, that rough local wine was the only kind produced here until the nineteenth century, following Argentina's independence from Spain, when a flood of immigrants began to arrive from Spain, Italy, and France. Most were farmers, and they brought with them treasured vine cuttings from the old country: Spanish tempranillo and torrontés, Italian barbera and sangiovese, and French cabernet sauvignon, viognier, and malbec.

However, things started to go downhill for the wine industry throughout the twentieth century, thanks to a variety of basket-case economic and political policies. But it was President Juan Perón who really sent wine consumption into decline when he imposed high domestic taxes in the 1950s. (Someone had to pay for his lavish lifestyle with Evita.)

The 1982 Falklands War with Britain also didn't help the economy or exports. Then there was hyperinflation that exceeded 3,000 percent a month, which discouraged foreign investment. Vintners made up for the lost revenue by producing high volumes of poor-quality wines that smelled like bananas rotting in an attic.

Meanwhile, neighboring Chile's economy was much more stable, and the country was already producing more wine than it could consume, so it was focused on export in the 1980s. Chile took advantage of this to position itself at the very low end of the market— bottles of wine under $10. (Ironically, Chile has struggled ever since to get up out of that category.) Argentina started to focus on exports in the 1990s, when government subsidies dried up for volume production and there were economic incentives to rip out inferior vines.

How did all this affect Nicolás Catena? In 1991, he shipped his first vintage to the United States and faced the dilemma of how to price his wines. At that time, the most expensive Argentine wines sold in the United States cost $4, and those from Chile cost $6. Nicolás made the gutsy move to price his chardonnay above the vinous ghetto at $13 and his cabernet sauvignon at $15. Fellow producers told him he was crazy, but word of the wine's quality spread, and he sold the entire vintage's production in two months. Still, it took another five years before the North American market fully accepted the Catena wines as part of that price segment.

I ask him which wines are the best in the world today. However, the professor dodges the question with a theoretical explanation. "If you accept that the dynamics of the market economy reflect the value judgments of its participants, then the best wine is the most expensive one."

And do critics influence which wines the market deems best?

"Critics increase market efficiency, but the consumer ultimately decides which is the best wine—and who is the best critic," he says, smiling at me. "I am market driven; I make wines that please people. If people did not like my wines, I would change them," he says.

Nicolás tells me he believes that wine allows people to show their affective side. "I cannot prove this theory, of course," he says earnestly, raising a finger. "But I have seen it many times. When you bring out a bottle of wine, something in your emotional, sensing nature is revealed. This is why people often drink wine with those they are fond of."

As it happens, I am terribly fond of this Catena Zapata Malbec. It floods my senses with a wanton perfume of violets and black plums. There's an unabashed Latin fire in the glass, with a lick of French polish.

"We're still scaling the Andes for cooler sites, taking vines to the very limit of cultivation," Nicolás says, his eyes moving up the mountains in front of us. "We are not producing our finest wines yet. That challenge is always ahead of us—we are always pursuing it."

* * *

THE NEXT DAY, I drive to meet Michael Halstrick of Bodega Norton, the country's sixth largest winery and exporter. Once I had changed my perception of Argentine wine, Norton was one of the first malbecs that I bought by the caseload. (I have a hard time with moderation in anything.) I even decided to serve it at a fancy dinner party one night, long before Argentina was thought to be a good producer. I can get away with this because everyone thinks that as a wine writer I will only serve them the best and most expensive wines. As usual, a Greek chorus chanted in my head, "Don't do it! Don't do it!" But I persisted and poured the wine into a decanter. My guests loved it, and I enjoyed having them guess at the wine's origins. They couldn't figure it out.

The sun burns a white hole in the sky. Flaming yellow and orange Alamos trees stand sentinel along the road, windbreaks for the vineyards behind them. Beyond the vines, creamy scrolls of sand stretch out into the blue distance. As I fly past, my mind keeps returning to my economics discussion with Nicolás Catena. How, I wonder, can a country like Argentina, with such great natural wealth, squander it so easily? But then, I'm always fascinated by beautifully flawed countries—and people. They have a thousand stories to tell.

Nicolás also gave me an idea of the extent of foreign investment in Argentina. Almost 50 percent of Argentine wine exports come from foreign-owned companies that have strong sales channels in other countries. Only two of the top ten exporters, Catena and Zuccardi, are owned by Argentines.

The devaluation of the peso not only made local wines inexpensive abroad but also attracted investors to the domestic industry. Making wine here is a tenth of the cost that it is in Europe, since the land, labor, and vineyard maintenance are all much less expensive. The

Argentine climate is also consistently warmer than Europe's, reducing crop losses, with sufficient warmth to ripen the grapes every year.

As a result, in the last ten years, foreign companies have invested more than $10 billion in the Argentine wine industry. In addition to the joint ventures I already mentioned between Château Cheval Blanc and Terrazas de los Andes (Cheval des Andes) and Nicolás's Catena Zapata and Château Lafite-Rothschild (Caro), other foreign-owned wineries include Bianchi (Seagram's, Canada), Navarro Correas (Diageo, Italy), Vina Patagonia (Concha y Toro, Chile), and Finca Flichmann (Sogrape, Portugal).

As well as bringing in cash from abroad, these companies also import winemaking expertise and technology. They train local vintners, often with the help of "flying winemakers"—international consultants who advise wineries in many countries. The most famous of these is the Bordeaux-based Michel Rolland, who owns the winery Val de Flores as well as part of the joint venture Clos de los Siete, both in Mendoza. He also consults for several other Argentine wineries. Foreign companies have also created a cadre of "flying interns," a new generation of young winemakers who choose to double their work experience by working in the Southern Hemisphere during the "reverse harvest."

One of the first foreigners to buy an Argentine winery was Gernot Langes-Swarovski, the Austrian crystal magnate, who purchased Bodega Norton in 1989. The winery was founded in 1895 by Sir Edmund Palmer Norton, a British engineer who came to Argentina to work for the Buenos Aires Railroad Company. In 1991, Swarovski's son, Michael Halstrick, took over as president.

I meet Michael, who's in his mid-forties, in the barrel room of Norton winery while I am on yet another obligatory tour with another export manager. Michael's broad smile and booming voice match his six-foot-six frame. Although he's made lots of changes at the winery, he still honors its traditions. For the last 105 years, local residents have gathered at the winery every Thursday afternoon to fill their bottles and demijohns with wine at cost. However, it was the opportunities for innovation in this country that drew him here.

"Unlike Europe, Argentina is a place where not everything has been done," Michael says with a clipped Austrian accent, as we walk through the shadowy cellar. His candor is a refreshing change from the euthanizing euphemisms in desperately perky wine press releases. "I came here because I wanted to create my own story."

His biggest challenge is to sell both his own brand and Argentina itself. Norton, which produces about eighteen million bottles a year, is one of the country's leading exporters. But for the past ten years, Argentina's wines haven't been able to gain a stronger foothold in foreign markets. The country is the world's fifth-largest wine producer today by volume, behind only France, Italy, Spain, and the United States, but it accounts for only 1 percent of global exports. Granted, it's hard to crack Europe's traditional 75 percent share of the $7 billion export market. But even Chile does better than Argentina, exporting twice as much, even though it produces a quarter of Argentina's output.

Yet many North Americans are gripped with a passion for Latin music, dance, cooking, and wine. So why isn't Argentine wine flying off liquor store shelves? Michael believes that the problem is image, or lack of one.

"Consumers drink a place in their minds when they drink wine," he theorizes. "When they drink Australia, they think of the Outback. When they drink California, they think of the beaches. But when they drink Argentina, they don't have a clear picture."

To combat the problem, the label on his Norton Lo Tengo wine features one of Argentina's most iconic images: a couple doing the tango. The label is actually a hologram that makes the dancers dip up and down as you change your viewing angle. You can always tell where the bottle is in the wine store: just look for the group of shoppers standing in front of it, tilting their heads one way, then the other.

Tango was born in the dockyards of Buenos Aires. As burly men waited for prostitutes, they danced with each other in a lusty expression of loneliness. The sad insistent notes of the accordion underscored their desire.

Eventually, women joined the dance, which became known as the vertical expression of a horizontal desire—about as close as two bodies can get with their clothes still on. The dance was further popularized in bars and nightclubs during the 1920s, especially by Carlos Gardel, the "King of Tango," with his buttery baritone voice. Hundreds of his recordings have been made into tango numbers. Today, tango is hotter than ever: there are Broadway-style shows, small crowded clubs called *milongas*, and even a twenty-four-hour tango cable channel, Solo Tango, devoted to national stars and competitions.

While I was still in Buenos Aires, I took in a tango show at a local club. I trained as a dancer for twenty years, so I respond with my body to most things. But watching tango made even the small muscles between my shoulder blades tighten with the dancer's arching back; my inner thighs shivered with memory when she straddled his leg with hers. Men and women pressed their foreheads together as they pushed against each other to get closer.

Domination, submission; rejection, passion; alienation, possession. Tango is as close as feet can get to talking to each other: a pointed toe placed there, another toe touching the floor beside it. Kinetic poetry.

Yes. No. Oh, yes!

"Journalists and the wine trade know Argentina, but most consumers don't," Michael says, snapping me out of my reverie. "In the past, most of our sales were accidental—a customer wandered into the Chilean section of the liquor store and mistakenly grabbed a bottle from Argentina. We're the Europe of South America, the last undiscovered jewel in the wine world, but we need to convince consumers of that."

We walk up to his tasting room beside the vineyard, where there are eight long-stemmed glasses of red wine on a long oak table. Shafts of sunlight pierce their violet-mulberry layers as the wine smolders in the glass, seducing my eyes.

"I fell in love with the color of the grapes first," Michael says as he hands me a glass of Norton Malbec. "The deep, saturated, bluish color that mirrors the depth of their fruit flavor."

He explains that the intensity of both color and flavor are produced by the climatic calibration of altitude and latitude. Argentine vineyards run down the spine of the Andes, spanning more than fifteen degrees of latitude, as far as the Champagne region of France is from northern Africa. In altitude, they range from twelve hundred to ten thousand feet above sea level. That's higher than most European Alps and more than a third of the way up Everest.

Of all the factors that influence Argentina's wine style, altitude has the most profound effect. For every three hundred feet higher up the mountainside vines are planted, they experience half a degree drop in temperature. This produces a different style of wine and often caters to a different grape.

Altitude also widens the difference between day and night temperatures by as much as twenty degrees. During the day, the vine absorbs sunlight through its leaves and converts it into carbohydrates, basic plant food. This is carried through the stems to its reserve organs, the grapes.

During the night, photosynthesis stops, and the plant consumes some of its stored carbohydrates. But at lower temperatures, less is consumed. This means the grapes keep more nutrients to enhance their color, flavor, and tannin structure. This long, slow ripening yields incredibly mature fruit flavors in the finished wine.

Higher-altitude wines tend to have darker floral aromas, such as roses and violets, while those produced at sea level have lighter floral notes, such as daisies and field flowers. As well, oxygen concentration is halved at higher levels, which reduces oxidation and intensifies the flavors. That's why we're short of breath and food takes twice as long to cook at higher elevations.

The benefits of altitude are such that among some producers, there's the inevitable "my vineyard is higher than your vineyard" braggadocio. Of course, at a certain point, more altitude (or length) becomes ridiculous, and it becomes too cold for the grapes to ripen.

Although Mendoza is the same distance from the equator as Napa (thirty-three degrees), the climate is much hotter and drier. The year averages 350 days of sunshine, with very little Pacific humidity making it past the Andes. Only dry winds roll down the mountains into Argentina. The most famous of these is called the Zonda, after the Greek god of wind. It can blow a hundred miles an hour and raise the temperature by twenty degrees in a couple of hours. This forces the grapes to produce thicker, protective skins, deepening the concentration of flavor.

Chilean vineyards, on the ocean side of the mountains, are planted according to how the Pacific breezes affect the vines as they glide inland and up through the river valleys. The country constantly battles humidity-related diseases, such as odium, mildew, mold, and botrytis. But Argentina's desert air almost eliminates such problems, so fungicides, herbicides, and pesticides are rarely needed. This makes organic and biodynamic farming much easier. In fact, most Argentine vineyards are organic in all but name. However, Michael, like many other Argentine producers, shies away from the organic marketing angle.

"Organic, inorganic; I don't believe in promoting that," he says. "All our wines are made naturally, so making that distinction doesn't help sales—and it hurts the ones we don't label as organic."

He pours me a glass of his Norton Malbec Barrel Select, a lovely weave of fruit and oak. It flows like a river of satin over my mouth, with vividly ripe black cherries and a smoky, mocha-infused finish.

The downside of a dry, desert climate is the challenge of finding enough water to keep the vines alive in a region that gets just eight inches of rain a year. (The great châteaux of Bordeaux get thirty-two inches, and even the dry-farmed vineyard of Australia's famed Henschke Hill of Grace gets twenty-four.) Argentina must depend on the torrents of crisp, clean meltwater that run down from the snowy peaks of the Andes and gurgle along a lacework of narrow canals that hug the vineyards and roads. The ditches were originally dug by Huarpe Indians a thousand years ago to irrigate their crops and cool their villages. The scarcity of this water limits how much land can be cultivated: only 3 percent of Mendoza has vineyards. Vineyard land without irrigation costs about $10,000 an acre; with irrigation, about $40,000.

The scarcity of water can be good for the vines. If they have enough to drink, the plants get lazy and their roots stay near the surface, drinking in only the water and nutrients at the top layers of soil. But if they're exposed to a little water stress, they're forced to push their roots much farther down into the soil to quench their thirst, allowing the roots to absorb the diverse nutrients of the lower soil layers, which deepens the grape flavors and expresses the terroir.

"The only thing we add is a little water," Michael says, winking, which sounds as though he's making instant soup. But the wines are anything but watery: they have the dark luxury of damson plums and peppered black raspberries. "We want the vines to be just a little grumpy."

Another reason to manage irrigation closely: during extrahot weather, the fruit sugars rise too quickly, before the grape's other elements—tannins, flavor, and color pigments—ripen. Wine made from such grapes is out of balance, with high alcohol, baked-fruit flavors, and a flat structure. But decreasing water to the vines slows that rapid rise in sugars, allowing the other elements to catch up. The result is wine with greater balance, maturity, and complexity.

Another advantage to canal irrigation is that it prevents the spread of the dreaded phylloxera, the aphids that eat vine roots and destroy entire vineyards. Although phylloxera does exist in Argentina, it doesn't cause damage because the pest's underground tunnels get washed away when the irrigation canals are flooded. As well, the flying variety of phylloxera is kept at bay by natural barriers: the sandy soils, the arid climate, and the Andes themselves.

Without the threat of phylloxera, the original Bordeaux vine cuttings of malbec have thrived here in splendid isolation for 150 years. Malbec is a stubbornly independent grape that prefers its own rootstock; it doesn't do well when grafted with other vines. The old vines produce tiny concentrated berries that yield wines of gorgeous concentration and deep spiced-berry flavors.

Although Malbec is the best-known grape here, there are more than a hundred varieties planted, many of them obscure and no longer grown in other regions. The weird and the wonderful thrive in this museum of lost grapes: primitivo, bonarda, corvina, mourvèdre, and especially torrontés—Argentina's most distinguished white wine. Michael pours me a glass of Norton Torrontés as we wrap up the tasting.

In the past, the warm climate made producing fresh whites difficult. However, modern controlled-temperature fermentation and storage changed that for many white wines, and none more so than torrontés, a crisp, aromatic tumble of daisies, lychees, and white peaches. The wine has been described as "the new viognier." Viognier's home is France, especially in the northern Rhône Valley regions of Condrieu and Château-Grillet, where it is the only white grape used and produces magnificently floral, voluptuous, and expensive wines.

To me, the Norton Torrontés seems closer aromatically to Alsatian gewürztraminer or muscat of Alexandria. It's a peach-fest of pungently floral aromas that makes you expect sweetness, but it's as bone-dry as chablis, with a crisp, feisty finish. It will thrill anyone looking for a value-priced condrieu, since it has the same mouth-filling, voluptuous texture as that rare Rhône Valley white.

The epicenter of torrontés is 850 miles north of Mendoza, in the Salta region near the Bolivian border. The light-skinned fruit was originally thought to be related to the Spanish grape of the same name. However, Carole Meredith, professor emerita of the University of California at Davis, has proved it to be a cross between the muscat grape of Alexandria and a local grape called criolla chica. Torrontés supposedly arrived in Argentina in the hatbox of a Jesuit priest.

Torrontés has since gone international, gaining a cultish following in Thailand, where its Turkish delight–tangerine essence suits the cuisine so well. It also pairs wonderfully with many spicy dishes and curries; works well with salads, seafood, shellfish, and vegetarian dishes; and makes a terrific aperitif. Torrontés is best consumed young, within a year or two of the vintage.

As we sip quietly on the wine, Michael leans back in his chair. "There are wines for thinking and wines for drinking," he says. "A very expensive wine makes only a few people happy. We want to make a lot of people happy."

THE SUN-BATHED UCO Valley, fifty miles southwest of the city of Mendoza, is bounded by the Cerrillos hills to the north and the San

Rafael Valley to the south. The challenge with visiting wineries here is that there are almost no road signs, so that pockmarked gravel path you just drove past was probably the one you should have taken. I discover this several times while trying to find Familia Zuccardi (Zuccardi Family Wines) before I finally pull up to a sleek building of glass and granite.

In 1973, Don Alberto Zuccardi, whose father had emigrated from Sicily, invented a deep-bore process to extract pure Andean meltwater from deep underground reservoirs to irrigate various crops. To prove that his invention could work, he bought land and planted vineyards here. His neighbors laughed, telling him that making wine in this dust-bowl region was impossible. Today, the family owns nearly fifteen hundred acres of vineyards, and the Uco Valley is the fastest-growing wine region in Mendoza. Don Alberto's irrigation company has since sold many systems to his neighbors.

I'm meeting Don Alberto's son José Alberto, who now runs the winery. Like his father, he studied engineering, but he also completed a degree in oenology. When he took over the company in 1985, he switched to organic farming and hand-harvesting to improve the quality of the wines. Today, the company produces fifteen million bottles a year, including some of the most successful brands in North America: Zuccardi Q, Fuzion, and Santa Julia, named after José's daughter, Julia, who runs their restaurant.

Although the company is large, it's also very much a family operation. His eldest son, Sebastian, is assistant winemaker; his second son, Miguel, makes the olive oils sold in the winery gift shop; and even Don Alberto, now in his late eighties, doesn't seem to realize that he's supposed to be retired. He still putters around the vineyards, plucking dead leaves off any vines within reach and gardening on the winery grounds.

José, an avuncular man in a gray cardigan, greets me as though

I'm a daughter returning after a long journey. "Welcome, welcome Natalie," he says, holding both my arms. "Shall we walk through the vineyard?"

Zuccardi's vines grow to six feet tall before spreading their tendrils horizontally across latticed wires overhead. This "parral" system of trellising forms a protective canopy roof for the grapes from the blistering sun. There is something *Secret Garden*–like about these leafy corridors, with bunches of grapes dangling overhead like purple chandeliers.

Many producers abandoned this method decades ago because they felt that it encouraged the vines to produce too many grapes of too little flavor. They preferred the European method of Guyot training, with vines planted more closely together and the cane of the vine only a few feet off the ground.

José disagrees. "Parral allows us to get more sunlight into the wine without the grapes getting sunburned," he says, as we stroll down one of the airy green hallways. "Grapes that are too exposed to the sun get scorched and give raisined flavors to the wine. For me, the age and care of the vines are more important than the trellising method."

Below us is dry, rocky soil—a geologist's wonderland. As the Andes rise, the stones get larger in size as measured by their "granulometry" (a word that I am dying to drop into casual conversation when I get home). This mother rock fractures into smaller pieces as it rolls down the mountainside or is swept down by meltwater. Loose-textured soil has much better drainage than sand or clay and contains fewer nutrients. Tough-love dirt makes vines work harder for their sustenance.

As we walk, I notice a number of large copper barrels hidden among the vines. These, José tells me, are essentially giant space heaters. Even though parral-trellised grapes are higher off the ground and thus more protected, frost still poses a threat. Every fall, there are a few nights when he must ring the bells to alert "the frost squad." A hundred or so farmhands, friends, and neighbors run to the vineyards in the darkness to light fires in these cauldrons. This generates just enough heat to prevent damage to the vines. José turns these evenings into festive occasions by roasting marshmallows and serving warm drinks.

The night also brings forward the wild, evident only the next morning from the dusty prints of rattlesnakes and pumas between the vineyard rows. But those creatures pose less of a threat to the vines than do the squawky green parrots in the daytime. Perched along a hydro line or rooftop, they give a beady-eyed expert's appraisal of the grapes' ripeness. A dawn raid could strip a hundred-acre vineyard in a few hours. Fortunately, the vines are protected by the vast hail nets that cover them.

Hail nets? It seems odd that in such an arid region, hail is a problem. In fact, Argentina suffers from the world's most violent hailstorms. Stones as big as golf balls can dent cars, kill grazing cows, and strip the leaves and fruit off vines in minutes. They can even damage the wood of the vine stalk, endangering next year's crop. José estimates that despite the netting (which costs about $8,000 per acre), he still loses 10 percent of the crop every year to hail.

Some larger producers also monitor hailstorm clouds with satellite technology and when they amass to dangerous levels, send up a plane to seed the clouds with silver nitrate. This forces them to precipitate their moisture as small, harmless pellets. The technique doesn't always work, though; sometimes the clouds are too large and high to be dissipated. Hail, frost, heat, draught: cue all the biblical afflictions. Who forgot to throw in flood, plague, and locusts?

We head back to the winery to see the "experimentation room." José opens two large barn doors to reveal a chamber gleaming with more than fifty small tanks and vats of various sizes. Lining the walls are panels of multicolored buttons, switches, and gauges.

"This is to make life more interesting. Wine constantly changes, so if you work with wine, you need to keep changing, too," he says enthusiastically, leaning in toward me to make his point. As a North American Scot, I have an emu's sense of personal space, so I tilt backward a little from the waist for every inch he moves closer in this cross-cultural conversational tango.

A tireless tester of winemaking techniques, José has tried micro-oxygenation, roto-fermenters, mechanical fermentation aids, and many other methods. He was the first producer to market a modern style of tempranillo in Argentina, and now he's experimenting with thirty-five varieties. His passion for the grapes is as sensual as it is intellectual. As we pass a large basket of pressed grapes, he grabs a bunch and extends his hand for me to smell the hedonistic perfume of crushed berries. Violently purple-black juice seeps between his fingers and drips to the ground.

As we continue around the winery, José greets every employee by name and *como estas?* Of the more than four hundred people who work here, most are locals who have been living in the vineyards since the vines were planted. Unlike many wineries, here they're employed year-round, not just for the harvest. José also believes in education: if new employees haven't completed high school, they attend school in the evenings at his expense.

"Terroir is as much about people as soil," he observes. "Making wine isn't just farming with fancy adjectives; it's about the deep connection between people and vines."

As the sun softens with evening, José invites me to join him for an *asado*, the traditional Argentine cookout. Most families in this beef-loving country have a barbecue in their backyard. Gauchos, the country's nomadic cowboys, started the tradition. Wherever they camped for the night on the great open grasslands of the pampas, they'd build a campfire and grill the least cooperative member of the herd for dinner.

At his home behind the winery, José lights the old knotty vines on the open grill. No wimpy charcoal briquettes or propane tanks here; the fuel is the old gray canes of the vines. And don't even think about chicken or tofu; beef is at the heart of Argentine cooking. *Parrillas* (steak houses) are to Argentina what cafés are to France, dotting the street corners of Buenos Aires and most small towns.

When families have an asado, they count on a couple of pounds of meat each. In this country of thirty-eight million people, there are two cattle for every person. (Fine with me as long as there's also a case of wine for everyone.) These cattle, which feed on the fertile grasslands, have juicier and more richly marbled meat than their corn-fed North American cousins. They don't have to walk far to feed. The younger the cattle and the less exercise it gets, the less muscle and fiber it develops and the more tender the meat.

The quality of Argentine beef has been recognized for centuries. When Charles Darwin stopped in for a visit two hundred years ago, he wrote in his diary that "the meat is as superior to common beef as venison is to mutton." Favored cuts include *lomo* (sirloin), *asada de tira* (short ribs), *vacio* (flank steak), and *bife de chorizo* (filet mignon). Steaks as thick as telephone directories are served with a sprig of parsley—a risible gesture toward vegetables.

A century ago, Argentine beef held 40 percent of the global export market. Today, it struggles to find a place on the foreign dinner table in an age that deems beef less healthful than white meat and seafood. Surely, Argentina must be a vegetarian's vision of hell: wherever you go, flame-broiled meat.

José and I sit at a small table under a shady trellis of vines while we wait for the burning wood to turn into coals hot enough for grilling. He hands me a glass of Santa Julia Malbec, with its heady scents of woodland berries and raspberry jam spread on warm bread.

"People don't care who makes Coca-Cola, but they *are* curious about who makes wine," he says. "They want to know the story behind it, the people, where it comes from, and how it's different from other wines."

Despite this, several years ago, José's Fuzion Malbec had the kind of product launch that Coke and Pepsi dream of. In just one year, it had sold five hundred thousand cases, the fastest ever sales spike in North America. A number of factors contributed to the wine's success: it was priced under $10, had a name that was easy to pronounce, and had an elegant label with lots of white space, which consumer tests show makes a wine look pricier. Most important, the wine tasted twice as expensive as it cost. Wine critics, always on the hunt for an undiscovered gem, gave it lots of free publicity. Fuzion sold so well that it didn't just take market share from similar wines; it brought new consumers into the wine market.

"There's no recipe for making wine," José tells me. This comment reminds me of the question from artist Rajinder Singh, whose work adorns the winery: "What is the numerical equivalent of lovely?"

"You can't make wine just to make money," he says earnestly, touching my arm gently. "Wine is personal; you need passion."

José certainly doesn't lack for passion. In 2005, at the age of fifty-one, he and his son Sebastian climbed nearby Aconcagua, the highest peak in the Andes at 22,851 feet.

"I live five hundred feet from the mountain, I wake up to it every day, my vines live in its shadow," he muses. "How could I not be curious enough to get closer to it?

"To climb a mountain is to know another dimension of time and space. It is 170 million years old and four thousand times larger than you are. You realize just how small and fleeting your life is. Better do what you can with the time you have!"

The smell from the burning wood wafts into our glasses. It's time to put the glistening slabs of meat onto the grill. José turns them gently in his hands and pats them with rock salt, as if to reassure them. Fine-grained salt would be absorbed completely into the meat, making it too salty. The Argentines also don't drown their beef in sugary barbecue sauces; salt is all the seasoning they use because it brings out the flavor without smothering the tender meat.

Once the juices start oozing, the meat on the grill is turned just once. In contrast to the quick searing of North American barbecues, asado is a slow cooking method that takes at least an hour, with several sets grilled in succession. The social event usually lasts an entire evening. Our filets hiss and sizzle, sending a smoky signal up to my reptilian brain that triggers ancestral memories of carnivorous feasts.

Finally, the meat is ready. José sets a large plate of steaming beef in front of me. I bite into a filet, as soft as freshly baked bread, and it falls apart in my mouth. I don't even have to chew; I just rub the meat against the roof of my mouth. Its sweet, slightly nutty flavor ripples across my tongue, its juices mingling with the figgy-rich notes of the malbec.

Slicing into my third piece, I realize that malbec was made for beef: the dark berry flavors pierce and soak the savory strands of meat. And the extra antioxidants make this defibrillation red the perfect foil for meat. Malbec is a knife-and-fork wine that not only suits anything grilled but also pairs well with tangy dishes, such as pasta in tomato sauce, pepperoni pizza, hard cheeses, and lamb with rosemary and thyme.

Malbec is a wonderfully in-between wine, more supple than cabernet sauvignon, more robust than merlot. Its velvet bite dances with the heat of Latin dishes, such as the ones José sets out before us now: tender pork with a spicy chimichurri sauce (a mix of spices such as oregano, garlic, parsley, paprika, pepper, and thyme in fresh balsamic vinegar); piping hot *chorizo* blood sausages; and warm empanadas, half-moon, scalloped-edged pastries filled with savory meat, onions, and cheese. These were baked in the igloo-shaped adobe oven beside the grill, another traditional feature of Argentine backyards.

As the evening deepens, the cool, limpid air of the mountain peaks slides in around us, and the trees and grass start to darken. José brings out a traditional dessert made by his eighty-three-year-old mother: slices of queen's jelly and the local Mantecosco cheese. It goes beautifully with his Malamado, a late-harvest blend of torrontés and viognier perfumed with ripe apricots and honeysuckle.

"No one retires in this company," he says, smiling and shrugging. "For us, work is a way to live; there is no separation between them. My father taught me that freedom is the equation between what you produce and what you need. If you don't need too much, you will always be free."

That's music to my cheapskate ears. But I think about how far away I am from my husband, my son, my life. It's a happy sadness I get when I travel on my own. Yet it's only when I'm away from my creature comforts that I'm more alert, more vulnerable, more prone to emotional cloudbursts. That's when I'm using more of my senses and synapses to write a good story.

Right now I'm flush with this emptiness as I lean back in my chair and take another drink of the malbec. The day's thoughts and worries and conversations fade into evening quiet. The sun drenches the mountains in sliding pinks and reds and then finally disappears behind their black-haloed peaks.

Field Notes from a
Wine Cheapskate

INSIDER TIPS

- Take a chance on lesser-known grapes. Varieties like malbec just don't have the brand awareness and cachet of cabernet sauvignon and merlot. Therefore, producers must compete more aggressively on price. In this book, you'll discover lots of grapes that you may not have heard of before.

- Go for regions where the currency gives you an advantage. Canadian and American dollars are much stronger than Argentina's pesos, so that builds in another discount on the import cost.

- Look for late bloomers: regions that entered the North American wine market after a number of other countries had already established themselves. These newcomers have to prove themselves, in terms of both price and quality.

WINERIES VISITED

Bodega Catena Zapata: www.catenawines.com
Bodega Norton: www.norton.com.ar
Cheval des Andes: www.chevaldesandes.com
Zuccardi Family Wines: www.familiazuccardi.com

BEST VALUE WINES

Alamos Malbec (Catena)
Alamos Torrontés (Catena)
Catena Zapata Malbec Cabernet
Fuzion Malbec Shiraz (Zuccardi)
Norton Malbec
Norton Torrontés
Santa Julia Malbec (Zuccardi)*
Zuccardi Malbec Series A

*My first pick for my own Friday dinner.

TOP VALUE PRODUCERS

Alamos	Luigi Bosca
Alta Vista	O. Fournier
Argento	Masi Tupungato
Benmarco	Michel Torino
Chakana	Navarro Correas
Conquista	Piattelli
Crios De Susana Balbo	Punto Final
Dominio Del Plata	Santa Julia
Doña Paula	Terrazas de los Andes
Finca El Origen	Tilia
Finca Flichman	Trapiche
Fuzion	Trivento
Gascón	Urban Eco
Graffigna	Vinecol
Kaiken	Viña Cobos
La Posta	

FRIDAY DINNER FOR A WINE CHEAPSKATE

You'll find José Alberto Zuccardi's recipes for the asado that we shared at www.nataliemaclean.com/food.

José Alberto's Best Barbecued Beef

Zuccardi Family Chimichurri Sauce

Warm Fuzion Empanadas

Emma's Queen Jelly

TERRIFIC PAIRINGS

The malbec grape produces wines that stylistically fall between cabernet sauvignon and merlot, with more plummy richness and roundness than cabernet but firmer tannins and structure than merlot. Signature aromas include plums, blackberries, black cherries, spices, earth, and wood smoke. Here are some of my favorite malbec pairings:

Barbecued beef ribs

Barbecued pork spareribs

Beef cooked in red wine

Beef stroganoff

Bison steak

Bittersweet chocolate

Braised lamb shanks

Brisket

Casseroles and stews

Cheddar cheese

Hamburgers, meat loaf

Herb-roasted lamb

Herb-rubbed roast chicken

Meat lovers' or pepperoni pizza

Peppercorn steak

Prime rib

Rack of lamb with rosemary

Rib roast with a coffee and
   pepper rub

Roast game

Spaghetti and meat balls   Steak fajitas
Steak and kidney pie   Venison

RESOURCES

For more information on Argentine wines and malbec:

*Vino Argentino: An Insider's Guide to the Wines and Wine
     Country of Argentina* by Laura Catena
The Wines of Argentina, Chile, and Latin America by
     Christopher Fielden
Wine Routes of Argentina by Alan Young
Wines of Argentina: www.winesofargentina.org/en
The Real Argentina: www.therealargentina.com
French Malbec: www.french-malbec.com
South World Wine Society: www.southworldwine.com/
     contactus.html

RELATED READING

The following books, while seemingly unrelated to the main subject
matter of this chapter, provided some enjoyable reading before, during, and after my travels:

Borges Collected Fictions by Jorge Luis Borges
Evita: The Real Life of Eva Perón by Nicholas Fraser and Marysa
     Navarro

SEVEN

SATURDAY

A Storm of Pleasure in Every Port

IF YOU REALLY want to know port, you can't loll about in the comfort of Oporto. You must go upriver to the wild heart of the Douro Valley of northern Portugal. Forget driving, though: the twisting mountain roads take forever. The best way is this ancient train, which left the coastal city an hour ago and is now wheezing its way past sheer granite walls. Over the millennia, the Douro River has carved a gorge that cuts some two thousand feet into the rock. As we follow the river deeper into the valley, I feel very Joseph Conrad on this May morning.

Black vultures circle in the sky above this remote, rugged landscape; more than a thousand square miles of cliffs dare anything to survive on them. The vines barely clinging to the rocky soil look as though they're threatening to jump. Others are abandoned, both men and plants having given up in exhaustion years ago. Nature teaches humility. Don't visit the Douro if you're lonely; it'll make you desolate. But for those who find some part of themselves in silence, it's perfect.

Boom! I hear an explosion in the distance, then another. It sounds like the invading forces are only a mile out. However, this is the echo of modernity on the Douro: they use dynamite to build new vineyard terraces into the rock face. Farming these steep slopes is expensive: it can cost up to $75,000 to develop one acre for Darwinianly low yields. Several wineries now use laser-guided bulldozers that calculate the angles of the slope precisely. However, a bulldozer still occasionally topples down the precipice into the water.

True port is only made here, in this valley, which stretches about eighty miles west from the central mountains of Spain down to the Atlantic Ocean. The climate is perfect for these grapes: the Serra do Marão mountains block the cool, moist air from the Atlantic, creating hot, arid growing conditions. The sun's intensity infuses port grapes with the extra ripening they need to sustain their flavor for decades. Port grapes love to bake in this ovenlike heat that can soar to 115°F. If they could, they'd probably slather on the suntan oil and roll over.

Although port isn't Europe's oldest wine style, the Douro is the world's oldest wine appellation: it was demarcated in 1756. For almost two hundred years, longboats with square sails and oars called *barcos rabelos* carried port down the Douro to Vila Nova de Gaia, at the mouth of the Atlantic. Trains and trucks have since replaced the boats—as well as the oarsmen who drank the port as they rowed and then topped up the barrels with river water.

The narrow cobblestone streets of Vila Nova de Gaia are lined with the historic port houses, which sit atop more than a hundred thousand barrels sleeping in their cellars. Some won't be moved for another fifty years. The wine is brought here to be aged beside the ocean because it's more humid than in the Douro, so there's less evaporation. Still, the aromas of caramelized alcohol and spiced oak waft out of the doorways, luring visitors into these alcoholic candy shops.

This charming town sits across the river from Oporto, the country's largest city after Lisbon and the one after which port is named. Oporto derived its name from the Latin word *portus*, or "haven." Legally, the wine can only be called port after it ships out of Oporto and leaves Portugal.

Now I have to confess that I've always enjoyed port a little more than I should—it brings me to my bliss point more quickly than any other wine. The high alcohol, at about 19 percent, helps, but its charm is more than that: the tangerine tints in the glass, the toffee richness on the tongue, the fireside warmth it creates inside you. You drink port to come alive in a time and a geography unknown to you.

I love those early October evenings when a chill in the air outside is countered by the warm contentment of a good meal inside. The dishes have been cleared; the rosy conversation becomes quieter with comfortable silences. You cradle a glass bowl of amber liquid in your palm. All that's missing is an Irish setter sleeping at your feet.

My favorite after-dinner consolation is to sink into a leather chair with a big book and a small glass of port—or, more often, a small book and a big glass of port. I also love finding references to port in literature. In George Meredith's eighteenth-century novel *The Egoist*, a professor tries to expose his daughter's fiancé as a fraud by tempting him with hundred-year-old port. As they descend into his cellar, he discusses what makes it different from other wines, such as Rhône Valley hermitage, German riesling (hock), and burgundy:

> Port is deep-sea deep. It is organic in conception, like a classic tragedy. An ancient Hermitage has the light of the antique. Neither of Hermitage nor of Hock can you say that it is the blood

of those long years, retaining the strength of youth with the wisdom of age. To Port for that! Port is our noblest legacy! I cherish the fancy that Port speaks the sentences of wisdom, Burgundy sings the inspired ode. Or put it that Port is the Homeric hexameter, Burgundy the Pindaric dithyramb. Pindar astounds. But his elder brings us the more sustaining cup. One is a fountain of prodigious ascent. One is the unsounded purple sea of marching billows.

It's a lovely ode to port, but she married the guy anyway. Another favorite passage comes from George Saintsbury's early-twentieth-century *Notes on a Cellar-Book*:

He drank it as a port should be drunk—a trial of the bouquet; a slow sip; a rather larger and slightly less slow one, and so on, but never a gulp; and during the drinking his face exchanged its usual bluff and almost brusque aspect for the peculiar blandness—which good wine gives to worthy countenances. And when he set the glass down he said, softly but cordially, "That won't do any harm."

It's such a seductive wine that the writer Samuel Johnson struggled to keep his daily ration to just four pints. And after one day in Portugal, I'm admiring the man's restraint. So it pains me to think that many people mistake port for a liqueur or a spirit because of its high alcohol and sweetness. In fact, it's a fortified wine like sherry. It starts off like regular wine, and then is made stronger with brandy. That's why I often enjoy it on a Saturday evening, when I don't have to get up early the next day.

Port also shares the dilemma of champagne: both terms are often used generically—though wrongly—for all fortified or sparkling wine, respectively. True, other countries do make port-style wines that offer good value, but they don't have the complexity and depth of flavor of true port. Like the Champenois, the Portuguese are trying to protect the name *port* as a trademark. In response, clever vintners in other regions have devised alternative names, such as starboard, export, or trop, which is *port* spelled backward—not exactly great marketing when it means "too much" in French.

However, this background can't help me with my current task, wickedly devised by George Thomas David Sandeman, the seventh-generation of the House of Sandeman, founded in 1790. A trim fifty-eight-year-old in a bespoke suit, George is the latest in a long line of master port blenders in his family firm. Despite his aristocratic bearing, he is quite a bon vivant, who almost bounces on the spot with enthusiasm as he talks. He's set a challenge for me: match his sample wine by blending the contents of three unmarked beakers of port, in the right proportions, by only smelling and tasting them.

Is this even possible, I wonder. Over the centuries, the Sandemans have perfected the art of blending dozens of wines from thirty or more vintages for their renowned tawny ports. The house style is one of elegance, finesse, power, and balance. Creating it takes years of daily practice to master: George tastes samples from his barrels every day so he can track the wines' maturity. If I tried to do that, they'd find me lying between barrels in the first week.

"How long did it take you to get an instinctive feel for blending?" I ask him.

"Oh, about twelve years," he says cheerfully. "But I'm sure you'll get it this afternoon." Beside him, his young assistant, Maria, muffles a laugh.

George hands me a white lab coat, an empty wine glass, a measuring cup, and a sample of the port that he's blended, with an encouraging nod. "The very first wine you make as a producer is the easiest," he explains. "It's every wine after that that's difficult because you're trying to keep the house style consistent. You have to remove all vintage variability and the differences in the aging capacity of each wine. There's very little room for error; consumers expect to taste the same style each year."

I feel my old nemesis, exam anxiety, rise in my gut, imaging the likely outcomes of this exercise. To calm myself, I mentally run through what I know about the Sandemans and about making port in general. I've heard that George's great-great-grandfather discovered the missing magic ingredient of port. He added a quarter barrel of brandy to a barrel of rough red wine before all the sugar in the grapes had been converted to alcohol. Since the brandy's high alcohol (77 percent) killed the remaining yeast cells, it stopped fermentation, resulting in a sweet wine with about 19 percent alcohol. Aging the result for twenty to thirty years ensured that the spirit was well integrated into the wine and that there was no burning sensation from the alcohol when consumed. This fortified wine also kept well during the long journey to foreign markets.

When it comes to aging, there are two broad categories of port: those aged in oak barrels and those aged in bottles. Wood-aged ports include white, ruby, tawny, and colheita; bottle-aged ports include vintage, late bottle vintage, and crusted. The result is two very different styles, which I think of as molten toffee versus primordial fruit. Those of the former style are aged in barrels, where their fruitiness makes a lovely trade with the barrel's toffee richness. Almost all wood-aged ports are blends of different vineyard parcels and vintages. The latter style comes from bottle aging, which preserves its core fruit character.

As I "evaluate" the blending for these samples, George watches me with merry but shrewd eyes. When I sip them, I taste a signature flavor that runs through them, yet they're also quite different from one another. How the hell am I going to do this? Where do I begin? I pour myself another comforting sample and gulp it down, then I whip out my notepad with a serious flourish and write down, "Buy Kleenex and toilet paper."

"You want to select your base wine first," George suggests. "That's your entrée wine; the other two will be condiments. Careful with your selection, though: you don't want to make the house style impossible to match next year."

Encouraged (and unnerved), I choose the second sample, my favorite, from the spectacular 2007 vintage. It has a generous nose that delivers rich aromas of almond and caramel, with just a hint of clementine, which adds a zing and lift to its toffeed heart.

"So should I make the blend mostly from the base wine and add only a dash of the other two?" I ask.

"Try it and see what happens," George says. "Remember that even a percent or two matters when your blend makes a hundred thousand cases."

Well, that really takes the pressure off. Not. I decide to try 70 percent of the 2007, then 20 percent of the 2006, and 10 percent of the 2008. I measure the proportions in a test tube, swirl the wines in a beaker to mix them, then I pour a sample of my new "blend" into all of our glasses. It tastes terrific, but nothing like George's sample, which is subtle and nuanced. The power and fruitiness of the 2007 has made my attempt far too exuberant.

George consoles me: it's an easy trap to fall into, he says, but an important one to avoid. Relying too heavily on one fine vintage would leave the business stranded in future years, when the vintage isn't as good.

I start over, swaying gently on my feet, as more port splashes on my lab coat. By this time, I've consumed more port than I've blended, so measuring the quantities is getting tricky. My effort to be scientifically thorough seems to be coming at the cost of basic precision. This time, quite uncharacteristically, I choose restraint. I stay my hand on the 2007, using only 20 percent of it, along with 30 percent of the 2008 and 50 percent of the 2006 as the base wine.

I swirl and pour into our glasses, and we all taste it. At this point, I imagine George exclaiming, "This is good—as a topping for ice cream! You fraud, get out!"

Instead, George asks Maria, "Should we tell her?"

Tell me what, I wonder. That I'm a complete idiot? I had thought my sample smelled a little closer to George's this time, but I bite my tongue rather than blather my neuroses.

"You've got it," George says, grinning.

"I've got what?" I ask, thinking anosmia or a cold sore on my upper lip.

"This is our house blend," he says. Maria is no longer smirking.

"No!"

"Yes."

Wow, I can't believe that I've stumbled onto the vinous equivalent of the Caramilk secret.

George smiles at me and takes my glass. "Good work," he says. "Let's go to the lounge."

I'm all for that; after all this tasting, I need a stiff drink. On the way downstairs, we pass a small museum with a collection of weird and wonderfully shaped port bottles from the sixteenth and seventeenth centuries. In those days, before brand names, labels, and advertising, it was the name of the buyer that was inscribed on the seal before shipping. Sandeman was an innovator in this regard, too, the first to create its own trademark in 1805, using an iron brand to stamp its barrels before shipping.

Sandeman was also among the first wine companies to advertise its wines. In 1928, George's great-grandfather Walter Sandeman bought the rights to "The Don," by the Scottish artist George Mas-siot Brown. The iconic drawing, a silhouetted man wearing a broad-brimmed Spanish hat and a Portuguese cloak, became the world's first wine logo.

Today, the Don is one of the three most recognized booze brands in the world, along with Johnny Walker and Captain Morgan. To me, he looks like a cross between Columbian coffee guy Juan Valdez and that 1950s radio drama *The Shadow*. The Sandeman tour guides wear the same outfit, giving the cellars here a mysterious cloak-and-dagger feel.

"For years, the Don was a flat figure, a cardboard cutout," George explains. "A few years ago, we gave him a makeover: we incorporated movement to his cape, added more three-dimensional shading, and even gave him feet for the first time. We had long meetings about his shoes, which started off looking like Hell's Angels boots, then eventually they morphed into something that was more in character and continues the mystery," he says.

"Some people scoff at brands as banal, but having a well-established brand is a tremendous responsibility to your customers who come back to you year after year, trusting that you'll deliver the experience that they expect."

As we sink into big lounge chairs, I'm reminded of the fine tradition of passing a decanter of port around the table. I've heard that it started with British sailors on those long sea voyages between Portugal and the homeland. Sitting after dinner in the officer's mess, the senior officer passed the decanter to the person on his left, or clockwise from "port to port." I ask George whether this etiquette is still practiced today in modern homes.

"The decanter still circles clockwise, symbolizing the passing of time," George explains. Tradition and manners require the decanter to keep moving from hand to hand, which is why some military decanters had rounded bottoms: they could never be set down. However, if the decanter gets held up anywhere on the table, it's considered bad manners to ask for it directly. The correct form is this:

"Do you know the bishop of Norwich?"

"No, I don't—why?"

"Well, the bishop is a good fellow, but he never passes the port, either."

Cue the forced laughter over the etiquette gaffe, and the decanter starts moving again. Serious drinkers kept the decanter moving around the table all night, and they challenged each other with "no heel-taps"—to finish the dregs so that a second bottle could be opened.

"There's also a practical reason to pass the port to your left," George adds. "Most people are right-handed, so it's easier to serve themselves when the decanter comes from that side."

One of the earliest references to decanting is in *The Iliad*, when Homer describes Hephaestus as pouring wine for the gods "from right to left." More recently, the ritual may come from the ancient Celtic superstition that all circular motions should be in the lucky direction, as they did in carrying a coffin around the grave three times before lowering it.

This reminds me of my favorite Scottish dance, the Highland reel, which I practiced several hours a day for eighteen years as a competitive dancer. (I also have a soft spot for it because it was the event in which I came fifth in the world championships in Scotland.) From left to right, four dancers weave in and out in a figure eight—essentially two connected circles. Like many Celtic symbols, this unending figure eight represented eternity.

Regardless of its origins, I love the tradition because the decanter becomes a little lighter as it passes from hand to hand, like our cares when shared with friends. However, it's the future of port rather than its glorious past that George wants to discuss. He believes that port can update its image by being the key ingredient in mixed cocktails. Wait a minute, port mixed cocktails? Isn't that as sacrilegious as putting ice into a single-malt scotch?

"Consumers are looking for low-alcohol, high-flavor cocktails," George says. "Port delivers that far better than spirits like gin, vodka, and rum. Those who go to bars and clubs are drinking fewer spirit-based cocktails so that they can drive home safely." As well, he points out, cocktails move port away from its old-fashioned ascots-and-monocles image. Mixed drinks adapt port to any season or social situation—on the deck in the summer, for example.

To prove his point, several of those mysteriously cloaked staffers whisk in trays of cocktails. Despite my reservations, I must admit I love his Porto Fizz, a jazzy mix of ruby port and champagne over ice, served in a wine glass and garnished with a slice of orange. The champagne diminishes the port's sweetness and gives the drink an effervescent zip.

Of the various types of port, ruby is the least expensive. It's made from the lowest-quality grapes and is aged only four to six years. The result is a young, fruity, vibrant wine that's ruby in color but lacks the complex depths and aging potential of vintage port. The cold temperatures of Portugal's winter help to precipitate the sediment from the young wine, naturally clarifying it. Then the wine is said to be "fallen bright," a lovely phrase that reminds me of a diamond dusting of snow across this rugged landscape.

George's sangria is equal parts ruby port and fresh orange juice in a long glass. Topping up with Sprite is optional, and I opt not to, of course, to keep the purity and concentration of the cocktail. After all, I still have my professional reputation to uphold, even if I can't stand up.

The crowning cocktail is the Sandeman Royale, a blend of tawny port and Chivas Regal whisky in a cocktail glass. It has a hypnotic fiery orange glow. When I ask about the name, George tells me he christened it after seeing the James Bond movie *Casino Royale*. It's a fitting name for the cocktail—and a fitting close to a day of being shaken, then stirred.

THE NEXT MORNING, I venture farther upriver on the train to meet Rupert Symington, of Symington Family Estates. Fourteen generations of Symingtons have been in the port business since 1652. Today, the family owns more than twenty-five-hundred acres of vineyards and twenty-six quintas (wineries), which produce more than 30 percent of all premium port. The Symingtons are the royal family of port.

The largest and oldest port producers all have British names: Sandeman, Churchill, Croft, and Taylor's, as well as Symington and their brands Graham, Dow, Warre, Cockburn, and Smith Woodhouse. Port may be made in Portugal, but it's a British invention—born of taste, error, and political intrigue. This has always fascinated me because I'm an anglophile, from my Jane Austen bonnet to my Charles Dickens spats. So I dug into several hundred years of history, which I'll summarize in a couple of paragraphs to explain the British connection.

In 1152, Eleanor of Aquitaine, a noblewoman in Bordeaux, whose marriage to Louis VII had recently been annulled, married the Duke of Normandy, Henry Plantagenet, who later became Henry II, making her the queen of England. (For the full story, see *The Lion in Winter*, with Peter O'Toole and Katharine Hepburn.) The Bordelais angled for preferential tax treatment for their wines in the English market. Like most lobbyists before and since, they got what they wanted after a lot of wining and dining. Henry wanted to be king of both countries.

The tax subsidies lasted about three hundred years, until England and France fell out again and went to war. In 1678, William of Orange imposed high taxes on French wine. The death and destruction of war was one thing, but losing their supply of their beloved claret from Bordeaux was really taking things too far. Portugal came to the rescue. In 1703, England signed the Methuen Treaty with Portugal to keep its seaports friendly to the British during the war. In exchange, Portugal won lower import tariffs on all of its products, including wine. British merchants started importing more of the lower-priced port and became the largest shippers of the wine.

As my train pulls into the sleepy, sun-drenched town of Pinhão, I can see Quinta do Bomfim, the most prestigious of Dow's quinta, perched next to the station on the riverbank. Rupert Symington comes out to meet me with a warm greeting. He reminds me of the Duke of Edinburgh, with his impeccable diction and consummate manners. The trim fifty-seven-year-old has two decades of corporate mergers and acquisitions under his Burberry belt, as well as five years as a stockbroker in London and graduate studies at INSEAD, France's most famous business school. He'd be the perfect model for the British Airways annual report photo, showing first-class passengers enjoying a glass of port.

The Quinta House, built by George Warre, of Warre's port, in 1890, is in the style of a Ceylonese tea planter's bungalow. Its walls are lined with sepia photographs of the hardy men and women who first settled this (formerly malarial) valley. Rupert escorts me to the back veranda, where he pours steaming coffee into Wedgwood cups. Like most Symington men, Rupert went to school locally until the age of thirteen, when he was shipped off to boarding school in Yorkshire, England—one known for making men out of boys. Before going on to Oxford for mathematics, he worked at several Australian wineries for a year.

"Running a family business is like managing your own household: it's about keeping harmony with other members, knowing what you can afford, and making ends meet," Rupert says, leaning back on his wicker chair, his steel blue eyes gazing out on the river.

He's referring to the fact that six family members run the business. Rupert's cousin Charles is the vineyard manager and master blender. Dominic oversees North and South American sales with Rupert; Paul manages U.K. sales; Johnny does the same for European sales; and Clare arranges auction sales.

Personally, I can't imagine working with my cousins and siblings all day. But then again, I'm an only child, so I can't imagine living with any siblings at all. So how do six Symingtons manage to work together, let alone keep the business thriving? The old adage about three generations of a family business is make it, spend it, break it.

"We actually like each other, so that helps," Rupert says, smiling. "We've always had consensus on major issues, and we've never taken a vote. We all have the same interest in making good wine. We're all working for our children and our children's children. After all, our reputation today depends on what my father did thirty years ago.

"Negotiants, like our family, were always just shippers of port, not growers and makers of it," he explains. "That's changed with our generation. Now we have much more control over the quality of the product, from start to finish."

Rupert believes that port is best managed by families, since the knowledge of how to make it is passed down from one generation to the next. As well, the long production cycle of ports—tawnies, for example, can be aged for up to forty years—ties up cash flow, making it unappealing to shareholders who want a return next year, not next generation. Producers are legally bound to carry huge inventories; their stock at the beginning of the year must be three times what it sold the previous year. This law, designed to prevent producers from flooding the market with young wine and driving prices down, also means tying up huge inventories and cash. This fact may be why several international conglomerates, such as Seagram's, Diageo, and Pernod Ricard/Allied Domecq, have divested their port interests in the last five years.

"It's a business for the tortoise, not the hare," Rupert says. "A family firm means that you never lock up the shop at five p.m. and go home. The business is also your home; in your mind, you never leave it.

He takes me down to the dock, where we jump into his speedboat. Out on the Douro, the water is sapphire blue, a liquid mirror of the sky. Rupert kicks up the speed and leans into the wind at the steering wheel as I tighten my grip on the edge of the boat. The summer heat has clamped down over the land like a steam-cooker lid: wavy transparent fireballs roll across the rocky hills. Words like *languid*, *torpor*, and *parched* hang in my mind until they wilt. The feral beauty of the scrub on the sun-baked slopes makes me want to lift language from the landscape, but the words melt and dissolve in the jet stream behind us.

Upriver, we slow down to watch some water tortoises warming themselves on rocks at the river's edge. Rupert laughs at the sight of them and tells me a story about his grandfather, an enthusiastic naturalist. He asked his assistant to collect one or two tortoises for him to study. After a week, he asked if the tortoises were ready. The answer: "Sorry, sir, we've only managed to collect 99 so far, but I'm sure we can get you 102."

For most of its history, the river dried up in the summer. Teams of oxen would pull the long *rabelos* boats over the riverbed of rocks for eighty miles down to Vila Nova de Gaia. To control this problem, several dams and locks were built in the 1950s. Now Rupert pulls the boat up to the towering Valeira dam: a 157-foot wall of steel. Someone far above must have spotted us; the wall starts to slowly creak open, like the portcullis of a medieval castle.

We glide into the dam like a water bug in a giant bathtub that can hold fifty-eight million gallons of water. As the wall shuts behind us, we're enclosed in silence and shadow. Then water starts to gush over the wall in front of us. We rise with the water to the equivalent of a ten-story building. Rupert ties the boat to a buoy and tells me about some inebriated tourists who once made the mistake of tying their yacht to the ladder on the wall. As they swigged their port and sang out of tune, the nose of the boat slowly started to point downward as the ladder submerged under the water. By the time they realized what was happening, they had to jump off the now-capsized boat.

After going through the dam, we continue upriver for about twenty minutes, then dock at another Dow property, Quinta da Senhora da Ribeira. I expect this flower-trimmed, white-washed winery to house the traditional *lagars*: the rectangular stone basins that are filled with grapes at harvest. Most are about three feet deep, so that the grapes sit thigh-high for the workers to crush them by foot. (Though a few cunning vintners built their lagars a little deeper so that women had to hitch their skirts up a little higher.)

A dozen men and women would stand side by side in the vat, linking their arms over one another's shoulders. Then they'd slowly march in unison down the length of the sixteen-foot basin to the sound of an accordion and to someone who called the beat. This lasted for three hours and was called the *corte* (cut). The last hour, called *liberdade* (freedom), was marginally more fun, as the treaders are free to dance, flirt, and sing folks songs.

Treading grapes (the Portuguese and French call it *pigeages* for "feet") is the best and gentlest way to extract as much color and flavor as possible from them. The human toe, instep, and heel are extremely effective tools for crushing grape flesh without breaking the seeds, which release bitter tannins. Wine drinkers worried about contaminants like athlete's foot can relax; the process of fermentation cleanses any unmentionables.

I try to imagine myself participating in a grape stomp, the feeling of slippery, squishy grape flesh against my own skin, cold where the fruit has just entered the vat and warm where it's fermenting. I smell the perfumed purple juice splashing my thighs under a hiked-up peasant dress and up across my arms and cheeks. It reminds me of *A Walk in the Clouds*, and the only scene in that ridiculous movie with Keanu Reeves that had any wine merit.

Perhaps grape stomping is how young people met each other in the Douro in the absence of Match.com. However, it sounds like too much work even for love—and I hate being sticky. Labor shortages and costs are also factors for their diminished use.

However, everything here is modern. Like the old-fashioned longboats, stomping grapes is another tradition no longer economically viable. Rupert explains the economics as we enter the winery. "It takes sixty people three hours to tread the grapes in one lagar," he says. "That gives us 1,200 cases, or 14,400 bottles. At 20 euros per person, that's 1,200 euros for just one vat. At this quinta, we crush twenty-five vats for the whole harvest; it could easily cost as much as 30,000 euros, or $40,000." He has a scary mind for figures that I find unsettling, so I just squint and nod, as though I'm mentally checking his calculations.

Not only is cost a factor, so too is convincing tired workers—who've just spent all day under this hot sun picking grapes—to come in for another four hours of marching around a vat. So treading grapes is a dying tradition: less than 5 percent of port today is made using this technique. Silicon and steel are replacing flesh and stone.

In 1998, instead of simply adopting a standard automated crusher, the Symingtons invented a robotic treader to simulate the shape and action of the human foot. They measured the motion and pressure exerted by the human foot, its temperature, and the average time a person takes to tread from one end of the vat to the other. The "feet" are large, flat steel paddles attached to a rail above the temperature-controlled tank, moving up and down on the grapes—their timing controlled by a computer program rather than an accordion. Silicon pads are attached to the bottoms of the feet, made of the same material as the rubber bungs that seal wine barrels, so they impart no color or flavor to the grape must—the squishy mass of pulp and juice starting to ferment.

In traditional lagars, it takes about two hours to run off the wine and shovel out the skins after the treading is finished, during which time the wine continues to ferment—meaning it can easily dry out and lose its fruit freshness. As a result, winemakers traditionally emptied the vat a few hours sooner than they preferred, reducing the optimal contact time between skins and juice. The mechanized vat, though, takes only five minutes, allowing for a longer soaking, with greater color and flavor going into the juice from the skins.

"This is the most significant technological advance for producing port in half a century," Rupert explains, showing me the gleaming steel basin and computer panel. The family now operates seventeen robotic lagars, and they are in widespread use in other Douro wineries. "The paddles' precisely calibrated pressure ruptures the grape skins, so they impart their color and flavor to the juice before fermentation starts."

This is more important in making port than in making most wines because copious amounts of tannin, flavor, and color must seep out of the skins and into the juice quickly, since fermentation is stopped halfway through with the addition of brandy. Port juice only has about thirty-six hours in contact with the skins, compared to five or six days for dry red wines.

Those massive tannins in port bond with the color and flavor elements so that the latter doesn't fall out of the wine along with other sediment—insoluble particles that settle to the bottom of the wine bottle over time. If too much color and flavor precipitates out of the wine, you're left with a faded, flavorless, high-alcohol drink. These depth charges of tannin give the wine "grip." Port must have a gathered density of tannin at its core that allows it to hang together for decades, which is why most ports are monstrous to drink before they've matured at twenty to thirty years or more.

Back in the 1600s, these rough young wines were called blackstrap and sold off to undiscriminating drinkers. Even today, tasting young port is like sensory waterboarding: you're almost drowning in high alcohol, extreme sweetness, and exaggerated fruit flavor. It's like gargling with blackberry-flavored vodka. After ten samples, you just want it to stop—and you'll tell whoever's leading the tasting whatever he wants to hear.

Rupert shows me Quinta da Senhora's barrel room, where we taste several ports. We start with the 2008 Vintage Port, a black core of mouthwatering plums, currants, and blackberries wrapped in vanilla smoke. It's still just a baby, so there's a tarry grip running through the middle. Nothing that a couple of decades won't solve.

The 1991 Dow's Vale do Bomfim Vintage Port, up next, seduces me with its cedary tobacco and truffled blackberry depths. It reminds me of the British wine merchant who wrote in 1754 that port should feel like "liquid fire in the stomach, burn like inflamed gunpowder; and have the tint of ink, the sugar of Brazil in sweetness, and the spices of India in aromatic flavor."

To me, this port is a voyage of spicy aromas and images. Acidity, alcohol, and tannin are the three-pronged scaffolding to hold the fruit vibrancy in place. In this age of instant messaging and gratification, it's pleasantly disjointing when someone comments (as Rupert does now) that even the 1927 is still a little young.

In case you're wondering, "vintage port" doesn't literally translate to "old port," even though it does age well. Vintage port is made from a single year rather than from many years, like tawny port. That year is always written on the label. Port and champagne are the only wines whose producers declare a vintage rather than just dating their wines every year. Port producers declare the vintage about eighteen months after harvest, once they assess the quality of the wines aging in the barrels. Usually no more than two or three years per decade are declared for port, and they are the very best years. Dow, for example, has declared a vintage in only twenty-five years of the last century. They're proud to be picky. The result is that vintage port accounts for just 2 percent of all the port made, and as you might expect, it's the most expensive.

In other years, when the weather hasn't been ideal so it's not worthy of declaring a vintage, some winemakers create a single-quinta port from the grapes in their best vineyards that year. Some of the most coveted include Dow's Quinta do Bomfim, Quinta do Noval National, Graham's Malvedos, and Quinta do Vesuvio.

The Douro has hundreds of microclimates, so any winemaker can declare a vintage independent of neighboring estates. However, in the second year after every harvest, the national Port Wine Institute must approve the declaration by tasting samples. When climatic conditions are so good that most producers have a great year, as they did in 2003, the vintage is "universally declared." Some of the best vintages for port over the last eighty years include 1931, 1945, 1950, 1963, 1970, 1977, 1980, 1983, 1985, 1991, 1992, 1994, 1997, 2000, 2003, and 2007.

Of all the age-worthy wines in the world, vintage port is the most talented. That's why so many people choose it when they lay down a case of the birth vintage for a child, grandchild, or the attentive, young trophy wife who stays by their side until their last respirator gasp. Lucky heirs get to collect this stash on their twenty-first birth-day (the grandchildren, not the trophy widow, who is presumably a few years older).

Usually, great aging potential in wine means premium prices: think Bordeaux, Burgundy, and Tuscany. Port is the exception, though, being often half the price, or less, of other coveted collectible wines. Why? History. The Portuguese have always priced their wines much lower than other prestigious regions and have yet to climb the price ladder that their longevity might command. Granted, a good bottle of port isn't cheap compared to, say, a Chilean cabernet, but among benchmark wines of the world, it's a bargain.

The one downside to vintage port is inseparable from the way it's made: that sludge at the bottom of the bottle. Unlike other wines, which are filtered, vintage ports can throw a sediment of up to an inch. (I love that phrase, "throw a sediment," as it makes me think that the wine is having a temper tantrum inside the bottle.) The sediment helps the wine to mature and gives it greater depth of flavor over the years. Other ports are filtered, which can decrease their ability to age and strip some of their fresh fruit character.

All ports, like all other wines, should be cellared on their side to keep the cork moist, at 70 percent humidity and about 55°F to 65°F. Older, unlabeled vintage ports have a white mark on one side of the bottle to indicate which way should face up when you lay the bottle down. If not, keep the label faceup. This ensures that the crust of sediment settles on one side, which makes decanting it easier.

Before I open a bottle of vintage port, I stand it upright for one day or two to let the sediment gradually settle at the bottom of the bottle rather than mixing throughout the wine, making it bitter tasting. I remove old corks gently: they can be dry and crumbly. For these corks, I sometimes use port tongs to open the bottle. I heat the tongs until hot, then clamp them around the bottle neck for a couple of minutes just above the shoulder, but below the cork. I remove the tongs and put a cold wet cloth on the same spot. The rapid temperature change makes the glass break cleanly across the neck, sparing me the struggle with the cork itself.

Once the bottle is open, I pour the wine in a slow, continuous motion into a mesh strainer over a decanter or jug. This catches the heaviest crust. When I see the black silt of sediment edging toward the neck of the bottle, I stop pouring and discard the rest—or I put it on my fern. Lighting a candle or standing a flashlight upright under the neck of the bottle helps me see when this trail is getting close to the opening.

If there's still a lot of sediment, I pour the wine from the first decanter into a second, filtering out the smaller debris with a cheesecloth. Even a nylon stocking—preferably unused—works. I just don't use paper coffee filters, as they can add unwanted flavors. I usually end up splashing port on myself whenever I do this. However, I'm comforted by the memory of Julia Child. In one of her 1950s television cooking shows, she drops the chicken she's stuffing on the floor. With her customary panache, she picks it up and tells viewers not to worry: "Only you know what happens in your kitchen!"

Fortunately, all this decanting fuss is necessary only for vintage and crusted ports because they're aged in the bottle and so keep their sediment. All other ports are aged in barrels and then filtered before bottling. As a result, they're ready to drink as soon as you open them and don't need decanting. They also last longer than vintage ports once opened, having already been exposed to air in the barrel and so being more resistant to oxidation. I enjoy tawny ports for up to a month or two after opening them. However, vintage port is best consumed within a day or two. So those decanters of dark vintage port that you see in movies have likely long-since turned to vinegar.

We then taste the 2001 Graham's Late Bottled Vintage, which

oozes decadent black fruit wrapped in pliable smoky leather. Late bottled vintage (LBV) has some of the character of vintage port, but it's more accessible and affordable. LBV blends wine from one vintage that has been aged four to six years in the vat (longer than vintage port) before being bottled. The bottle has two dates on it: the year of the harvest and the year it was bottled. I hold my glass up to the sunlight slanting through the cellar door and watch the amethyst droplets slide slowly down the glass.

I wish I had a Mars bar right now. I wouldn't dare confess this to Rupert, but their chocolate-coated nougat layers are irresistible with LBV port. Another favorite indulgence, Skor, is best paired with tawny port. My hedonistic fantasy is to layer three Skor bars and marinate-melt them in my mouth with a twenty-year-old tawny.

The Dow's Crusted Port has an elemental taste of earth and spice, along with a volcanic warmth that gains momentum as it slides down my throat. (Spit out this wine? You must be kidding.) Crusted port, as the name implies, isn't filtered, so it also throws a sediment that must be decanted. Unlike vintage port, though, this style is a blend of two or three years, aged for two years in the barrel, then bottled and aged for another two to three years. It gives you a mature wine taste without having to wait ten to fifteen years, as you do for vintage port.

As Rupert and I taste, we discuss the market for port. There are two big challenges. First, port, like champagne, suffers from its seasonal and occasional associations. I call it the Christmas-cake dilemma: both wines are pigeonholed with the holidays, and we forget to drink them at other times of the year. In fact, more than 60 percent of port is sold in the six weeks before Christmas. Second, sales have been almost flat for more than a decade. Much of that has to do with the drink's image: tradition isn't exactly the sexiest marketing angle.

"We can't just sell to retired generals and bankers in their clubs," Rupert observes. Port buyers are dying off—or as he puts it more delicately, "The consumer is not being renewed. We need to attract new customers without scaring off the old ones."

Rupert should know; the Symingtons are also the largest producers of Portugal's other fortified wine, madeira, now mostly relegated to sauces. The lesson from madeira and sherry: innovate or die.

"There are more taste barriers for madeira and sherry than port," he explains. "Port is easy to like immediately, with its flavors of toffee, toasted almond, and caramel. To a novice palate, sherry can have a bitter taste, and madeira can taste baked. We need to take a lesson from whisky, especially single-malt scotch. They've marketed successfully to a younger generation and made the drink part of a daily repertoire."

Two of the trendy new Symington ports are Dow's Midnight and Warre's Otima, which have won prizes for their marketing and bottle design. Dow's Midnight has a sleek, elongated form, and Otima looks like a perfume bottle. You might say the redesign is overdue: the shape hasn't changed since 1775, when the Portuguese created the first cylindrical wine bottles that we know today. (The French borrowed the innovation and the concept of vintage dating: their first was the 1787 Château-Lafite from Bordeaux.)

Other producers are also trying to keep up with the current century. Another port family, Taylor's, launched the first pink port under their Croft label several years ago. My instinctive response: could there be a better way to raise the antimarketing hackles of a woman wine writer? I imagined it would taste like a patronizing cotton-candy slap on the palate. The company described it as rosé-style port, which to me sounded as contradictory as Manolo Blahnik sneakers. Then I tried it and, grudgingly, had to admit that it was pretty good. It tasted like the lightest essence of port with wild raspberries, especially when served chilled over ice with a twist of orange. It reminded me of hot summer nights when I'd open the fridge freezer and stand in its cold embrace for a few minutes before hauling out another tub of mint chocolate chip Häagen-Dazs.

Traditionally, women didn't even drink port. After dinner, they'd retire to the drawing room to discuss domestic issues as they sipped on sherry. The men lingered around the dining room table, drank port, puffed cigars, and decided how to run the world. So I was surprised to learn that sales figures refute this cultural image: worldwide, women consume 47 percent of the port sold. In France and Belgium, women actually drink more than men because they enjoy it as an aperitif on the rocks. Chilling reduces the perception of heat, sweetness, and alcoholic strength, making port seem like a pleasant cocktail anytime of the year.

After we've sampled the best of this cellar, Rupert and I jump back in the boat to cross the river to another Symington property, Quinta do Vesuvio. This historic winery is considered one of the finest port producers in the country. It was the first estate to make single-quinta ports and now also produces dry red wines. Perched high on the bank above the river, the winery looks like an Asian dynasty: a white palace with gold-trimmed spires and jeweled tiles that glint in the sun.

As we walk up from the dock, Rupert asks, "Shall we tickle the palate before lunch?" I'm all for a liquid tickle and respond a little too enthusiastically. Up on the quinta's shady veranda, he pours Dow's Fine White Port over ice, with a splash of tonic water and a slice of lemon. White port, the least known of ports, is made from white grapes, then matured for three years in the barrel to give it a light straw color. It may have a slightly lower alcohol level than other ports, at 17 percent.

The drink has a lovely refreshing flavor, somewhere between a light tawny port and a dry fino sherry. Pair it with green olives, spicy prawns, cold crab, fried oysters, steamed clams, smoked fish, or, best of all, a long afternoon nap. It calls to mind summer evenings in a chaise longue under a rustling tree, ice clinking on glass, the coolness of the tumbler in my hand bringing down the day's heat and energy. Rupert and I sink into large cushioned chairs to wait for lunch, eating handfuls of fresh salted almonds grown on the estate. The almonds make me thirsty and the port makes me peckish; it's a pleasantly vicious circle.

After a half hour of idle chat and river gazing, we move over to a linen-crisp table. The quinta's cook brings out a large steaming dish of *bacalhau*, the traditional Portuguese casserole made with fresh salt cod, new potatoes, hard-boiled eggs, onions, garlic, olives, parsley, and paprika. To my surprise, Rupert pours his 2007 Quinta Vesuvio, a dry red wine with flavors of plush blueberry and blackberry. It's another revelation; thanks to the spicy notes in the dish, it actually pairs well with the wine.

These days, most of the surprises in the Douro are coming from dry table wines. More and more producers like Rupert realize that they need to diversify their fortified wine portfolio to attract younger drinkers. To do this, they also have to overcome the unfortunate reputation for table wine that Portugal developed in the 1970s, when vinstrosities like Mateus and Lancers rosés were perpetrated on unsuspecting drinkers.

Table wines have never been Portugal's strength, because the best grapes have always been used for port under a strict classification system known as the *benefício*. The premium vineyards are close to the river, at lower altitudes and warmer temperatures, so they produce the ripest grapes for the powerfully concentrated ports. Grapes for dry wines were grown on less-desirable real estate higher up on hillsides, so they were always the lower-quality leftovers from the harvest.

However, winemakers have recently discovered that the best grapes for dry table wines come from the higher altitudes, allowing for slower maturation without intense sugar levels. So in a happy coincidence, the two styles can complement each other: port grapes at the lower levels, table grapes at the upper levels. The quality of the dry table grapes is improving, and these wines are becoming less of an afterthought.

"The magic of the Douro is in all the different altitudes and exposures that create all the different wine styles," Rupert tells me. "The slopes are mostly schist with intrusions of granite. Schist drains well and captures the sun's warmth reflecting off its shiny facets."

Today, the region produces some eight million cases of port a year and twelve million cases of dry wine. Even so, the only way to economically justify dry red wine production is to assign all the fixed costs of production to port. Like most top Douro reds, the Symington wines are varying blends of the five primary grapes used to make port: touriga franca, touriga nacional, tinta roriz, tinta cão, and tinta barroca.

Touriga franca is the most widely planted grape, accounting for more than 20 percent of vineyards. It infuses blends with aromas of wild violet. Touriga nacional has the most character and acidity but accounts for just 2 percent of the country's grapes, being difficult to grow and requiring stringently low yields. Michel Chapoutier, the famous Rhône Valley producer who also makes wine here, compares touriga nacional to syrah because of its aromas of red plum and savory herbs. Tinta roriz, the Portuguese name for the Spanish grape tempranillo, has notes of spicy cherry; tinta cão gives black cherry and acidity, and tinta barroca adds chocolate and fig notes.

Unlike modern vineyards devoted to single grapes, older Portuguese vineyards are often haphazardly mixed plantings. When vines died, vintners would plant whatever they had on hand to fill the gap. As a result, even today single-variety wines are rare. The challenge is trying to isolate diseases or pests that may afflict one particular variety, as well as trying to manage different ripening speeds in order to choose optimal harvest dates. Tinta barroca ripens first, followed by roriz, touriga nacional, and tinta cão, with touriga francesa always the last by about three to four weeks. This moving window of maturity changes each year.

However, there are some advantages: a mix of grapes in the vineyard strengthens pollination. There's also the curious phenomenon that winemakers have noticed. "Vines are like people," Rupert observes. "The longer they live together, the more alike they become. Eventually, they start to flower and mature at the same time, even if they're from different stocks."

As he pours his 2008 Altano Reserva into my glass, Rupert observes, "The Douro is a lot like the Rhône—a rustic, earthy character but with fresh fruit flavors." The Symingtons have four non–port wine labels: Altano, Quinta de Roriz, Quinta do Vesuvio, and Chryseia, a partnership with Bruno Prats, formerly of Bordeaux's second growth Château Cos d'Estournel. The sweetly spiced cherry and raspberry aromas of the Altano are held in a racy tension by its acidity. It would pair beautifully with other traditional Portuguese dishes, such as sausage stuffed with garlic, venison, partridge in a port reduction sauce, and the local specialty *cabrito*—goat casserole.

Next we try his 2007 Quinta do Vesuvio, alive with vivid black raspberry aromas inflected with peppery spices, with some acidity for freshness. There's also a pent-up power in the wine, like a leopard dozing in a tree, ready in an instant to pounce. We finish with the 2007 Quinta do Vesuvio Vintage Port, a rip-roaring good wine with mounting levels of flavor and pleasure the more you drink. Its black fruit seems bathed in coffee treacle. Rupert and I finish with an espresso, which gives me a much-needed energy boost for my next visit farther downriver with the legendary Dirk Niepoort.

* * *

AFTER MY THREE-HOUR lunch with Rupert, I barely have time to freshen up for the seven-course dinner this evening with Dirk. I had heard much about him before even arriving in Portugal: viticultural philosopher, savvy-sharp marketer, *enfant terrible* of the Douro. He reminds me of what the poet Fernando Pessoa once said: "The Portuguese cannot live within the restraints of a single personality, nation, or faith." (Pessoa was drinking himself silly in a Lisbon bar when he said this, so perhaps he may have just been seeing double.)

Dirk, who now runs the eponymous family business that was established in 1842, is the first generation to actually make wine rather than just ship it. After he graduated with a degree in economics in Switzerland, he worked for the Swiss food company Mövenpick, where two of the company directors gave him "the bug to like wine." He did an internship at Cuvaison winery in Napa Valley and returned home to work in 1987.

While his Dutch ancestors may have worn wooden clogs and circumnavigated the globe, Dirk prefers rubber Crocs as he walks around his kitchen. On this lemony evening, I'm ushered in by his housekeeper, Maria José da Fonseca Mansilha—a small woman in her sixties who looks me up and down with her nose wrinkled, like I'm an eight-day-old sausage. Dirk doesn't seem to notice me; he's busy stirring an array of steaming pots and pans on the stove. The long counter is covered with bowls of green, red, and yellow vegetables; shiitake mushrooms; spices; and two massive slabs of uncooked fish. With his stern expression and runaway curly hair, this culinary Beethoven holds a spatula for a conductor's baton.

Finally, he swims up from his thoughts and notices me. "Ah, you're here; hello," he says. A smile plays at the corners of his mouth as he hands me a bowl of sun-dried tomatoes and a small knife: "First, if you are not comfortable here, this is your fault, not mine." His brusque manner is the defense of the shy. When I heard that Dirk was also a terrific cook, I had emailed him to ask if I could help him make dinner. His terse reply: "There are no recipes. Come at seven."

Following his quick instructions, I start to dice the tomatoes while he debones the fish. "This is the hardest, most complex, and most expressive wine region in the world," he says, eschewing small talk as he dives into his favorite topic. "In the Douro, we have 110,000 acres under vine; 39,000 growers, with vineyards ranging from 250 to 2,500 square feet; and thousands of different exposures to the sun. More than eighty indigenous grape varieties have been grown here for three centuries." This translates to many pockets of nuance that only the old people know about, he continues. "They know their parcels, which grapes to plant. We must keep their small-grower logic. There's power in genetic diversity to craft compelling red wine flavors here."

Dirk cherishes those mixed plantings, and with his Dutch name, German heritage, and Portuguese passport, Dirk is a bit of field blend himself. He's always on the hunt for old, north-facing vineyards, prowling the hills for those hidden crevices that give him the intense dark berry flavors he craves but have a paradoxically fresh brightness in their acidity.

"If we follow the modern logic of ripping up old vineyards and replanting, we will end up in five years where the New World is now—except they know how to do it better. We will be fighting them with uninteresting wines, and it won't matter where we come from."

Still, he doesn't ignore modernity. Dirk has teamed up with five other producers in their thirties and forties, calling themselves the

Douro Boys. ("Some people think we are a boy band," he says, smiling.) The others include Quinta do Crasto, Quinta do Vale Dona Maria, Quinta do Vallado, and Quinta do Vale Meão. "We need to lead with our best here, as Bordeaux does. The five first-growths lift the reputation of the whole region."

He stirs, I chop. We're both relieved that this isn't a face-to-face interview without anything for our hands to do. He's peeling tiny squid now, so I ask what he's making.

"I don't know," he says. "They looked interesting in the market, but I'm not sure what to do with them. If you start with respect for raw products, something good will happen." Then abruptly changing the subject, he asks, "What kind of wine do you like?"

"Your wines!" I almost say, but I know he'll despise sycophancy. Instead, I blurt out, "Old wines!"

Old wines? Why did I say "old wines," I wonder. Why not "mature wines" or "wines from the upper Douro, especially the spectacular 1978 and 1982 vintages"? But no, all I've managed is something that sounds as though I've just graduated from vodka coolers.

"Old wines?" he asks, squinting at me as though I'm dangerously stupid. I nod and decide to shut up.

"Come," he says, leading the way out of the kitchen and downstairs. He opens a door and I follow him into his cellar, with rows and rows of cobwebbed bottles, many so encased you can't see the labels.

"Old wines," he says, pointing. There must be thousands of bottles here, and from the few labels I can see, they date back decades, if not centuries. They're not just Portuguese; there are also some of the finest wines from Burgundy, Bordeaux, Spain, and other regions.

"How about this one?" he asks, pulling out a bottle. The amber liquid shows through streaks of dirt, and the ragged, moldy label barely clings to the glass, but I can just make out the vintage: 1893.

"Yes, please," I whisper.

Back in the kitchen, Dirk pours his tawny port into a decanter, and the amber essence of another century wafts out of the bottle. He gently swirls the decanter to aerate the wine that has been waiting for us for 117 years. He pours us a small glass each, we clink, and, hand shaking, I lift the glass to my lips.

The wine isn't oxidized as I had expected. In fact, it's absolutely fresh. It's not robust or rich, either; it's just a slip of a wine. Still, its aromas swirl around my head, like I'm sitting in a steam room billowing with spice-smoke. Fleeting whiffs of pan-seared tangerines, honey-dipped violets, and plums dusted with cinnamon appear, then vanish. This is a wine to chase all the way to the bottom of the decanter.

Tawny ports start out like ruby ports, but they're aged in wood for much longer. There are four types: fine tawny, tawny, tawny with an indication of age, and colheita. Fine tawny, contrary to what it suggests, is not the best type, just the simplest; it's made by blending ruby and white port, and results in a style even lighter than ruby. It's a quick and inexpensive production method, like mixing red and white wines to make cheap rosé. Tawny from the second category is also fairly simple and usually blended with white port.

Tawnies with an indication of age are labeled by their decade, as ten, twenty, thirty, or forty years old. Each of these is the average age, not the absolute age of the wine. So a ten-year-old tawny may contain some wine that was aged for seven years and some for thirty years. The Port Institute makes the final call when their tasters evaluate a sample to determine if the blend has the character of a ten-, twenty-, thirty-, or forty-year tawny. Colheitas are tawnies that come from a single vintage and are aged for at least seven years in the barrel, but often for decades. These are the rarest of all ports, comprising less than half a percent of total production. On the whole, ruby and tawny port account for 90 percent of sales, but vintage port drives profitability and sales growth.

We continue to sip on the port and chop vegetables until the other dinner guests arrive. The first is Dirk's cellar master, Luís Seabra, who is mesmerizingly charming and, I sense, quite a cad, with those flashing dark eyes and suggestive eyebrow action. He, too, drinks some of the 1893, toasting us with the traditional "Saude!" More guests arrive; few bother ringing the doorbell—most just stroll into the kitchen, deposit a bottle or two on the table, have a drink, and then drift out to the living room to chat. There's an orthopedic surgeon, a landscape photographer, a woman who makes jewelry, and several people from the Port Wine Institute, presumably writing off the evening as media relations work. One of the latter asks me where the 1893 is. I shrug and say that I think it's out in the living room— hoping he doesn't see the decanter behind me on the counter.

Dirk starts frying Galicia pimentos in olive oil, salting them so they lose their toughness and their skins peel off. He looks over at my sun-dried tomatoes and says, "There must be twenty-five pieces all the same size, not twenty-four, not twenty-six."

"I thought you said there are no recipes?" I ask, feeling flustered.

He smiles. "We are guided by intuition, not science—twenty-five feels right."

He turns back to the fish, which he's flipping deftly in the saucepan. "It's easy to overcook fish," he says. "You must understand how high heat affects food. The best cook I ever knew was Joerg Woerther from Austria. I never met anyone so sensitive to heat—he would take the pan on and off the heat constantly, as though he were cooking himself. We try to do the same thing with wine: to feel the outer limits of the wine . . . how far can we take it without ruining it?" He nods as though satisfied with his analogy and with the crispy fish that he teases out of the pan to a large plate. "Yes, to cook and to make wine—to create at the moment of destruction."

The kitchen is now filled with savory cooking aromas and chatty guests. It's so crowded that when I try to move the bowl of chopped tomatoes nearer to Dirk at the stove, I bump into Maria. She glowers at me, turns her back, and starts chopping the celery furiously. I slink back to my corner to console myself with another nip of the 1893 as I angle my body to hide it.

Dirk serves a starter of the steaming grilled squid to anyone in the kitchen not too wrapped up in conversation to notice the food. Then he, Maria, and I carry out the platters of roasted vegetables and fried fish to the dining room. He sits at the head of a long table, and sixteen of us slide into chairs. As the platters are passed around, the conversation continues unabated—Dirk seems to have invited the gastronomic equivalent of a literary salon. Fortunately, I'm seated at his right, because he mostly just chats quietly with the people closest to him. The languages around us weave in and out of French, English, Portuguese, and Spanish. Again, Dirk has an apt analogy: "Making wine is like speaking English: easy to learn but difficult to master."

Dirk pours his 2004 Redoma, an expressive white wine made from a cooler site in the Douro. Its acidity is an electric spine, holding together the flesh of the wine. He explains that a former assistant winemaker with obsessive tendencies had the entire staff, including Dirk, de-stemming the grapes by hand for days.

"Did it make a difference?" I ask.

"To the wine, no. To us, yes, it changed our lives. I'll never do it again, and he's gone," Dirk says, smiling.

As we continue to enjoy the tender fish, Dirk pours his Charme, a blend of tinta roriz and touriga grapes. They come from vines that are seventy to a hundred years old and were trodden by foot in the old lagars. It's a lovely, delicate wine, with great length and polish.

"Fruity wines are a modern disease," Dirk says, clearly moved by his own words. "If I want to drink fruit, I'll have cherry juice. Fruit just sits there on top of wine, facing outward to impress; it's psychopathic. The point of wine is deeper than fruit—it's the essence of the land."

He has a particular passion for Old World pinot noir, which seems to me almost the antithesis of port. However, he seeks to infuse his wines with Burgundian elegance. "We live in a region that gives us rich, ripe wines, but we don't want heavy, fat wines—we want elegance and finesse," he explains. "Most modern wines hurt you; they flatten your senses. We need wines that make us sing."

I ask him what he means by elegance and finesse. His response: "Wines that are of one sensory piece from start to finish."

Turning a question on me, he asks, "So what do you say when you think a wine is complete crap?"

As I search for an answer, my mouth opens and closes, opens and closes, like a fish dying on a dock. Finally, I splutter, "Interesting, very interesting—unlike anything I've ever tasted before."

"*Interesting* answer," he replies, with a sidelong glance and wolfish smile.

He pours his forty-year-old tawny, brimming with aromas of toffee, butterscotch, cedar, and almonds. Dirk explains that this port is drier than younger tawnies and will pair better with the dessert. How can one port be "drier" than another, I ask him—aren't they all sweet? He tells me to think of the difference between a caramel candy and the caramelized but slightly bitter top of crème brûlée. The toffee signature is in both, but there's a wide spectrum of sweetness.

"A great sweet wine finishes dry," Dirk declares. "It starts sweet in your mouth, but the acidity acts like little brushes, sweeping away the sweetness and making your palate feel clean, refreshed, and ready for the next sip. Acidity is the cleanup crew."

Tawny is both lighter and sweeter than vintage port, so it marries well with any egg-based dessert: crème brûlée, sabayon, sponge cake, or custard pudding. The lighter, berry-fresh aromas of ruby ports go better with fruit-based desserts, such as flans, pies, cobblers, and crumbles. These don't go well with the caramel notes in tawnies, which do better with dried, toasted, or spiced fruit, including fruit-cake, toasted almonds, nut-based tarts, pear frangipane, almond cake, tarte tatin, crème caramel, or on their own. Tawny also loves to tango with salty, pungent blue cheeses, such as Stilton, Bleu d'Auvergne, and Gorgonzola. It's the liquid line drawn after the meal.

Port is also autumn in a glass, with its fiery tawny-red tones. It pairs well with many harvest dishes, such as foie gras, pumpkin pie, and pecan tart. However, Dirk even pairs tawny port with game meats and birds, such as smoked duck, quail with black figs, and boar in a red wine reduction sauce, because it brings out their darker, savory flavors. However, it won't obliterate the flavors of the meat itself because it doesn't slink across your mouth the way some sweet wines do. Many people don't understand the concept of sweet. A lot of what they eat is sweet, and not just for dessert. Think of glazed ham, teriyaki sauce, sweet potatoes, creamed corn. Dirk likes vintage port with pepper steak because the pepper reduces the perception of sweetness so that the robust flavors in the dish and glass marry well.

In North America, we don't have much of a history with port, as we don't pair them with our entrées. We drink 75 percent of our wine with dinner, rather than afterward. By the time dinner's over, we're usually too stuffed (or drunk) to have a digestif. When did we lose the pleasant ritual of lingering after dinner for more talk and drink?

So just as you might propose other daring ideas at the end of a meal when your companion is more open to suggestion, try a little port. The ideal way to enjoy it is about a two- to three-ounce serving, only about half the amount of a dry wine; thus, one bottle can easily serve eight to thirteen people. Being a bit greedy, I find the traditional port glasses too small; I prefer drinking my port from the luxurious roundness of a brandy snifter, so I can cradle it in my hands. Although some wine lovers advise serving port slightly chilled, I prefer the aromatic sensuality of a tawny cupped in my hand.

"You can drink tawnies anytime, they're like wearing jeans; but drinking vintage port makes you feel like you should be wearing a tuxedo," Dirk says, as we clink glasses.

He tells me that as tawnies age, they lose about 3 percent of their volume every year through evaporation from the barrel. So they're topped up by younger, fruiter wine to "refresh" them. This builds differing layers of freshness, maturity, flavor, and complexity, much like a modified version of the *solera* system used to make sherry. The oldest barrel is topped up with younger wine. Without careful blending, the wines can taste disjointed: the young fruit doesn't marry the mature character. The longer the wine stays in the barrel, the more its color changes, from the deep violet of youth to the fiery amber and topaz of maturity. This creates a smooth wine of luminescent amber that doesn't need to be decanted because it was filtered before being barreled.

It also doesn't need aging by the buyer, since the winemaker has already matured the port before bottling and selling it. In fact, most tawnies are best consumed within two to three years of bottling. In the liquor store, ten-year-old tawnies are the best value: prices double with every decade, but the hedonistic pleasure doesn't. This was quite a revelation to me—and one that's saved me a lot of money.

Ten-year tawnies have the most vibrant fruit flavors, twenty-year-olds display candied fruits wrapped in toffee, thirty-year tawnies start to taste drier and more honeyed, and by forty, tawnies have darker depths of dried figs and spice-coated clementines. For years I felt less evolved because I loved tawny more than vintage ports.

Now I've just accepted myself as an uncomplicated, unrepentant hedonist: I can't resist tangerine zest, cinnamon, and butterscotch.

Another advantage tawnies have over vintage ports: they retain their taste for one to two months after opening the bottle rather than having to be consumed within a day or two. That's an enormous benefit when you just want to sip an ounce or two a few evenings a week. They've already had to toughen up against oxidation during the aging process, when they're exposed to air as they're transferred (racked) from barrel to barrel several times.

Before I came to Portugal, I didn't even know what made a colheita different from a tawny, but I'm learning quickly now. Dirk has an amazing vertical collection of them: the oldest colheita is from 1906 and spent seventy-two years in cask before being bottled. Some winemakers believe that colheitas confuse the consumer and shouldn't be produced (most tawnies are a blend of years, whereas colheitas are tawnies from a single vintage and are bottle-dated).

Naturally, Dirk disagrees. "Port needs to have different expressions; they make it exciting. Colheitas have always been some of our very best wines."

He pours one for me now but covers the label. Oh joy, we're going to play my favorite game: make the wine writer guess that vintage for a slow and measured disgracing that yields maximum satisfaction to the vintner. This colheita has a surprisingly vibrant freshness that reminds me of the verbal zingers my grandmother used to fling from her corner of the kitchen during dinner.

"I don't like selling these old wines," he surprises me by saying. "I prefer to drink them with my family and friends."

I am so very glad he feels this way. I glance around the room, now saturated with the rich heady haze of honey, spices, and toffee. This wine hasn't been ruined with words—it seems to have been created around a longing.

Dirk prompts me for my answer, and so I guess a few vintages, all too old or too young, of course. Finally, unable to resist, he tells me: he did a little research himself to find what year I was born and has opened a 1966. I'm touched. Families here reserve heirloom wines from various vintages the way we in North America pass down antique watches, cars, and paintings.

This port reminds me of a dessert I created when I was six: tangerine slices rolled in brown sugar. These aromas re-create the entire atmosphere in my mind, and I'm on my grandparents' veranda again. I have such a feeling of beautiful resignation that I sit there smiling at nothing. Stravinsky said that music is the best way to digest time. I think port is better—and certainly tastier. This bottle is a memory palace.

Field Notes from a
Wine Cheapskate

Although port tends to be more expensive per bottle than dry table wines, a little goes a long way, since we usually only indulge in a few ounces at a time. Therefore, a bottle can serve many more people or, in the case of non-vintage ports, be enjoyed over a month or two.

INSIDER TIPS

- Ten-year-old tawnies represent the best value on the liquor store shelf because their prices roughly double with every decade, but their quality doesn't.

- Portugal's native grapes are not well-known to North Americans, but that translates to great values. Varieties like tinta roriz and tinta barroca just don't have the brand awareness and cachet of cabernet sauvignon and merlot. Therefore, producers must compete more aggressively on price.

- The best-known vintages for port will always command the highest prices, just as they do in Bordeaux and Tuscany. So seek out the well-rated vintages close to a star vintage. For example, 2007 is considered one of the best in decades, so try 2006.

WINERIES VISITED

Dow's: www.dows-port.com
Graham's: www.grahams-port.com
Niepoort: www.niepoort-vinhos.com
Sandeman: www.sandeman.eu
Symington Family Estates: www.symington.com
Warre's: www.warre.com

BEST VALUE WINES

Croft Pink Port
Dow's Crusted Port
Dow's Fine White Port
Graham's Late Bottled Vintage
Niepoort 10 Years Old Tawny Port*
Sandeman Ruby Port
Sandeman Tawny Port
Warre's Otima Tawny Port

My first pick for my own Saturday dinner.

TOP VALUE PRODUCERS

Altano (Symington)	Quinta do Bomfim
Cálem	Quinta do Casal
Callabriga (Sogrape)	Da Coelheira
Croft	Quinta do Cerrado
Delaforce	Quinta do Crasto
Duas Quintas	Quinta do Portal
(Ramos Pinto)	Quinta do Vallado
Ferreira	Quinta do Vesuvio
Fonseca	Quinta dos Aciprestes
Kopke	Ramos Pinto
Monte da Cal	Taylor's
Quinta de Cabriz	Vinha Longa

SATURDAY DINNER FOR A WINE CHEAPSKATE

You'll find the recipes for the dishes I enjoyed with Rupert Symington at www.nataliemaclean.com/food.

Bacalhau in Cream Sauce (Fresh Cod Casserole)

Wood-Oven Baked Lamb

Duck Rice

Crème Queimado (Crème Brûlée)

TERRIFIC PAIRINGS

Port is a magnificent, rich, and long-lived dessert wine, with signature aromas of toffee and almonds in the tawnies, and black fruits in the vintage ports. My favorite pairings include:

Almond desserts
Apples: baked, pie, tart
Baked Alaska
Biscotti
Brownies: chocolate
Cheese: cheddar, Stilton, Roquefort
Chicken with dates
Chocolate: all types, with nuts or caramel

Chocolate-chip cookies
Crème caramel
Donuts: chocolate with sprinkles
Pavlova
Pecan pie
Pizza: blue cheese and buffalo chicken
Toffee pudding

RESOURCES

For more information about Portuguese wines and port:

Wine and Food Lover's Guide to Portugal by Charles Metcalfe
The Wines and Vineyards of Portugal by Richard Mayson
Portugal's Wines and Wine Makers: Port Madeira and Regional Wines by Richard Mayson
Wineries of Portugal: www.nataliemaclean.com/wineries
Institute of Port Wines: www.ivdp.pt
Wines of Portugal: www.viniportugal.pt
Body and Soul of Portugal Wine Club Toronto: www.bodyand soulwine.com
For the Love of Port: www.fortheloveofport.com

RELATED READING

The following books, while seemingly unrelated to the main subject matter of this chapter, provided some enjoyable reading before, during, and after my travels:

Heart of Darkness by Joseph Conrad
The Egoist by George Meredith
Notes on a Cellar-Book by George Saintsbury

EIGHT

SUNDAY

La Vie en Rosé en Provence

As I DRIVE down the autoroute du Soleil, the yellow fields of Provence around me are ablaze with the red and blue of poppies and lavender. I can see orchards heavy with apricots and plums, and smell the wild thyme and rosemary that grow around Roman ruins and the villages of cream-colored cottages. Everything is drenched in golden Mediterranean light.

Cypress trees flit by my open car windows: *fwip—fwip—fwip*. Henry IV of France planted those trees along the roads to help buffer the mistral, the infamous wind that sweeps down into Provence from the Rhône Valley. It can reach speeds of fifty-five miles an hour, hard enough to knock people off their feet. The mistral has even been cited as an extenuating circumstance in murder trials: its unceasing howl can drive a person crazy. The wind is most intense during the winter; but even now, on a quiet summer evening, the ivy rippling along a stone wall is a reminder that the mistral is never far away.

Still, the mistral also blows in fresh weather to Provence, keeping the vines dry and preventing disease and rot. That is one reason why winemaking is an ancient tradition here: Phoenicians or Greeks are believed to have planted the first vines sometime in the sixth century BCE, making this France's oldest wine region. After Julius Caesar ousted the Greeks, he considered this region his favorite among the many provinces he owned and affectionately named it "my provence." The name stuck, as did the Romans who continued to cultivate vines there until their eventual decline. Today, there are more than eighty thousand acres of vineyards here and some four hundred producers.

Provence's most famous wine is its deliciously carefree rosé. As a knock-it-back drinker, I love the indiscriminate guzzling of this pink wine—especially over a long Sunday lunch. It combines the fleshy fruit flavors of red wine with the airy lightness of white. Rosé is the world's greatest mindless wine. Every time I taste it, I wonder why I don't drink more of it.

Actually, I *do* know why: for many of us, rosé has never managed to shake that cheap and nasty image from the 1970s. Cast your mind back to the saccharine pink bog-wash we downed in college: Mateus, Lancers, Piat d'Or. Ugh. None of those wines came from Provence, but they still influence how we think of rosé: Kool-Aid with a kick, seemingly a blend of alcohol and fuchsia food coloring—with no fruit flavor and little balancing acidity.

The biggest brand was Mateus, that syrupy concoction in the squat bottle inspired by a World War I water canteen. Although we may shudder at its taste now, it was pure marketing brilliance when first launched back in 1943. Designed by a committee in a Portuguese conglomerate, it paired perfectly with 1950s fare: hotdog wedges on toothpicks and canned fruit trapped in Jell-O. The bonus: when the bottle was empty, you could use it as a candleholder.

By the 1960s, Mateus was the world's biggest selling wine brand; twenty years later, it still accounted for 40 percent of Portugal's wine export. Mateus was the favorite of both royalty and celebrity: Queen Elizabeth, crooner Sir Cliff Richard, and even Saddam Hussein. (In 2002, U.S. inspectors reportedly found several cases of the wine stockpiled in the dictator's palace. There was some debate as to whether these qualified as weapons of mass destruction.)

In the 1970s, North American drinkers moved on from Mateus to even sweeter Californian white zinfandels, which tasted more like the Coca-Cola they had grown up drinking. Bob Trinchero of the Sutter Home winery first popularized the style: he bottled and sold the light pink runoff juice from pressing red zinfandel grapes. The third year he made the wine, the fermentation got stuck, leaving a lot of unfermented sugar in the wine. It sold even better than his dry version—he could barely keep up with demand. Other wineries jumped on his blush bandwagon.

However, most of the buyers of these wines tended to be women, because rosés had cultural associations that gave burly men pause: Mary Kay Cadillacs, Jackie Collins book covers, and heart-shaped resort beds in Niagara Falls. Even today, many people still think of these wines as the vinous equivalent of love beads, lava lamps, and Tom Jones, with his open shirts and gold chains. (After a glass or two of rosé, I've been known to perform a hairdryer-microphone solo in the bathroom of "It's Not Unusual.")

Still viewed as the Rodney Dangerfield of wine, rosé gets little respect. That fact spurred the formation, in 2005, of a group of U.S. wine lovers called Rosé Avengers and Producers (RAP). Every year, they host "Pink Out" tastings across the country to convince consumers, retailers, and sommeliers that rosé can be both versatile and tasty.

What a difference a few decades can make. Rosé is now the new white—a light, approachable wine without oak or heavy flavors. North American sales have jumped 26 percent in the past five years. By comparison, the entire category of table wines increased only

7 percent. Dry rosés are popping up on many restaurant wine lists and liquor store shelves. Younger drinkers are discovering rosé as a bridge between sweet coolers and dry wines. The beautiful bonus is that most of these wines are less than $20, often $15.

However, one challenge remains: few wine regions specialize in the style. Most vintners stake their reputation on "serious" red or white wines: chardonnay, riesling, pinot noir, cabernet sauvignon, or merlot. Not so in Provence, where rosé makes up more than 80 percent of its production. The remaining 20 percent is mostly red wine, with just a little white. That makes Provence the world's largest producer of good rosé, which is why I'm here.

I turn off the autoroute and drive down increasingly narrow back roads. The cicadas make their wheezy summer song. An indigo sky stretches out ahead, with a few corrugated clouds rippling over the hills. It looks like some of them have actually landed on the road itself, but as I get closer, I realize it's a herd of more than a hundred sheep wandering across the lane. I honk, a few of them look at me with their bored gray eyes, and then they go back to grazing. It takes a good fifteen minutes until the woolly scavengers amble on, giving me time to slow down my internal clock.

The vineyards of Provence hug the Mediterranean coast from Marseille to Nice. It's the land of daydream getaways and the playground of the rich: Monte Carlo gambling, the Cannes film festival, Saint-Tropez sunglasses bigger than the bikinis. The shimmering luminous light streaming in my windows has also drawn many artists here: Pablo Picasso, Henri Matisse, Marc Chagall, Paul Cézanne. In fact, it feels like I'm driving through a Van Gogh painting as I pass sun-dappled bales of hay and swaying sunflowers. The artist once wrote how much he loved this countryside for "the limpidity of its atmosphere and gay color effects."

I've always been fascinated by Van Gogh's prodigiously crazed

talent, epitomized by his cutting off of his own ear. After that incident, he checked himself into a local asylum, where he could see the
swirling stars above the fields. Apparently, when he painted, he no
longer saw the bars on his bedroom window. A year later, he checked
out, walked into one of those fields, and shot himself. He was thirty-
seven years old and left the world with 189 paintings.

I believe that Van Gogh would have painted many more master-
pieces had he drunk the local wine rather than absinthe, a spirit
distilled from wormwood at 140 proof. (I vaguely recall the one
evening I ever drank absinthe. The next morning, I prayed for quick
and painless death, but it did not come. I spent the day with my head
in the green fairy's vise grip.) Van Gogh wrote to his brother Theo
that "to attain the high yellow note, I really had to be pretty well
keyed up." Such a hallucinatory drink was hardly the ideal tipple for
a bipolar artist, yet perhaps it was this mad mixture that gave us
Starry Night.

These thoughts bring me back to the present-day genius I'm on
my way to see now: vintner Raimond Villeneuve. I became intrigued
with him when I read the back label of a bottle of his Château de
Roquefort wine, written by Tim Johnson, owner of the renowned
Willi's Wine Bar in Paris:

> These wines are the result of the courage of a man who once
> could easily have been the Court Jester, a man with a touch of
> madness and a genuine love for what he does best: make wine!
>
> —TIM JOHNSON

When I drank his rosé, I knew I had to meet Raimond, and as I
get out of my car in front of Château de Roquefort, I hear his deep,
sonorous voice before I see him. As he emerges from the cellar into
the sunlight, the picture matches the sound—a tanned, muscular

man in his forties, who looks like a war correspondent: multipocketed khaki vest, cargo shorts, hiking boots. He pushes his sunglasses up onto his head as he says hello, revealing electric blue eyes.

"Let me show you the vineyards," he says with a rolling French accent. I follow him up the castle steps and through the one-room apartment where he lives. *"Pas de luxe,"* he acknowledges, smiling. ("No luxury.") The walls are covered with maps, old photos, and rusting farm tools; the kitchen table is stacked with viticultural and history books. Raimond evicted himself from the other twenty-three rooms in his grand château in favor of storing almost two hundred thousand bottles of his precious wine.

"Voilà!" he says, taking me out onto a small balcony and gesturing at the sweeping rows of vines below us that run up to the opposite rock face. We're twelve hundred feet above the turquoise Mediterranean sparkling off in the distance—its breezes keep the fruit cool, allowing the grapes to ripen slowly and to be picked later in the fall, when their flavors have matured. The vineyard is sheltered in a stony, amphitheater-shaped hollow. The soil, mostly clay and limestone, rests on beds of fossilized shells and intrusions of flint.

Outside the vineyard is the wild, harsh countryside, dotted with tough little shrubs where the ground is uncultivated. The Romans built this fortified castle to defend their settlements in Marseilles and Cassis, and named it after the rocky hillside (*rocca fortis*), which became Roquefort in French. Over the centuries, the property has been variously owned by the princes of Baux and the bishops of Marseilles.

Wine has been made in these cellars since the Middle Ages. The place has been in Raimond's family since 1812, when his ancestor, the Earl of Gardanne, bought it. When I admire the château's beautiful bell tower, he tells me that his grandmother built it in 1880. "But the house is much older, 1568."

Raimond takes me through one shadowy ballroom after another, stacked with boxes of wine. The once-stately rooms are uninhabited otherwise: chandeliers darkened, gold-embossed paper peeling from the walls, and dusty velvet curtains shutting out the sunlight. I almost expect to find Miss Havisham here, with her yellowing wedding dress and cobwebbed gray hair. I imagine her sampling Raimond's wine and haughtily dismissing it into the spittoon—great expectorations.

As we wander though the box-filled rooms, Raimond tells me that although he was raised at the family château, where his father made bulk wine for other wineries, his first love was antique wood furniture. He originally trained as an artisanal carpenter and "learned the value of natural materials and craftsmanship." But after several years in that business, Raimond yearned to be back in the wine industry, so he became the export manager for the big Burgundian firm Mommessin. After six years, in 1995, he returned home and took over from his father, making better quality wines under the Château de Roquefort label.

The château has some fifty acres under vine, more than one-third of which are older than forty years. All are farmed biodynamically. Raimond replaced chemicals with manure, and insecticides with wild grasses and beneficial insects. He also uses the natural yeasts on the grape skins to start fermentation, rather than commercially cultivated ones. "I'm not religious about biodynamic farming, but I do see the value in trying to make natural liquids born of experience and observation."

Through an open window, I hear a donkey bray, then again. "Ah, that's Polie—she knows I have a guest, and she gets so jealous." Raimond chuckles. "Would you like to meet her?"

We go down the stone steps of the château and over to a hayfield, where a life-sized Eeyore trots over to greet us. She angles her body to the fence sideways, eyeing me suspiciously, her long gray velvet ears cocked back so as not to miss any of our conversation. Raimond strokes her nose affectionately, and she looks at me as if to say, see, he's still mine.

"Mules are better at tilling vineyard rows than horses or machines," he says. "They're smaller and more careful where they step. But unlike horses, they need lots of companionship. We go for long walks, don't we, Polie? She carries the picnic basket."

Raimond usually allows Polie to wander freely on the estate, and she often follows him on his chores. Laughing, he tells me about one evening when he was hosting an outdoor dinner party. His friends were mingling by the campfire, and he set down a platter of sardines and several open bottles of rosé on a picnic table before going down to the cellar to fetch more wine. When he came back, Polie had already polished off all the sardines and was lifting a bottle of wine in her teeth—drinking what wasn't splashing over her mouth.

"You like your rosé, don't you, Polie?" Raimond asks, as she paws the ground, presumably in agreement.

On our way back to the château, I ask the impertinent question that's been topmost in my mind since I arrived. "Raimond, why is Provence better known for rosé than anywhere else? I know you make a lot of it, but the Rhône Valley produces great rosés, too, and hardly anyone knows about them. What gives?"

"In the Rhône Valley, rosé is the afterthought of red wine," he says, smiling. "But in Provence, rosé is all we think of."

The big difference between the Rhône and Provence is how rosé is made. When red grapes are first crushed, the resulting juice is a light pinkish color. Only after a long soak with the skins does the juice take on a deeper ruby hue, after its acidity breaks down the skins to release their color and flavor. The longer this period of maceration, the more color the juice absorbs. Dark red wines often macerate for several weeks to a month, whereas white wines usually spend no more than twenty-four hours in contact with the skins.

When winemakers want to produce a particularly strong and deep red wine, as they do in the Rhône, they can concentrate the skin-to-juice ratio by removing some of the pink juice early in the process. This "bleeding the vats" is known as *saignée*, which sounds to me like a medieval operation involving leeches. The siphoned-off juice is then fermented like white wine and bottled early in the spring to capture its exuberant fruit flavors. "One advantage of the saignée method," Raimond says, "is that it allows vignerons to create two rivers of wine from one harvest. But it doesn't always make the best rosés—they have high alcohol, like the reds, and too much tannin for my taste."

He has a point. Rhône rosés tend to be beefy vino, often weighing in at 14 percent alcohol, with chewy red fruit flavors. They hint at the big bruiser reds this region can produce. But to me, rosé with that much heft is like a hairy man in a tutu: it just doesn't fly. And if the juice soaks too long on the skins, there's the danger of too much bitter tannin for such a delicate wine, not to mention the lurid lipstick red color of the wine. Conversely, if the grapes don't soak for long enough, the wine looks and tastes pallid. Some vintners try to correct this by adding a little red wine, but that can cause the rosé to lose its ethereal vivacity.

The best-known rosé region in the Rhône is Tavel—a small town just south of Châteauneuf-du-Pape—where all they think of is rosé as well. In fact, it's the only appellation in France that produces nothing but rosé—and has done so for more than five hundred years. At just two thousand acres, the growing area is only 2.5 percent of the size of Provence. Nevertheless, I love the robust style of Tavel rosé, which still manages to be refreshing. Fans throughout history have included Honoré de Balzac, King Louis XIV, and King Philippe le Bel. The latter, traveling through the area in the thirteenth century, reportedly declared, "There is no good wine but for the wine of Tavel!" (Always a politic thing to say about the local wine, wherever you are.)

"We don't use the saignée method here," Raimond says. "We pick the grapes at a ripeness level for a lively rosé, not a big red, then we gently press whole bunches of grapes rather than crushing them individually, so we don't extract too much color and tannin from the skins." Provençal winemakers cold-soak the grapes and skins for just a few hours, or at most, a day, to preserve their delicate flavor and color. The invention of temperature-controlled fermentation has also helped to keep the fruit fresh and lively.

"There is no miracle in my wine," Raimond says. "It's just the quality of the grapes. We use the same grapes here as they do in the Rhône: grenache, mourvèdre, carignan, cinsault. They make great rosé, but they create too tannic red wines here because of the heat." The ideal grapes for red wine in other regions don't necessarily work as well for rosé. Cabernet sauvignon, for example, is too tannic a base—though its parent, cabernet franc, is terrific because it creates a lighter, more aromatic wine.

The best Provençal rosé is perfumed with the lighter spectrum of red wine aromas, such as field raspberries and strawberries, but with the structure and lightness of white wine. Yet those ripe fruit flavors don't mean that the wine is sweet, even though it may taste that way. In fact, all Provençal rosés are bone-dry: they don't even make a sweet style. Wine is sweet only if the vintner stops fermentation before the yeast consumes all the sugar, leaving some sweetness and less alcohol. Usually the higher the alcohol level, the drier the wine; a wine with 12 percent or more is usually dry.

However, in other regions, an insouciant touch of sweetness can be charming in a pert little pink wine, like a coquettish flutter of eyelashes. It tames the tannins and highlights the fresh fruit flavors, like sprinkling sugar over fresh berries and cream.

"Making white wine is more difficult than making red wine, and making rosé is the most difficult," Raimond explains. "If you make the smallest mistake, you throw the acidity out of balance and end up with a wine that's too flabby or too tart. You can't hide your mistakes behind oak, as you can with red wine and some whites, because you want the fresh fruit flavors. It's like cooking: it's easier to ruin a delicate fish than a hearty steak."

The third way to make rosé is the down-market method of mixing red and white wines. It takes only 3 percent of red wine blended into white to make rosé. Even with this small amount, the red wine tannins and bitterness are apparent, so the taste is quite different from the other production methods. This method is illegal in most of Europe. In 2010, when the European Union proposed legalizing this blending method to give producers a way to use up cheap wines, the Provençal wine council lobbied hard against it. They argued that French rosé had finally achieved a reputation as a quality wine, and cheap knockoffs would ruin the whole industry. Fortunately, they were successful, and the legislation was quashed.

That was only the latest salvo in the ongoing battle for the good name of Provence. Back in the 1970s, the government paid vintners to grub up inferior vines and replant with better ones, such as syrah and grenache. Other regions around the world slowly followed suit, and the quality of rosé started improving as more and more wineries planted better vines and improved their techniques. Despite this, wine quality in Provence, like in the rest of France, ranges from the most basic *vin de table* (table wine) to *vin de pays* (country wine) to the highest quality in nine designated growing areas, or *appellation d'origine contrôlée* (AOC). The largest and most important appellation is Côtes de Provence with 115,000 acres, France's sixth largest appellation.

Regardless of how it's made, rosé has traditionally filled a vinous gap in many regions when the locals wanted something to drink while they waited for the red wines to mature. In areas too warm to produce crisp white wines, such as the Rhône Valley, Provence, Portugal, and Spain, rosés are the wines of refreshment. Conversely, cool regions that can make crisp whites, like the Loire Valley, aren't warm enough to produce rich, deep reds. So those places use the thin-skinned, quick-ripening pinot noir and gamay grapes to produce rosés that have a little more weight than their whites.

Fashion has turned to pale rosé, boosting the popularity of Provençal wines. The most ragingly stylish rosé is Domaines Ott, with its distinctive curvy bottle that looks like the glass-blowing machine had a meltdown. The Ott family still runs the winery today, even though Louis Roederer, producer of the prestigious Cristal Champagne, bought a controlling interest in 2004. The wine is a perennial favorite of the jet set, who dubbed it "D.O." Casually drop that moniker into your conversation and everyone will know that you've wintered on the Côte d'Azur or at Cap d'Antibes.

To achieve a color range between translucent onionskin to ballet-slipper pink, the Provençal grape of choice is often grenache, which dominates Raimond's vineyards. Its skin is only lightly pigmented because it has low levels of anthocyanin, the compound that gives red grapes their deep bluish tint. Still, color can be deceiving: it doesn't indicate the wine's quality or body. Pale rosés can be full-bodied, and raspberry-red ones can be lightweights. Some Provençal rosés pack a surprising alcoholic punch, known as "pink pain." Drinking them can give you that same feeling of disbelief after sunbathing on a cloudy day, then discovering that you look like a radioactive lobster.

The challenge with grenache is that it can oxidize quickly because it has low acidity, so it can easily lose its freshness and color after a couple years. This is why most rosé is best drunk young. (The wine, that is, not the drinker.) Ideally, the rosé you drink is from the current vintage or, at most, one to two years old. That said, there are a few exceptions, such as robust rosés from the Rhône, which can age well for five to ten years. But beware if you see that the wine's pink color has acquired an orange-brown tint; that means it's most likely oxidized and will taste tired and faded.

Color is so important to Raimond that he names his wines for their hues. Les Mures, French for "blackberry," is a rich dark red blend of grenache noir, carignan, and syrah; Rubrum Obscrum, the Latin for "obscure red," is mostly old grenache. Corail, or "coral," is a rosé made mostly from grenache, syrah, and cinsault. He pours me a glass as we walk through his cellar, a luminous pink wine with salmon highlights. I inhale its vibrant scents of strawberry and summer-flush raspberries. It's a vivacious wine, made for immediate rejoicing.

Raimond also pours me his other rosé: Sémiramis, a bone-dry, delicate, herb-scented wonder that perfumes my mind. It tastes of the season's first fruit and fresh fields; sipping it, I can feel the juice of ripe grapes running through my fingers.

As we taste, Raimond reflects on his career change. "When I was a carpenter, I was able to see the chair within the tree," he says. "That required observation, creativity, and stillness. Now I have to see the wine within the grape. But either way, craftsmanship is the combination of work and energy—and art as intellect applied to good raw materials," he says, as we emerge back into the sunlight.

"The only escape in this world is through what you produce," he explains. "You cannot escape your fate. When I'm not busy with the vines, I don't feel well."

One of his pockets starts ringing, and he feels in his vest and pulls out a cell phone. It's not the right one, so he pulls out another and answers it. When he's done, he says to me, smiling, "This one is for the cellar—I can drop it on the floor.

"*Alors!* Shall we get some lunch?"

Oui, oui, merci! I am always hungry—tasting wine builds the appetite.

Raimond's battered jeep proves that transportation, like accommodation, is a much lower priority to him than wine. On the glove compartment, scribbled in gold pen, is a note by his friend Tim Johnson, the Paris wine bar owner: "Stick with me and I'll show you the world! TJ, 1995." It's the record of a road trip they took together when Raimond was just starting to sell his first small production of rosé to restaurants in the countryside.

In the heart of bustling Cassis, Raimond parks the jeep half up onto a sidewalk, right under a sign with a severe warning that all cars will be towed. He sticks one of his wine labels on the dashboard—the local police enjoy free samples of his wines.

On a vine-covered terrace overlooking the Mediterranean, the day's heat hasn't released its hold, though it's relieved by a breeze from the ocean. Below us, bathers sprawl on the creamy sand, children's voices trail across the water, and heady gusts of thyme, rosemary, and pine from the hillside fill my lungs. Our server pours a cool coral stream of Raimond's rosé into my glass, misting it over. Its raspberry ripeness mixes with the dried salt of sun-baked sweat on my lips. I lick them and gulp some more, feeling it wash away the dust.

Rosé is one of the few wines that satisfies a searing thirst. As I slosh it down, I feel myself reviving, like my dried-out ferns when I remember to water them. Don't get me wrong, I like a good palate-whacking shiraz as much as the next gal—but not when it's so hot that the pavement is curdling.

Rosé should be served almost as cool as most dry white wines: about 60°F. Low temperatures tame those riotous fruit flavors and highlight the wine's acidity, making it more refreshing and less cloying, rather than a mushy mess of hot strawberries. Another bonus is that this wine's soft tannins enable it to chill without losing its fruity flavors. In fact, several rosé producers encourage drinkers to drop in an ice cube. The South African brand Frozé, for instance, is a dark, concentrated, off-dry rosé that's been crafted to be diluted with ice. The producers claim it actually tastes better on the rocks, like an instant sangria.

Despite their delicate reputation, rosés can hold their own against the strong aromas of al fresco dining, like freshly cut grass, barbecue smoke, and suntan lotion. The notes of raspberry, strawberry, cherry, pomegranate, guava, and watermelon are never jammy or candied. Underlying these exuberant fruits is often a mouthwatering layer of herbal, spice, and mineral notes. A brisk finish is like the invigorating "Ah!" of an Alpine hike.

Rosé's association with hot weather is why some wine critics advise us to start drinking it when we get our first sunburn and to stop after Labor Day—when we stop wearing white. Nonsense. We don't drink white wine only in the summer. Rosé is also a year-round pleasure, especially with food. In fact, with their eyes closed, many people can't tell the difference between an aromatic rosé and a light red wine.

"Rosé is a wine of climate, not terroir," Raimond says, lifting his glass to the light. "My wines are free of 'mass terroir-ism,'" he says, referring to the overused wine term that confuses more than illuminates. "This is the wine to drink when you want to be on permanent vacation."

Indeed, Provençal rosé seduces you because you want to live the life here, not just drink the wine. With the sun on my shoulders and a cool river of wine running down my center, I haven't moved in an hour and feel in touch with my inner amoeba. But is drinking rosé back in a North American apartment on a cold, rainy day like looking at the photos you took of Niagara Falls: just not the same thing?

Great wines are often described as tasting of the place from which they come, but I think the best wines are those that take you back to the places that mean the most to you. They unlock those times and places at the edge of memory. This wine will always take me back to this hilltop terrace. In my mind, I will taste again the glistening ivory-satin fish and grilled vegetables, the bowl of sun-warmed cherries topped with a cool dollop of mascarpone, and the rosé that released me from myself for a few hours.

AFTER I SAY good-bye to Raimond and drive off to my next visit, I think about the other regions that produce rosé. Burgundy and Bordeaux, for instance, though best known for their red wines, also make blush wine. Burgundy's finest is Rosé de Marsannay, made from pinot noir grapes; Bordeaux makes it from merlot and cabernet sauvignon. The result is called clairet, to differentiate it from the deep-red wine known as claret.

The Languedoc region of southern France makes deeper-colored rosés, with riper red fruit flavors from mourvèdre and other grapes. However, a lighter, sparkling version from the region's Domaine de Boyer is called TendreBulle Gay Vin. The label shows two stylized heads almost kissing, and on the capsule are the letters *G* and *L*, for *gay* and *lesbian*. In a similar playful vein, New Zealand winery Kim Crawford called their wine Pansy Rosé.

Rosés from the Loire Valley in northern France, where the climate is cooler, tend to be lighter, with more acidity, fresher fruit flavors, and even a little carbon-dioxide fizz. Vintners use the thin-skinned pinot noir grape to make *vin gris*, or "gray wine"—it doesn't sound appetizing (and it's not actually gray, but copper pink), but it's the term the French use because this rosé is paler than most others. It's produced like white wine, only with red grapes. The grapes are pressed to extract the juice and a tiny amount of color from the skins, but there is no further skin contact. The eastern Loire also uses pinot noir, which gives the wine its copper-pink tone. None of these should be confused with inferior rosés made elsewhere from cheap grapes, whose juice is filtered through charcoal to get the pink color.

However, not all Loire rosés have a good reputation. Rosé d'Anjou, for instance, is known for its cheap and nasty sweet blends made from malbec, gamay, and groslot. The latter grape, so aptly named, is remarkable only for its ability to produce oceans of insipid wine. Cabernet d'Anjou, made from cabernet franc, is drier and more palatable, with some pleasant herbal notes. Chinon, farther west in the Loire, makes rich rosés from cabernet franc.

Outside France, many other countries make rosé. In Spain they're called rosados. Navarra, in the northeast, is the traditional heart of production. The wines are usually made from either tempranillo or garnacha (the Spanish name for grenache). Cheaper Spanish rosés are made from the little-known bobal grape—one of the world's most widely planted, even though it's only grown in Spain. Rosado juice gets a teasingly short contact with the skins: less than twenty-four hours. That's why the wine is known as *vino de una noche*, or "one-night wine." (Sounds like a fleeting summer romance.)

The most famous fan of rosados was Ernest Hemingway, who reportedly gulped down two bottles a day during those sultry after-noons spent watching the bullfights in Pamplona, Navarra's capital. He also filled wineskins to take with him when he went off to fight in the mountains during the country's civil war. Who says pink can't be manly? I love the way Hemingway described the taste of rosado in *Dangerous Summer*: "The wine was as good as when you were twenty-one."

Italy also makes some rosé, though most of it is consumed locally. Known as rosato, it's usually made from the sangiovese grape, the base for chianti, which has juicy red fruit flavors and good acidity. Some vintners prefer to use the white grape pinot grigio, which has a natural copper tinge to it. Left on the skins for an extended maceration, the wine emerges a lovely salmon color.

Then there's the New World. In North America, many wineries now produce dry rosé. In Canada, both Ontario and British Columbia make some great wines in the cool-climate style of the Loire, usually from the same grapes: cabernet franc or gamay. Several Canadian producers, such as Malivoire, Flat Rock, and Southbrook Vineyards, specialize in rosé. They believe that it's a natural wine for Canada, where ripening red grapes can be a challenge.

The California winery Bonny Doon makes Vin Gris de Cigare, a delicious blend of grenache, marsanne, cinsault, sangiovese, colombard, syrah, viognier, barbera, and dolcetto. It's impertinently labeled as "Pink Wine." In fact, there must be something about rosé that makes producers cheeky. My favorite description on the Napa winery Renard Rosé's label: "The nose suggests smoky strawberries, raspberry cigars and blah, blah, blah . . . Isn't wine indescribably fun? Just enjoy it!"

Personally, one of my favorite styles of rosés is sparkling, now that I've managed to move past those early awful associations with the saccharine fizz of Baby Duck and the like. I love the naughty color of a rosé sparkler and its sexy raspberry aroma. It conjures up the decadence of a weekday afternoon picnic beside the Seine, eating caviar and quaffing pink bubbles with a seductive Frenchman whom you have to slap occasionally. I read recently that a poll in Switzerland revealed that when those stoic Swiss see a man drinking rosé champagne with a woman, two out of three conclude that she is *not* his wife.

For winemakers, it's especially difficult to get the color of pink bubbly right. In the Champagne region of France, the most common method is to blend chardonnay, pinot meunier, and pinot noir so that the pinot noir dominates. An even more difficult and time-consuming approach allows the juice of all three grapes to sit on the skins for a short time to create the coveted pale-salmon color known as *oeil de perdrix*, or "eye of the partridge." The challenge is to produce the same color, year after year, even though the proportions of the grapes may change. But the reward is a wine with a wonderful delicate flavor. Rosés are considered among Champagne's most prestigious wines and comprise just 5 percent of all champagne production. They're priced accordingly: bottles sell for $80 or more.

JUST OUTSIDE THE village of Saint-Antonin, Domaine du Clos d'Alari is hidden among the trees on the slope of Saint-Antoninus. Inside this fifteenth-century stone winery in the heart of Provence, Nathalie Vautrin-Vancoillie and her family produce wonderfully aromatic rosés. I've heard that Nathalie loves to cook local dishes and pair them with rosé: what better way to spend this evening?

As I get out of my car, Nathalie, an athletic woman in a T-shirt and jeans, comes to meet me. "I'm surprised you found us," she says, smiling.

Nathalie grew up in the old farmhouse, a creamy yellow stone building with blue shutters—a palette typical of the region. Her parents sold their grapes to local winemakers for years but began making their own wine in 1998. A year later, Nathalie joined them to make wine.

"Dad was also in the meat business, and mother loved to cook," she says as we walk into her kitchen—a warm, blue-and-white-tiled cavern filled with wooden tables laden with fresh prosciutto and melon, gorgeously red tomatoes, glistening olives, and bushy heads of romaine lettuce. At the far end, her oven, gas stove, and microwave are winking red-and-orange-eyed creatures, beckoning us to come deeper into the cave. "They transmitted that love of food to me. Then I married Paul."

Her husband, Paul Vautrin, who owns a gourmet deli in Paris, works all week in the city and comes home only on the weekends. Some of his specialty products are on the kitchen shelves: mustard blended with truffle oil, Bloody Mary ketchup, caviar-brined pickles.

Their children's artwork covers the walls throughout the house— colorful pictures on paper as well as crayon drawings on the walls themselves. They feature smiling stick children holding hands, climbing trees, and running through the vineyards. There's also a large photograph of Nathalie and Paul facing each other and laughing, bare shouldered and presumably with no clothes below the frame. It's signed by hundreds of friends. The children have drawn dialogue bubbles for each of them and printed inside "J'taime!" [sic] Nathalie's son and daughter are in their early twenties now, both in university.

"I love discovering new flavors, whether it's food or wine," Nathalie says, pushing her thick, dark hair behind her ears. "And I love feeling the products in my hands: the small roundness of a grape, the smoothness of a tomato, spices running through my fingers."

Just as I'm feeling those first stirrings of hunger, Nathalie suggests that we "go pick dinner." We walk through the golden September evening, heady scents of sage, rosemary, and lavender wafting up from the warm earth. I finally understand that wine descriptor *garrigue*: the savory blend of wild herbs, cedar, and shrubs.

"Welcome to the field," she says quietly, gesturing to the land beyond the garden. Vintners here refer to their vineyards as "the field." It's a romantic, rolled-up-sleeves notion that evokes the struggle to cultivate one patch of dirt all your life. Of the family's twenty hectares, seven are planted with syrah, grenache, carignan, mourvèdre, merlot, cinsault, and rolle grapes, which the family pick by hand and press lightly using a low-tech method called "the drop": only the weight of the grapes themselves for first-run juice. The result is about thirty thousand bottles a year of wine.

I watch as Nathalie squats down to snip some fennel, her weathered, scarred hands marking her intimate knowledge of this field. "The old people used to call this wild salad," she says, pointing to the tangle of herbs and other plants around us. She offers me a bouquet of wispy yellow fennel. I bury my nose in it and inhale childhood memories of eating licorice on my grandparents' veranda.

We pass a shimmering silvery grove of more than three hundred olive trees, from which Nathalie produces about four hundred litres of olive oil a year. Nearby is a cluster of massive, century-old oak trees. I'm curious about the circle of dead-looking yellow grass around each tree.

"That's from the fungus on the tree roots," Nathalie explains. "That's how you know there are truffles underground."

Ah, truffles: those glorious, exotic cousins of potatoes, with their pungent aromas of wet, musky fall leaves; fresh-turned soil; ripe cheese; and underground caves. Unlike other kinds of fungus, which are parasites on their hosts, truffles are beneficial: they feed minerals to the tree along its roots as they absorb small amounts of sugar from it. The Cadillac of French truffles is the coveted "black diamond" from the Périgord region of Provence. More than 90 percent of French truffles grow in the southeast: Provence, Languedoc, and the Rhône Valley.

To the uninitiated, a truffle can seem almost repellent: a black, lumpy growth that looks like a diseased potato. However, in the right dishes, they're slivers of the netherworld. My most memorable meal was at Alain Ducasse restaurant in New York several years ago, when my husband, Andrew, and I were celebrating a James Beard journalism award. We ordered the eight-course truffle menu. By the time our server was shaving truffle onto our pistachio pastry cream atop a Napoleon of raspberries, I begged for mercy and chocolate sauce.

Nathalie's truffles aren't ready yet, since the season runs from mid-December to March. But even if they were here, nature doesn't give up her treasures easily. "That's the mystery of the truffle," she says, shrugging. "You can't cultivate them; you can only discover them and hope they grow back the next year."

Finding truffles is famously difficult, since they grow about six inches underground—and not necessarily in the same spot as the previous year. The best detection is scent, so most truffle hunters use a dog to sniff them out. Pigs have keen truffle noses, too, but unfortunately, they love them as much as humans do and will gobble down their discoveries if the handler doesn't pay close attention. Nathalie's dog Ubu is a dachshund, more popularly (and aptly in this case) known as a sausage dog. "He's king of the truffles!" she says, smiling. Ubu is enjoying an off-season romp on Nathalie's parents' farm a few miles away. She trained him from a pup, hiding a truffle in a sock and rewarding him every time he found it in ever more difficult and buried locations.

Now when he finds a truffle, he paws the ground and points his nose at the exact spot until Nathalie walks over. She gently digs around the precious tuber with a trowel—breaking it would decrease its value and freshness. The market in truffles is a lucrative one, and often as black as the fungus itself. A good-sized truffle is worth about $2,000 a pound at the local outdoor market, where they're often sold in stealthy cash transactions from a farmer's car (often a Mercedes or BMW). By the time the mushrooms reach fancy restaurants in cities such as Toronto, London, or New York, they've tripled in price. No wonder Nathalie hesitates when I ask her how many truffles she finds in a year—sources and yields are closely guarded secrets. Nobody wants to attract midnight poachers, and dark stories are told of truffle dogs that mysteriously disappear.

Under one of the trees, we see that the ground has been dug up even though truffle season doesn't start for another three months. *"Sanglier!"* Nathalie spits out. It sounds like a swear word until she translates. "Wild boar," she explains, kneeling down to fill the dirt back into the holes. Wild pigs have the same penchant for truffles as the tame ones, and will dig them up and eat them whenever they can. They also enjoy the vineyard grapes for dessert. "That's okay," Nathalie says, smiling. "The boars eat the truffles, and then we eat the boars." As we walk to the house, she tells me about her spice-marinated rack of wild boar with pistachio crust.

Back in the kitchen, Nathalie flits from counter to fridge to stove, while I try to anticipate her next move to stay out of her way. As she inserts a laurel bay leaf into the center of each half-boiled potato on a tray, coats them with olive oil, and slips them into the oven, she explains that Provençal cuisine is lighter than most French fare. It relies on olive oil more than butter, on fresh vegetables and seafood more than heavy meats, and it's seasoned with garlic and herbs rather than with salt. Most Provençal recipes seem to begin with the words "Peel one clove of garlic." This is the dream of the Mediterranean diet: eat as much as you want of delicious, flavorful foods and still maintain your weight. And yes, you get to drink wine—especially rosé.

Rosé is brilliant with the herbed dishes of Provençal cooking: basil-infused *pistou* vegetable soup, roasted chicken with rosemary, and succulently stewed tomatoes and vegetables in ratatouille. Many styles of wine work well with herbs because those same aromas are often found in both, especially sauvignon blanc, syrah, and cabernet sauvignon. For example, the tomatoes in a tomato sauce require an acidic red, such as chianti, whereas the basil in a pesto sauce might pair better with a crisp white, such as sauvignon blanc. The beautiful thing about rosé is that it works with both, having the flavor to pair with many foods.

"Rosé doesn't have the interfering elements of heavy oak, alcohol, big fruit, and butter notes," Nathalie says, pouring us each a glass of her wine. After a few sips, I can taste how its ripe berry aromas and natural acidity would allow it to pair with foods that might defeat other wines: ones with sharp, salty, spicy, or smoky flavors, such as green olives, anchovies, pesto, and tapenade. This wine would be perfect on a sultry summer evening; it would flesh out the flavors of mild dishes and lighten the richer fare. Well-made rosés are fragrant with field berries and often sprinkled with pepper notes.

Another challenging ingredient in the game of pairing is garlic, which is so potent that it can make almost any wine taste sour. That's true even of cooked garlic, which is relatively mild. Raw garlic, such as in pesto sauce, is tougher on wine because it numbs the palate the way chili peppers do. But rosé works with both, a crisp counterpoint that cools a seared palate. My mouth waters just thinking of rosé with bouillabaisse, the traditional fish stew of Marseilles. The pairing will mentally transport you to a bistro in the Vieux Port—you may even mistakenly call your husband Jean-Jacques, as I did the other evening while enjoying the dish.

Nathalie is now pouring olive oil into a roasting pan and shredding tiny bits of fennel into it. She also inserts slivers of fennel into some half-slit chicken breasts, turns them over in the oil, and pops them into the oven with the potatoes. Olive oil, one of the delicious staples here in Provence, coats the mouth and makes it hard to taste the wine. Fortunately, it's rarely alone in a dish, like aioli, that masterful blend of just three ingredients: olive oil, garlic, and egg yolk. Rosé cuts through this luxuriously rich mayonnaise.

As the savory aromas of the baking chicken and potatoes waft out from the oven, Nathalie prepares us a simple starter dish of diced fresh tomatoes adorned with salt, pepper, and shredded leaves of fresh thyme. Over this she scoops a dollop of chèvre, meadow-fresh goat cheese. There's nothing I love more than a chin-drippingly juicy tomato, so I'm delighted that they feature in many Provençal dishes, from vegetable soup to ratatouille. While they're terrific at flavoring food, their acidity is hard on wine: like lemon and vinegar, tomatoes can make most wines taste dull. Rosé, however, matches their acidic tang. Rosé dances with acidic citrus sauces, like duck à l'orange. The wine's acidity also cuts through the fat in soft cheeses like Nathalie's chèvre, as well as cream sauces and fried foods. Rosé is revolutionary with a cheeseburger.

My pet theory, though, is that pink wine and pink food go best together. I love a pale, crisp rosé with raw or lightly cooked seafood, such as tuna tartare and cod carpaccio. Think of lobsters cooking over a fire on the beach, glowing roseate as the sun slowly sinks into the ocean. On a picnic table are platters of freshly steamed crabs and barbecued salmon. A row of rosé bottles beside them have the frivolous symmetry of lipstick samples.

While I've been counting the ways that rosé pairs with food, Nathalie has finished cooking. We take our plates outside to an old wooden farm table and sit under an ancient cypress tree, through which sparkles the shattered crystal of a thousand stars around a shard of moon. I'm feeling quite twinkly myself. The September evening is warm, and I'm pleasantly hungry. Nathalie's rosé pairs beautifully with the tomato and goat cheese as well as the fennel-infused chicken and potatoes. This gossamer wine is a midnight run through a field of raspberries in a sheer nightdress shot through with moonlight.

"I hate big, body-builder wines," Nathalie says, as we sip contemplatively on the rosé. "These wines are slender, like the body of a woman. Wine is seduction—women are better at that, yes?" she asks with a sly smile. Certainly, the steroid of the wine world, oak, is absent from this transparent, limpid wine. Notions of lingering over another glass, or four, come to mind.

As we talk in the darkness, I love listening to Nathalie's voice; her laugh is free and uneven, the kind loosed among friends. I believe that as the evening progressed, toasts were made, backs were slapped, promises were not kept. I do recall informing Nathalie that she was *très sympa* and that we were both marvelous citizens of a marvelous world.

Eventually, Nathalie's steaming apricot tart magically appears on the table. (Perhaps Nathalie nipped into the kitchen to bring it out, but I don't recall pausing from sharing my brilliant observations with her.) For all its versatility, Provençal rosé does have a limitation: desserts make the bone-dry wine taste bitter. So we drink a dessert wine from the Languedoc instead.

By this time it's nearly midnight, I'm feeling contentedly wine-heavy, and realize I'm emitting a low, sybaritic purr. Nathalie and I bid each other a drowsy good evening, and I trudge upstairs to bed. I immediately plunge into a deep sleep. But at 2:47 a.m., I'm jerked awake by a thousand bullfrogs that had organized themselves below my window during the night and are now croaking in unison. "Those damn frogs!" I shout. Then I hope no one has heard me. Eventually, I fall back to sleep and spend the rest of the night dreaming of *cuisses de grenouille*—tender frogs' legs sautéed in finely chopped onions and garlic, garnished with a sprig of revenge parsley.

Early the next morning, I throw open the bedroom shutters to watch the sun brush over the dark violet hills, slowly painting them into lavender and pink. Mercifully, the frogs have dispersed. I had thought I'd skip breakfast so I wouldn't be charged for extra luggage on the flight home. However, I can't resist sharing warm homemade bread, local cheeses, and peach preserves with Nathalie before leaving. As she says, "It's a good way to live."

My FINAL VISIT in Provence isn't with a winery but rather with the man who put this region and its wines in my daydreams. Certain writers are associated with certain places: Émile Zola with Paris, E. M. Forster with India, Woody Allen with New York. And for this heavenly place, it's an author whose book *A Year in Provence* has sold more than six million copies in forty languages. In fact, the man who's been called the Pied Piper of Provence created a whole new genre of travel memoir: leave a dreary job, move to a warm climate, renovate a derelict farmhouse. Think of the books that have followed: *A Piano in the Pyrenees* by Tony Hawks, *Driving Over Lemons* by Chris Stewart, *Under the Tuscan Sun* by Frances Mayes, and even a parody, published in France, called *An Eternity in Provence*.

Peter's book celebrates life here: the abundant fresh food and wine, the long, lazy walks in the herb-scented countryside, the sunny afternoons in the hammock, the quaint and odd village folk and local customs. Since that first bestseller, he's written more than twenty books, most about his beloved Provence. I love them all, so I'm more than a little nervous about meeting him for drinks this afternoon. My heart thuds heavily, like dough flipped over and over as it's kneaded.

"Are you Peter Mayle?" I pose the ridiculous question in a bat-squeak to the only man in the lobby of the inn where we're to meet.

He smiles warmly at me as we shake hands, his bronzed face radiant under silver hair.

"Nice to meet you, Natalie," he says in a soft British accent. He wears an untucked Ralph Lauren shirt, blue trousers, leather loafers without socks, and no watch. At seventy-one, he's Mediterranean cool.

As we walk down into the postcard village of Lourmarin (a thousand inhabitants and eleven restaurants), Peter tells me he decided to become a writer because he was "useless at mathematics and anything technical. I was not drawn to politics or big business, or to any endeavor where I had to report to committees and bosses. English was my favorite subject at school, and the only one at which I was any good. I wanted independence and thought that writing would give me that." Journalism didn't appeal to him, but "advertising seemed like much more fun, and it was better paid."

Peter found breaking into the field difficult. Despite the aristocratic Oxbridge accent, he doesn't have a university degree. "The Brits are sticklers for that sort of thing, so I couldn't get an advertising job in London." So in the early 1960s, he moved to New York and worked for advertising giants David Ogilvy and George Lois, first as a copywriter and eventually as a creative director. He was one of the real-life *Mad Men* on Madison Avenue. He looks back on that time now as good training for his future career as a novelist. "You have to stick to the plot—to be concise, informative, and if possible entertaining. If one idea didn't work, you tried something else. No one was going to wait for your muse to inspire you."

Even though he was successful in the field, he decided to leave Madison Avenue in 1975 and become a full-time writer. Was it hard, I ask him, to leave the security of an advertising-executive income to become a writer? He laughs and tells me that advertising was always a precarious occupation. "But I was able to leave the business because my first books were starting to make money, and I was able to get freelance advertising work."

The stories about Provence were far from his first foray into print; by the time *A Year in Provence* was published in 1989, he had already been an author for sixteen years. His first book, a children's sex-education primer called *Where Did I Come From?* was published in 1973. This was followed by several more as part of a series, then by the hilarious *Wicked Willie* series of cartoon books. They're still in print today, having sold more than three million copies.

"Here we are," Peter says, as we walk up to the patio of a small bistro. Ever the gentleman, he pulls out a seat for me at a table. We sit in the bright sunshine sipping on icy rosé, watching villagers walk by. He tells me that after readers found out that this café was his favorite spot for drinks, they started sending letters and gifts here.

"I've had some addressed simply to 'Peter Mayle, France,'" he says, shaking his head. "I've also received many, many jars of marmalade, because I mentioned in an interview that's what I missed most about Britain."

We talk about England, America, and France. What's the key difference among them? Peter pauses for a moment, then responds, "Lunch. Sunday lunch, in particular. Until you've watched a Frenchman enjoying his Sunday lunch, you can't possibly imagine how religious an experience eating can be in France," he says, smiling. "It's not just rich people at fancy restaurants, either; it goes all the way through society. Farmers and plumbers have their favorite restaurants and their own special recipes, and they like to talk about them. This fascination with the stomach is a very pleasant addition to life."

So why don't those outside France enjoy their food and wine the same way, I ask. "The North American business ethic says that if you're having a two-hour lunch, you're being unproductive, wasting time," Peter responds. "The French are not ashamed to admit to liking pleasure, whether it's two hours for lunch or a month's holiday in August. They like to have a good time, and they're not guilty about it. Let me put it this way: When an American looks at a duck, he says, 'Oh, how cute.' When a Frenchman looks at a duck, he wonders, 'How shall I cook him?'"

In 1986, Peter and his wife, Jean, were on vacation on the Côte d'Azur when they stumbled upon the Lubéron valley, in the heart of Provence. They loved the area so much that a year later, they bought an old farmhouse, figuring they had just enough money to last them while Peter wrote his first novel.

"We started to renovate our home, but I became completely distracted—and much more taken with the curiosities of life in Provence than with getting down to work on the novel," he explains. "The daily dose of education I was getting from the stonemason, the mushroom hunter, the lady with the stubborn donkey, the electrician, the farmer next door, and so on, was infinitely more interesting than anything I could invent. Months went by without my committing a word to paper. Eventually, I felt so guilty that I sent my agent a long letter explaining why I hadn't even started the novel and describing some of the distractions. To my enormous surprise and relief, he wrote back saying that if I could do another two hundred and fifty pages like the letter, he might be able to find a publisher."

The agent was right, but the publisher evidently didn't expect much: he printed only three thousand copies, and told Peter that there'd be plenty of unsold ones that he could give as Christmas presents. But six weeks after the book went on sale, his agent called to say that every copy had been bought. The reprints started, and by the end of the year, it had become a runaway bestseller. Its popularity was such that over the next few years, Peter followed up with *Encore Provence*, *Toujours Provence*, and *A Good Year*, another escapist novel with a London stockbroker who inherits his uncle's Lubéron château and vineyard. The book was later made into a film by Peter's vacation-home neighbor, the film director Ridley Scott, and starred Russell Crowe.

Such was the success of his books that some people accused Peter of spoiling Provence by fueling an invasion of tourists: more than ten million tourists now visit the region every year. "I've been accused of causing everything from the village baker running out of bread to a surfeit of Germans in the café," he says, smiling. "But the tourist in Provence is an unfairly maligned creature—the good they bring far outweighs the bad." Peter argues that without tourism, there wouldn't be money to maintain the churches, châteaux, and other historic buildings. Most Provençaux recognize this fact, and their reaction has generally been positive. "They know tourism is an important part of the local economy, and they're happy that a foreigner has fallen so publicly in love with their region."

I love that Peter proudly declares himself a "permanent tourist" rather than the more fashionable and intellectual descriptor of traveler. Like rosé itself, he shrugs off snobbery and admits to simple pleasures.

Peter didn't change the names of the people in his book or disguise the village. He thought that would make the story less authentic. "Besides, I never expected many people to actually read it," he confesses, chuckling. The result is that many of the characters, unintended beneficiaries of Peter's success, have become minor local celebrities—like the builder Didier Andreis, described in *A Year in Provence* as "half man, half forklift truck." Since then, he and his wife have opened a flourishing guesthouse. Visitors often bring a well-thumbed copy of the book with them to help them savor Peter's eye for the cultural peculiarities of France.

As we're sitting there, for instance, a small man with a mustache roars up in his open-top convertible, stops in the middle of the cobblestone street, hops out over the door, and goes into a bar. "The

French have such imaginative ways of parking," Peter says with affectionate humor.

Peter had his first notion of the book's success when strangers started showing up on his doorstep. "I remember the first fan well—a man in a BMW," he says. "I invited him in, plied him with wine, and signed his book at least twice. At first it was exciting. People came from Australia, Germany, England, Sweden, America. Then it increased until we had four, five, six visits a day."

One February day, Peter discovered a photographer from a British tabloid newspaper hiding in his bushes. The cameraman explained, "Well, you never know . . . someone might be outdoors naked." Another day, a bus pulled up in front of his home and let out twenty Japanese tourists; their Tokyo travel agent had told them that their tour of Provence included a visit to Peter Mayle's house. Several local bars started selling maps to his house. The final straw came one Sunday. As Peter and Jean were sitting down to lunch, they heard splashing water in the backyard. Peter walked around to find a group of Italians videotaping themselves swimming in his pool.

To escape their unwanted celebrity, Peter and Jean sold their home and fled to America. They settled in Long Island, New York, and Peter entered himself into the self-devised Author Protection Program. "That's the great thing about America: you can be anonymous if you want," he says. They were content there for four years, especially since four of his five adult children lived in the United States. But eventually, the lure of Provence proved too strong. In 1997, after Peter and Jean watched a video of friends enjoying Sunday lunch there, they knew they had to return. "You can live outside eight months a year there, and the rhythm of daily life is slower. In America, I missed the moments that make up the daily texture of life. In America, I felt deprived of oxygen."

So they moved back and found another farmhouse just outside the village of Lourmarin—Peter's cagey now about the address. He writes in the mornings, but keeps afternoons and evenings free for friends, family, food, and appreciating the life he chronicles. As one of his characters says, "Nowhere else in the world can you keep busy doing so little, and enjoying it so much." Indeed, that's the reason not much has changed in his life since publishing his books. "I drink better wine," he says, noting that he drinks about a liter a day. "It sounds like a lot, but you have two or three glasses at lunch and two or three at dinner, and that's a bottle gone."

His latest book, *The Vintage Caper*, is a lighthearted mystery novel about the theft of a $3 million wine cellar. The plot takes a private investigator to Marseilles, Bordeaux, Paris, and Hollywood in a wonderful romp that displays Peter's deep knowledge of wine. When I tell him so, he responds, "I'm light entertainment; I'm not Proust. Writing, like wine, doesn't have to be complicated to be good. I can tell a good story because I enjoy what I write about."

That's probably why I—and millions of other readers—love Peter's books so much. Like a chilly glass of rosé, they wash away thoughts of finishing chores, making plans, returning from vacation, getting old. Rosé is a great wine because it's fleeting, reminding us that all things end, so seize the day.

"I've got this scene worked out for my death," Peter says, as he smiles and pours us more wine from the carafe. "I've just had the most extraordinary three-hour lunch. As I raise my hand for another glass of wine, I have a mammoth heart attack—just before the bill arrives."

And until then?

"Learning about food and wine is a series of edible adventures and surprises—you never finish."

Field Notes from a
Wine Cheapskate

INSIDER TIPS

- Forget those notions of pink wine being sweet: today's rosés are bone-dry and refreshing. With Provence, you're guaranteed to get a dry rosé.

- Look for wines that have never been taken seriously by connoisseurs, always considered lightweights. You'll find pleasure at a pittance there.

- Rosé is best served chilled, as it's more refreshing. So here's a tip that will give wine snobs a coronary: if your wine's too warm, drop an ice cube in it for ten seconds, then scoop it out. It has an immediate chilling effect and doesn't dilute the flavors—and after all, we're not trying to ice Châteaux Margaux, just an everyday good value wine. Consider this your license to chill.

WINERIES VISITED

Château de Roquefort: www.deroquefort.com
Domaine du Clos d'Alari: www.leclosdalari.fr

BEST VALUE WINES

Château de Roquefort Corail*
Château de Roquefort Les Mûres

Château de Roquefort Sémiramis
Domaine du Clos d'Alari Côtes de Provence Rosé
Domaine du Clos d'Alari Grand Clos Rosé

My first pick for my own Sunday lunch.

TOP VALUE PRODUCERS

Bieler Père et Fils
Carte Noire
Château Barbeyrolles
Château Calissanne
Château Constantin-
  Chevalier
Château de
  Fonscolombe
Château la Tour
  de l'Évêque
Château Routas
  Rouvière
Château Simone
Clos Mireille
Domaine de la Petite
  Cassagne

Domaine de la Sauveuse
Domaine de l'Olivette
Domaine de Suriane
Domaine de Trévallon
Domaine des Peirecèdes
Domaine Houchart
Domaine Sorin
Domaine Tempier
Domaines Ott
La Bastide Blanche
Les Vignerons de la
  Cadierenne
Sables d'Azur

SUNDAY LUNCH FOR A WINE CHEAPSKATE

You'll find Nathalie Vautrin-Vancoillie's recipes for the dinner we made together and shared at her home at www.nataliemaclean.com/food.

Tomato with Goat Cheese

Chicken with Fennel

Baked Potatoes with Bay Laurel Leaf

Apricot Tart

TERRIFIC PAIRINGS

Asian, Indian, and
  Thai dishes
Charcuterie
Cheese: Brie,
  Camembert,
  Parmesan
Chicken club sandwich
Curries: mild and spicy
Pasta with tomato and
  seafood sauces
Pâté
Pizza: cheese, pepperoni
Pork roast
Quiche
Salmon with herbs
Tuna: grilled
Turkey: roast
Veal piccata
Vegetables and salads

RESOURCES

For more information about Provence and rosés:

Adventures on the Wine Route by Kermit Lynch
Extremely Pale Rosé: A Very Pale Adventure by Jamie Ivey
Touring in Wine Country: Provence by Hubrecht Duijker
Wines of Provence: www.vinsdeprovence.com
Provence Wines USA: www.provencewineusa.com
Rosé Avengers and Producers: www.rapwine.com
Wines of Provence: www.nataliemaclean.com/wineries

RELATED READING

A Year in Provence by Peter Mayle
Toujours Provence by Peter Mayle
The Vintage Caper by Peter Mayle
Encore Provence: New Adventures in the South of France by Peter
    Mayle
Provence A–Z: A Francophile's Essential Handbook by Peter
    Mayle

DRINKING MY WORDS

Closing-Time Comments

CANDY-COLORED BOTTLES OF spirits glow against the mirrors behind the bar of the Algonquin Hotel. I've perched myself on a bar stool on this brisk May evening after having found the collected essays of my favorite New York City writer with the acid pen, Dorothy Parker, at a nearby bookstore. I've mentioned more than twenty books throughout the chapters. I'm often reading the work of one of the country's beloved authors while I'm traveling in a region to sharpen my observations, whether it's *The Leopard* by Sicily's Giuseppe di Lampedusa, the short stories of Argentina's Jorge Luis Borges, or Peter Mayle's books about Provence. This gets me thinking about my journey and the connection between writing and drinking as a way of understanding a place and its people.

Now that my own book of adventures is coming to an end, I can contemplate all that I've seen through a wine-soaked looking glass. Frankly, I just want a drink (or four) without making even one tasting note, so perhaps I'll go with cocktails tonight. And what better place than the Algonquin Hotel? Rich aromas of leather, oak, and booze fill the air. A man sitting in one corner of the bar seems as remote as a lighthouse, looking down on the afterwork tipplers at the tables throughout the room. The buttery tones of Ella Fitzgerald fill the spaces between their scattered conversations.

The Algonquin is famous as the gathering spot of the city's leading wits in the 1920s: humorist Robert Benchley, theater critic Alexander Woollcott, playwrights Edna Ferber and George Kaufman, *New Yorker* founder Harold Ross, and Dorothy Parker.

Almost a century later, their boozy lives still speak to us almost as eloquently as their literary legacy. Their writing back then had a prominence impossible in today's multimedia clutter, though they'd all be brilliantly pithy on Twitter. Still, they remain memorable. My favorite Parker lines come from her comments at the wake of a fellow writer. A friend by the open coffin remarked, "Doesn't he look wonderful?"

"Why shouldn't he?" Parker replied. "He hasn't had a drink in three days."

Perhaps these writers fascinate me, as this book surely attests, because I've always freely admitted to loving the hedonistic joys of wine (okay, the buzz). Alcohol makes me happy and stops me from being a tightly wound control freak, as some people (*quite* unjustly) characterize me. After a few glasses, I magnanimously forgive those people . . . for now.

James Joyce said that drinking is the revenge of shy people, but I'd say it's the passport of the socially awkward. Wine is a universal language of pleasure that has helped me connect with hundreds of people around the world for this book. It has allowed me to slip into social situations and feel an immediate connection. Many of the vintners I met along the way were scary smart or famous or forbidding. But exchanging a few oenophile-geeky references made the initial bond that allowed our conversation to flow with the wine.

Establishing a trust that says "you share my passion; you're like me" enabled my questions and their answers to become less protected and get downright indiscreet in some cases. As a fully immersive writer, much of this book was written while I was abuzz with my subject. (Fortunately, a very sober editor went through it before it arrived in your hands.) But why do most wine writers never mention the buzz they get from drinking? Are they afraid of not being taken seriously if they're having fun? This reminds me of the critic who observed that the splendid Irish novelist, Edna O'Brien, was one of the "first writers to have sex in her novels; all the other writers just had children."

The title of my first book—*Red, White, and Drunk All Over*—made people smile, but it also drew some criticism. I claimed, rather weakly, that "drunk all over" simply referred to savoring wines in many places around the world. That said, I'm an equal-opportunity drinker: cocktails, cognac, vodka, whisky, saké, wine, you name it. I got called to the bar years ago for the affirmative action in my glass.

Unwinding at the Algonquin, cocktail in hand, is a welcome respite from my professional focus on wine, and a liquid punctuation for the end of a long journey in this book. Earlier in the day, I was one of twenty journalists at a tasting of more than a hundred Californian cabernets, hosted by their agents. This type of event, when you compare one type of wine made during the same year from many producers, is called a horizontal tasting. (Not to be confused with your likely position by the time you finish.) A vertical tasting, by contrast, would mean tasting many different vintages of one producer's cabernets.

I remember all the times I've tried to convince friends that tasting wine and traveling to far-flung, exotic locales is hard work. The usual response is an amused smile or outright laughter. Ah, the glamorous life of a wine writer, they think: tasting delicious wines in gorgeous settings, being wined and dined by witty people in fine restaurants, getting effusive emails from admiring readers. But tasting wine as a professional is like being a driver in a foreign city—unlike the passenger who's just along for the sensory ride, you have to pay attention and use your wits.

I wish those friends could see me now, after 8 countries, 312 wineries, and 15,267 wines: a crimson flower blooms inside my mouth, its fiery tendrils licking at the back of my throat. I think my lips are starting to peel off. I've definitely lost a layer of enamel from my teeth; bathing them in acidity for three hours will do that. My mouth is a fire-blackened building; my cheeks glow like red-hot metal.

Many of the wines I tasted for this book were high in alcohol, especially port, Australian shiraz, and Argentine malbec. But that was the style they needed to be. Wines such as Niagara pinot noir, German riesling, and Provençal rosé are all creatures of lightness. Tasting this incredible stylistic range made me respect that each wine needs to be true to its own character, and that as drinkers, we need to be true to our own taste rather than follow what's fashionable or expensive.

Wine fascinates us, so it's easy to get caught up in its aroma, flavor, body, and structure. What matters, though, when we lift a glass to our lips, are the experiences that become woven into that wine, including where we are and who we're with. Time after time, when I breathe in the aromas of a wine I've had before, those memories are summoned instantly: I see and smell the first time I had the wine, rather than a fruit salad of descriptors. That's what we overlook when we dismiss inexpensive wine as uninteresting; it's we, as drinkers, who make a wine interesting with what we bring to the wine. You won't find this complete experience of wine in tasting notes. It's a lot like this book: your experience of it will depend on who you are.

Many of the winemakers I met understood this because they bring generations of family struggle to every glass. Their legacy is in the blend, and they know what sacrifices have been made to create it. When they taste their wine, they're back in the harvest, dealing with the issues farmers face, wondering how to pay for the new grape press, or remembering the celebratory dinner after the picking was done.

As I flip through my Parker anthology, the old Chinese bartender, whose name tag reads Mr. Hoy, hands me a cocktail list. I order the Parker: vodka, cassis, and fresh lemon juice. The vodka sluices through the crimson liqueur like rain tearing the sky open. The stem of the glass, cool and smooth in my hand, feels as familiar as my own skin. Like Parker's wit, the drink tastes sweet up front but finishes with a nasty bite.

It makes me wonder about the connection between alcohol and the creative process. Does booze loosen writers' inhibitions and heighten their feelings? Are they more susceptible to drink than other artists? Perhaps Tolstoy grasped it better when he observed, "Writing requires two people: the writer and the critic. Alcohol silences the critic until the writer is done." My subject matter relaxes me about my subject. That helps not just because I'm a puddle of neuroses but also because I'm drawn to fully immersive experiences in foreign places, rather than to sitting at a table and interviewing someone who visits my hometown. I've always searched for flesh knowledge—an understanding of life skinned of its social protocols. But all that flitting from experience to experience, emotion to emotion, is draining.

For my first book, I tried the day-in-the-life approach of working as a sommelier, a liquor store staffer, a winemaker, and a grape picker. For this book, and strangely for someone who usually avoids animals, I threw myself into odd situations where I encountered them in almost every chapter: sharks, snakes, sheep, goats, horses, donkeys, dogs, baboons, kangaroos, kookaburras, magpies, ladybugs, and hawks. Perhaps I knew at a gut level that being uncomfortable is the starting point for a good story. You use more of your senses and synapses when you're on strange terrain. Perhaps the animals were also part of my desire to stay connected with nature, especially in a world that's increasingly mediated by social media and technology. I never want to lose my awe of the land, yet I don't want to be overwhelmed by it. It is grand and I am small, but I rise and respond to it. That narrative pattern emerges only when you're finished.

A few more people have seated themselves at the bar. Their cocktails glow like tiny campfires along the dark wood surface. The chatter in the room is cheerful and loud, and their pink faces radiate goodwill. A flowering tenderness floods me with love for all these *beautiful* people.

I ask Mr. Hoy for a cocktail called the New Yorker. As he mixes the tequila, fruit nectar, and a squeeze of fresh lime, I listen drowsily to the clicking ice and chatter from the other end of the room, where a group of women are celebrating someone's birthday. A couple at a nearby table lean into each other, foreheads touching. All these details seem magnified and precious to me, worth recording for posterity. In fact, I think I'll start making a few notes for the brilliant novel that now seems entirely possible to write this week.

The woman at the other end of the bar slowly sips a martini in which three olives float like commas. Her pale skin rests on her face like sheets draped over furniture in an empty summer home. Maybe it's the preponderance here of women drinkers, but it occurs to me that most of the celebrated writer-drinkers were men. Hemingway-style boozing gave a man an attractive aura of both manliness and vulnerability, but a drinking woman was viewed as unladylike and promiscuous.

Drink like a man, write like a man. Parker once prayed, "Dear God, please make me stop writing like a woman." So where does that leave me, a woman who writes about wine and comes from a long line of alcoholics? Does my interest in alcoholic writers bode ill for my own sobriety, or is it an encouraging portent for a spectacular boozy memoir that starts with how well-maintained the tennis courts are at the Betty Ford Clinic? There's no doubt that wine tasting is not a profession for lily livers, even though you're supposed to spit out the sample after tasting it. Wine professionals also like to drink for pleasure.

After I started writing about wine, it bothered me that I wasn't a doctor helping to heal people or a teacher guiding children to enlightenment. What ideal had I given my life to? Facilitating bourgeois hedonism? Consumerism? Sloth? I needed a drink to sort it all out. The more I thought about it, the more I realized that there is honor in helping people find pleasure and relaxation. We all work hard, and there are many stresses in our lives. We need the simple joys in life, like a good glass of inexpensive wine, to regain a sense of ourselves. No worrying about how much it cost or what it scored; simply, do I like it, and do I like who I'm with?

I'm on my own, but tonight, the answer is yes. I finish with a small snifter of brandy. My fingers wrap around the bowl of the glass the way two lovers cradle each other lying side by side. It's past midnight now, and most people have left; the remaining drinkers look like party debris.

After communing with spirits all evening—both the bottled and the writerly kind—I feel as though I'm now putting away a family album of faded photographs. As I bid good night to Mr. Hoy and walk out of the Algonquin, an inky drizzle almost hisses as it hits my warm skin. Behind me, I believe I can hear those writers stumbling out, calling cheery, drunken good-byes as they head home to a bed or a desk. I think we all agree with the Irish poet and *New Yorker* writer Brendan Behan's self-assessment: I'm a drinker with a writing problem.

ACKNOWLEDGMENTS

Most of those who make wine are hospitable by nature, but the winemakers I met for this book were congenitally kind, inviting me into their homes and lives. Without their help, this would just be a transcript of dull interviews rather than a tapestry of human stories: Nicolas Audebert, Thomas Bachelder, Charles Back, Giuseppe Benanti, Wolf Blass, Norbret Breit, Nicolás and Laura Catena, Marco de Grazia, Tom Drieseberg, Louise Engel, Andrea Franchetti, Peter Gago, Michael Halstrick, Anthony and Olive Hamilton Russell, Stephen and Prue Henschke, Bevan Johnson, David Johnson, Ernie Loosen, Martin Malivoire, Rusty Myers, Dirk Niepoort, Diego Planeta, Katharina Prüm, George Sandeman, Carmen Stevens, Rupert Symington, Nathalie Vautrin-Vancoillie, Raimond Villeneuve, Nik Weis, and José Alberto Zuccardi.

A special thank-you to Peter Mayle, who helped me wrap up these edible adventures in the last chapter. Peter's irrepressible zest for food, drink, and life is my model. The next bottle is on me, Peter.

In a book about wine, there are thousands of facts that you can screw up. That became clear to me when I sent my manuscript to several wine wizards, whose depth of knowledge and incisive comments made me realize just how much I had yet to learn. They could have been brutal, even mocking, but they were all gentlemen: Steve Beckta, Kent Benson, Ken Goosens, Craig Hosbach, Kevin Keith, Bob McConnell, Grayson McDiarmid, and

Scott Richards. Any remaining errors are entirely my own—they could only do so much given what they had to work with.

Did I mention I can't cook? I just pull corks and twist caps. My deepest thanks to those who tested hundreds of recipes for this book that are now on my website: Pat Anderson, Stephanie Arsenault, Terra Baltosiewich, Kim Beavers, Vicki Bensinger, Tracey Black, Susan Blomeley, Maxine Borcherding, Betty Brown, Tim Brown, Leanna Bullock, Mark Busse, Don Chow, Beryl Cohen, Andrew Coppolino, David Crowley, Kari Cunningham, Veronique Deblois, Kathy Dimson, Lynnmarie Donner, Philippe Dupuy, Steff Ehm, Michelle Gibeau, Winona Godwin, Jacqueline Gomes, Peggy Grace, Deanna Hostler, Nadine Hughes, Heather Jones, Jennifer Kingsley, Honna Kozik, Tracy Lawson, Jennifer Lim, Richard Mahoney, Susie Majesky, Meghan Malloy, Alona Martinez, Jennifer Massolo, Ian McKichan, Craig McKnight, Lisa McKnight, Javier Merino, Liz Milender, Stéphanie Montreuil, Jessica Vilani Nanna, Debbie Patterson, Shari Reed, Ryan Reichert, Anna and Dave Russell, Sylvia Sicuso, Rebecca Stanisic, Lesley Stowe, Coleen Thompson, Lori Tinella, Sandy Trojansek, Maia Welbourne, Kathy Weldy, Robin White, Deborah Wickins, Dianne Willis, Lisa Wood, and Kristin Zangrilli.

For their assistance with the daunting task of planning the logistics of my trips abroad, I would like to acknowledge the help of Ulrike Bahm, Denis Boucher, Maria Cabral, Liz Clement, Ron Fiorelli, Louisa Fry, Magdalena Kaiser-Smit, Laurel Keenan, Valérie Lelong, Giuseppe Longo, Ariel Menniti, François Millo, Andre Morgenthal, and Rebel Neary.

I'd like to thank Antonia Morton, whom I affectionately call my personal word trainer. Antonia has read everything I have ever written professionally—buffing and polishing it before the world saw it.

This book would have remained a Microsoft Word document without the support of my Canadian publishers, Kristin Cochrane and Brad Martin, and my U.S. publisher and editor, John Duff. Working with my editors, Amy Black and John, felt like an intriguing conversation over a long, satisfying dinner. They gently prodded and posed questions that made me believe I had come up with their skillful insights on my own. And when

I stubbornly ignored them, they delivered the necessary unvarnished direction.

I am grateful to my agent, Jackie Kaiser, who provided critical guidance in conceiving the idea for this book and its organization. Jackie is, and always has been, steadfast and gracious.

I considered changing the last name of my superstar assistant, Helena Cody, in these acknowledgments so that you can't find her or hire her. (Note to self: send flowers.)

Most profoundly, I'd like to thank my life editor and dreams agent, Ann MacLean. You're on every page of this book, Mom.

The burden of putting up with my obsession for wine rests most heavily on my husband, Andrew, and my son, Rian. Andrew, universally curious and brilliant, has adopted my field as a subject of interest to him, too. His efforts to make this a shared passion have brought us closer together. Rian, now twelve, kept me afloat with his wry humor and optimism for the book's success, asking earnest questions about how royalties are transferred to relatives when an author dies. Let's hope this book sends your grandkids to college, Rian!

INDEX

Australian wine, 36–37
French wine, 313
German wine, 78
Niagara (Canadian) wine, 119
Portuguese wine and port, 275
Sicilian wine, 198
South African wine, 162–63
torrontés, 211, 220–21
Toujours Provence (Mayle), 308, 315
touriga grapes, 261, 262, 268
Touring in Wine Country: Provence
(Duijker), 314
trade bans and competition, 138–39, 161
trademark name of port, 239
traditionalists vs. modernists, 193
"Transatlantic Upset," 107
Trapped in Paradise (film), 90
traveling in
Argentina, 202, 213
Australia, 11, 20–21, 25
Canada, 83, 84–86, 89
Germany, 41, 53, 55, 60, 61, 71
Niagara (Canada), 83, 84–86, 89
Portugal, 235, 247, 249–50
Sicily, 177, 183
South Africa, 124
treading grapes *(pigeages)*, 250–51, 268
Treadwell Restaurant, 100–101
Treasury Wine Estates, 10
trellising, 30, 63, 174, 223
Trinchero, Bob (Sutter Home winery), 281
trockenbeerenauslese (TBA) riesling, 65,
69–70, 80
"trop" (port-style wine), 239
"True Love Chardonnay," xi
truffles, 299–301
Tuesday dinner, 111, 115, 118, 119
Tukulu, 140, 143–44, 148
Tuscany, Italy, xi, 43, 172, 197, 203, 255
Tutu, Desmond, 125
Twain, Shania, 114
Twitter, xiv, xix, 318
Two Oceans, 128, 163

U-boats, 64
U.K., 138
Under the Tuscan Sun (Mayes), 305
ungrafted *(pied frau)* vines, 176
United States, 86, 138, 215
"universally declared" vintage, 254
University of Adelaide, Australia, 12, 18,
22, 34

unquenchable journey, xv–xvi
See also bargain wines
Urban, Saint (Pope Urban I), 61
Ürziger Würzgarten Riesling Spätlese, 57

Valckenberg family, 54
Valeira dam, Portugal, 249–50
value, relativity of, 117–18
van der Stel, Simon, 126–27
Van Gogh, Theo, 283
Van Gogh, Vincent, 282–83
Vanity Fair (Thackeray), 154
van Riebeeck, Jan, 126
Vautrin, Paul, 298
Vautrin-Vancoillie, Nathalie (Domaine du
Clos d'Alari), 297–99, 300, 301,
302–4, 305, 313
Vergine marsala, 171
vertical tastings, 319
Vesuvius, 176
Victoria (Queen of England), 47
Vila Nova de Gaia, Portugal, 236–37, 249
Villeneuve, Raimond (Château de
Roquefort), 283–87, 288, 289, 290,
291–92, 293, 294
Vina Patagonia (Concha y Toro, Chile), 214
Vincor, 108, 110
Vin Gris de Cigare, 296
Vinicola Benanti, 177–80, 181–83, 193,
197, 198
*Vino Argentino: An Insider's Guide to the
Wines and Wine Country of Argentina*
(Catena), 233
Vino-Lok glass stoppers, 31
Vintage Caper, The (Mayle), 311, 315
vintage port, 254–56, 257, 271, 272
vintages, xvii–xviii, 258
Vintners Quality Alliance (VQA), 87, 116
viognier, 211, 220–21, 296
virtual glass of wine, sharing, xiv, xx
volcanic viticulture, 167, 176–77, 179, 181,
186, 192–93, 194, 196
Volgyesi, Andrew, 96
Volnay, 115
von Bismarck, Otto, 127
von Söetern, Christoph (Bernkasteler
Doctor), 72
Vulcan, 176, 192

Walk in the Clouds, A (film), 251
warm-climate vs. cold-climate regions, 35
War of 1812, 86